Studies in Public Choice

For further volumes, go to
http://www.springer.com/series/6550

Thomas König • George Tsebelis • Marc Debus
Editors

Reform Processes and Policy Change

Veto Players and Decision-Making in Modern Democracies

Springer

Editors
Thomas König
University of Mannheim
Department of Political Science
Professor of Political Science II
(International Relations) A5, 6
68131 Mannheim
Germany
koenig@uni-mannheim.de

George Tsebelis
Department of Political Science
University of Michigan
Haven Hall
505 S. State St.
Ann Arbor, MI 48109-1045
tsebelis@umich.edu

Marc Debus
University of Mannheim
Mannheim Centre for European Social Research
Senior Research Fellow in Political Science A5, 6
68131 Mannheim
Germany
marc.debus@mzes.uni-mannheim.de

ISBN 978-1-4419-5808-2 e-ISBN 978-1-4419-5809-9
DOI 10.1007/978-1-4419-5809-9
Springer New York Dordrecht Heidelberg London

Library of Congress Control Number: 2010932407

Printed on acid-free paper

Springer is part of Springer Science+Business Media (www.springer.com)

Acknowledgements

This book originates from a series of papers presented at a Workshop on "Reform processes and policy change: How do veto players determine decision making in modern democracies", held at the Mannheim Centre for European Social Research (MZES), Germany, in May 2009. We would like to thank all the participants who attended this workshop for their valuable contributions. In addition, we thank the MZES and Fritz-Thyssen-Foundation for their organisational and financial support. Moreover, we also wish to thank the executive editor of European Union Politics, Gerald Schneider, for granting us permission to reprint an article entitled 'Why Don't Veto Players Use Their Power?' by Thomas König and Dirk Junge (2009) 10:507–534. This contribution is reproduced as Chap. 8 of this book.

Contents

Contributors

Thomas Bräuninger University of Mannheim, Mannheim, Germany, thomas.braeuninger@uni-mannheim.de

Luigi Curini University of Milan, Milan, Italy, luigi.curini@unimi.it

Marc Debus University of Mannheim, Mannheim, Germany, marc.debus@mzes.uni-mannheim.de

Mark Hallerberg Hertie School of Governance, Berlin, Germany, hallerberg@hertie-school.org

Simon Hug University of Geneva, Geneva, Switzerland, simon.hug@unige.ch

Detlef Jahn University of Greifswald, Greifswald, Germany, djahn@uni-greifswald.de

Dirk Junge University of Mannheim, Mannheim, Germany, djunge@mail.uni-mannheim.de

Thomas König University of Mannheim, Mannheim, Germany, t.koenig@uni-mannheim.de

Bernd Luig University of Mannheim, Mannheim, Germany, bernd.luig@mzes.uni-mannheim.de

Thomas M. Meyer University of Mannheim, Mannheim, Germany, tmeyer@mail.uni-mannheim.de

Wolfgang C. Müller University of Vienna, Vienna, Austria, wolfgang.mueller@univie.ac.at

Sven-Oliver Proksch University of Mannheim, Mannheim, Germany, proksch@uni-mannheim.de

Thomas Saalfeld University of Bamberg, Bamberg, Germany, thomas.saalfeld@uni-bamberg.de

Jonathan B. Slapin University of Houston, Houston, TX, USA, jonslapin@gmail.com

Bernard Steunenberg Leiden University, Leiden, The Netherlands, steunenberg@fsw.leidenuniv.nl

George Tsebelis University of Michigan, Ann Arbor, MI, USA, tsebelis@umich.edu

Francesco Zucchini University of Milan, Milan, Italy, francesco.zucchini@unimi.it

Part I
Introduction

Chapter 1
Veto Player Theory and Policy Change: An Introduction

George Tsebelis

Some months ago I had the honor to be invited to Mannheim for a conference organized by Thomas Koenig and Marc Debus. The subject matter was "Reform Processes and Policy Change," and the organizers thought that my book *Veto Players* would be a good starting point for their study. I thought that the conference was an excellent idea, particularly since the reputation of Mannheim on policy studies is outstanding. Little did I know that this would be only a first step, because they now have received an interdisciplinary multimillion grant from the German Government (SFB 884) to "Political Economy of Reforms" (http://reforms.uni-mannheim.de/english/startpage/index.html).

I was excited to see the work of a number of colleagues on topics and methods related to my own research. I think I speak not only about myself, but about most of them when I say that I (we) came out of these meetings knowing and understanding a lot more about a series of topics related to the political economy of institutions and policymaking. This is why the organizers and I decided to bring this work to the attention of the scholarly public. I am contributing the introduction to this edited volume, and the organizers (along with their individual contributions) will draw the conclusions.

This Introduction will address issues raised both in *Veto Players* and in the works of the participants of that conference. The reader will be able to study this book without having read *Veto Players* previously and will be able to understand that, besides the common interests in substance and methodology which the authors of this book share, and aside from the appreciation of each other's work and contribution, we also have disagreements. And it is the combination of appreciation and disagreement that is essential to the growth of knowledge. We read each other's work and are fascinated by it, but we express our disagreements openly and sincerely, trying to persuade each other about the validity of our arguments, and argue that our expectations are corroborated by the data.

G. Tsebelis (✉)
Anotol Rapoport Collegiate Professor of Political Science, University of Michigan, Ann Arbor, MI, USA
e-mail: tsebelis@umich.edu

T. König et al. (eds.), *Reform Processes and Policy Change: Veto Players and Decision-Making in Modern Democracies*, Studies in Public Choice 16,
DOI 10.1007/978-1-4419-5809-9_1, © Springer Science+Business Media, LLC 2010

This introduction has two parts: the first introduces the reader to elements of *Veto Players* that will be addressed by the subsequent chapters; the second points out the differences between the specific chapters and the original book. These differences range from disagreements in some auxiliary assumptions that lead to different conclusions, to the significance and applicability of the model to different phenomena, to the methods applied in the chapters, to evaluating the preferences of actors, to estimating the accuracy of predictions, etc.

Arguments Made in *Veto Players*

This book connects political institutions to policy outcomes. Focussing on policy outcomes is important because the impact of public policies on the life of citizens is overwhelming. If we think about it, the most important events in our life (besides significant developments in the immediate family like deaths, births of children, etc.) are decisions made within the political system to expand or contract healthcare, or unemployment benefits, or educational privileges, or taxes etc.

While individual citizens are interested in specific policies, and have strong preferences in one dimension (like tax reduction) or another (such as education), the way one can address all of these potential changes in a systematic comparative way is to assess the possibility of changing the status quo policy (no matter what the status quo is). This is the goal of *Veto Players.* Most of the propositions developed in the book regard the impact of particular institutional settings on "policy stability," that is, the difficulty of making a significant change to the status quo. The book argues that policy stability is the effect of a constellation of "veto players" (vp): individual or collective actors whose agreement is necessary for the change of the status quo.

From these two definitions, a series of propositions follows, some of them known through folk knowledge for millennia. One analytical truth connecting veto players with policy stability is that as the number of vp increases, policy stability does not decrease (a change of the status quo does not becomes easier, though it may not become more difficult). I call this proposition an analytical truth–because it is the consequence of the definition of the terms alone–and it is logically inconceivable that it will be otherwise, no matter what additional assumptions one would make. For example, if a veto player decides to veto some of the policies that others accept for changes to the status quo, then the player's existence will make the change to the status quo more difficult, while if s(he) agrees with everything that the others agree to, this player's addition will not change anything in terms of policy outcomes. What is not possible under any set of conditions is to add a veto player and make changes in the status quo easier.

Another analytic truth concerns the ideological distances of veto players. What is required for this proposition are two different assumptions: First, common knowledge of the location of the different veto players in the policy space, and second, that they exercise their veto only on the basis of their policy preferences, not on the basis of other considerations (say electoral goals, appeal to their constituency, etc). If a vp is located in the Pareto set (the set of outcomes that makes no actor worse off than the status quo) of the rest of the vp, (s)he will be "absorbed" (i.e., will not exercise veto powers). As I show in the original book, there is no position accepted by all other veto players that will not be approved by this particular one if (s)he is located within the Pareto set of the others. I argue that in this case, the absorbed player will not count as an additional vp. A trivial application of this statement is that if there are two vp with identical preferences, they will act as though they were a single vp, because they will always agree on any policy change. Another application is that if the policy positions of three vps are on the same straight line, then the one in the middle is absorbed and, as a result, what matters is the distance between the two extreme vps, not the location of the one in between. Again, as a consequence, in a one-dimensional setting of vps, the *only* thing that matters is their "range" (the distance of the two most extreme vps), not their number. Given the analytic status of this proposition, if some empirical study finds that the number of vp matters and not the range, the *only* possible inference is that the single dimensional assumption is not a reasonable approximation of reality in the case under study.

Figure 1.1 gives a graphic representation of the argument above. Veto player B is located between A and C, and there is nothing that A and C can agree to (the intersection of their preferences is the thin lens in the picture) that B would disagree to (his/her preferences over the status quo include this thin lens). It is easy to verify that as long as B is located between A and C, this statement will be true. The reader can experiment by herself and verify that if B is not on the line AC, there will always be some parts on the lens that are not preferred by B to the status quo.

A last empirical application is in two dimensions: if a vp is located inside the triangle generated by three others, (s)he will be absorbed. Again, if under these conditions an empirical application finds that this particular vp exercises a veto it is because one of the initial assumptions is violated: either the vp exercises veto on

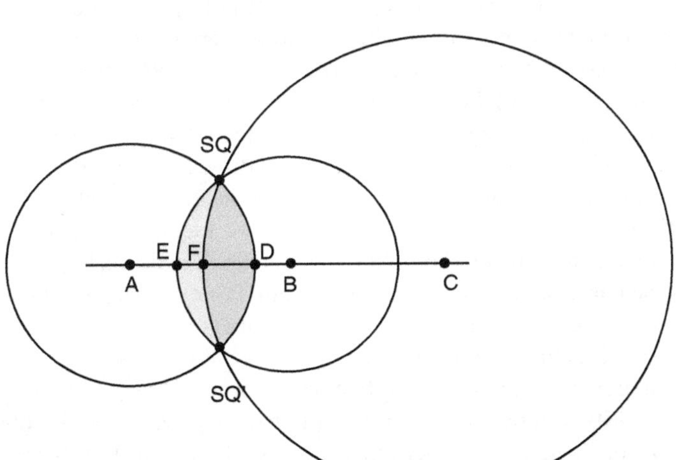

Fig. 1.1 Winset of VPs A and C is contained within Winset of VPs A and B (B is absorbed)

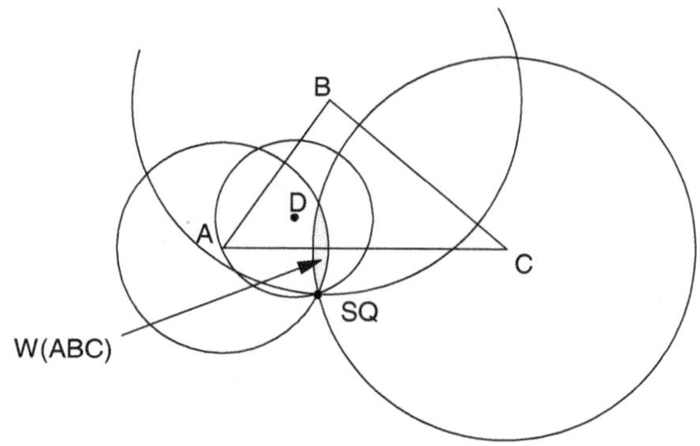

Fig. 1.2 Winset of VPs A, B, and C is contained in Winset of D (D is absorbed)

the basis of motives other than policy preferences (say electoral considerations) or s(he) is not located inside the triangle of the three others (say s(he) is outside the plane generated by them).

Figure 1.2 gives the graphic representation of the argument. D is a veto player located in the triangle created by the positions of vp A, B, and C. Consequently, anything that A, B, and C prefer to the status quo (the area W(ABC) in the picture) is preferred by D to the status quo. Again, the proposition will not be true if D is located outside the triangle (or outside the plane).

These propositions are mentioned here because they are discussed in some of the chapters of this book. They do not exhaust the implications of the theory of veto players, but, as I said, this chapter is not a summary of the book but of the parts of the veto players theory that are relevant to what follows.

Another part of the veto players book that will be discussed is the counting rules of vps. The first step in mapping the vp constellation of a country (a necessary step in assessing the impact of political institutions on policy outcomes) is to establish the number and identity of its institutional veto players by determining how many institutions are required to agree for a new policy to be adopted (stipulated within the constitution of the country). For example, in the United States, there are a minimum of three institutions whose agreement is needed (President, House, and Senate), in Germany most of the time two need to consent (Bundestag and Bundesrat), while just one institution must agree to policy changes in France (National Assembly) and the UK (House of Commons).[1] Once we have identified the institutional vp of a country, we can focus on the political conditions inside each institutional that determines the partisan veto players of the system. For example, if a stable coalition prevails inside a legislature, then the parties members of this coalition are the vp. Figure 1.3 illustrates this argument.

Think of a legislature composed of five parties where three of them are required to form a majority. Suppose that it is a parliamentary system with cohesive parties, and three of them are in government (say A, B, and C). In this case, one can

[1] I will omit here a discussion of constitutional courts as vps (see Tsebelis 2002).

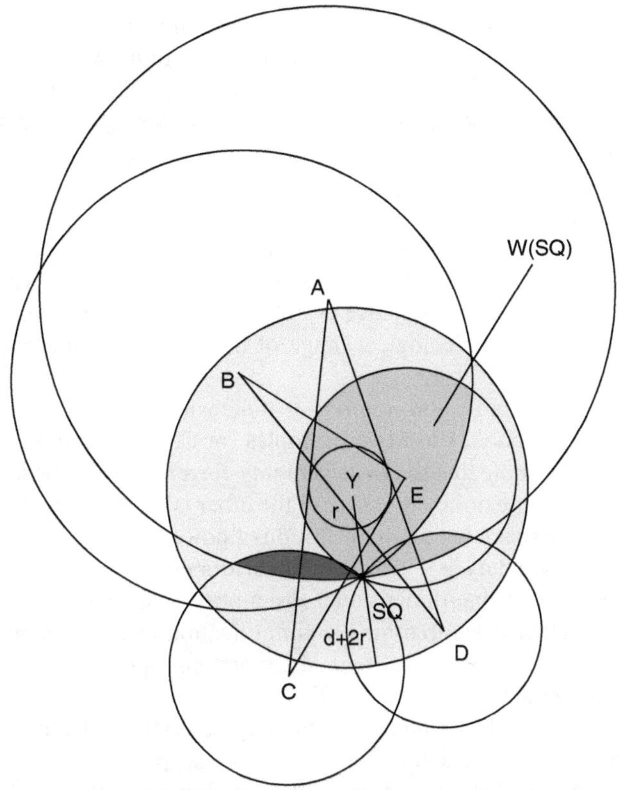

Fig. 1.3 Circle (Y. $d + 2r$) contains the Winset of the status quo of collective VP (ABCDE)

predict the outcomes that can replace the status quo quite accurately: it is the heavily shaded lens in Fig. 1.3. If, however, parties can form multiple coalitions, then there are a number of coalitions that can form to replace the status quo, and the prediction cannot be very accurate. Policy outcomes could lie within any one of the three lenses that are lightly or heavily shaded. Tsebelis (2002) demonstrates that this irregular shape can be included inside a circle (with centre Y and radius $d + 2r$ in the figure), so that one can think of this parliament as a collective vp and approximate its preferences. If parties are cohesive but different majorities prevail in each chamber of a bicameral legislature, then one would have to include the required parties for concurrent majorities in both chambers. For example, in Germany in 2004, there was a majority coalition of the Social Democrats and the Greens in the Bundestag, but the addition of the Christian Democratic Party was necessary to achieve a majority in the Bundesrat, as a result there were three veto players in Germany.[2]

[2] Actually the situation is slightly more complicated because for some laws the Bundesrat does not have veto power, which will mean that for these laws, the only veto players are the Social Democrats and the Greens, while in the most significant legislation, the agreement of the Bundesrat is required.

It is not enough, however, to simply count the number of partisan vp (parties required to achieve a simple majority) within the institutional vp: we must also pay attention to significant additional details of the political system. For example, it is necessary to determine the decision-making rule inside each institutional vp as this determines who the partisan vp are (as the vote required to adopt a that proposal increases the number of partisan vp may also increase as additional actors are necessary to meet the voting threshold).[3]

Measuring the number of veto players is relatively easy: one has to identify institutional vp, and then open each of them (see who the partisan vp are as a function of the decision-making rule, the existence or not of stable coalitions, and the cohesion of parties). Assessing the ideological range of the particular vp constellation is a more challenging matter.

First, one has to identify the number of dimensions of the underlying policy space. In the original book, I use two examples (in Chaps. 7 and 8): one on labor legislation where I assume that the issue is highly correlated with the left–right axis, so I use this as the single policy dimension; the other is on the budget where I use a two-dimensional approach (as a demonstration of how one can increase the number of dimensions in the analysis). The number of dimensions is usually ignored in empirical studies, and a one-dimensional assumption is adopted without adequate concern about whether it is a reasonable simplification of the phenomenon that is studied. The more complicated the issue, the more appropriate is the adoption of a multidimensional model.

Second, one has to select a dataset from which to extract ideological positions. There are three methods that have been used in the past: expert survey assessments that do not introduce very much variation over time, the manifesto project that assesses policy positions of parties in each election, and, more recently, computerized programs that are based on any documents the researcher would like to analyze. Several of the chapters in this book deal with the issues of measuring the underlying policy space, so the reader will be immersed in this methodology below, and throughout the book.

This is a summary of the issues relevant to veto players and policy stability. However, there are implications of veto players for the formation of coalitions and for structural characteristics of countries, like the importance of bureaucracies and the judiciary. Since coalitions are studied and discussed in several chapters, let me present a summary of the veto players approach to coalitions.

Given that both range and number of vp affect policy stability, the expectation is that whenever a country is faced with a significant exogenous shock (like an increase in oil prices, a financial meltdown, or prolonged social strife around a particular issue such as unemployment, healthcare, or education), a government with multiple distinct vp will not be able to produce policies to overcome the crisis, and consequently (in a parliamentary system) will have to resign, and be replaced by another coalition government. There are two implications of this analysis (though only the

[3] For the details of analyzing institutions that decide by qualified majority, see Tsebelis (2002).

first is included in the book): The duration of governments with large ranges or multiple vp will be shorter; the second is that, given that government duration of coalitions with a large ideological range and many vp is shorter, this will affect the composition of governments. While this is an important and interesting phenomenon in itself, I will not discuss this issue any further.

While it is clear in parliamentary systems who the veto players are, this is not true about the identity of agenda setters. In a general way, the agenda setting institution in parliamentary systems is "the government," but this statement is very vague. First, it does not identify the real agenda setter except in the rare case of single party governments. Second, it does not identify the exact powers of the government. Let me deal with each one of these issues in turn.

With respect to the first issue (who within a government is the real agenda setter), I explicitly and purposely adopted the position that all the parties of the coalition participate in the process. Other analyses on this point make a different assumption: they assume that it is solely the prime minister, or the corresponding minister, or underline the contribution of the finance minister who sets the legislative agenda. I do not doubt that in some cases one can find significant contribution from the prime minister or the corresponding minister in shaping a particular policy. However, I believe that none of these individuals would have exclusive jurisdiction, because by virtue of being a veto player, if ministers have a significant policy difference with a member of the coalition, either the policy will not go forward or the coalition will collapse because they will use their veto power.

With respect to the second issue (agenda setting power of different governments), this is a new independent variable in the study of parliamentary systems. The best analysis of this subject was conducted by Döring (1995) and I have consequently adopted his analysis. As we will see, several of the chapters in this volume deal with this issue, and we will address it again in the second part of this introduction.

To conclude the discussion of the relevant aspects of veto players theory, the veto players' analysis is based on a partial equilibrium assumption: as long as the government is in place, it will have a series of properties determined by its vp configuration. If faced with a shock, the government may survive or may change and then we will have a different government with similar or different properties. This statement ignores elections, as well as other exogenous shocks. Should we include them in the analysis in order to produce a more general theory? Of course, we should. However, it is unclear at this point how this can be done in a systematic way. In addition, all the reasoning in the analysis is based on complete information models – that is, the model assumes that parties know each other's positions in a multidimensional space. I think this is a reasonable assumption, but should we be restricted by it for everything we study? No, and the reader will find that several chapters remove this assumption and proceed further in the analysis. I have been assuming single bill consideration by the political system on the basis of policy preferences. No side payments were used, no log rolling could occur. Is it because I believe that these phenomena never occur? No, but I did not allow for these options in the original book because if you allow for these possibilities everything becomes possible, and you cannot test theories on the basis of this assumption. Again, the reader will see that this argument is disputed in this book in a meaningful and creative way. There have been a series of simplifying assumptions in the original book, and most of them are challenged in the pages that follow.

Arguments Made in This Book

It is time now to apply the arguments developed above to the studies presented in this book. Mark Hallerberg first presents an overview of the veto players literature. He has done an exhaustive study that covers legislative politics as well as political economy issues (to which he has widely contributed). He argues that institutions designed by a specific configuration of veto players may not function as well with a different constellation. I have two points of disagreement to raise with his thorough analysis.

The first is that he (rightfully) considers not only my approach to the analysis of political institutions but a number of other approaches that speak to the policy consequences of institutions. He identifies in them different counting rules and argues that empirical evidence will show which one is better. Let me give to empirical evidence what is due to empirical evidence, but let me also point out that logical consistency is a necessary condition for the development of a theory. In the absence of logical consistency, corroboration (no matter how rigorous the tests and no matter how strong the results) *does not* matter. Take, for example, the issue of veto players in the way it was developed in the original book, and veto points or veto gates, that is, the veto players determined by the constitution alone. The difference between the two concepts is significant, and the difference arises from two causes. First, some institutional veto players may be absorbed. For example, two chambers of a bicameral legislature may both have veto power, but they may have identical compositions (Italy). If this is the case, in veto players theory, one is absorbed by the other, while they both constitute equally important veto points, or veto gates. Conversely, a single institutional veto point or veto gate may be composed of multiple partisan veto players (see discussion surrounding Fig. 1.3), where one single institutional veto player can be composed of three partisan ones.

The point I am making here is that the veto points or veto gates analyses are inconsistent if one takes into account the preferences of the different political actors. Of course, if such positions are unknown or unknowable (think of studies covering hundreds of countries for centuries, like some analyses of economic growth (Henisz)), then veto points are the best approximation of veto players, and as such it should be used. However, when we can assess the preferences of the potential veto players, we should use that information.

So, veto players and veto points are not two different ways of counting wherein one can use whichever method s(he) prefers, or test them and see which is more accurate. One logically supersedes the other, and if both veto points and the ideological composition of the groups that compose those points are available, the veto players' framework should be used; if this information is not available, veto points are probably the best approximation. I do not need to develop the point any further. The reader will verify that most chapters in this volume use both institutions and preferences, and some of them go to great lengths to develop means of assessing one or the other or their combination.

Another difference between the veto players and veto points counting mechanisms arises from the issue of "enabling" and "encompassing" veto players. As I explained in the previous section, it follows from the definition of veto players that adding veto players necessarily leads to policy change becoming equally or more difficult. It does not matter what one chooses to call them. If the argument is that policy change becomes easier as the term "enabling" suggests, then, the argument is that parties in government are not veto players, and this argument should be presented and assessed.

The second point that Hallerberg makes (and it is connected to his own work) is that some veto player configurations may generate results that are better under the initial configuration than under the subsequent alternatives. I have tried to avoid normative implications of veto player throughout my work on the theory. I never said that few or many veto players are better. On the contrary, my argument was that reasonable people may disagree and the best approximation for whether one prefers more or fewer veto players is their attitude towards the status quo. I made this argument even discussing the economic growth argument that multiple veto players are better than few for growth, because they create policy stability and enable the market to fully develop. While policy stability may be a good condition for growth, it may also be the case that the ability of the political actors for change policy quickly may improve economic results (think of the Obama stimulus package). Finally, different actors may have different assessments of policies and as a result of the institutions that promote or inhibit those policies. Therefore, normative assessments about veto players will be equally controversial.

Jahn (Chap. 3) proceeds through a careful reconstruction of all existing indexes (both veto player and veto point) incorporating all available information about changes in institutions and in preferences. Although he shares my theoretical assessment of veto points in comparison to veto players, he nevertheless proceeds in a careful reconstruction of all indexes in order to be able to construct a correlation matrix of all of them.

There are two important contributions that Jahn introduces in his analysis, both of them depend on the time dimension. Preferences of actors change over time. This change was not included in my original work, so Jahn clearly proceeds one step further. However, this analysis will also soon become dated because, as we will see in the discussion of the subsequent chapter, we are today at the verge of major methodological discoveries with respect to preference assessment. As we will see, preferences can be assessed not only by voting in legislatures (as is the case in the US congress) but also by textual analysis of party documents or parliamentary speeches, or laws, and consequently, the manifesto approach that measures policy position only before elections and inter- or extra-polates in between will be soon be set aside.

The other significant change that Jahn introduces is the change in institutions. This second change does not produce a significant empirical result (the indices, Jahn 1 and 2, are correlated at 0.98) but it is nevertheless a significant contribution.

I do not know how "medium"-strength chambers are included in the index in his measure. While (as Jahn cites) I have argued that any second chamber has influence in the legislative output, it does not mean that it is a "veto player." For example, both the House of Lords and the French Senate can be over-ruled by the lower chambers, and consequently their agreement is not necessary for a modification of the status quo. It is essential that we keep the same rules across countries when we construct summary indices, otherwise it will not be clear what differences can be attributed to institutions and what to changes in rules. Similarly, the President of the French Republic is not a veto player (whether under cohabitation or not) because he cannot veto a bill (he can send a bill back to the National Assembly for reconsideration, but it is re-examined under the same rules). Now, the dynamics of the French government are very different if the elected President is the leader of the government coalition, or if he has to form a government from opposing parties. In the first case, he is the indisputable leader of the country; in the second, he falls back into the position of a President of a parliamentary democracy (with the most significant difference that he can dissolve the national Assembly whenever he wants). But in either case, he is not a distinct veto player.

One final point of disagreement with Jahn's conclusions is his statement that "[a]nalyses in which Henisz' indicator is applied and in which results are interpreted according to Tsebelis' theory are invalid." While I do not for a moment dispute Jahn's findings that the index I calculated correlates with "Crepaz 1" at 0.51 and with Henisz's "polcon 3" at only 0.40 I find the intellectual, conceptual, and methodological affinity with the latter to be much stronger (and I have used it when the time period or the spread of countries was much larger than my own dataset).

The Koenig et al. chapter presents a new methodology for the estimation of preferences of political actors. Compared with the preference specification I used in the veto players book, this methodology is several steps ahead. It uses legislation to identify verbal expressions relevant to different ministries and traces these expressions back to party documents. Then, with a computerized method like wordfish, they approximate the ideological conflict that generates these words and produce the ideological positions of the different parties. The method is impressive: it updates the information constantly (as a function of laws enacted (or if one wants simply debated)), it produces outcomes in multiple dimensions, and the dimensions are correlated with the different government ministries as opposed to decisions of some researcher.

The results of the analysis are remarkable: one can see the movement of the FDP from left to right as a coalition partner of the SPD first, and the CDU-CSU later. All of these movements are lost in the analyses in my book. The authors are kind to point out that in the last period when the government parties are the closest together they produce no legislation (against the veto players theory); the result can be explained by the fact that the status quo was presumably very close to the parties to begin with (which is consistent with the theory).

Yet, all this precision comes at the loss of comparability. The reason that veto players has a negative coefficient for the law production function is not the difference in the ideological distance of parties in German government, but the fact that countries like Germany or Italy produce few significant laws, while Greece or the UK produce a lot of them. And this requires compatibility among the ideological range of different countries. The Koenig et al. approach is extremely significant for the study of each country, but the results cannot be compared cross-nationally, because the legislation varies, and the smart tags of one country are not relevant to the next.

This is a similar problem with the ideological positions of legislators in the US House and Senate on the basis of their voting records: given that different amendments are presented in each chamber, there is no comparability of voting in the two chambers. Different researchers have found different "anchors" to produce comparable results: some amendments may be identical and produce a (limited) way for making comparative judgments; some legislators move from one chamber to the other, so, assuming that they have the same positions (over time), can become the means of comparing one chamber with the other etc. Still, no method has been able to place the President in these ideological continuums, and this is the reason I have not been able to include the United States in my dataset (to respond here to Jahn's criticism).

So, Koenig et al. produce "country expertise" with their analysis, but they do not have the ability to make cross-country comparisons (yet). If they are able to make comparisons, they will achieve immediate recognition. But what they have already achieved is an immense step forward in the identification of policy preferences. This is not an achievement just related to veto players, but a big step forward in political and social sciences more generally. Because preference identification is a necessary step for the analysis of any rational behavior since by definition rationality is maximization of goal achievement, this methodological advancement is a step forward for the social sciences more generally.

The Mueller and Meyer chapter deals with the way coalitions over-rule parties in performing government business. They start from the well-known Shepsle and Laver model according to which ministers have exclusive jurisdictions over policy-making in their area and address a series of mechanisms by which coalitions are able to reign them in and make them promote the coalition platform as opposed to their partisan wishes, despite the fact that their commitment to the party is long-term, and their career payoffs are controlled by the party and not the coalition.

There are means by which coalitions can reduce the independence of ministers, most of which have already been described in the literature: ex ante mechanisms (policy agreement, coalition discipline, election rule, and screening of ministers), ex post mechanisms (monitoring by parliamentary committees, coalition committees, and watchdog junior ministers), and environmental factors (familiarity, bargaining complexity, parliamentary polarization, cabinet preference divergence, time until next election, prime ministerial powers, and additional veto players). The original contribution of the argument is not the identification of any particular mechanism of supervision but the combination of all of them and the demonstration that all these mechanisms perform the same duties, and are connected with each other so that if the environment provides a lot of them, only a few additional ones are needed. In addition to the theoretical argument, empirical analysis using some 260 coalition governments in 17 West European countries beginning with the first post-war (or current regime) cabinet until 1999, corroborates the theoretical expectations of the authors. The bottom line is that the best conceptual approximation of how coalition governments work is that the parties composing these governments are veto players – that is, exercise veto over each other's proposals, so that the government policies are approved by all coalition partners. So, what in my book was essentially taken for granted is now carefully analyzed and corroborated by empirical evidence. Beyond that, the chapter is an important contribution to the very wide literature on coalitions, and explains how the most important institution in parliamentary democracies (government coalitions) works.

Saafeld's chapter derives a series of five assumptions on government duration from veto players, and tests them with the same dataset as Mueller and Meyer. The arguments are sound, the methodology appropriate, and the conclusions are very nuanced: some of the expectations are corroborated, whereas others do not produce results at the traditional levels of significance. The major finding of this chapter is a negative one, in contradiction of both expectations of veto players theory as well as of previous empirical work from Warwick: the ideological distance of veto players in the right–left dimension does not significantly affect the longevity of governments, although the number of veto players does. Saafeld's argument is that the significance of the number of veto players could be attributed to transaction costs, and not to veto players. This is a plausible explanation, but this is not the only study that finds the number of vps more significant than their range in one dimension. For example, Franseze, analyzing the size of budgets in democracies found the number of veto players mattered more than their range, and concluded that the evidence corroborated the veto players' argument.

This is an important issue deserving more extensive discussion. *All* spatial models agree that the results of single dimensional analysis do not extrapolate to multiple dimensions. The basic difference is that in one-dimensional models, there is always an equilibrium (the median voter), whereas in multidimensional models, the equilibrium disappears (the most accurate statement is that it exists with probability 0). In addition, the core (set of points that cannot be defeated by application of the decision-making rule) may or may not exist as a function of the number of underlying policy dimensions. So, the number of underlying dimensions is of crucial significance for spatial reasoning. Actually, the reason that I produced the veto player theory and did not use the equilibrium of a one-dimensional model nor analyze the core of different political systems is that these concepts are not guaranteed to exist. Veto players theory has an advantage over such analyses that the results hold *regardless* of the number of underlying dimensions.

Let us now take Saafeld's results (number of vps matters, but not range in one dimension), and let us assume that three government parties were located in an equilateral triangle or a similar shape. Obviously, the ideological conflicts cannot be understood in one dimension. In this case, one would have to go to two dimensions, or, would have the number of veto players as a proxy for the existence of multiple dimensions. So, the significance of number of veto players may be an indication of multidimensionality of the underlying space. How many dimensions? Spatial theory tells us that with n veto players (i.e., parties in government plus additional institutional ones), the number of dimensions can be up to $n - 1$. If it turns out that the first two dimensions eliminate the argument that it is the number of veto players that matters for policy outcomes, the interpretation would be that it is not transaction costs. So, we could test Saafeld's conjecture against mine (actually, in the veto players book I have a two dimensional analysis that could be replicated for any number of dimensions).

The chapter by Bräuninger and Debus deals with a phenomenon that has not been studied before. Bipartisan policy proposals, that is, bills that have been proposed jointly by members of the government and the opposition are the subject of their chapter. The reason that the subject has not been studied is that the canonical configuration of parliamentary systems is government versus opposition, given that the discipline of parties in parliamentary democracies was considered "Prussian," political scientists started studying parliamentary voting only recently. Bräuninger and Debus go one step further, and argue that agenda setting is even less restricted than votes, and so focus on this unusual for parliamentary system phenomenon. They find out that there is a significant percentage of bipartisan bills (although the number of those that becomes law is limited; but then again, any non-government bill has low probability of success in a parliamentary democracy). What is the reason even the existence of such bills? The authors cannot explain bipartisan bills on the basis of the veto players' assumption (that parties are policy oriented and preferences are determined by policy goals alone) and so, modify the assumption: what if MPs are interested in their reputation and reelection? Then, they would have independent desire to create a certain image about themselves, and they would be proposing bipartisan laws more frequently before elections. Such bills would be on minor issues rather than major ones (which government would be interested in the latter), and should occur more frequently the larger the distance among parties in the government, and the smaller the distance between government and opposition parties. All these expectations are corroborated by an extensive dataset covering legislation in both Germany and Belgium.

What is interesting to notice in this chapter is the discovery of a new phenomenon, and the generation of an explanation that bridges what happens with what we know about how politics works, in other words, the creation of a bridge between realism and rationalism.

The König and Junge chapter deals with an important puzzle: while the member countries of the EU have disagreements in terms of policies, they tend to vote unanimously in favour of Commission proposals. Since this appears to be a contradiction, the authors have to justify their claim. They provide several pieces of evidence to support claims of divergent policy preferences among member countries, the most significant being that the member states have attempted several times to revise EU institutions because they perceive them as impeding decision making. Given these disagreements over policy, why do they vote in favour of (most) of

Commission proposals? One possible explanation is that the Commission chooses to present only (or predominantly) legislation that can gain the required support of the member countries. The second (and this is the subject matter of the chapter) is that members may be logrolling across bills in the same jurisdiction, or across bills in different jurisdictions that are decided at the same time. The authors present a series of simulations according to which a small number of such bills are enough to eliminate disagreements. This is a very original contribution because logrolling (like side payments) is a well-known explanation for the question of why veto players would not exercise their veto powers. Logrolling, because it increases the dimensionality of the underlying policyspace until the aggregate bill is preferred by all relevant actors, and side payments, because they make disagreeing players change their mind (if the price is high enough), are two explanations of how veto players can overcome the institutional hurdles of policymaking. The reason that such explanations are not discussed very much in the literature (including the veto players book) is because such explanations (if accepted) would explain everything: for every instance of deviant behaviour there is a price (either in money or in policy) that can explain the deviation, and consequently, any behaviour can be explained. This chapter, however, demonstrates that a *small* number of bills, either in the same jurisdiction or in the same time period, are enough to produce the observed result. The authors claim that logrolling over a large number of bills is unrealistic because of the associated transaction costs. What is more interesting, in my view, is that they present one case where logrolling does *not* work, which indicates that their argument is not trivial: in Fig. 8.2, one can see that logrolling in the area of Justice and Home Affairs does not work (I presume because the few bills that exist in their data set are too similar to generate the necessary benefits). So, this chapter has produced an impressive algorithm to test the possibilities of logrolling.

The Curini and Zucchini chapter is the first paper that uses roll call votes to investigate institutions in a parliamentary system. It goes through a painstaking analysis of different models elaborated for the US system, translates veto players into the necessary context (one-dimensional politics, identification of the pivotal voter(s), and identification of the agenda setter) in order to produce specific expectations for roll call analysis, and compares four different models using this methodology.

One point that needs to be underlined is that for their analysis the agenda setting powers of the government have to be included. However, as I said above (Sect. 1), I consider agenda setting power an independent variable and use Doering's analysis to provide summary statements for different countries. So, the chapter by Curini and Zucchini tests two alternative assumptions of the veto players model: one where the government has the ability to propose bills under closed rule and one under open rule.

They provide extensive analysis of models and predictions, finding that the model of veto players model under open rule has the best results overall. However, I would be unjust to their paper if I did not underline that they produce a much more detailed analysis of different governments and party system configurations in Italy, and nuance their results identifying better models for different cases.

This is a fine piece of work both in terms of deriving specific predictions from different models and analyzing Italian politics. I want to state these points clearly so that what follows is not perceived as criticism, but as suggestion for further research: I am not as comfortable as the authors with the single dimensional models. They find it reasonable that, given government control of the agenda, what is brought to the floor is what the government wants, so that if the government is centrist, extreme left and right can only say "no," meaning that sometimes there is no difference between opposition left and opposition right. However, they cite cases where legislation comes from MPs, not the government, and cases that enable them to tell the moderate left and right from the extremes. I think that, had they not applied the W-Nominate scoring method, and had they not separated governments, they would have produced a multi-dimensional underlying space that would be more credible. But, as I said, it is only because I have read this creative analysis that I have these questions and look forward to future research building on this piece of scholarship.

The chapter by Steunenberg deals with implementation of European policy by EU member states. More precisely, it examines the conditions under which different countries will implement exactly (or deviate slightly from) regulations approved by the EU legislative system. The problem is complicated, the diversity of domestic institutions enormous, so the model is significantly simplified – complicated institutions are assigned names like "national authority" in order to examine their role in a summary way. Steunenberg produces a series of necessary conditions for implementation at the national level to deviate from the status quo (which is the decision made by the legislative institutions of the EU). These conditions include agreement between the Commission and the (national) veto players. What is interesting to note is that while the previous statement may seem trivial, as Steunenberg argues it is not true in the case that one deals with a sequential game between the Commission and not simply one (as this model) but a series of countries: since any action with the Commission with respect to one country will be considered by the others as information about the preferences of the Commission in their subsequent implementation decisions. This model deals with a very significant and very specific EU problem, and as the author many times iterates, it is a first attempt to understand how the multiple layers of decision makers interact.

The chapter on bicameralism (Hug) persistently emphasizes the point that under lots of different plausible configurations, the two chambers of a bicameral legislature interact in a strategic way. Unless this interaction is modeled explicitly, the results from the study of one chamber alone are biased. This is a simple and clear point, and it has been ignored for a long time by the literature. One may think that this is not a significant problem, since after all only one-third of the legislatures in the world are bicameral and the number where the second chamber has a significant say in policy and has a different composition from the first can be counted on one's hands. Yet, most of the countries that produce studies of legislatures (United States, Germany, Switzerland, and EU) belong in this category, so, the misspecification is of consequence. So, Hug's point is a very significant one.

Having said that, here is a case where the underlying number of dimensions is of critical importance. Hug can make all the calculations of backwards induction in complete and (some cases incomplete) information models because he assumes a single dimension, and a median voter result in all cases. If one assumes a two or higher dimension underlying space, the median voter disappears and so does backwards induction, leading us back to the Krehbiel and Rivers (1990) argument according to which strategic voting should not be a major concern. Given the heuristic character of Hug's models, the assumption of single dimensionality of the underlying space determines the credibility of his analysis.

Finally, the Junge chapter comes in the intersection of two different literatures: the study of European institutions that, despite their recent creation (in comparative perspective), are the second most studied institutions (after the United States) and empirical analysis that, of course, has a prevalent value in contemporary social sciences. What Junge does is apply a method that replicates the multiple steps of the analysis of game theoretic models and generates a coefficient for each one of them through simulations that involve small deviations from the point predictions. This way, if the studied institution is the unanimity rule and one of the members fails to agree the mistake is not considered as large as if a whole group of members failed to agree, despite the fact that, strictly speaking, the theory predicts that both situations are impossible.

Junge is able to analyze a series of models of the EU, some of them predicting an important influence of the Parliament, others of the Commission, and still others of the Council. While at the theoretical level disagreements among the authors of these different models have existed for many years, it is refreshing and encouraging that empirical studies can now shed light on the empirical accuracy of different approaches (characterized by assumptions concerning game trees, preferences, permitted and prohibited moves, agenda setting, vetoes, etc.). To my knowledge this is the first time that the quantal response approach has been applied to institutional analysis, and it has the ability to generate a whole industry of empirical investigations comparing the accuracy of specific assumptions concerning institutions. In particular, with respect to the EU where the institutional structure is young and complicated (the reader is referred to the other chapters on the EU in this volume), the potential of this method is remarkable and the potential impact really impressive.

To conclude, I have tried my best to understand how institutions work, and a series of colleagues took the approach I developed and applied it to new phenomena, or disputed some of the assumptions, and produced new and interesting explanations – that is, they produced added value. Either they identified phenomena that we did not know about before reading their chapter or explanations of problems that we had not identified or we did not know how to resolve. The reader will verify that each chapter has something to offer along one of these dimensions, or maybe several of them.

References

Döring H (1995) Parliaments and Majority Rule in Western Europe. St. Martin's Press, New York
Krehbiel K, Rivers D (1990) Sophisticated voting in congress: a reconsideration. J Polit 52:548–78
Tsebelis G (2002) Veto players: how politcal institutions work. Princeton University Press, Princeton, NJ

Part II
Identification of Veto Players

Chapter 2
Empirical Applications of Veto Player Analysis and Institutional Effectiveness

Mark Hallerberg

Introduction

Following the initial publications of Immergut (1992), Huber et al. (1993), and, especially Tsebelis (1995, 2002), the veto player approach has justifiably received increasing attention during the last decade. It is a good theory according to the standards of political science. It is parsimonious, it is testable, and, as Sartori (1970) would want to know, it travels well. Indeed, one of the principal appeals of the approach is its claim that it allows one to compare the effects of institutions in a wide variety of settings, be it presidential or parliamentary democracy, one-party or multi-party government, or Spain and South Korea.

However, despite recent empirical advances as well as clear theoretical claims, we do not know how widely applicable the approach is in empirical work. This essay begins with a discussion of the definition of "veto players." It relies on the definition that Tsebelis provides, but it also presents alternative conceptualizations. The discussion places an emphasis on how the authors translate the theory into testable concepts. The section concludes with a review of the difficulties in operationalizing what constitutes a "veto player" in practice, with some of the problems conceptual and others practical. The second part of this chapter evaluates the empirical evidence in support of the approach. To date, the evidence is quite encouraging and the findings are more supportive of the veto player approach than findings for most theories that are no more than a decade old. However, there are limitations in the cases scholars have studied as well as in the policy areas they have explored. Most empirical studies examine the effects of veto players in developed countries with parliamentary systems. They also, generally, restrict their dependent variables either to law production or to some type of economic policy. The third part of the chapter extends the analysis to the effectiveness of institutions. Certain institutions work best under specific veto player configurations. If the veto player configuration changes but the

M. Hallerberg (✉)
Hertie School of Governance, Berlin, Germany
e-mail: hallerberg@hertie-school.org

T. König et al. (eds.), *Reform Processes and Policy Change: Veto Players and Decision-Making in Modern Democracies*, Studies in Public Choice 16,
DOI 10.1007/978-1-4419-5809-9_2,

institutions remain the same, one would expect that the institutional effectiveness would decline. This section illustrates the argument with examples from the fiscal policy realm. The final section concludes the discussion.

Veto Players: Definitional Issues

The veto player approach in comparative politics is young; indeed, it is difficult to find work older than two decades, which explicitly considers "veto players." Immergut (1992) and Huber et al. (1993) discuss "veto points" and "constitutional structures" respectively, and, as indicated below, each of these concepts is at least in the veto player family. Tsebelis (1995) wrote a key article that introduced the term "veto player." Since his 1995 article, the term has come into vogue. Yet, as Tsebelis (1995, 2002) himself points out, this approach is rooted in a rich tradition that considers the role of institutions. The potential policy effects of multiple "checks and balances" show up at least as early as Montesquieu and this argument motivates Madison in Federalist Paper #10. Romer and Rosenthal (1978) use spatial models to develop an argument about the importance of agenda-setting control as well as the critical role a "reversion point" can play in determining the final outcome. Scholars of presidential systems may wonder what is new about any discussion of a "veto player."

Nevertheless, there is something new and the contemporary use of the concept is most associated with George Tsebelis's work (1995, 1999, 2002). I begin my discussion with his definition: "A veto player is an individual or collective actor whose agreement is required for policy decisions (1995, 293)." In principle, the relevant veto players vary across countries and even within countries. In the American system, for example, the president is usually a relevant veto player because his assent is needed for a bill to become law unless two-third of the House and the Senate override his veto. In Germany, the president is expected to sign all legislation unless he regards it as unconstitutional. The president is therefore a relevant veto player in the United States but not in Germany.[1] The relevant player(s) can also vary within countries. Tsebelis (1995) points out that on defense policy one Senator, Sam Nunn, constituted a "veto player" by himself, while in other dimensions he was simply a member of the Democratic Party.

To understand the relevance of different veto players one needs to know three things: their number, their congruence in relevant policy directions, and their cohesion (Tsebelis 1995, 301). If there is just one veto player, then that player gets his policy choice and there remains nothing more to explain. If there are multiple players, then one must determine where they stand on relevant policy issues and whether it is realistic to treat them as one actor. If there are many actors and they

[1] Note that, in the consideration of the 2002 immigration bill, the German President, Johannes Rau, did serve as a true veto player. Yet such occasions are quite rare in the German system.

all hold the same policy preferences, then according to the "absorption rule," the researcher should treat them all as one. Cohesion refers to the policy positions of the different individual actors who constitute the collective actor (Tsebelis 1995, 311).

How should one apply this argument in empirical work? Tsebelis (1995) focusses especially on how to define and to count relevant veto players. What one does ultimately depends on the type of study one is undertaking. If one is doing a case study, then it is important to examine all relevant players. Less frequent veto players, such as the courts, referenda, or even a single legislator like Sam Nunn, can constitute a veto player and must enter the analysis.[2] If one is doing a large-*n* study, the less frequent players essentially cancel out and become background "noise." The scholar should focus on the relevant institutional and the relevant partisan veto players. The American constitution, for example, requires that the House, the Senate, and the President approve most types of bills unless the Congress can overrule the President's veto. There are therefore three institutional players in the United States. One then determines the number of partisan veto players whose assent is needed in the institutional veto players while keeping the "absorption rule" in mind. The United States has one veto player when a single party controls all three institutional veto players (under President Obama's Administration from 2009) or two veto players at all other times. In countries with only one institutional veto player, the number of veto players is simply the number of parties in government. One should note that, according to Tsebelis (1995), whether or not does the government have a majority status in the parliament does not matter. Minority governments as a rule hold a central position in the ideological spectrum, and, combined with their agenda-setting powers as the party in government, the outcome is essentially the same that would have existed under a majority government with the same parties.[3]

Tsebelis (1999), Tsebelis and Chang (2004), and Tsebelis (2002) refine the application of the model further. The emphasis during the first two works is much more on the ideological distance among veto players. In his article, Tsebelis (1999) adopts the model to a single, left–right dimension. He computes two variables in practice – a "range" variable, which computes the absolute value of the ideological distance between the two players who are most distant and an "alternation" variable, which computes the mid-range position of each coalition and takes the absolute difference between two successive coalitions. His prediction is that greater the ideological distance between the veto players the lower the probability that there will be significant change from the status quo. Moreover, the larger the alternation the greater the probability of change, because governments that are much different from previous governments will want to move away from the status quo. Tsebelis (1999) places empirical focus on significant law production in 15 European parliamentary democracies during 1981–1991. To compute his two independent variables, he averaged the standardized values of three measures of partisanship: Warwick (1994),

[2] It should be noted that Tsebelis makes this argument in his original formulation of the theory. Many authors focus only on his coding rules for large-*n* studies, which are necessarily less detailed.

[3] See Ganghof and Bräuninger (2006) for a spatial analysis and application to Denmark in particular that disputes this view.

Castles and Mair (1984), and Laver and Hunt (1992). He found that both "distance" and "partisanship" have significant effects on the number of laws produced in these democracies.

Tsebelis and Chang (2004) took the analysis to the budgetary realm. They found that increase in "distance" lead to smaller changes in budget composition across 19 advanced industrial countries during 1973–1995.[4] Similarly, a larger "alternation" in the average position of the veto players leads to greater change in the composition of the budget. In their empirical tests, they use the same measure for ideological distance with one change – they take the average of the ideological distance of the three measures in the article by Tsebelis and average this figure with ideological distance in the foreign policy dimension provided by Laver and Hunt (1992), which is the given party's position vis-à-vis the Soviet Union. To determine the location of the previous government's status quo to calculate the measure of "alternation," Tsebelis and Tsebelis and Chang (2004, 457) assume in practice that it is the average position of the government; as Tsebelis and Chang write, "we will consider the average position of the veto players in the previous government as a proxy for the position of the status quo."

Finally, Tsebelis (2002) addresses most completely the issue of cohesion of collective veto players. In Chap. 2, he derives the finding that the type of decision rule within a collective veto player is critical. Under simple majority voting, more cohesion leads to higher policy stability, whereas under qualified majority voting, cohesion leads to *less* policy stability. Yet, he also notes that in practice "collective veto players approximate the behavior of individual ones. We can approximate their preferences by a wincircle (which includes the actual winset) whether they decide by simple or qualified majorities… (63)."

A theoretically powerful claim of this approach is that it can integrate other types of institutional analyses into its framework. The key difference between autocracies and democracies is the way these systems select their veto players. One moves to a democracy when there is competitive selection of veto players. Within the democratic institutions' literature, Lijphart's (1999) majoritarian and consensual forms of democracy can be reformulated as systems with few (or one) veto players and systems with many veto players. This approach also clarifies normative discussions about the choice of institutions. If one desires a government that changes policies quickly, then one should choose a system with one veto player. If one wants to make it difficult for the government to change the status quo unless there is general consensus in society, one should design a system with multiple veto players who have different policy preferences.

Tsebelis (2002) also considers differences between parliamentary and presidential systems. In his article, Tsebelis (1995) treats presidential and parliamentary systems equally concerning the "absorption" rule – if a political party controls two institutional veto players, there is only one veto player in practice. Tsebelis (2002)

---

[4] They compute change in budget composition as the square root of the square of the change in nine budget categories as provided by the IMF's *Government Finance Statistics Yearbook.*

revises this formulation. He argues that the first difference between the two systems concerns who is the agenda setter. In parliamentary systems the agenda setter is the government, whereas in presidential systems the agenda setter is the legislature on non-financial bills (only). He adds that the actual agenda-setting power of the executive may vary considerably, but he uses the differentiation as part of his working definition of the two types of systems.[5] The second difference concerns veto player cohesion. Collective veto players, and particularly political parties, are more disciplined in parliamentary systems than in presidential systems. This discussion has important implications for the counting of veto players. He contends that "the fact that parties lack discipline in presidential systems makes it difficult or even impossible to identify the origins of particular votes. As a result, it is difficult to identify partisan veto players in presidential systems. Whenever this is the case, we will be confined to the study of institutional veto players (85)." A further refinement comes in Alemán and Tsebelis (2005; see also Tsebelis and Alemán 2005). The focus is on the agenda-setting powers of the president across Latin America. One institutional feature that especially strengthens the role of the president is the ability to amend legislation that Congress already has passed. In practice, these "positive" powers of amendment are more powerful than the more "negative" role of a straight veto.

Taken together, the theory that Tsebelis has developed is impressive. Tsebelis is certainly correct when he emphasizes that the veto player approach allows one to analyze seemingly unrelated theoretical literatures in political science; this is an important point. As Tsebelis (1995, 292) emphasizes, "one important contribution of such an approach is that by permitting a simple and conceptually consistent method of making comparisons across systems, it helps resolve a pervasive problem of comparative politics: small sample size."

Additional strengths of the theory include its parsimony and its ready application to empirical work. All of Tsebelis's written work is clear on how to test his arguments, and where there is any question, he addresses the potential glitch in his next chapter or book. The one potential weakness comes from the distinction between presidential and parliamentary democracy in Tsebelis's latest work (2002). The recommendation that he makes empirically is to count partisan players across parliamentary systems on the basis of the number of parties. For presidential systems, one must first consider party discipline and *then* aggregate at the party level only if party discipline is high. Given that his argument is that presidential systems usually have lower party discipline, his expectation is that this will rarely be the case. In the United States, his example of the applicability of the absorption rule in practice is the party discipline that was found during the first 100 days of the Roosevelt Administration (78). This is a high standard to meet. Admittedly, this addition, as applied to presidential systems, makes the theory more realistic and the focus on agenda setting in presidential democracies by Alemán and Tsebelis (2005) suggests a more fruitful way to go for empirical work.

[5] As Tsebelis (2002, 84) notes, "some presidential systems may provide so many agenda setting powers to the president that they look parliamentary, and some parliamentary systems may take away so many agenda setting initiatives from the government that they look presidential."

Yet, the change in the theory concerning veto players in presidential systems does complicate matters. A study of veto players in Latin America, for example, will now need to consider party discipline in every country. To make matters worse, as far as I know, there is no acceptable, comparative measure of party discipline in any event even if one reads the article by Tsebelis (2002) and decides to use such a concept empirically.

Tsebelis is not, however, the only application of the veto player approach and three further distinct arguments about the definition of veto players deserve some discussion before moving on. One argument limits the focus to institutional players only. For Shugart and Haggard (2001), such institutions are "veto gates." A gate is any institution that is required to approve a change from the status quo. An assembly is a veto gate, for example, and, in a unicameral parliamentary system, it is the *only* veto gate. The addition of a second legislature or a president with veto power would add veto gates. The concept is therefore related to the Tsebelis definition – Tsebelis too requires the scholar to consider every relevant institution – but in this case there is not an emphasis on party control. This line of work therefore rejects the use of the "absorption rule" to determine relevant players. Counting veto gates can consequently lead to different counting rules from Tsebelis. A parliamentary democracy like the Netherlands, for example, has just one veto gate according to Shugart and Haggard (2001) but three veto players according to Tsebelis because of the presence of a three-party coalition. Similarly, there is no "absorption rule" in practice. The United States has three veto gates under both "united" and "divided" governments.

This leads to potentially different predictions about the likelihood and scope of change. The very presence of a veto gate represents a potential check to changes from the status quo. The reasoning for a focus on the institutions is best developed by Immergut's (1992) discussion of the politics of health care. Veto points (or gates) provide the opportunity for interest groups to block changes.[6] Tsebelis (1995) does discuss interest groups as potential veto players, but he does not discuss how they matter in practice and how the institutional structure of the policy process may offer a given interest group a veto over policy change even if the group's assent is not formally required for a bill to become law.

Huber et al. (1993), whose definition of "multiple points of influence" approximates Immergut's "veto points," also derive different implications of the choice of electoral system for the effective number of veto players. If parties are well disciplined, interest groups must lobby the whole party (see Huber et al. 1993, 722, footnote 10). Hence a (closed list) proportional representation system decreases the potential level of influence of interest groups. Tsebelis would similarly interpret the use of closed list proportional representation (PR) as eliminating the "personal vote," and in his framework, this makes political parties more cohesive. Yet, to the extent that such systems lead to multiple parties represented in parliament and

[6] To be clear, Immergut (1992) in practice discusses "veto points" instead of "veto gates," but the concept is the same – one should pay attention to the number of veto points that a bill must traverse to become law.

decrease the probability of a one-party majority government, PR systems increase the number of veto players and, so long as the do not share the same ideology in all dimensions, they decrease the scope for change from the status quo.

The second argument calls for separating out the effects of partisan and institutional players while keeping the fundamental division in place. Birchfield and Crepaz (1998) and Crepaz (2002) make the distinction between "collective" and "competitive" veto points, with the latter Tsebelisian institutional players and the former partisan players, respectively, in practice.[7] The predicted effects of the two differ from Tsebelis. The assumption is that "collective" players interact with each other constantly, and they tend to pass legislation through internal logrolling. Therefore, potentially, one expects more change with more collective players. Increase in "competitive" veto players, however, is likely to lead to gridlock. Moreover, which party controls which competitive player is not a concern.[8] This approach therefore is consistent with elements of the veto gate literature, but it adds an assumption about the role of "collective" (or partisan) that is contrary to what Tsebelis argues.

Tsebelis's aggregation of partisan and institutional veto players also troubles Strøm (2000). He contends that it is misleading to aggregate institutional and partisan veto players. Partisan veto players may have motive to veto something but lack the opportunity, whereas institutional veto players may have opportunity but no motive. He notes that Tsebelis agrees with the latter – this is why party control of two chambers can be aggregated – and Tsebelis should add the former as well. Ganghof (2003) has a similar criticism. A veto player may be close in a policy space to another, so that in practice he should agree readily to changes in the status quo with the second player. Yet, he may have motive to block changes in the status quo that the other veto player proposes. The key player here is the voter – a party may have an incentive to differentiate itself in the eyes of voters, which means that it will not accept a position that is readily identified with another player, although ideologically the parties are more or less identical.

Tsebelis (2002, 86–88) responds directly to Strøm's criticism. He argues that it does not make sense for veto players to have motive but no opportunity. Political parties in government work hard to negotiate coalition agreements and try to enact most of their agreement. If they disagree with a change to the status quo they can bring down the government. It therefore is not logical that a veto player could have a motive but no opportunity.

Theoretically, the difference between the two authors may be a difference in conceptualizations about how (parliamentary) governments form and how they function in everyday affairs. Strøm's (2000) argument is consistent with Laver and Shepsle's (1996) view of parliamentary politics. Coalition formation is a game to determine party control of portfolios. Once a minister is selected, that minister determines policy in that ministry. This means that the minister's party selects the policy

---

[7] Crepaz' (2002) competitive players include "federalism, bi-cameralism, central bank independence, and rigid constitutional structures (183)."

[8] Wagschal's (1999a, b) analyses have a similar coding.

in a given dimension. Other parties have no veto power in practice after portfolio distribution. Crepaz (2002) would add that the partisan players then logroll their preferred policies and in the end spending increases. The deal among the parties is that they respect the autonomy of each other's ministers. Tsebelis's response would be that the parties collectively agree on a coalition agreement that spells out the government's position in every policy dimension. Moreover, a party can pull down the government if a minister does something the party does not like.

Ultimately, which argument is right may be an empirical question. Hallerberg (2004) argues that the degree of minister autonomy within a government is a variable. In his study of budget policy, he contends that there are cases of "fiefdom governance" where the individual ministers have fairly wide latitude to set policy. Italy's "pentapartito" governments in the 1980s are good examples. There are also cases where the coalition partners negotiate detailed "fiscal contracts" that set budgets and policy positions for the expected life of the coalition. The parties negotiate expenditure levels in every ministry for the upcoming 4 years. This type of "commitment governance" has been the norm in the Netherlands since 1994. Only after parties have agreed on the fiscal contract do they discuss portfolio allocation. Then the job of the minister is to execute the contract in his/her ministry. Generally, and in Tsebelis's defense, coalition agreements have become more detailed, and have covered more policy areas, in recent years, as Strøm (2000) edited volume convincingly demonstrates. The Tsebelis argument certainly has more applicability in the last two decades.

While Americanists rarely discuss "veto players" as meant in this chapter, there is a rich literature on "divided government" that deserves to be mentioned before moving on to the empirical section.[9] "Divided government" exists whenever different parties control the presidency and at least one of the houses of Congress. It augments the constitutional separation of powers (Cox and Kernell 1991). Moreover, divided government generally means that less gets done. Alesina and Rosenthal (1995) make an argument very much in the spirit of Madison – voters intentionally support different parties for the different offices because they want to increase the checks on the policies that any one party would implement on its own. This argument is, in general, broadly consistent with Tsebelis; an increase in the number of parties that control at least one of the three institutions at the federal (i.e., national) level leads to greater preservation of the status quo. The one difference is that Americanists are generally not willing to give too much credit to the idea of "absorption" of parties. Separation of powers still matters because the three institutions are elected differently (Hansen 1998).

Finally, there is a loose literature that counts simply the number of parties whose assent is needed to pass a bill (Roubini and Sachs 1989; Hallerberg and Basinger 1998; Franzese 2002). The idea is that the fragmentation of government increases the transaction costs to changing the status quo.

[9] See also Cox and McCubbins (2005). Many thanks to Christopher Carman for help wading through the Americanist literature.

Taken together, a common theme that emerges is that increase in veto players usually leads to less policy change (the exception here is Crepaz 2002). The next section reviews the literature to examine whether this is the case in studies done to date.

Empirical Application of the Veto Player Approach

This section reviews empirical work using the veto player approach to explain differences in policy outputs. It can only be a partial review; Tsebelis (2002) does a terrific job in summarizing empirical work that finds support for veto players, and a chapter-length treatment cannot be as comprehensive. Instead, I would like to highlight for which policy fields, and in which parts of the world, the approach has been most successful and also where it has been tested less often and where theory tells us it should be examined further.[10] This way of reviewing the work is constructive because it illustrates where more work can, and should, be done. The discussion below indicates that there are common themes, such as legislative passage of bills and the composition of budgets, where scholars have used the approach. Political economists in the US and in Germany in particular have tested the theoretical implications. Moreover, the data set that analysts use has usually been composed of industrialized democracies and usually (though not always) parliamentary democracies. One indication that the veto player approach is growing more mature is that there are increasing disagreements among the scholars who do this type of work about how best to apply it. The application of the approach to developing countries as well as presidential systems appears less frequently and the results are more mixed.

Legislatures in Parliamentary Democracies

One branch of veto player theory examines legislative outputs broadly defined. Little work has been done in this area outside of Tsebelis and his students, but the reason for the lack of empirical work has as much to do with the state of legislative studies as with the use (or non-use) of veto players in broadly comparative studies. There are simply few legislative studies that are both comparative and quantitative.[11] Tsebelis (1999) does apply his framework to the production of important laws across 15 European democracies during 1981–1991. Increase in the ideological distance between the most extreme veto players in a one-dimensional space leads to decrease

[10] Another way to do this type of review is to break down the work according to the somewhat different definitions of veto players that appear in the literature.

[11] Exceptions include the edited volumes of Herbert Döring (1995) and Döring and Hallerberg (2004).

in the number of important bills that pass parliament. Kreppel (1997) similarly focusses on legislative output in Italy. She finds that increase in the number of political parties leads to decreases in legislative output.[12]

Political Economy Outputs in Developed Countries

Much of the veto player literature in practice has been applied to political economy outputs in developed countries. The initial works focussed on the composition of budgets, and it looked at the number of players only in time-series cross-section analyses of OECD countries. The classic article in budgeting is Roubini and Sachs (1989). They argue that one-party majority governments' consistently maintained tighter fiscal policy than coalition governments with 2–3 parties, whereas the latter governments performed better than majority governments with 4–5 parties. The worst performers were minority governments. Although the authors do not use the term "veto players," their results are consistent with arguments that focus on the number of parties whose assent is required for changes from the status quo. Their empirical results, however, have been questioned both because of their use of an ordinal variable instead of separate dummy variables (Edin and Ohlsson 1991) and because of many miscoded values for their political variables (De Haan and Sturm, 1997; Beck et al. 2000). On the basis of a data set of Organisation of Economic Cooperation and Development (OECD) countries during 1955–1990, Franzese (2002) found that increasing the fragmentation of the government made change from the status quo stickier – government with many players in government tended to maintain either high budget deficits or low budget deficits. Volkerink and De Haan (2001) find that increased fragmentation of the cabinet in terms of the number of parties leads to higher budget deficits. Interestingly, for a comparison with Tsebelis, both Franzese (2001) and Volkerink and De Haan (2001) test ideological distance explicitly but do not find evidence that the ideological distance among coalition partners matters; only the actual *number* of veto players is statistically significant.[13]

In his own work on budgets with Chang, Tsebelis and Chang (2004) found the opposite result, namely ideological distance is statistically significant and leads to less change in the budget because distance increases while the absolute number of veto players is not significant. They examine the degree of change in different categories of the budget with a data set of 19 OECD countries for the period 1973–1990. A potential criticism of their work concerns their coding of ideological distance. As explained in the previous section, they average three measures of the location of political parties on a simple left–right scale and then they average this average with Laver and Hunt's scoring of the ideological position of a given party's foreign

[12] See also Zucchini (1998).

[13] Volkerink and De Haan (2001) operationalize distance as "political fragmentation," and they use the same formula as Franzese (2001) in one case and, following Tsebelis (1995), they also examine the maximum ideological distance between parties in coalition.

policy position vis-à-vis the Soviet Union. One question concerns whether party positions change over time; the indices that Tsebelis and Chang (2004) use, assume that party positions remain constant over time. The second question concerns the use of foreign policy. The rationale in Tsebelis and Chang (2004) is that foreign policy captures truly a second dimension, but one can ask whether foreign policy positions have any relation to budget outcomes.

Bräuninger (2002) addresses these criticisms, and his examination of changes in budget policy represents a rigorous test of the argument. He uses data from the party manifesto project to classify the ideological positions of parties in every dimension. He then runs similar regressions on central government expenditure data from 14 OECD countries during the time period 1973–1997. He finds that the simple one-dimensional coding of ideological distance performs better than the more complex versions that take account of policy positions in multiple dimensions. His results are reassuring to scholars who use simpler measures of veto players.

There have also been a few articles that examine budgetary policy in a given country instead of across a set of countries, although as far as this author knows the analyses have been restricted to one country, namely Germany. Bawn (1999) examines German's spending patterns during 1961–1989. She classifies spending items according to whether they are SPD items, such as educational grants and loans, labor market policy, and sport; whether they are CDU items, such as defense, roads, and housing; and whether the (party) benefits of a given spending item are ambiguous. She finds support for a veto player's explanation of government spending. Spending for SPD items, for example, increased in 1967 when the SPD first affected the budget after forming a Grand Coalition with the CDU in 1966, but, as a veto player argument would anticipate, spending did not change in 1970 after the party formed a coalition with the Free Democratic Party (FDP). König and Troeger (2001) look at the composition of German budgets for a somewhat longer period, from 1961 to 1998. There are some differences between their study and that of Bawn's. They treat the government as a potentially separate actor from the majority parties in the Bundestag. The government has agenda-setting power on the budget, and, because the Bundesrat's approval is not necessary for the annual budget, the game is restricted to the government and to the Bundestag as institutional actors. They also do not assume that the FDP always wants lower spending across the board as Bawn does; instead, there are some budget categories, such as spending on research and development, where the FDP would like more spending. Even with these changes, their results are broadly in line with those reported by Bawn (1999). It should be noted that each article takes ideological distance seriously and hence supports Tsebelis's empirical application of the argument.

Huber et al. (1993) look at the composition of one part of the budget, namely spending on the welfare state. They use generalized least square techniques to estimate the effects of "constitutional structures" on "welfare state effort," which they measure as either social security transfers as a percentage of GDP, social security benefits as a percentage of GDP, or total revenue as a percentage of GDP (733). They find that an increase in the number of constitutional structures reduces welfare effort. Crepaz (2002), examining a factor that size of the welfare state presumably affects, for example, income inequality, arrives at much the same conclusion. An increase in his "competitive" veto players, which largely overlaps Huber's, Ragin's, and Stephens's "constitutional structure," increases income inequality. His findings on "collective veto players," however, contradict much of the previous literature. He contends that increase in partisan veto players leads to higher government spending and lower income inequality. The previous studies that look at budgets more generally, all assume some level of gridlock with more players so that spending should not increase.

There has also been work that examines the other side of the budget, namely taxation. Hallerberg and Basinger (1998) look at the reaction of OECD countries to the 1986 tax reform in the United States. This reform lowered the marginal tax rate on corporations as well as the top marginal rate on personal incomes. Using a cross-section regression of 18 countries, they found that countries with more than one veto player made smaller changes to their marginal tax rates than countries with one veto player during 1986–1990. Although they count the players according to Tsebelis (1995), they look only at the number, not the ideological distance between them. Their conclusions, however, have not gone uncontested. In a "Controversy" section of the journal *Politische Vierteljahresschrift*, Ganghof (1999) criticizes the article on several counts.[14] While Hallerberg and von Hagen (1999) respond to the criticisms directly, and interested readers in the debate are asked to read both articles. As one of the co-authors of the original article, I freely admit that Ganghof (1999) has a point – there are alternative ways to formulate the regression equations and to code some of the cases, under some alternatives, the veto player effects disappear, whereas under others, the veto player effects are clear. With an *n* of just 18, one can put only so much confidence in the results.

Basinger and Hallerberg (2004) attempt to address two weaknesses they saw in Hallerberg and Basinger (1998) as well as some of Ganghof's (1999) criticism. First, in the original article there was no underlying model how veto players mattered in an interactive fashion, that is, the authors assume that countries see a cut in the United States and make a decision at home and ignore what the rest of the world is doing. Second, the empirical analysis in the original article is rather primitive. In this chapter, they begin with a formal model of tax competition. The model's key insight is that political costs that accompany tax reforms have both direct and indirect effects on the likelihood and scale of tax reforms. While countries with higher political costs for reforming are less likely themselves to reduce taxes, these costs also reduce competing countries' incentives to reform regardless of their own political costs. In veto player terms, the model predicts that countries consider the likelihood of reform in competitor countries on the basis of their competitors' veto player structures when making decisions about their tax rate on a mobile factor. In their empirical work, they examine the tax burden on capital in 20 OECD countries during 1980–1997.[15]

[14] Ganghof (1999) also critiques earlier work by Uwe Wagschal (1999a) on the connection between veto players and tax reform; see Wagschal (1999b) for his response.

[15] The calculation of tax burdens is based on the data set provided in Carey and Tchilinguirian (2000). Such calculations are not unproblematic, and Hallerberg and Basinger (2004) should be

They find that decision makers are indeed sensitive to the likelihood of change in competitor countries on the basis of their competitors' veto player constellations. They also find evidence in a time-series cross-sectional framework for the original Hallerberg and Basinger (1998) thesis. Increasing the ideological distance of domestic veto players decreases the sensitivity of the government to actual changes in tax burdens in competitor countries in the previous year.

Finally, two works roughly a decade apart used a case study approach to examine how veto points affect the development of specific policy areas. Immergut (1992) finds that increasing the number of veto points increases specialized interest group influence over health care reform, and they can stall reforms. The number and location of veto points also influence the *strategies* that interest groups use in their lobbying of the government. Bonoli (2001) focusses on pension reform. He finds that increase in the number of veto points leads to concessions to key (narrowly defined) constituencies in countries like Switzerland, whereas few veto points allow the government to pass its reform more or less as is and not to target specific constituencies.

As this summary indicates, the application of the veto player approach to political economy outputs in developed countries is becoming fairly sophisticated. Different methodological approaches, be it case studies, cross-sectional regressions, or time-series cross-sectional work, all find support for the core contention that increasing veto players leads to increasing policy stability.

The next subsections turn to cases where institutions, be it political parties, presidents, or legislatures, tend to be less well defined and less cohesive, than in the developed world. *A priori*, one would therefore expect to find less evidence in support of the approach.

Application in Developing Countries

Scholars have employed the veto player approach less frequently to the developing world, although the results so far are broadly encouraging. Like in the developed world, some of the work has been case study in nature and some large *n*. Because large *n* studies usually have mostly developing countries as cases even when developed countries are included in the analysis, I include such studies in this subsection as well.

In an empirical chapter in the Haggard and McCubbins (2001) edited volume, Heller and McCubbins (2001) explain how different configurations of veto gates affected the development of the regulation of electric utility regulation in Argentina and in Chile. They argue that "an increase in the number of veto players, while making no other changes, will be more biased towards preserving the reversionary policy (232)." Consistent results with a more Immergutian conceptualization of veto

humble about how much they can read into their results. Yet they do use what is "best practice" among the different measures available.

points come from Henisz and Zelner (2001). They examine electricity investment in a panel data set of 78 countries. They find that more veto points leads to overinvestment in "white elephant" projects or projects that concentrate political benefits but are not justified based on their costs to the general population. They contend that there are more "white elephants" where there are many veto points. They conclude that policymakers are better able to withstand interest group pressure when there are few veto points.[16] This work follows Henisz (2000a, b), where he similarly looks at a large *n* data set that covers most of the world to argue that veto points affect economic growth and multi-national investment. Increase in the number of veto points leads to higher economic growth and higher investment as it becomes harder for governments to change the economic rules of the game.[17]

MacIntyre (2001) similarly looks at investment decisions, but, unlike Henisz, he hypothesizes a non-linear relationship between veto players and investment levels. In his view, public policy is the intervening variable between underlying political institutions and the level of capital investment in a given country. Many veto players can lead to stark policy rigidity, which makes governments too slow in responding to crises, whereas few veto players can lead to excessive policy volatility. Both extremes can scare capital. Instead, an intermediate level reduces volatility and increases rigidity, and the level fosters investment. Empirically, he uses an analytic narrative framework to examine fluctuations in the level of investment in four countries that suffered under the East Asia crisis during 1996–1998.

Satyanath's solo or co-authored work with David LeBlang suggests that veto players are especially problematic during economic crises. In response to the East Asian crisis (Satyanath 2006) and in causing currency crises in the first place (LeBlang and Satyanath 2006), increasing veto players meant an inability to act quickly to address the crisis. His more general finding that gridlock may be "good" in normal times but "bad" in a crisis is an interesting extension of Tsebelis' arguments.

Treisman (2000) examines changes in inflation in 87 countries during the 1970s and 1980s. He argues that federalism allows more veto players into macro-economic policy, and it tends to "fix" the level of central bank independence at either high or low (I will discuss central banking in more detail below). Similarly, states with more veto players tend to "lock in" their previous inflation rates. If the rates were high they remain high, whereas if they were low they remain low.

The results for developing countries, whether as case studies or as large *n* studies, are consistent with the veto player approach. In comparison to research on developed countries, however, there are comparatively fewer articles. It may be that

[16] Their index for veto points runs from 0 to 1. It considers party fragmentation within specific institutional veto players, their congruence, and whether or not there are strong courts. The original index is presented in Henisz (2000).

[17] See also Henisz et al. (2005), where they find that increased veto players make it more likely that small investors come to a country because they have greater confidence that the policy environment will remain stable. In this way, veto players may make certain types of changes *more* likely – the possibility of stability makes reforms that open up markets feasible.

there is much less faith in institutional approaches among those who do work on developing countries. Yet, this lack of faith should not discourage rigorous testing of a theory that has proven its use in the developed world and has had encouraging evidence in the studies that have used it, to date.

Transition Countries

Transition countries are located in Eastern Europe. They all experienced some form of collapse of Communist regime around 1989–1990 and are transitioning from a command economy to a market economy. They are therefore in need of significant changes to their status quo. The new democracies would seem to constitute a good data set to test the effects of veto players.

Yet, the research that has been done to date on this part of the world has been less confirmatory of the veto player approach. Indeed, Hellman (1998) seems to find the opposite effect. He argues that increasing the number of parties in government *increases* the degree of change from the status quo. Short-term winners from the initial transition process, such as enterprise insiders who benefit from subsidies and who strip away remaining assets, bankers who thrive because of arbitrage opportunities, etc., fight further moves towards consolidation. They insist that the status quo remains, so that they can continue to collect their rents to the great disadvantage of the population at large. Reform then stalls where government coalitions have narrow bases. Where government coalitions are broad-based and include many parties, parties against further reforms are watered down. In his empirical analysis, he finds strong empirical support for his argument.

Kitschelt (2001) test is not a true test of the veto player approach, but the weak to non-existent results he finds for constitutional design measures reinforce the perception that institutional differences have little practical effect in these countries. He measures constitutional design as the relative strength of the president as well as whether there is parliamentarism. His empirical results provide weak support for the effects of constitutional design on market liberalization in his statistical analysis but no effects on institutional economic reform. Yet, further analysis as well as detailed case knowledge makes him "somewhat skeptical (39)" even of these results.

Bodenstein (2002), in an examination of the determinants of trade liberalization in transition countries, finds no relationship between the assessment of Beck et al.'s (2000) checks and balances and a negative impact of strength of the presidency. Like Kitschelt (2001), he does not test the Tsebelis argument directly, but the results nevertheless are consistent.

Do these three articles together constitute an indictment of the veto player approach, at least as applied to transition countries? On the face of it, the answer is no–political parties are simply not cohesive in any East European country, with the last incarnation of the party "Solidarity" in Poland almost an absurd extreme. Indeed, one can tell a Tsebelisian story even with the results in Hellman (1998). The narrow party coalitions Hellman discusses arise to protect the initial change during the transition process, and they have no interest in change from the status quo. A large coalition with loose party discipline, however, may very well increase the size of the winset and make greater change possible. If a reformer is the agenda setter, then that change will occur.[18] Political institutions are similarly fragile and subject to change.

Moreover, to the extent that presidents are relevant in former Communist countries, Tsebelis and Rizova (2007) find similar evidence for the strength of the president in roughly one-third of countries in the region where the president has the same power to amend legislation as is found in some Latin American countries.

Veto Players and Institutions

There is also a growing literature that looks at how veto players determine the relative effectiveness, and the choice, of institutions. Tsebelis (2002) emphasizes that the ideological distance between/among veto players determines the amount of discretion that certain institutions have in a given policy area. For example, large ideological differences among parties in government would allow the bureaucracy, relatively greater reign, to do what it wants than a government with just one veto player. Tsebelis applies this framework to the checking power of referenda on the government (Hug and Tsebelis 2002; Tsebelis 2002, Chap. 5), legislative veto players on judges (Tsebelis 2002, Chap. 10), and the Council of Ministers on European Commission proposals (Tsebelis 2002, Chap. 11).

Others have made similar arguments concerning the relative independence of central banks. The application of the theory to central banking is more developed than to other institutions and Tsebelis (2002) does a good job of summarizing the effects of veto players on other institutions, so I will focus especially on the central banking literature here.[19]

Lohmann (1998a), Bernhard (1998), Moser (1999), and Keefer and Stasavage (2003) all consider how increase in the number of some type of "veto player" increases the discretion of the central bank to determine monetary policy. It becomes harder for the government to unite to overturn the decision of the central bank when there are more veto players.

Who these "veto players" are, however, and the exact role that they play, differ. Lohmann's (1998a) focus is on Germany, and she notes that the discretion of the Bundesbank increases when the government's parties do not hold a majority of seats in the upper house of parliament, the Bundesrat. Discretion therefore increases when Germany experiences periods of divided government; the number of partisan players *in* government is not consequential. Bernhard focusses primarily

---

[18] Indeed, an interesting extension of Hellman (1998) would be to look at the agenda-setter in the various governments.

[19] The next two pages received inspiration from a shorter summary of the central bank literature in Hallerberg (2002).

on the dichotomy between one-party and multi-party governments. States that have coalition governments are more likely to have independent central banks. Keefer and Stasavage (2003) come closer to the original Tsebelis coding of veto players. Like Tsebelis, they include partisan players for parliamentary systems, but they count the number of veto points in presidential systems depending on whether or not the same parties control the different institutions. They also make a series of adjustments depending on whether a country uses an open or closed list proportional representation system and whether they judge the electoral system as being competitive.[20] They find that the effectiveness of central banks in pursuing low inflation increases with an increase in the number of (logged) veto players. In the empirical results they include 78 countries.

Bernhard (1998) considers a combination of institutional and partisan veto players. He codes countries with "strong bi-cameralism" and indicates that such states are more likely to have independent central banks. In practice, those states are Australia, Germany, Switzerland, and the United States. He also creates a "punishment index" where increase in the index lead to greater independence. This index includes polarization, parliamentary or congressional committee strength, and whether or not a country has a coalition or minority government. Neither of his variables match completely the Tsebelis definition for veto players – strong bi-cameral states are coded the same way whether one party or more than one party controls them, whereas the punishment index codes coalition governments and one-party minority governments the same way – but Bernhard's (1998) results are consistent with an argument that an increase in veto players increases independence of the bank.

Moser (1999, 2000), in contrast, focusses on the level of institutional checks and balances for a cross-section of 22 OECD countries rather than partisan control. He creates dummy variables for countries with strong checks and balances, weak checks and balances, and no checks and balances. Countries with bi-cameral chambers that have equal power and have different rules to elect them to assure different "compositions" are coded "strong," those where the lower chamber dominates but where there is still a different composition are coded "weak," and all others are coded with no strong checks and balances. One should note that "composition" is meant to represent, in most cases, the *potential* for different partisan majorities to control the two houses, which makes the argument distinct from Tsebelis (1995, 1999), who counts only *actual* differences in partisan control.[21] Moser (1999, 2000) produces results to argue that states with strong institutional checks and balances have lower inflation rates than states without them even controlling for the level of central bank independence. He also emphasizes that it is harder for governments with strong checks and balances to change bank charters that grant banks independence, and he finds that states with more checks and balances have more independent banks.

---

[20] They also take the log of the value before they include it in regressions.

[21] Moser (2000) does note that, in cases where the coding is unclear, he looks at partisan control and rules a country as having no checks and balances if the same parties always control both houses. He does this in his coding for three countries – Belgium, Italy, and Japan.

Hallerberg (2002) examines the joint choice of exchange rate regime and the level of central bank independence. He argues that two types of veto players matter, partisan veto players and the presence or absence of subnational veto players in the form of federalism. A crucial issue for partisan players is whether voters can readily identify the benefits, and the costs, of the manipulation of the economy with the partisan players. A second issue concerns the veto player's controllability of a given type of policy.

The Role of Veto Players in Institutional Effectiveness

Analyses of budget policy in the European Union (Hallerberg and von Hagen 1999; Hallerberg 2004) have also assessed how the number of veto players affects the fiscal institutions that parliamentary democracies in the European Union put in place to make decisions on the budget. "Good" fiscal governance arises from packages of rules, norms, and institutions that centralize the budget process. In game-theoretic terms, all governments face a common pool resource (CPR) problem. This problem arises whenever the decision makers consider the full benefits of spending only part of the tax burden. A centralization of the budget process that forces the actors to internalize the full tax externality leads to lower spending and, over multiple periods, lower budget deficits. They argue that there are two ways to solve CPR problems that which arise in all governments because decision makers on spending rarely have an incentive to consider the full tax burden of their decisions. One way to solve this problem, which they term "delegation," involves delegating strategic problems to one central player who considers the full tax burden. In practice, this player is usually the finance minister. In contrast to this discretionary approach, "fiscal contracts" involve clear rules on the budget. Coalition partners sign such "contracts" for the life of the coalition and in the process of the negotiations internalize the tax externality. The discretionary approach works only in countries with one veto player in government or where the policy positions of the players are close. The reason is that coalition partners would not trust a strong finance minister where ideological distances are larger. Instead, countries with veto players where the ideological distance is large prefer explicit fiscal contracts that all parties can monitor.

The work discussed in Hallerberg et al. (2009) extends this analysis and is particularly relevant for institutional analysis and suggests some avenues for future work. They consider cases where the fiscal institutions remain in place but where the ideological distance of veto players' changes. For example, the Greek Communist–Conservative coalition in 1989 brought together two parties that had no trust on each other. Although the fiscal institutions in support of the Greek finance minister were weak to begin with, there was no political will to delegate the power to one central player to consolidate public finances, and fiscal performance deteriorated. Similarly, when the veto player distance narrowed in countries that were expected "contract" states, a "delegation" form of fiscal governance would have been more appropriate and fiscal performance similarly worsened. An example here would be the Irish government in 1989 or the Dutch government in 1994 (see Chap. 4 for further details).

The point here is that veto player distance can affect both the choice of fiscal institutions as well as their effectiveness. When institutions are designed for the long-term average, but there is a short-term deviation from this average, the institutions will remain in place but they will not function well.

Conclusion

This chapter argues that the veto player approach is intuitive, testable, and transparent. A principal strength is that it offers researchers a theoretical tool to compare across seemingly incomparable systems, be they democracies, non-democracies, single- or multi-party systems, or presidential and parliamentary systems. The approach therefore furthers our knowledge of comparative politics. The discussion of empirical evidence indicates that the approach has already demonstrated its empirical value when applied to political economy outputs in developed parliamentary democracies. Yet, the applicability to the rest of the world so far, although relatively thin, has been encouraging. Moreover, the relative paucity of work outside of the developed world has less to do with explicit evidence that the theory is false than with the fact that the theory is yet to be tested. There is so much more that can be, and should be, done in the future.

This chapter also suggests that more work should be done on how veto players affect the design of other institutions. Most work puts some variable for "veto player" on the right-hand side as an independent variable and some outcome variable like economic growth on the left-hand side. As the example from fiscal policy illustrates, there may be institutions that also bear explanation. The configuration of veto players leads to different types of coordination problems within government. Under one-party governments, the issue is to make decisions where the base preferences are essentially the same but where policymakers have incentives to consider only the tax burden that their constituencies bear, and this burden is usually less than the burden on the whole party (or country). One central player in the form of a finance minister can then act as the central coordinator. As the ideological distance among veto players increases, however, the nature of the coordination game changes. Parties with clear differences in what they consider to be an ideal policy must nevertheless make agreements. In the fiscal policy case, fiscal contracts that set clear rules and that are transparent for all players are preferable to granting discretion to one player who is common when ideological distance is zero or low.

Tsebelis's work also reminds us of where to begin any analysis. He expects that we focus on actors whose assent is required to change the status quo. One must begin with the question, who matters? This in itself is important. Too many approaches and too many authors, forget this guiding question. Without knowing who matters it is hard to explain anything.

References

Alemán E, Tsebelis G (2005) The origins of presidential conditional agenda-setting power in Latin America. Lat Am Res Rev 40(2):3–26

Alesina A, Rosenthal H (1995) Partisan politics, divided government, and the economy. Cambridge University Press, Cambridge and New York

Basinger S, Hallerberg M (2004) Remodeling the competition for capital: how domestic politics erases the Race-to-the-Bottom. Am Polit Sci Rev 98(2):261–276

Bawn K (1999) Money and majorities in the Federal Republic of Germany: evidence for a veto players model of government spending. Am J Pol Sci 43(3):707–736

Beck T, Clarke G, Groff A, Keefer P, Walsh P (2000) New tools and new tests in comparative political economy: the database of political institutions. Working Paper # 2283, World Bank

Bernhard W (1998) A political explanation of variations in central bank independence. Am Polit Sci Rev 92(2):311–327

Birchfield V, Crepaz MML (1998) The impact of constitutional structures and collective and competitive veto points on income inequality in industrialized democracies. Eur J Polit Res 34,175–200

Bodenstein T (2002) The domestic and international sources of trade openness in transition countries Paper Presented at the 2002 Meetings of the European Consortium of Political Research Meetings, Turin, Italy, March

Bräuninger T (2002) Partisan veto players, party preferences, and the composition of government expenditures. Paper presented at the Annual Meeting of the Public Choice Society, Nashville, 2003

Carey D, Tchilinguirian H (2000) Average effective tax rates on capital, labour and consumption. OECD Economic Working Paper 258

Castles F, Mair P (1984) Left-right political scales: some expert judgments. Eur J Polit Res 12, 73–88

Cox GW, Kernell S (eds) (1991) The politics of divided government. Westview Press, Boulder

Cox GW, McCubbins MD (2005) Setting the agenda: responsible party government in the US House of Representatives. Princeton University Press, Princeton

Crepaz MML (2002) Global, constitutional, and partisan determinants of redistribution in fifteen OECD countries. Comp Polit 34(2):169–188

De Haan J, Sturm J-E (1997) Political and economic determinants of OECD budget deficits and government expenditures: A reinvestigation. Eur J Polit Econ 13: 739–750

Döring, H (1995) Parliaments and majority rule in Western Europe. Campus Verlag, Frankfurt am Main

Döring H, Hallerberg M (eds) (2004) Patterns of parliamentary behaviour: passage of legislation across Western Europe. Ashgate Publishing Limited, Aldershot

Edin P-A, Ohlsson H (1991) Political determinants of budget deficits: coalition effects versus minority effects. Eur Econ Rev 35:1597–1603

Franzese RJ (2002) Macroeconomic policies of developed democracies. University of Michigan Press, Ann Arbor

Ganghof S (1999) Steuerwettbewerb und Vetospieler: Stimmt die These der blockierten Anpassung? Polit Vierteljahresschr 40:458–472

Ganghof S (2003) Promises and pitfalls of veto player analysis. Swiss Polit Sci Rev 9(2):1–25

Ganghof S, Bräuninger T (2006) Government status and legislative behavior. Party Polit 12(4): 521–539

Haggard S, McCubbins MD (2001) Presidents, parliaments, and policy. Cambridge University Press, Cambridge

Hallerberg M (2002) Veto players and monetary commitment technologies. Int Organ 56(4): 775–802

Hallerberg M (2004) Domestic budgets in a united Europe: fiscal governance from the end of Bretton Woods to EMU. Cornell University Press, Ithaca, NY

Hallerberg M, Basinger S (1998) Internationalization and changes in tax policy in OECD countries: the importance of domestic veto players. Comp Polit Stud 31:321–353
Hallerberg M, Basinger S (1999) Globalization and tax reform: an updated case for the importance of veto players. Polit Vierteljahresschr 40:618–627
Hallerberg M, von Hagen J (1999) Electoral institutions, cabinet negotiations, and budget deficits within the European Union. In: Poterba J, von Hagen J (eds) Fiscal institutions and fiscal performance. University of Chicago Press, Chicago, pp 209–232
Hallerberg M, Strauch R, von Hagen J (2009) Fiscal governance: evidence from Europe. Cambridge University Press, Cambridge
Hansen MJ (1998) Individuals, institutions, and public preferences over public finance. Am Polit Sci Rev 92 (3):513–531
Heller WB, McCubbins MD (2001) Political institutions and economic development: the case of electric utility regulation in Argentina and Chile. In: Haggard S, McCubbins MD (eds) Presidents, parliaments, and policy. Cambridge University Press, Cambridge, pp 229–255
Hellman JS (1998) Winners take all: the politics of partial reform in Postcommunist transitions. World Polit 50(2):203–234
Henisz WJ (2000a) The institutional environment for economic growth. Econ Polit 12:1–31
Henisz WJ (2000b) The institutional environment for multinational investment. J Law Econ Organ 16(2):334–364
Henisz WJ, Zelner BA (2001) Interest groups, political institutions and electricity investment. Paper Presented at the 2001 American Political Science Association Meetings, San Francisco, CA
Henisz WJ, Zelner BA, Guillén MF (2005) The worldwide diffusion of market-oriented infrastructure reform,1977–1999. Am Sociol Rev 70(6):871–897
Huber E, Ragin C, Stephens JD (1993) Social democracy, Christian democracy, constitutional structure, and the welfare state. Am J Sociol 99(3):711–749
Hug S, Tsebelis G (2002) Veto players and referenda around the world. J Theor Polit 14(4):465–515
Immergut E (1992) The political construction of interests: national health insurance politics in Switzerland, France and Sweden, 1930–1970. Cambridge University Press, New York
Keefer P, Stasavage D (2003) The limits of delegation: veto players, central bank independence, and the credibility of monetary policy. Am Polit Sci Rev 97(3):407–423
Kitschelt H (2001) Post-communist economic reform. Causal mechanisms and concomitant properties. Paper prepared for the 2001 Annual Meeting of the American Political Science Association, San Francisco, CA
König T, Troeger V (2001) Haushaltspolitik und Vetospieler. Manuscript, University of Constance (May)
Kreppel A (1997) The impact of parties in government on legislative output in Italy. Eur J Polit Res 31:327–350
Laver M, Hunt WB (1992) Policy and party competition. Routledge, Chapman, & Hall, New York
Laver M, Shepsle K (1996) Making and breaking governments. Cambridge University Press, Cambridge
LeBlang D, Satyanath S (2006) Institutions, expectations, and currency crises. Int Organ 60(1):245–262
Lijphart A (1999) Patterns of democracy. Government forms and performance in thirty-six countries. Yale University Press, New Haven
Lohmann S (1998a) Federalism and central bank independence: the politics of German monetary policy, 1957–92. World Polit 50(April):401–446
Lohmann S (1998b) Institutional checks and balances and the political control of the money supply. Oxf Econ Pap 50:360–377
MacIntyre A (2001) Institutions and investors: the politics of the economic crisis in Southeast Asia. Int Organ 55(1):81–122
Moser P (1999) Checks and balances, and the supply of central bank independence. Eur Econ Rev 43(8):1569–1593

Moser P (2000) The political economy of democratic institutions. Edward Elgar, Cheltenham
Romer T, Rosenthal H (1978) Political resource allocation, controlled agendas, and the status quo. Public Choice 33(4):27–43
Roubini N, Sachs JD (1989) Political and economic determinants of budget deficits in the industrial democracies. Eur Econ Rev 33:903–938
Sartori G (1970) Concept misformation in comparative politics. Am Polit Sci Rev 64(4): 1033–1053
Satyanath S (2006) Globalization, politics, and financial turmoil: Asia's banking crisis. Cambridge University Press, Cambridge
Shugart MS, Haggard S (2001) Institutions and public policy in presidential systems. In: Haggard S, McCubbins (eds) Presidents, parliaments, and policy. Cambridge University Press, Cambridge, pp 64–104
Strøm K (2000) Delegation and accountability in parliamentary democracies. Eur J Polit Res 37: 261–289
Strøm K, Müller W (eds) (2000) Coalition governments in Western Europe. Oxford University Press, Oxford
Treisman D (2000) Decentralization and inflation: commitment, collective action, or continuity? Am Polit Sci Rev 94(4):837–857
Tsebelis G (1995) Decision making in political systems: veto players in presidentialism, parliamentarism, multicameralism and multipartyism. Br J Polit Sci 25(3):289–325
Tsebelis G (1999) Veto players and law production in parliamentary democracies: an empirical analysis. Am Polit Sci Rev 93(3):591–608
Tsebelis G (2002) Veto players: how political institutions work. Russell Sage Foundation, New York City; and Princeton University Press, Princeton
Tsebelis G, Chang ECC (2004) Veto players and the structure of budgets in industrialized countries. Eur J Polit Res 43:449–476
Tsebelis G, Alemán E (2005) Presidential conditional agenda setting in Latin America. World Polit 57(3):396–420
Tsebelis G, Rizova TP (2007) Presidential conditional agenda setting in the former Communist countries. Comp Polit Stud 40(10):1155–1182
Volkerink B, De Haan J (2001) Fragmented government effects on fiscal policy: new evidence. Public Choice 109:221–242
Wagschal U (1999a) Schranken staatlicher Steuerungspolitik: Warum Steuerreformen scheitern können. In: Busch A, Plümper T (eds) Nationaler Staat und internationale Wirtschaft. Nomos, Baden-Baden, pp 223–247
Wagschal W (1999b) Blockieren Vetospieler Steuerreformen? Polit Vierteljahresschr 40(4): 628–640
Warwick P (1994) Government survival in western European parliamentary democracies. Cambridge University Press, New York
Zucchini F (1998) Italian divided government: veto players in executive-legislative interaction. Manuscript, University of Milan

Chapter 3
The Veto Player Approach in Macro-Comparative Politics: Concepts and Measurement[1]

Detlef Jahn

The veto player approach is one of the most prominent analytical strategies in current comparative politics research. It has been applied in both qualitative and quantitative comparative analysis as well as in formal modelling of decision-making processes. This chapter focusses on the veto player approach in macro-quantitative research designs. Macro-quantitative analysis requires a relatively large number of observations in order to allow for comparison by statistical analysis. In recent years, highly sophisticated statistical methods of causal inference have been developed for macro-comparative analysis. This is a welcome development because statistical analysis is becoming increasingly important in political science research. This is particularly true for the so-called time-series–cross-sectional (TSCS) analysis, which is the state-of-the art method of the discipline and considers variables that are potentially variant between countries and over time. Both the comparison of a large number of countries over ample periods of time as well as the modelling of sophisticated causality place high demands on the variables used. While variables have to be sufficiently abstract in order to travel across cases (Sartori 1984), the downside of abstractness is that it renders the specification of causal relationships difficult. For this reason, some scholars are highly suspicious of macro-quantitative comparative analysis (Kittel 2006). In order to overcome this problem, macro-quantitative analysis needs a theoretical micro-foundation as well as variables that are sensitive to variations between countries and time.

[1]The first version of this chapter was presented at the conference "Reform processes and policy change: How do veto players determine decision-making in modern democracies" at the Mannheim Centre for European Social Research (MZES), 14–16 May 2009. I thank the participants of this workshop and George Tsebelis for comments and encouragement. The results of this chapter are derived from the research project "Environmental Pollution as a Global Phenomenon" funded by the German Research Foundation (DFG). I thank Christoph Oberst, Nils Düpont, Thomas Behm, Konstantin Baltz, Jesse Lehrke and Stefanie Korte for data collection and helpful comments. Further, I thank Esther Seha for commenting on and editing the chapter.

D. Jahn (✉)
Baderstr. 6/7, 17489 Greifswald, University of Greifswald, Germany
e-mail: djahn@uni-greifswald.de

T. König et al. (eds.), *Reform Processes and Policy Change: Veto Players and Decision-Making in Modern Democracies*, Studies in Public Choice 16,
DOI 10.1007/978-1-4419-5809-9_3, © Springer Science+Business Media, LLC 2010

In this chapter, I review how these requirements have been dealt with in the literature. I focus on the conceptualization of the veto player approach and the examination of the concept's measurement and aggregation. As more and more indices are on offer and often used without further reflection, this analysis is of increasing importance. It is necessary to assess empirical indices with regard to their conceptual and empirical benefits in order to provide guidelines for their use in analytical models. This concerns not only the handling of the veto player approach but also the use of other indices. For instance, democracy indices have recently been reviewed by Munck and Verkuilen (2002) from the same perspective. In their assessment they have differentiated between concerns of conceptualization, measurement, and aggregation. I follow their line of argument by considering a variety of veto player indices in this way.

Here I first outline the essential aspects of assessing the conceptualization of the veto player approach. Then I summarize its core analytical foundation that results in the differentiation between veto point and veto player analysis. After reviewing major indices of veto point and veto player analysis in the third and fourth part, I elaborate on some empirical requirements an enhanced veto player index would have to meet. These improvements make the veto player analysis sensitive to changes in both institutional settings and preferences of veto players. In addition, the approach enables us to analyze multi-dimensional preferences and shorter time units. The chapter concludes by discussing the contribution of the enhanced veto player index, embedding the results into the debate on the development of more powerful analytical and empirical tools for veto player analysis.

Conceptualizing and Measuring Veto Players in Macro-comparative Analysis

Our concern with developing highly complex causal theories and revealing causal inferences between variables by sophisticated data analysis over-shadows the equally important problem of conceptualization and measurement. This is even true for a parsimonious theory such as the veto player approach. Applying elaborated concepts always involves a trade-off between analytical clarity and parsimony on the one hand and a concept's validity in its empirical context on the other hand. Sartori (1984) forcefully argues that concepts must be able to travel while also making sense for individual cases without becoming idiographic. Some might, metaphorically speaking, throw the baby out with the bath water when suggesting case-specific improvements to veto player analysis (Ganghof 2003 discusses this point). However, over-simplistic operationalizations run the risk of undermining the validity of an analysis.

In this chapter, I follow the lead of other scholars and evaluate various veto player approaches with regard to their conceptualization, measurement, and aggregation (Smelser 1976; Adcock and Collier 2001; Munck and Verkuilen 2002). Conceptualization translates the theoretical concept into the empirical world. Theoretical concepts should generate explicit hypotheses that reflect their effects in empirical terms. We have to be clear about causal mechanisms that yield certain effects (Hedström and Swedberg 1998). For instance, causal mechanisms can be established by substantiating analytical concepts with a micro-foundation.

Conceptualization also implies the identification of a concept's relevant empirical attributes. One is best advised to opt for a parsimonious approach that neither includes too many specifications (maximalistic) nor too few (minimalistic). In the field of veto player analysis, this mainly concerns the identification of veto players as well as their preferences. Hypothetically, many stakeholders can act as veto players in certain policy fields. For macro-comparative analysis however, we need to focus on the most relevant ones in order to obtain general conclusions. In this respect, one important aspect is the problem of redundancy. Some empirical concepts measure the same analytical aspect by means of various empirical indicators, which entails an implicit over-estimation of some of the concept's elements. Political actors' preferences are the driving force of veto player analysis and must be clearly specified in order to provide a basis for causal hypotheses.

Measurements link the conceptual attributes to observations. As mentioned above, the most important conceptual attributes of veto player analysis are the number of veto players and their respective preferences. How are data collected for these attributes? A technical issue in this context is the level of measurement. Although this may seem rather trivial, it is not. Highly sophisticated empirical analysis such as TSCS analysis presupposes a certain level of measurement. Regression analysis normally calls for metric variables. Ordinal or count variables are unsuitable for regression analysis as they yield biased coefficients. In turn, downgrading ordinal variables to dummy variables – which are suitable for regression analysis – leads to a substantial information loss.

Modern data analysis also needs variation over time, meaning that if a concept such as the function of veto players were to be time-variant, it would have to be taken into account. This aspect actually refers to both attributes of the veto player approach: the number of veto players as well as their preferences. As both may vary over time, empirical concepts have to account for this aspect.

Once a concept's measurement is completed with the assignment of scores to each of the relevant attributes, the next step is to aggregate the concept's disaggregated scores. This step has to do with the conceptualization of the theoretical concept. How does causal inference work in theoretical terms? In veto player analysis, some scholars focus on the number of (potential) veto players. When advancing this view, one has to determine whether (potential) veto players have the same effect and must thus be counted equally. Other veto player approaches assume a different theoretical assumption. Tsebelis contends that the number of veto players is second – rank as opposed to their respective ideological distances. In order to grasp this aspect empirically, we need to measure the ideological range of the veto players that are spaced farthest from one another. In this case we do not have the problem of weighing various veto players differently.

In the following text, I address the three aspects of conceptualization, measurement, and aggregation by referring to four commonly used veto player indices. Since there are two approaches which differ in their focus I begin by pointing out the differences. The following two parts then focus on veto point and veto player analysis. While the first part is mainly of an analytical nature, the two subsequent ones also present empirical data applied in various approaches.

Competing Concepts of Veto Player and Veto Point Analysis

The basic premise of the veto player approach is simple. Governments as agenda setters[2] strive for implementing their favoured policies. In the case of government inactivity, the policies remain unchanged. If governments were free and willing to act without obstruction, they would move the status quo to satisfy their preferences. Granted that there are other actors with divergent preferences that have decision-making power (veto players), the result would be a compromise between the government's preferences on the one hand and the veto player's preferences on the other. Formally, government activity can be measured by comparing the policy or policy outcome at time point t_1 with that of at t_2. The policy or policy outcome at t_1 is called *status quo*. If the status quo is 30 (e.g. 30% of the GDP is invested in social expenditure) and the preference of the government is 35 (for instance, it wants to improve unemployment benefits), the policy shift from t_1 to t_2 would change from 30 to 35. This would be true, other things being equal, if there were no veto players. Veto players can alter the outcome since they are "... actors whose agreement is required for a change of the status quo." (Tsebelis 2002: 17). Referring to the example this means that if a veto player prefers 32, a compromise between 35 and 32 has to be reached and the government's target of 35 is unattainable. If a veto player were to prefer 25, making a compromise could even mean the continuance of the status quo. Since agenda setters control the agenda, they do not have to make compromises that are further away from their ideal points than the status quo. If they risk reaching a result that, in their view, is less favourable than the status quo, they simply do not put the issue on the agenda and make do with the status quo.

There are basically two notions of veto players and their operationalization in macro-comparative politics. One strand counts the number of veto players. As this perspective does not take preferences and veto player interaction into account, I assign these approaches to the veto *points* category. The veto function is measured by the number of veto points. Scholars in this research tradition contend that the status quo is more likely to change in political systems with few or no veto points than in political systems with many veto points.

---

[2] In modern democracies, there could also be agenda setters other than governments. However, I neglect this aspect since in parliamentary democracies governments are the agenda setter most of the time (Döring et al. 1995; Bräuninger and Debus 2009). In the political system of the United States, the Congress acts as an agenda setter above all the majority parties (Krehbiel 1998; Cameron 2000; Cox and McCubbins 2005). Another exception is the European Union's increased status as agenda setter. This aspect is not accounted for as it would complicate veto player illustration and its inclusion would not change the basic idea of the chapter.

The analysis of veto points does not incorporate actor preferences: neither those of the agenda setter (e.g. governments) nor those of veto points. In fact this presupposition makes speculating on the range of potential compromise impossible. This is different in approaches under the label of veto *player* analysis. Veto player analysis considers the preferences of veto players. The veto function is the ideological range between the preferences of veto players. The closer the preferences of potential veto players, the easier it is to change the status quo. The relevant ideological range for analysis is the distance between the two veto players with the greatest differences. For instance, if there were five veto players with social expenditure preferences of 31, 32, 33, 34, and 35% of GDP, the relevant range would be 4 (from 31 to 35), meaning that three veto players in between 31 and 35 would be absorbed. Veto player analysis builds on rational choice theory and is theoretically complex (Tsebelis 2002). The empirical measure of the ideological range of the two opposite veto players is merely an empirical proxy for the win set, the area within which a compromise between veto players is possible.[3]

Veto point and veto player analysis focus on different empirical aspects. Veto point analysis intends to count all *potential* veto points. A basic problem of this analytical concept is that it cannot capture when a potential veto point actually exercises its veto power. This is easier in veto player analysis. If veto players have identical preferences, their veto function is zero; if the preferences differ by five points on an ideological scale, the veto function is five and so on.

The theoretical underpinning of both approaches is substantially different. While the analysis of veto points aims at identifying the number of veto points that perform institutional constraints on the manoeuvrability of central governments, veto player analysis starts out from models of interaction of political actors and institutions, which are based on rational choice theory. Therefore, causal mechanisms in veto point analysis are much more difficult to trace than in veto player analysis, which has a micro-foundation.

To be sure, veto player theory – both the notions of veto points and veto players – cannot make assumptions about the direction of policy change. For instance, with regard to the positive or negative effects of veto players on economic growth, George Tsebelis explicitly states: "It is not clear whether many veto players will lead to higher or lower growth, because they will 'lock' a country to whatever policies they inherited, and it depends whether such policies induce or inhibit growth." (Tsebelis 2002: 204). Veto player analysis is also flawed when the status quo shifts, which is common in political reality (e.g. changes in the economic situation, unemployment rates, trade, demographic factors, etc.). Even though this aspect is crucial for veto player analysis, I will not focus on it and will instead concentrate on a

[3] The analytical tools for identifying the win set of collective actors are (a) preferences, (b) status quo, and (c) the cohesion of individual veto players in a particular issue area. I do not consider the complex interaction of variables in this chapter and focus instead on established operationalizations of the veto player approach in macro-comparative analysis. However, I will get back to these aspects in the conclusion of this chapter.

discussion of the established indices of veto point/player analysis. I next discuss certain concepts and their operationalization in the tradition of veto point analysis in macro-comparative politics before turning to veto player analysis.

Measurement and Aggregation of Veto Points in Macro-comparative Analysis

Indices about institutional constraints on central governments were introduced for the first time in the early 1990s (Huber et al. 1993; Colomer 1996; Schmidt 1996, Kaiser 1997). These indices refer to the theoretical work of semi-sovereign states (Katzenstein 1987) and try to specify the "degree of semi-sovereignty" (Schmidt 1996: 171) or the "patterns of institutional pluralism" (Colomer 1996). The analysis of institutional constraints on the manoeuvrability of central governments concentrates on potential veto points which may obstruct decision-making. These approaches can be divided into two categories: simple indices which count a country's number of veto points and veto point analyses which aim at identifying the general goal of veto points. The latter approach distinguishes between veto points that either obstruct or support governments. Strictly speaking, supportive veto points are a contradiction in terms, and may have substantially different functions than vetoing a government's policies. Since the distinction between obstructive and supportive veto points is not clear, analysis of the latter – or collective or consensus veto points as they are sometimes labeled – might measure something else than veto points.

The empirical analysis of these indices is based on the number of veto points in a respective political system. All veto points count the same and are designed to remain stable over the time. I illustrate this by presenting Manfred G. Schmidt's (1996) indicator.[4] The index of institutional constraints on central governments ranges from 0 to 6. High values indicate powerful constraints on central governments, whereas low values show room to manoeuvre. The additive index is composed of six dummy-variables ("1" = constraints, "0" = else) (1) EU membership = 1, (2) degree of centralization of state structures (federalism = 1), (3) difficulty of amending constitutions (very difficult = 1), (4) strong bicameralism =1, (5) central bank autonomy = 1, and finally, (6) frequent referenda = 1 (Schmidt 1996: 172).

The conceptual logic seems to be clear. Institutional veto points limit a government's action space. However, there are at least three conceptual problems. First, it is not at all clear if the index includes all potential veto points. Constitutional courts,

---

[4] The indices of Colomer and Huber et al. are rather similar in empirical terms to Schmidt's index although they analytically stress slightly different aspects. Schmidt's index correlates with 0.79 with Colomer's and Huber et al.'s indices for the 23 OECD countries considered in this chapter. The latter two correlate with 0.87. We included the 23 OECD countries because we could obtain data for only these countries concerning the preferences over time, that is, available party manifesto data (see below).

presidents, or strong interest groups and even mass media could be additional veto points. Secondly, not all potential veto points are veto points in all policy areas and there might be additional veto points in different policy areas. For instance, central banks are not veto points in the field of environmental or social policy. Instead, environmental NGOs or influential enterprises might be potential veto points in the area of environmental policy while employer associations and trade unions might be additional veto points in labour or social policy. Thirdly, potential veto points may not use their veto power in certain policy fields or situations. They could even support the government policy. For instance, the EU and central banks might support a government which aims at privatizing sectors but at the same time might obstruct government initiatives in other policy areas. These policy-related factors make it difficult to identify the key veto points.

The aggregation of veto point analysis does not follow specific theoretical guidelines. All veto points are assigned equal weight even though it is plausible that some veto points have a stronger veto power than others. For instance, Schmidt counts "strong" bicameralism but does not provide criteria for when bicameralism is strong enough to be counted as a veto point. This is also a problem of double counting. For example, federalism and bicameralism may measure the same thing (dispersion of power to sub-units). Including both aspects into an index gives double weight to sub-national power dispersion. Another problem of Schmidt's index is that it is constructed for cross-sectional analysis (valid for the mid-1990s), so that it does not consider changes in the number of veto points over time.

The failure to consider changes over time can easily be remedied by recoding the index for empirical analysis in order to make it time-variant. I have accounted for the abolishment of the Danish and Swedish second chambers (in 1953 and 1970) and marked the respective years of EU membership. I also factored in that the Bank of England became independent in 1998 and that some countries had to abide by European Central Bank rules on joining the Euro zone. Figure 3.1 gives an overview of the number of veto points in 23 OECD countries from 1950 to 2005. I did not include Greece, Portugal, and Spain during periods of dictatorship.

Schmidt's index is relatively stable over time. Switzerland, the United States, and Germany have the most institutional constraints. In contrast, New Zealand has no institutional constraints. The number of institutional constraints mainly increases because of EU membership and joining the Euro zone (Central European Bank). Denmark and Sweden lost one institutional constraint when they abolished the second chamber but gained one due to joining the EU. The United Kingdom's institutional constraints are EU membership (1973) and the independent Bank of England (1998).

Since the late 1990s, a more differentiated approach for veto point analysis has been published. Birchfield and Crepaz (1998; see also Crepaz and Moser 2004) as well as Wagschal (2005) distinguish between consensual and competitive veto points. While consensual veto points support rather than obstruct central government policies and therefore are not real veto points, competitive veto points result in the blocking of central government's policy reform attempts.

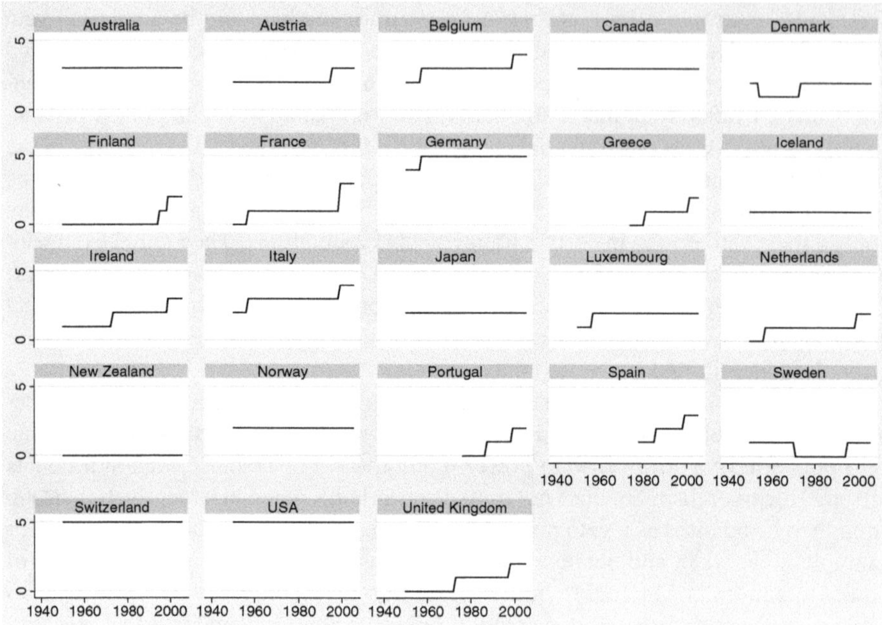

Fig. 3.1 Institutional constraints on central governments (Schmidt)

In Crepaz' view, collective veto points – which is his term for supportive veto points – are a measure of institutional diffusion that necessitates the sharing of political power in a collective fashion. It is a composite indicator that consists of three elements: (a) the proportionality of the electoral system, (b) the effective number of legislative parties, and (c) the degree of corporatism. Competitive veto points encompass federalism and bicameralism. Crepaz operationalized collective and competitive veto players by using Lijphart's (1999) measure for two distinct patterns of democracy.[5] Hence Lijphart's executives-parties dimension corresponds to collective veto points, whereas the federal-unitary dimension matches the competitive dimension. According to the conceptual logic of Crepaz' index, consensus democracies have more collective veto points that support government policy. However, the causal links are not always clear. Why, for instance, should a proportional election system promote government policy?

Although Crepaz uses two time periods (Lijphart's data from 1945 to 1996 for the period from 1960 to 1970 and the data from 1971 to 1996 for the period from 1971 to 1996), his measure of veto points is not really time-variant. Following Crepaz' coding, I have used his index with a breakpoint in 1971 and extended the data to

[5] Based on Crepaz' publications, it appears as if he has significantly altered Lijphart's indices. In fact however, he has adopted Lijphart's measures one-to-one. I thank Markus Crepaz for sending me his data set.

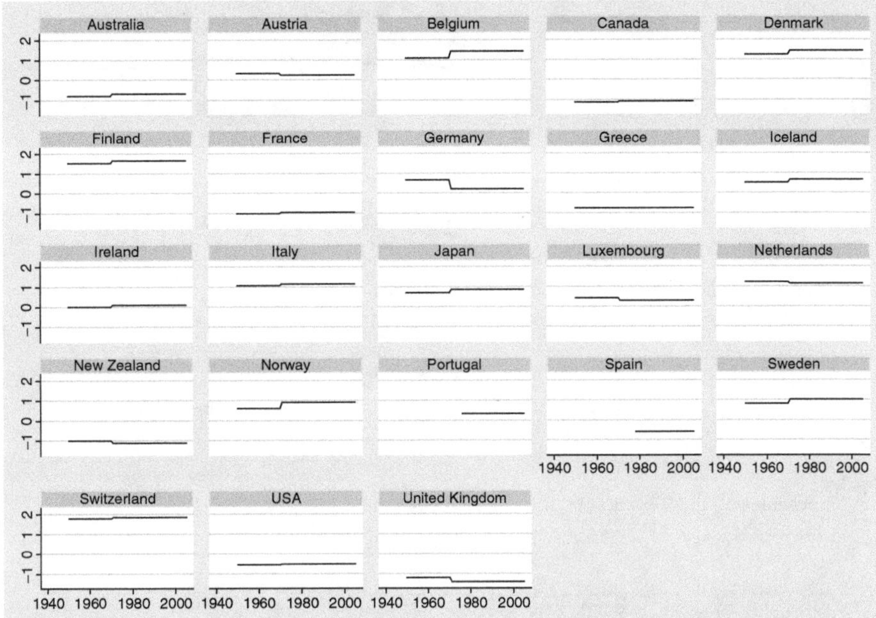

Fig. 3.2 Collective veto points (Crepaz 1)

1950 and 2005. I have also included the collective veto player index because this indicator is identical to Lijphart's major dimension of consensus democracy. Consequently, collective veto points are an indicator for a different logic of politics: the consensual policy style. Crepaz, or Lijphart for that matter, has aggregated veto points by way of factor analysis, meaning that the factor scores weigh the empirical strength of individual veto points. The inductive weighting of veto points might be more appropriate than simply adding them up like Schmidt did. Figures 3.2 and 3.3 show the scores for collective and competitive veto points.

Since Crepaz' veto point indices are based on Lijphart's highly aggregated concepts, it is difficult to deduce the major elements and causal mechanisms which may have an impact on policies and outcomes. A more transparent and elaborated index of veto points which also distinguishes between consensual and competitive veto points has been compiled by Uwe Wagschal. Wagschal (2005) contends that coalition governments and constitutional courts are consensual veto players which do not have the same policy obstructing functions as competitive veto points. In his view, competitive veto points are (a) strong federalism, (b) EU membership, (c) direct democracy, (d) strong bicameralism, (e) strong presidents, (f) proportional representation, and (g) independent central banks. The variables have a dichotomous coding and are added up. Direct democracy, constitutional courts, and presidentialism have a .5 coding (Fig. 3.4).

As with Schmidt's and Crepaz' indices, it is not always easy to see the causal mechanisms which result from Wagschal's veto point index. Coalition parties might

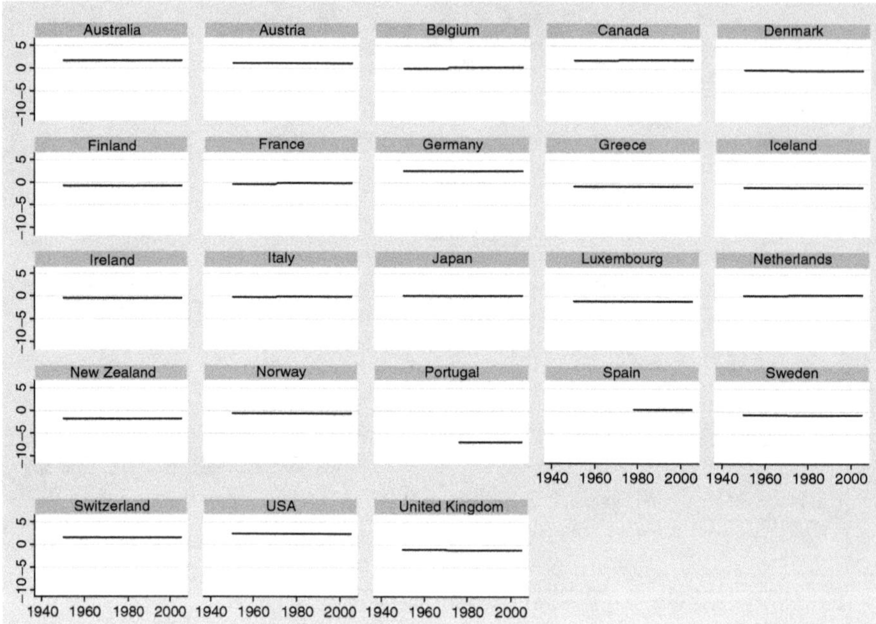

Fig. 3.3 Competitive veto points (Crepaz 2)

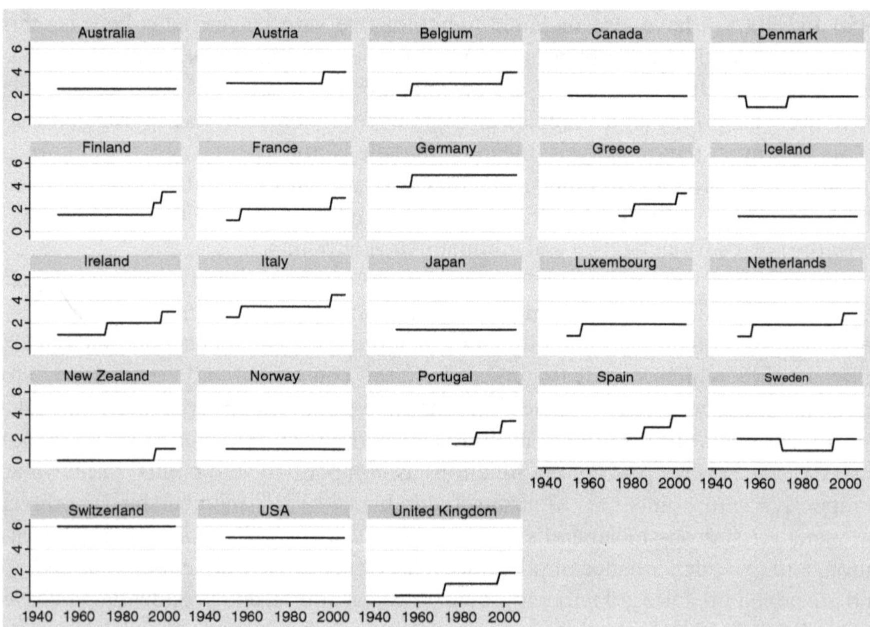

Fig. 3.4 Competitive veto points (Wagschal)

not be an obstructive veto point, yet claiming that they support government policy more strongly than single party governments is a daring assumption. The same is true for constitutional courts. Both analytically and empirically the claim that political systems with constitutional courts call for more government support than political systems without constitutional courts is not sustainable. The same is true for "strong" federalism and bicameralism (cf. comments on Schmidt's index). With regard to the veto function of proportional election systems, Crepaz and Wagschal arrive at opposite conclusions. While Crepaz considers proportional elections systems to be consensual, Wagschal rates them as competitive.

Considering aggregation, Wagschal weights some indicators less than others. It is not always clear why a .5 weighting is appropriate and why all "strong" presidents have the same weight. The President of the United States could, for instance, be stronger than the President of Finland.

Analogous to Schmidt's index, I have also updated Wagschal's index and made it time-variant. In addition to the changes made in Schmidt's index, I have included an additional veto point for New Zealand due to the change from a majoritarian to a proportional electoral system in 1996.

Apart from conceptual and theoretical problems, veto point indices face substantial technical problems. The analysis of veto points has the shortcoming that all variables are count variables. The use of count variables as independent variables is difficult in regression analysis, in particular given the ambiguity about whether all veto points exercise the same constraints on policy. Wagschal seems to pay attention to this aspect because he attributes only half of the impact to some veto points. However, this measurement seems to be very arbitrary. Another detriment of veto point analysis is that it seems to count some veto functions twice. This is particularly obvious with regard to federalism and bicameralism. Countries with strong bicameralism are often organized federally with the second chamber representing the interests of the sub-national units. Furthermore, most veto point analyses are to a large extent time-invariant, which means that they often bring about effects that are difficult to distinguish from country effects in TSCS analysis. This is problematic when applying fixed effects in statistical analysis, and is particularly relevant for Crepaz' indices, which do not really change over time. Although his data aggregation is more appropriate than that of Schmidt and Wagschal, his concepts present severe theoretical problems. It is not at all clear whether to interpret Crepaz' veto point indices in the light of veto player theory or of consensus democracy. After all, Crepaz' veto point indicators are identical with Lijphart's indicators for consensus democracy. This confusion makes causal inferences extremely difficult.

As mentioned above, the analysis of veto points is substantially different from the analysis of veto players. While veto points are structural characteristics of political systems which change only infrequently, veto player analysis combines structural characteristics with the strategic behaviour of political actors within institutional settings. Consequently, veto player analysis is more ambitious as it calls not only for information about the institutional setting but also about the preferences of political actors. As both institutional settings and actor preferences can change over time, empirical analysis is highly demanding. In the following section, I focus on two veto player approaches: Witold Henisz's (2000, 2002) analysis of political constraints of policy change and George Tsebelis's (2002) analysis of veto players.

Measurement and Aggregation of Veto Players in Macro-Comparative Analysis

Witold Henisz (2000, 2002) introduces two measures of political constraints. He identifies the number of independent branches of government with veto power over policy change in various countries on a yearly basis from 1800 to 2004. The preferences of each of these branches and the *status quo* policy are assumed to be independent and identical and are drawn from a uniform, one-dimensional policy space. Thus, Henisz works with assumed preferences rather than empirical ones. This assumption allows the derivation of a quantitative measure of institutional hazards using a simple spatial model of political interaction. This initial measure is then modified to take into account the extent of alignments across the branches of government by using data on the composition of parties in veto player branches. Such an alignment increases the feasibility of policy change. The measure is further modified to capture the extent of preference heterogeneity within each veto player branch, which increases (decreases) decision costs of over-turning policy for aligned (opposed) executive branches. The main results of the calculations are that (1) each additional veto point (a branch of government that is both constitutionally effective and controlled by a party different from other branches) provides a positive but diminishing effect on the total level of constraints on policy change and (2) homogeneity (heterogeneity) of party preferences within an opposition (aligned) branch of government is positively correlated with constraints on policy change. Henisz supplies two measures: The first measure includes three independent branches of government (executive, lower house, and upper house) (polcon3), whereas the second contains five independent branches of government (additionally sub-federal units and the judiciary) (polcon5).

As Henisz points out, his approach has some weaknesses. One is that actor preferences are estimated. The range between the independent branches of government is deduced from a simple spatial model, which is applied to all countries. George Tsebelis (2002: 204/205) argues that Henisz' approach of political constraints approximates veto player theory but that its operationalization features important deviations that consequently make it impossible to predict a high correlation between the two indices. Furthermore, Tsebelis criticizes Henisz' approach with regard to the fact that the judiciary does not always have veto power and that federalism has been counted twice because it is included in both the concepts of federalism and bicameralism. In addition, legislative constraint is captured by taking into account all parties that are represented in parliament. At least in parliamentary systems the government has control over the legislative game and therefore the opposition parties impose no constraints on legislation.

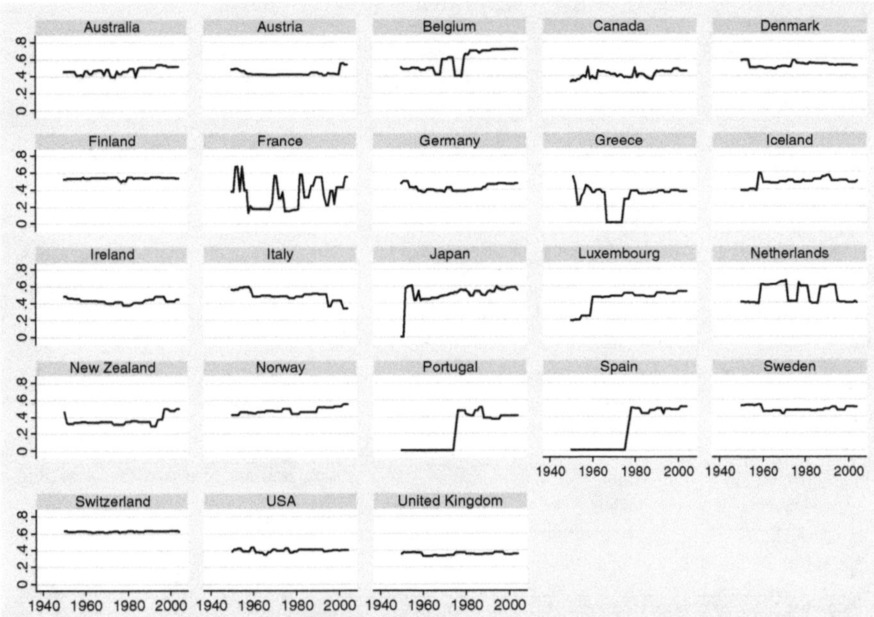

Fig. 3.5 Political constraints on policy change (polcon3)

Figures 3.5 and 3.6 show the variation of political constraints over recent decades. Figure 3.5 uses data for three independent branches of government (polcon3), whereas Fig. 3.6 uses data for five (polcon5). While the former index is available for the period 1950–2004 (even longer for some countries), the latter index is only available for the period 1960–2004.

The inclusion of sub-federal units and the judiciary increases the level of political constraints (mean for polcon3 = 0.44; for polcon5 = 0.75) and the variance between countries, but it equalizes the political constraints within countries, which may cause problems when using fixed effects in regression models.[6] The aggregation rules of Henisz' indices follow the veto player approach and use the ideological range between the two most opposing veto players. Thus, Henisz' indices are metric and suitable for modern regression analysis. With regard to preferences, Henisz is restricted to an estimated one-dimensional analysis. It remains unclear though what this dimension is intended to represent.

The analysis of veto player function in macro-comparative studies is exclusively based on George Tsebelis' (2002) theoretical elaborations. Therefore, we should pay close attention to the operationalization of his concept for macro-comparative analysis. He points out that the veto player function can be calculated by means of (a) the

[6] The average index of variance (standard deviation/mean) within the 23 OECD countries is for polcon3 = 0.211 and for polcon5 = 0.084.

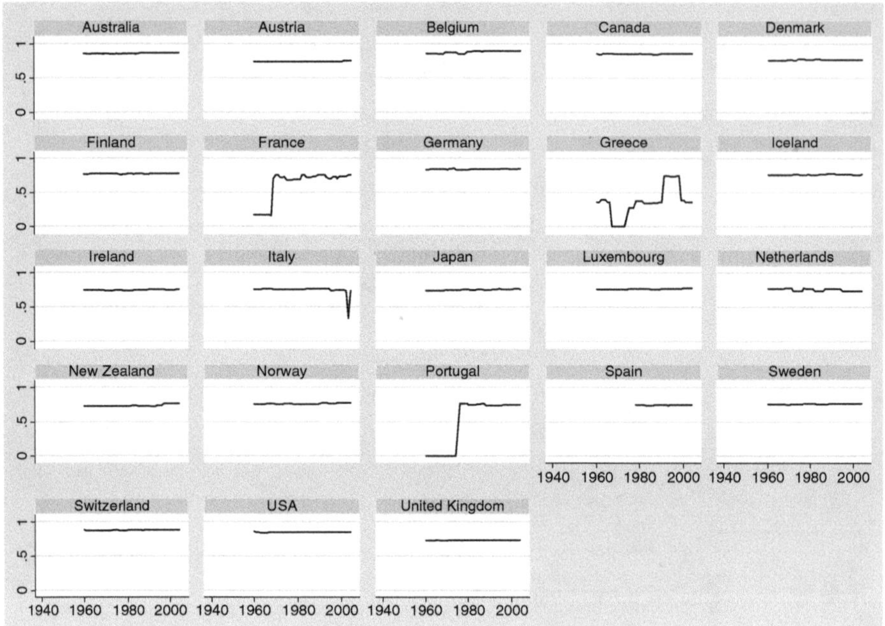

Fig. 3.6 Political constraints on policy change (polcon5)

number of veto players, (b) their maximum ideological distance, and (c) the coherence of individual veto players. In his macro-comparative studies, Tsebelis (2002: Chaps. 7 and 8; Tsebelis and Chang 2004) uses the ideological distances of the two most opposite veto players as a proxy, as derived from expert judgements. I use George Tsebelis' data and have updated the data set until 2005 with data from Benoit and Laver (2006) (Fig. 3.7).[7]

Tsebelis' operationalization of veto players is transparent and consistent with his theory (Tsebelis 2002). However, even here shortcomings can be identified. The most important flaw is that party positions and institutional settings are considered to be invariant over time. Party positions are derived from average counts of expert judgements assembled over several decades. Furthermore, it is not clear why Tsebelis does not include the United States and Greece in his analysis. As data on party preferences in Switzerland were lacking in the Laver/Hunt expert judgement data set (Tsebelis 2002: 170; for the original data set, see Laver and Hunt (1992), Swiss party preferences were replaced with data from Finland. Tsebelis' approach has exclusively been applied to the Right/Left dimension, and no serious attempts have been made to transfer it to other dimensions.[8]

[7] The data is available on George Tsebelis' webpage: http://sitemaker.umich.edu/tsebelis/veto_players_data.

[8] Tsebelis (2002: Chap. 8; Tsebelis and Chang 2004) uses a two-dimensional model. However, these data are not open to the public and the two dimensions chosen (three left/right indices from

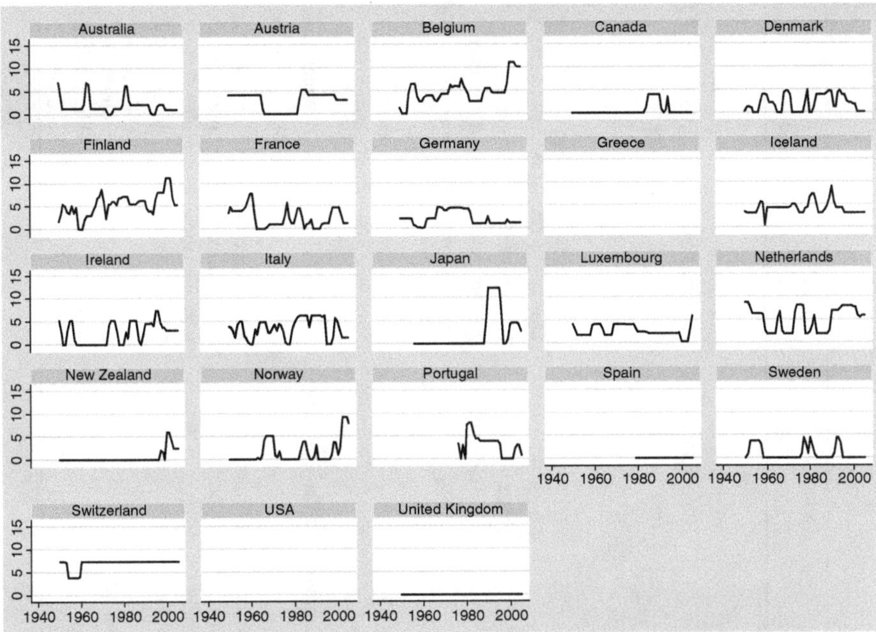

Fig. 3.7 Veto player analysis (Tsebelis)

To sum up to this point, it is obvious from Table 3.1 that the approaches have some common and some special features in terms of conceptualization, measurement, and aggregation.

In terms of conceptualization, one should strive for a balance between maximalist and minimalist definitions (Munck and Verkuilen 2002: 9). In this respect, veto point analysis and polcon5 are rather maximalist which contains the risk of redundancy. Polcon3 and Tsebelis' approach are minimalist. With regard to the conceptualization of preferences, Tsebelis is the only one to use an empirical measure. Henisz' two indices use a hypothetical measure, which is problematic. Veto point indices ignore preferences in extenso and attribute opposition preferences to all veto points outside of government. The greatest advantage of veto player over veto point approaches is their theoretical micro-foundation that allows the formulation of hypotheses about causal mechanisms. This has been explained in book length by Tsebelis (2002).

The measurements for veto points/players have been obtained by different means. Schmidt's and Wagschal's indices count the number of veto points, whereas Crepaz uses factor analysis for the identification of differences in political systems. After

expert judgements on the one hand and a "pro-friendly relationship to the USSR versus anti" from Laver and Hunt's expert judgements on the other) may not be independent and analytically distinct. All indicators measure various aspects of the left/right dimension.

Table 3.1 Conceptualization, measurement, and aggregation of veto points/player analysis

	Schmidt	Crepaz	Wagschal	Henizs (polcon3)	Henizs (polcon5)	Tsebelis
Conceptualization						
• Number of veto points/players	Maximum	Maximum	Maximum	Minimum	Maximum	Minimum
• Preferences	None	None	None	Hypothetical	Hypothetical	Empirical
• Micro-foundation	No	No	No	Yes	Yes	Yes
• Redundancy	Yes	Yes	Yes	No	Yes	No
Measurement						
• Veto points/veto players	Counting	Factor analysis	Counting	Preferences	Preferences	Preferences
• Level of measurement	Ordinal	Metric	Ordinal	Metric	Metric	Metric
• Preferences	None	None	None	Hypothetical Preferences	Hypothetical Preferences	Empirical Preferences
• Time variance						
– Preference of actors	No	No	No	No	No	No
– Through changing majorities	No	Very little	No	Yes	Yes	Yes
– Institutional setting	No	Very little	No	No	No	No
Aggregation	Unweighted summing up	Factor scores	Weighted summing up	Ideological range	Ideological range	Ideological range
Major weakness	• No preferences • Redundancy • Time invariant • Little over all variance for TSCS-analysis	• No preferences • Redundancy • Time invariant • Little over all variance for TSCS-analysis	• No preferences • Redundancy • Time invariant • Little over all variance for TSCS-analysis	• Hypothetical preferences	• Hypothetical preferences • Redundancy • Little over all variance for TSCS-analysis	• Time invariant preferences and institutional settings • Exclusion of United States and Greece

having identified relevant veto players, Henisz and Tsebelis use their respective preferences as measurement for the estimation of veto player effects.

The measurement of veto points/players also influences the aggregation of the veto function into an overall index. Both Schmidt and Wagschal obtain aggregation by summing up individual veto players. While Wagschal uses weighting procedures, Schmidt does not. However, strictly speaking, count variables are not suitable for regression analysis (King 1986: 666). Crepaz uses the factor scores for further analysis. Although the factor analysis includes some ordinal variables, the factor scores are interval data. However, the biggest drawback of Crepaz' index is that it is time invariant. All veto player approaches use the ideological range of the two most opposite veto players. This aggregation measure has an interval scaling and is therefore suitable for regression analysis.

The bottom line is that veto player analysis is superior to veto point analysis. This is true with regard to all three categories: conceptualization, measurement, and aggregation. When comparing the two veto player approaches, the lack of empirical data for veto player preferences stands out as a major weakness of Henisz' approach. Yet his inclusion of more countries and years presents a substantial advantage over Tsebelis' measurement. It is particularly disappointing that Tsebelis does not include Greece and the United States. Above all, the omission of the United States makes it difficult to use Tsebelis' approach for studies of highly industrialized countries. An additional drawback of Tsebelis' approach is that empirical preferences of veto players are time-invariant. Finally, another weakness of both veto player analyses is that they concentrate on a one-dimensional ideological space. This is often not suitable for an empirical analysis. Therefore, I would like to elaborate on Tsebelis' veto player index by using time-variant preferences and by including Greece and the United States as well as changes in institutional settings.

Towards a More Refined Veto Player Analysis

In this section, I offer two new veto player indices. In a first step, I update and complement Tsebelis' veto player index by using time-variant veto player preferences. In a next step, I elaborate the concept by considering changes in the institutional settings. I also include additional second chambers and presidents since they may exercise an "anticipated veto."

In order to update and complement Tsebelis' veto player index, I modify this by using time-variant veto player preferences. Furthermore, I include Greece and the United States in the analysis. I also replace the Finnish data which was used for Switzerland with data on Swiss parties. Greece was easy to add to the sample of countries since data are available, but there will always remain a question why it was not included in Tsebelis' analyses. There might be substantial objections with regard to the inclusion of the United States since the programmatic standpoints of American parties are difficult to determine. However, there is a substantial amount of literature which claims that parties in the United States are well-structured and have a systematic impact on the political process as well as policies (Cox and McCubbins 2005; Theriault 2008). I used the largest ideological range between the President, the Senate, and the House.[9]

In order to obtain a time-variant index of party preferences, I used data from the Comparative Manifestos Project (Budge et al. 2001; Klingemann et al. 2006). In order to determine the range of veto players from party manifesto data, I attributed the estimated party position to each party in government. As party manifesto data are only available for election times, data for the remaining years were imputed. In this analysis, I used a Left/Right index that has been deduced from political theory and deviates from the inductive measures offered by the Party Manifesto Group (RILE) (Jahn 2010a). The advantage of this measure for preferences is that it allows the use of the same method for other ideological dimensions as well. So far it is possible to use data for the familiar Left/Right dimension and for other ideological dimensions such as the environmental Green/Growth dimension (Jahn 2010b).[10]

My veto player index is sensitive both to changes in governments and the majority of second chambers. The second chambers are included in the analysis with their median position.[11] Where the median was situated outside the coalition parties' ideological range, the range was respectively extended. The same has been done for the President of Portugal, the only president included in Tsebelis' analysis. The development of the veto player function with time-variant party positions in 23 OECD countries is shown in Fig. 3.8.

While this index (Jahn1) is conceptually similar to Tsebelis' index, the major difference is the replacement of time-invariant preferences from expert judgements with time-variant preferences deduced from party manifesto data. In the next step, I consider changes of institutional settings in various countries and relax the criteria for including second chambers as veto players. Following to Tsebelis' analysis, the data in Fig. 3.8 only includes second chambers in Australia, Canada, Germany, and Switzerland. In addition, I have included the US Senate. In spite of second chambers being crucial institutions in veto player analysis, their analytical status and operationalization remain inconsistent. In this respect, it has been stated "... that second chambers always exercise an influence on final outcomes of legislation. This is a

[9] I did, however, not consider the two super-majority rules characteristic of the US' political system, the filibuster in the Senate and the President's veto that may both have expanded the US' range.

[10] This method of identifying party preferences has further advantages. First, it is possible to obtain a measure for the saliency of respective issue dimensions. Thereby, one can construct indifference curves which are essential to veto player theory (Jahn 2010a). Second, this measure of preferences also allows for measuring the coherence of individual parties over time. This is also pivotal for veto player analysis since actors' coherence is another important feature of veto player theory (Jahn and Oberst 2009). As the inclusion of these factors would increase the complexity of this chapter, I leave the elaboration of these concepts to later publications. The data can be downloaded from http://partypositions.uni-greifswald.de/

[11] Tsebelis seems to use the second chamber party which is ideologically furthest away from the most radical party in government and which takes a stand on the opposite side of an ideological dimension. However, this is not really appropriate because the second chambers are collective actors.

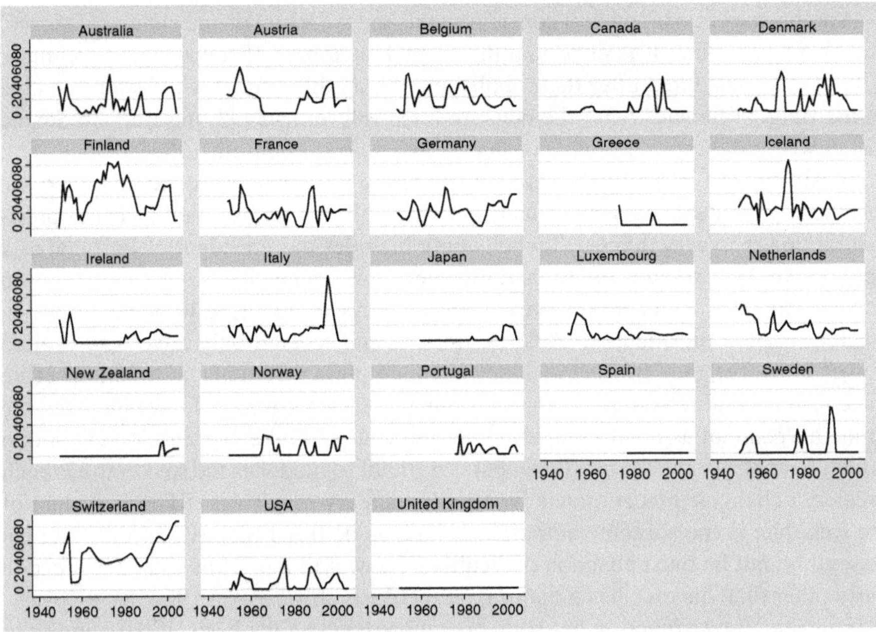

Fig. 3.8 Veto player analysis (Jahn 1)

trivial point when upper chambers can veto legislation, as in the United States, Switzerland, and Germany. However, it is our contention that all second chambers exercise influence even if they are considered weak or insignificant" (Tsebelis and Money 1997: 211). Yet, when it comes to empirical analysis, Tsebelis (2002: Chaps. 7 and 8; Tsebelis and Chang 2004) only includes the German *Bundesrat* and the Australian, Canadian, and Swiss second chambers. However, it remains unclear why the Belgian, Japanese, Italian, Dutch, Danish, Swedish, French, and Spanish second chambers (which are perceived as strong or medium-strong (Lijphart 1999: 211–213)) are not included in the analysis. This might be true with regard to formal decision-making structures. Yet, informal anticipatory effects call for the inclusion of other second chambers as well. Although the German second chamber is perceived as strong in the literature, it has been demonstrated that the formal intervention competences of the *Bundesrat* are rather modest and that many decisions are influenced by a so-called veto-anticipation (Burkhardt and Manow 2006).[12] The same could also be true for the other second chambers mentioned above. Almost all second chambers can delay the political process. If governments want to produce political results in a timely fashion, they are dependent on the cooperation of second chambers. In order to get along, governments have to be prepared to compromise on policy goals. In this way, second chambers can influence policies.

[12] The same logic of anticipated impact has been analyzed in terms of "the politics of negative power" for the President of the United States (Cameron 2000).

Another aspect which I will consider in this index (Jahn2) is the change of second chambers over time. It is clear that the second chambers of Sweden and Denmark will not be considered after their abolishment. Another aspect is the status change of the Belgian Senate. After the constitutional reform in 1993, the Belgian Senate lost power and therefore I only consider it as a veto player until 1993.

Presidents are institutional veto players along the lines of second chambers. In theory, all presidents have an influence on the political process but in reality presidential power is very diverse. Tsebelis only includes the President of Portugal as a veto player. He excludes the French President from his analysis and does not even consider the presidents of Austria, Finland, Ireland, and Iceland to be veto players. I agree that the presidents in Austria, Ireland, and Iceland only have very limited power. However, the Finnish President had an important veto player function before the constitutional reform in 2000 (Nousiainen 2001). Therefore, I have included the Finnish President as a veto player before the change in the constitution came into effect. In contrast, the French President is difficult to model as the role of the French President changes in accordance with parliamentary majorities: "The President of the Republic is the supreme authority as long as he has a majority in the National Assembly; but he must abandon the reality of power to the prime minister if ever a party other than his own has a majority in the Assembly" (Aron 1982: 8).

The veto player function has been operationalized on the basis of the number of veto players and their ideological distances measured on the Left/Right dimension. Veto players are (a) coalition governments, (b) second chambers, and (c) presidents. I have always included the widest ideological range. A veto player situated within this range was absorbed (absorption rule; Tsebelis 2002: 26–30). I accounted for second chambers and presidents granted that they have an impact on the political process (Tsebelis and Money 1997; Lijphart 1999). For Austria, Greece, Ireland, New Zealand, Norway, Iceland, and the United Kingdom I used ideological ranges of coalitions (if existent). This entails that I disregarded second chambers in Austria, Ireland, and the United Kingdom.[13] Countries with strong (symmetrical) second chambers are Australia, Germany, United States, Italy, Japan, the Netherlands, Sweden (until 1970), Denmark (until 1953), Belgium (until 1993), and Switzerland. Although Canada, France, and Spain have moderate bicameralism (Lijphart 1999: 212), I included them in the group of countries with second chambers which exert influence on the policy process. Portugal and Finland (until 2000) are countries with strong presidents. For the United States, I used the range between Senate, House, and President as described above. For Belgium, I included the second chamber until 1993. After the reform I only analyzed the coalition range. In France, the situation is more complicated. In periods without *cohabitation* I treated the French system as presidential. Although the French President has few formal powers (Huber 1996: 24–30) he has informal power positions in his own (governmental) party during periods of united government. Thus, I have used the range between the coalition, the

[13] I also do not consider the Norwegian "second chamber" (*lagting*) as it is part of the parliament (*storting*). The same applies to the Icelandic second chamber (*Nethri Deild*) which was abolished in 1991 (Eythorsson and Jahn 2009: 197).

Senate, and the President as the veto player range. However, since the position of the president is identical with the president's party position in our analysis,[14] the president's position is situated within the range of the coalition and is therefore absorbed. In times of *cohabitation*, I have ignored the position of the president: "Cohabitation demonstrates that in the absence of a coherent majority in support of the president, the president is relatively powerless in influencing even the direction of political change" (Huber 1996: 29). Therefore, I have used the range between the coalition parties and the second chamber in cases of *cohabitation*. The French Senate is normally considered to be a medium-strong second chamber (Lijphart 1999). However, it has been demonstrated that the French Senate has a profound impact on the legislative process (Tsebelis and Money 1997: Chap. 7). In particular, in periods of non-cohabitation with the Left in power, the Senate was often able to influence policy.

The index also includes a factor that is often neglected in macro-comparative research. Normally, data for variables are collected on an annual basis. However, most legislative processes proceed faster. Analyzing 17 Western European parliaments, Becker and Saalfeld (2004) conclude that the legislative process on average takes around 4–5 months. Yet it is also common that bills are negotiated for 2 or even 3 years. Consequently, most legislative procedures have a time lag of between 0 and 1 year. Therefore, it is important to construct data files that have time units that are shorter than 1 year. The data set presented for the revised veto player index is based on quarterly changes in institutional settings.[15] This enables more refined lag-structures for empirical analysis. The result of this operationalization is displayed in Fig. 3.9.

The correlation matrix shows that the various indices correlate quite differently with each other and thus measure different things. There is a clear divide between veto point and veto player indices, which do not correlate. However, veto point indices (Schmidt, Wagschal, Crepaz 2) are closely connected. Tsebelis' index is quite isolated and correlates highly with Lijphart's executives-parties dimension (!) (Crepaz1) meaning that the index potentially measures something other than veto player impact. We find the same high correlation between Crepaz' collective veto points (which is Lijphart's consensus democracy index) and polcon3. The correlation also explicitly confirms that Tsebelis' index is very different from Henisz' polcon indices, above all polcon5. Thus, one should avoid applying Henisz' indices when referring to Tsebelis' veto player theory as Henisz measures something other than veto player effects. Finally, the correlation matrix in Table 3.2 demonstrates that time-variant policy positions of veto players (Jahn1) differ considerably from time-invariant measures (Tsebelis).

My own indices correlate highly. Although the latter index (Jahn 2) is theoretically and empirically more elaborated than the time-variant and complemented improved Tsebelis index (Jahn 1), the distinctly high correlation seems to indicate that the analytical gains do not fully translate into empirical ones. However, my

[14] Since I have no data for the preferences of the presidents over time, I use the party preferences of the president's party from Party Manifesto Data.

[15] Since it is difficult to include all government changes, I have decided for units of analysis on a quarterly basis for each country from 1950 to 2005.

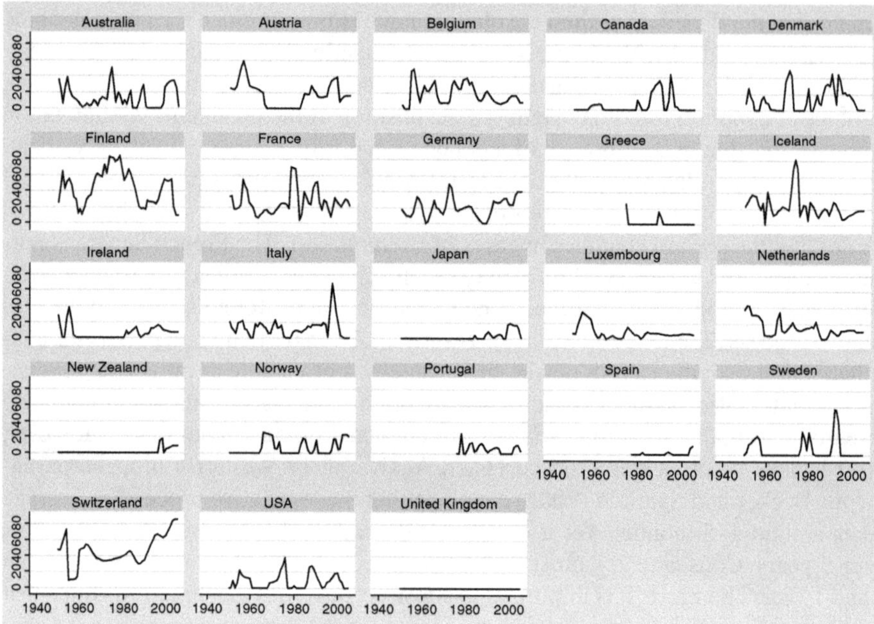

Fig. 3.9 Veto player analysis (Jahn 2)

Table 3.2 Correlation matrix of various veto points and veto players indices

	Schmidt	Crepaz1	Crepaz2	Wagschal	Polcon3	Polcon5	Tsebelis	Jahn1	Jahn2
Schmidt	1.0000								
	1210								
Crepaz1	0.1182	1.0000							
	1210	1227							
Crepaz2	**0.6845**	−0.0242	1.0000						
	1210	1227	1227						
Wagschal	**0.8834**	0.2568	**0.5461**	1.0000					
	1210	1210	**1210**	1210					
Polcon3	0.2044	**0.6366**	0.1158	0.2517	1.0000				
	1187	**1203**	1203	1187	1261				
Polcon5	0.4805	0.2502	0.3305	0.3232	**0.7013**	1.0000			
	986	993	993	986	**1015**	1015			
Tsebelis	0.2026	**0.5093**	0.0588	0.3736	0.3979	0.1869	1.0000		
	1114	**1114**	1114	1114	1093	910	1114		
Jahn1	0.1639	0.4243	0.1625	0.3193	0.2970	0.2197	**0.5809**	1.0000	
	1199	1199	1199	1199	1176	985	**1109**	1200	
Jahn2	0.1464	0.3936	0.1567	0.3111	0.2599	0.2041	**0.5733**	**0.9764**	1.0000
	1210	1210	1210	1210	1187	986	**1114**	**1200**	1211

Note: All correlations >0.5 are bold. Upper line is Pearson's r; lower line is number of observations

indices have the highest degree of correlation with Tsebelis' index. Further they are considerably set apart from the veto point and polcon indices. We can therefore assert that the new indices measure the veto player concept more accurately than the others.

Conclusion

The chapter demonstrates that veto player analysis is distinct from veto point analysis and superior with regard to conceptualization, measurement, and aggregation. Theoretically, veto player analysis has a micro-foundation that allows for compiling hypotheses about causal mechanisms to be tested in macro-comparative analysis. However, the chapter also clarified that similar analytical concepts are measured in very different ways. This has severe consequences for causal analysis and interpretation. If we test our theoretical concepts with alternative empirical indicators our results are bound to be highly ambiguous. Similar analytical concepts have to be operationalized with indicators that produce similar results. This concern is particularly relevant when operationalizing Tsebelis' veto player approach with the indicator developed by Henizs. Empirically, Tsebelis' and Henisz' indicators have very little in common. Analyses in which Henisz' indicator is applied and in which results are interpreted according to Tsebelis' theory are flawed.

This chapter also showed ways to overcome some empirical weaknesses of established veto player indices. Based on the theoretical foundation of George Tsebelis' veto player approach, I have developed a new index that includes changes in preferences and institutional settings. Furthermore, this index is available for different ideological dimensions (so far the Left/Right and Green/Growth dimensions) in annual as well as quarterly units. In particular, the shorter units make more sophisticated legislative studies possible.

However, the elaborations of this chapter only constitute the first step on the way to improving veto player analysis. In particular, two aspects deserve detailed examination in the years to come: First, the cohesion of political actors and secondly, the inclusion of the European Union as veto player (O'Reilly 2005; Jones and Lee 2008). The former is mainly an empirical question since coherence plays an important analytical role in veto player theory. However, there are thus far very few reliable indicators for party or government coherence which cover a substantial number of countries (for a review of literature for his own index, see Powell 2000: 58–67; also see Depauw and Martin 2009). Furthermore these measures are time-invariant.[16] Up to now, few approaches have attempted

[16] Jones and Lee (2008) draw conclusions about party coherence in party systems from the incentives of personal votes (the stronger the element of personal votes, the more incoherent the parties in the party system). However, this indicator is also time-invariant and treats all parties within a party system similarly. Both assumptions are not realistic. The same applies to Depauw and Martin (2009) index which is based on roll-call analysis. So far the only systematic comparative study, even though still time-invariant, which uses parties as a unit of analysis has recently been presented by Warwick (2006) in the context of his analysis of policy horizons. However, his study includes only parties in those West European countries with a tradition of coalition governments.

to draw inferences about time-variant government parties' coherence (Jahn and Oberst 2009).

The second challenge concerns the inclusion of international veto players. There is disagreement about which veto players should be included in the analysis. The spectrum includes minimalist approaches (Tsebelis and Chang 2004: 460–461) as well as maximalist ones (Wagschal 2005). Parsimonious approaches are favoured as they have a sharper analytical focus than maximalist ones, which often run the risk of measuring something else and thus make tracing causal mechanisms difficult. The research on the impact of international factors on domestic policies has gained momentum in recent years (Jahn 2006). In future research, especially the European Union has to be taken into account since it increasingly shapes its member states' domestic policies. In this context, it is not adequate to model the EU as a dummy variable assuming the same effect for all countries. Instead a measure is required that grasps the EU's position and relates the results back to individual countries. In turn, this means that the EU's positions need to be identified. In consequence, further research is required to refine macro-comparative analysis of veto players.

Moreover, we need a more sophisticated index of second chamber strength. It is inadequate to include either only the most relevant or all relevant second chambers. Lijphart's ordinal scale is a good start (see also Tsebelis and Money 1997; Bergman et al. 2003: 117–120). Yet what we need is an interval-scaled index of second chamber strength.

Turning away from the dichotomy of policy stability versus change presents an even bigger challenge. It would be a major improvement if we were able to say more about the direction of change. This could be achieved by combining veto player with agenda-setting analysis. However, this research is still in its early stages and presupposes a basic theoretical elaboration of both the veto player and agenda-setting approaches.

To sum up, much remains to be done in veto player analysis. However, the veto player approach has the potential to combine sophisticated empirical analysis with solid social theory and may thus promote a new phase of theoretically informed empirical analysis in macro-comparative research. I hope that the veto player indices developed here are helpful for conducting more refined empirical analysis to this end.

References

Adcock R, Collier D (2001) Measurement validity: a shared standard for qualitative and quantitative research. Am Polit Sci Rev 95(3):529–546

Aron R (1982) Alternation in government in the industrialized countries. Gov Opposit 17(1):3–21

Becker R, Saalfeld T (2004) The life and times of bills. In: Döring H, Hallerberg M (eds) Patterns of parliamentary behavior. Passages of legislation across Western Europe. Ashgate, Aldershot, pp 57–90

Benoit K, Laver M (2006) Party policy in modern democracies. Routledge, London

Bergman T, Müller WC, Strøm K, Blomgren M (2003) Democratic delegation and accountability: cross-national patterns. In: Strøm K, Müller WC, Bergman T (eds) Delegation and accountability in parliamentary democracies. Oxford University Press, Oxford

Birchfield VL, Crepaz MML (1998) The impact of constitutional structures and collective and competitive veto points on income inequality in industrialized democracies. Eur J Polit Res 34:175–200

Bräuninger T, Debus M (2009) Legislative agenda-setting in parliametary democracies. Eur J Polit Res 48(6):804–839

Budge I, Klingemann H-D, Volkens A, Bara J, Tannenbaum E (2001) Mapping policy preferences: estimates for parties, electors, and governments, 1945–1998. University Press, Oxford

Burkhardt S, Manow P (2006) Veto-Antizipation. Gesetzgebung im deutschen Bikameralismus. MPIfG Discussion Paper 06/3

Cameron C (2000) Veto bargaining: presidents and the politics of negative power. Cambridge University Press, Cambridge

Colomer JM (1996) Introduction. In: Colomer JM (ed) Political institutions in Europe. Routledge, London, pp 1–17

Cox GW, McCubbins MD (2005) Setting the agenda: responsible party government in the US House of Representatives. Cambridge University Press, Cambridge

Crepaz MML, Moser A (2004) The impact of collective and competitive veto points on public expenditures in the global age. Comp Polit Stud 37(3):259–285

Depauw S, Martin S (2009) Legislative party discipline and cohesion in comparative perspective. In: Giannetti D, Benoit K (eds) Intra-party politics and coelition governments. Routledge, London, pp 103–120

Döring H (ed) (1995) Parliaments and majority rule in Western Europe. Campus/St. Martin's Press, Frankfurt/New York

Eythorsson G, Jahn D (2009) Das politische System Islands. In: W Ismayr (ed) Die politischen systeme westeuropas. VS Verlag, Wiesbaden, pp 195–218

Ganghof S (2003) Promises and pitfalls of veto player analysis. Swiss Polit Sci Rev 9(2):1–25

Hedström P, Swedberg R (eds) (1998) Social mechanisms: an analytical approach in social theory. Cambridge University Press, Cambridge

Henisz WJ (2000) The institutional environment for economic growth. Econ Polit 12(1):1–31

Henisz WJ (2002) The institutional environment for infrastructure investment. Ind Corp Change 11(2):355–389

Huber JD (1996) Rationalizing parliament: legislative institutions and party politics in France. Cambridge University Press, Cambridge

Huber E, Ragin CC, Stephens JD (1993) Social democracy, christian democracy, constitutional structure and the welfare state. Am J Sociol 99(3):711–749

Jahn D (2006) Globalization as "Galton's problem": the missing link in the analysis of diffusion patterns in welfare state development. Int Org 60(2):401–431

Jahn D (2010a) Conceptualizing Left and Right in Comparative Politics: Towards a Deductive Approach, Party Politcs (forthcoming)

Jahn D (2010b) Mapping political dimensions from party manifesto data, unpublished manuscript, University of Greifswald

Jahn D, Oberst C (2009) Cohesion of Nordic Social democratic parties in comparative perspective. Paper prepared for presentation at the 5th ECPR General Conference, Potsdam 10–12 September, 2009 in the panel on "Conflict and Cohesion in North European Political Parties" organized by Nicholas Aylott

Jones KA, Lee H (2008) Veto players revisited: internal and external influences on policy stability. Presented at the 2008 annual meeting of the Midwest Political Science Association, Chicago, IL

Kaiser A (1997) Types of democracy: from classical to new institutionalism. J Theor Polit 9(4):419–444

Katzenstein P (1987) Policy and politics in West Germany: the growth of a semi-Sovereign State. Temple University Press, Philadelphia

King G (1986) How not to lie with statistics: avoiding common mistakes in quantitative political science. Am J Polit Sci 30(3):666–687

Kittel B (2006) Crazy methodology? on the limits of macroquantitative social science research. Int Sociol 21(5):647–677

Klingemann H-D, Volkens A, Bara JL, Budge I, McDonald MD (2006) Mapping policy preferences ii: estimates for parties, electors, and governments, 1990–2003. Oxford University Press, Oxford

Krehbiel K (1998) Pivotal politics: a theory of U.S. lawmaking. University of Chicago Press, Chicago

Laver M, Hunt WB (1992) Policy and party competition. Routledge, New York, NY

Lijphart A (1999) Patterns of democracy. government forms and performance in thirty-six countries. Yale University Press, New Haven, CT

Munck GL, Verkuilen J (2002) Conceptualizing and measuring democracy: evaluating alternative indices. Comp Polit Stud 35(1):5–34

Nousiainen J (2001) From semi-presidentialism to parliamentary government: political and constitutional developments in Finland. Scand Popul Stud 24:95–109

O'Reilly RF (2005) Veto points, veto players, and international trade policy. Comp Polit Stud 38:652–675

Powell GB (2000) Elections as instruments of democracy: majoritarian and proportional visions. Yale University Press, New Haven, CT

Sartori G (1984) Guidelines for concept analysis. In: Sartori G (ed) Social science concepts: a systematic analysis. Sage, Beverly Hills, CA, pp 15–85

Schmidt MG (1996) When parties matter: a review of the possibilities and limits of partisan influence on public policy. Eur J Polit Res 30:155–183

Smelser NJ (1976) Comparative methods in the social sciences: Prentice-Hall methods of social science series. Prentice-Hall, Englewood Cliffs, NJ

Theriault SM (2008) Party polarization in congress. Cambridge University Press, Cambridge

Tsebelis G (2002) Veto players. how political institutions work. Princeton University Press, Princeton, NJ

Tsebelis G, Money J (1997) Bicameralism. Cambridge University Press, Cambridge

Tsebelis G, Chang ECC (2004) Veto player and the structure of budgets in advanced industrialized countries. Eur J Polit Res 43:449–476

Wagschal U (2005) Steuerpolitik und Steuerreformen im internationalen Vergleich. LIT Verlag, Münster

Warwick PV (2006) Policy horizon and parliamentary government. Palgrave MacMillan, New York, NY

Chapter 4
Measuring Policy Positions of Veto Players in Parliamentary Democracies

Thomas König, Bernd Luig, Sven-Oliver Proksch, and Jonathan B. Slapin

Introduction

In recent years, scholars have made an enormous effort to understand the impact and relevance of the interaction of preferences and political institutions on government formation and policy making in parliamentary democracies (e.g., Laver and Shepsle 1996; Laver and Schofield 1998; Lijphart 1999; Tsebelis 2002; Tsebelis and Money 1997; Martin and Vanberg 2004, 2005). One of the most prominent examples of these theories is the veto players framework introduced by George Tsebelis (1995, 1999, 2002). The parsimonious framework, which focuses on variation in policy positions of partisan and institutional veto players and their agenda-setting power, has fostered the integration of different strands of literature on parliamentary and presidential systems, bicameral legislatures, and party systems. At its core, the veto players framework is a policy-focused theory. Veto players, such as political parties in a government coalition, may have different preferences over policies, and the distances between these positions of veto players explain their ability to change the status quo. Veto players theory is not the only policy-focused theory which relies on the variation of policy positions. Laver and Shepsle's (1996) policy-focused portfolio model, for example, suggests that the making and breaking of governments is endogenous to party preferences over legislative policy making. Likewise, Martin and Vanberg (2004, 2005) propose and test a policy-focused theory of legislative review and parliamentary scrutiny of coalition policy making in parliamentary democracies.

T. König (✉), B. Luig, and S.-O. Proksch
University of Mannheim, Mannheim, Germany
e-mail: t.koenig@uni-mannheim.de; bernd.luig@mzes.uni-mannheim.de; proksch@uni-mannheim.de

J.B. Slapin
University of Houston, Houston, TX, USA
e-mail: jonslapin@gmail.com

T. König et al. (eds.), *Reform Processes and Policy Change: Veto Players and Decision-Making in Modern Democracies*, Studies in Public Choice 16,
DOI 10.1007/978-1-4419-5809-9_4, © Springer Science+Business Media, LLC 2010

To test these theories, scholars have developed several techniques to measure party positions on policy dimensions that reflect legislative activity. However, existing methods based on party manifestos or on expert judgments inadequately consider the legislative context and dynamic nature of preferences on multiple policy dimensions. Typically, estimates only partially cover the scope of government policy making, and researchers must often impute data or make simplifying assumptions about the nature of the policy conflict. For example, a general left–right dimension is frequently used to explain the presence or absence of change, despite a theoretical emphasis on multidimensional policy spaces. When controlling for portfolios, these studies commonly find significant variation across policy areas. Furthermore, the time-invariant nature of many existing estimates leads scholars to induce variation by multiplying ideology with other institutional variables, such as seat shares, that are not central to, or – in the veto players context – go against, their theoretical claims.

In sum, there is a lack of dynamic portfolio-specific party position estimates on policy dimensions that truly reflect the context of legislative activities, meaning that empirical tests of policy-focused theories in parliamentary democracies often rely on less than adequate measures of actors positions. In response, we propose a new automated technique to identify policy-specific language in political texts using keywords from legislative databases. We use these legislative keywords of distinct portfolios to "smart tag" sentences in party election manifestos. On the basis of these tagged sentences, we estimate positions for political parties on dimensions related to ministerial portfolios. We apply our new technique to labor policy, the area investigated by Tsebelis (1999, 2002), as well as to thirteen additional policy portfolios in Germany over time. Furthermore, we describe how the same approach can be applied to other parliamentary systems. We argue that our approach provides more complete and reliable estimates for empirical studies of legislative productivity and government policy making by increasing variation in ideological variables.

Veto Players, Policy Dimensionality, and Legislative Activity

In the veto players framework, the policy positions of political parties in governments are used to explain the presence or absence of policy change in parliamentary systems (Tsebelis 1995, 1999, 2002).[1] But empirical estimates of party positions do not cover the full range of policies over which legislation is introduced, and they often fail to capture the dynamic nature of ideology over time.

To solve the problem of inadequate policy-specific context, researchers typically resort to one of two strategies. The first is to choose a specific combination of dimensions in modelling ideological conflict, the second is to reduce the data sample

[1] Although Veto Players Theory is applicable to all democratic political systems, our focus in this paper is on parliamentary democracies. This is because we are interested in estimating policy portfolio specific positions for partisan veto players.

according to available policy dimension estimates. Yet, these approaches may cause concern regarding the adequacy of the data sample and the partisan conflicts over the total distribution of dimensions and portfolios (e.g., Strøm and Leipart 1993; Laver and Shepsle 1996; Warwick 2005). The lack of available scores often means that the data sample as a whole is significantly reduced (e.g., Martin and Vanberg 2004, 2005). Therefore, available estimates may not be specific enough to perform the necessary statistical tests of dimensional- and portfolio-based models. Equally, problematic is the use of general "left–right" dimension scores, which only partially describe policy conflict in multiparty legislatures (see Castles and Mair 1984; Roozendaal 1992; Strøm and Leipart 1993; Tsebelis 1999; Gabel and Huber 2000; Huber and McCarty 2001; Druckman and Thies 2002; Martin and Stevenson 2001; Martin and Vanberg 2003; Volden and Carrubba 2004; Adams et al. 2006; Bawn and Rosenbluth 2006; Adams and Somer-Topcu 2009).

The second challenge is that party positions are likely to change over time. Given that parliaments and their representatives are confronted with changing agendas and issues, it would be surprising if ideological distances between these actors remained stable. Hence, the static nature of party position estimates hampers the evaluation of policy-focused theories; their invariant nature can only be overcome using a large cross-sectional dataset or by mixing them with other institutional variables (e.g., Huber and McCarty 2001; Martin and Vanberg 2004, 2005). However, such an interaction generates nonlinear scales, and researchers may no longer be able to distinguish between the impact of institutional and policy-specific variables.

In our view, policy position estimates that are used to test veto players and other policy-focused theories need to fulfill three criteria: *completeness, reliability, and construct validity*. The first criterion states that the estimates should cover the entire policy space of legislative activities. Ideally, all policy dimensions need to be included and this is by no means a trivial task, as we will discuss later. The second criterion ensures that the procedure for generating the scores must be reliable. Researchers should be able to reach similar conclusions in repeated trials. Finally, the measures should be valid in the sense that inferences drawn from the estimates should legitimately reflect significant policy differences between governments and political parties as well as the changes in these differences over time. In the following we discuss these criteria for expert survey estimates, the dominant source of policy-specific party position estimates.

Policy Dimensionality in Expert Surveys

Expert surveys are one of the primary sources for party positions. Regarding policy context, most surveys take an *a priori* approach to the estimation of policy dimensions by asking experts to evaluate party positions on a range of issues (e.g., Castles and Mair 1984; Laver and Hunt 1992; Benoit and Laver 2006).[2] Given that the experts are usually asked about the policy positions of all parties on several dimensions in a particular country, the surveyors require them to possess a great deal of information and to spend some time on responses. An expert may be asked to place five to ten parties on ten or more dimensions. Unsurprisingly, experts diverge in their estimates of the positions of political parties or are unable to locate them in the policy space (König et al. 2005). Often, the substantive content is presented to experts through definitions of the end points of preselected policy dimensions. In the extreme, this context is reduced to a left/right-dimension on a standardized scale, on which experts provide an aggregated view of the political parties.

For the study of policy-focused theories, the most common expert survey questions originate from a study conducted in 1988–1989 by Laver and Hunt (1992). These data have been used to explain all sorts of political phenomena, including coalition formation (Laver and Shepsle 1996; Warwick 1996), coalition policy making (Martin and Vanberg 2004, 2005), law production (Tsebelis 1999), judicial independence (Santoni and Zucchini 2004) and political budget cycles (Alt and Lassen 2006), to name just a few examples. Laver and Hunt devised a questionnaire with eight questions regarding parties' stances on "taxes vs. public services," "foreign policy," "public ownership," "social policy," "religion," "urban vs. rural interests," "centralization of decision-making," and "environmental policy." The questions asked on these dimensions were fairly specific and often defined in a concrete manner. For instance, the "social policy" dimension was defined as the promotion vs. opposition regarding permissive policies on matters such as abortion and homosexuality. Similarly, "foreign policy" referred to the extent of development of friendly relations with the Soviet Union. More recently, Benoit and Laver (2006) updated and expanded the Laver and Hunt expert survey in 2002–2003. They kept a core set of policy dimensions defined in the same manner as those used by Laver and Hunt, but they also included new ones and they increased the number of countries and the number of experts surveyed.

The amount of information required to complete an expert survey is quite substantial. "Experts" in the Laver & Hunt and Benoit & Laver surveys were for the most part political scientists who were targeted using political science association membership lists, or through snowball techniques in which new experts were recommended by known ones. The implicit assumption in expert surveys on party positions is that political science scholars use outside sources, such as manifestos, party speeches, and voting records, when estimating a party position *and* they do not use the knowledge on party ideology generated by the political science discipline. In the extreme, if the latter were the case, but not the former, then expert surveys would simply be a recycled summary of existing knowledge. In fact, many political scientists who would otherwise consider themselves to be country experts may not feel comfortable assessing parties on different issue dimensions. For those who

[2] Other prominent expert surveys have been conducted specifically on the issue of European integration, see Rohrschneider and Whitefield (2007), Steenbergen and Marks (2007), and Hooghe et al. (2010).

responded in their expert survey, Benoit and Laver (2006, p. 163) find a small but statistically significant effect of survey complexity on the standard deviations of expert placements. But the average response rate in both surveys did not exceed 30%. Ideally, we would like the responding experts to be the ones who know the most, but unfortunately we do not know anything about the sample that did not respond, nor do we have a good understanding of the population of country experts.[3]

Furthermore, it is not known how experts reach their judgment about the party positions on specific dimensions (Mair 2001, p. 24). If experts do not have sufficient information about parties on each dimension (in fact, are not experts), they may simply report similar scores across dimensions because they estimate, for example, a given party to be right-wing. They may also believe right-wing parties must support policies x, y, and z. Therefore, the expert believes the party in question must support x, y, z regardless of whether the party truly supports these policies. Empirically, the expert scores within each country may, therefore, be highly correlated. We do not know, however, whether this is actually correlation between party positions across policies, or an artifact of the expert survey methodology. To our knowledge, expert surveys do not actually test the factual knowledge of the expert respondents.

A related problem may arise if experts, rather than reporting party intentions, infer their positions based upon past behavior (Budge 2000, p. 109). For example, experts may be more likely to assign similar scores to past coalition partners, not because the parties truly hold similar positions, but because the experts believe the parties must have been close on the policy dimensions because of past membership in the same coalition government. A prominent example for this confusion might be the position of the German liberal party FDP, which formed coalitions with Social Democrats during the 1970s and after 1982 with the Christian Democrats. If experts assign scores in this manner, then using the scores to explain coalition formation borders on tautology. It is not uncommon, however, that expert scores generated in a particular year are used to explain events that happened prior to the survey, simply because alternative data sources are scarce.[4]

Additionally, when experts are asked about positions of parties on a scale that implicitly contains a status quo, and this issue question is repeated over time in surveys, comparisons become difficult. The undefined status quo may change over time, thereby shifting the positions on the scale in an unknown manner. An example of such an issue question is Laver & Hunt's and Benoit & Laver's question regarding services vs. taxes. The endpoints of this dimension were defined as "promotes raising taxes to increase public services" and as "promotes cutting public services

[3] Note that the statistical inference problem in expert surveys is different from that in voter surveys. Whereas in the latter we are interested in inferring the attitudes of a population (i.e., all citizens or voters) from information about a sample, the goal in expert surveys is to "uncover an assumed underlying truth, the spatial location of a party's policy positions" (Benoit and Laver 2006). Nevertheless, the reasons for expert participation in surveys remain unexplored, as do issues of expert pool contamination due to multiple surveys directed repeatedly at the same experts.

[4] Even more problematic are expert surveys that ask experts at point t to "remember" and indicate the positions of parties held at point $t - x$.

to cut taxes." Implicitly, a status quo is the reference point because the questions ask for more or less taxation or spending with regard to the current policy. If the status quo changes over time (e.g., taxes or spending levels increase), and experts know this, then party position estimates on this scale change simply because the status quo has changed, and not because the positions did. To our knowledge, this issue has been completely ignored by the expert survey literature.

We now examine how Tsebelis (1999, 2002) uses expert survey data to test veto players theory, and describe the problems which he encounters. Our purpose is not to cast doubt on Tsebelis's results, but to use his work as an example of how a lack of dynamic, context-specific party position data limits the research designs of even the best empirical studies.[5]

Tsebelis: Veto Players and Law Production

In his work on veto players and law production in parliamentary democracies, Tsebelis (1999, 2002) analyzes the impact of ideological differences of government parties on legislative output. One of his central hypotheses is that the ideological range of a government coalition negatively affects the number of significant laws produced in parliamentary systems (Tsebelis 1999, p. 596). Moreover, ideological differences between successive governments (alternation) should positively affect the labor law production because new governments with a different ideological composition are expected to make more changes to legislation. In the empirical analysis, Tsebelis investigates the relationship between the ideological range of governments, i.e., the maximum ideological distance between coalition parties, and the number of significant pieces of labor legislation, mainly regarding working time and conditions, in 16 European countries for the period between 1981 and 1991. The data on labor laws stems from the NATLEX database (International Labor Organization) and the significance of these laws was identified using the Encyclopedia of Labor Law (Blanpain 1995), which contains the most important acts of parliament and government decrees in the field of social and labor politics. In the dataset, successive coalition governments with identical composition are counted as one government, even if the governments were separated by an election or a resignation. Tsebelis argues that this best reflects the theoretical concept of the veto players framework, because identical governments may use several legislative terms to accomplish their legislative agenda. However, it does exclude the possibility that the positions differ between a governmental agenda setter and the political parties and that they change over time, because the "merged" governments are essentially treated as one observation.

The ideological range is calculated using party positions generated from expert surveys – the Laver and Hunt (1992) survey, an earlier survey conducted by

---

[5] We thank George Tsebelis for making the replication data available to us.

Castles and Mair (1984), and from a study based on a single expert interpretation by Dodd (1976). The surveys roughly cover the beginning and the end of the period under investigation. In the Castles and Mair survey, experts were asked to place all parties in their national parliaments on a general left–right scale. From the Laver and Hunt survey, Tsebelis uses the question regarding taxation, with one end of the dimension meaning that a party would "promote raising taxes to increase public services" and the other that a party would "promote cutting public services to cut taxes." Finally, Tsebelis uses placements of parties on an economic conflict scale generated by Dodd (1976), updated by Browne et al. (1984) and used by Warwick (1994). Thus, the three measures focus on a broad socio-economic dimension of partisan conflict. Because the measures do not provide estimates for all parties in the sample, Tsebelis must construct an index that does.

He first calculates the ideological range of governments and alternation variables separately for each measure. In a next step, each index is standardized and then an average of the standardized scores is generated from the data.[6] Although the three indices are proxies for the left–right positions of parties, the measure raises several questions. First, the expert scores cover different time periods, with some scores generated in the 1970s (later updated), and others at the beginning and the end of the 1980s. Taking the average of all three therefore flattens out any dynamic differences between the scores. Second, the three measures cover different issues. The policy-focused measure by Laver and Hunt (1992) refers to the trade-off between taxation and public services, but does not directly relate to the context of labor laws, which mainly concern individual employment regulations and collective labor law (Scholtz and Trantas 1995, p. 652). The other two measures deal either with an unspecified left–right dimension or with economic conflict. Third, the different indices sometimes create different orderings of the parties in each country. As Tsebelis remarks himself, this means that the most extreme parties of a coalition are not always the same for all three indices (Tsebelis 1999, p. 599). Thus, the average ideological distance of a government coalition is not always derived from the same government parties.

This prominent study relies on available expert surveys to test veto players theory, a theory that hinges on party positions. But the expert surveys fall short as a measure of those positions. They likely mask variation in policy positions, in particular over time. Likewise, the estimates do not offer Tsebelis a dimension directly related to labor law legislation, his dimension of interest. The study is also exemplary of an instance in which a cross-country design is necessary to introduce variation in the independent variables. The study, though, does not test the effects of country-specific institutions that would theoretically necessitate a cross-sectional design.

---

[6] In cases for which all three indices exist, the average was calculated on the basis of all three; for countries covered by two indices, only the two standardized indices were used. The same logic was applied for cases covered only by one index.

The Method

The example in the previous section demonstrates that expert estimates may provide inadequate data to test policy-centered theories of policy making such as veto players. Not all government portfolios are covered and the dynamic nature of positions is insufficiently reflected in the data. Scholars have, therefore, turned to alternative sources of party positions in the form of documents, such as election manifestos. Election manifestos provide a first-hand source of party intentions, and as such may eliminate many of the problems of expert surveys. These documents are authorized by the parties, and published before elections, and therefore provide excellent time-series data from which to estimate party positions. However, existing applications exploit the complete text of party manifestos, even though these manifestos serve different purposes, such as signaling messages to voters and party members or preparing coalition bargains. Our method will provide an automated technique to identify policy relevant content in political texts. This means that we only consider those manifesto passages which relate to legislative activities in the ministerial portfolios of parliamentary democracies. Positions can then be obtained by applying any of the available text scaling techniques to the subsets of sentences that we have identified as policy relevant.

Policy Dimensionality in Manifesto-Based Approaches

Before explaining our approach, it is useful to consider how election manifestos have been used in the past. Currently, there are two major schools using party manifestos for estimating political parties preferences, automated and manual content analysis. The Comparative Manifesto Project (CMP) has conducted the most comprehensive manual content analysis of these documents (Budge et al. 1987, 2001; Klingemann et al. 2006).[7] Our point here is not to further criticize the CMP approach of manual content analysis, but simply to demonstrate that these data are not always adequate for the type of multidimensional time-series analysis of policy-focused theories. The nature of dimensionality is fixed across time because it is enforced through the CMP coding scheme. The coding scheme was devised to test theories of representation, not policy-focused theories of legislative and executive politics. Therefore, the CMP data make it difficult to construct dimensions that match cabinet portfolios and reflect legislative activities. To extract meaningful positions from the categories, researchers often employ scaling techniques to extract principal dimensions from these categories (e.g., Crombez 1996; Warwick 1998; Gabel and Huber

[7] The CMP data contain information on 56 categories, indicating the relative frequency of manifesto quasi-sentences that fit into each of these categories. There has been much criticism of this approach on grounds of reliability and misclassification of the CMP codings (e.g., Mikhaylov et al. 2008; Benoit et al. 2009).

2000). But in doing so, the context-specific nature of the data is lost. Even if more than one dimension is extracted, it is difficult to know what, precisely, the dimensions represent and how such data can be used to study portfolio-specific theories.

An alternative to the manual coding of party manifestos is quantitative content analysis. The use of quantitative text analysis tools in political science has exploded over the last several years, in particular in the field of political parties.[8] Party manifestos have been at the center of this analysis (e.g. Laver and Garry 2000; Laver et al. 2003; Slapin and Proksch 2008; Proksch and Slapin 2009). The assumption underlying such analysis is that party texts reveal positions in a latent space.[9] Quantitative content analysis techniques have been applied successfully in a broad range of institutional settings, in different languages, and across time (Proksch and Slapin forthcoming). Moreover, the numerous quantitative position estimation techniques often produce relatively similar results, and are often based on the same underlying model of text (Lowe 2008).

Until now, there have been two major obstacles for the wide application of these techniques. First, there was the inability to produce refined position estimates that reflect government policy-making activities in parliamentary democracies. Second, even though it is possible to leave the estimation of positions to statistical scaling algorithms, the substantive definition of policy and the text selection has remained within the realm of the researchers' own judgment. This is a source of error that has not received much attention in the literature. While it is a straightforward matter to estimate the major conflict on a single dimension from the total word frequency distributions in election manifestos, it is not trivial to use the algorithms to extract positions on narrowly defined policy dimensions that reflect cabinet policy making, such as labor policy, environmental policy, defense policy, or interior policy. Laver and Garry (2000) were among the first to manually construct a dictionary of policy-relevant words endogenously from manifestos for two major policy areas, which were then used in computer-assisted content analysis to extract positions. Similarly, the *Wordscores* technique introduced by Laver et al. (2003) uses "reference texts" (i.e., other party manifestos) as dictionaries. Word frequencies in manifestos are compared to those in the reference texts to estimate positions. However, the policy specific content of text is ignored, as the technique simply uses all the information in manifestos to extract scores on different policy dimensions. Estimates in Wordscores vary across dimensions *only* because different expert evaluations are used to anchor the reference texts on the "dimensions," not because the text input varies according to the policy area of interest.[10] In other words, the estimation of the policy dimension hinges on the assessments of experts rather than the policy-relevant

[8] See, for example, a recent special issue on the topic: The Statistical Analysis of Political Text. *Political Analysis* 16(4), edited by Burt L. Monroe and Philip A. Schrodt.

[9] This is different from the CMP measurement approach, which assumes that there is a true coding of quasi-sentences (the CMP "gold standard") according to which each coder should be evaluated.

[10] Only if researchers assign different party documents as reference texts does this approach use different text for different dimensions, but in any case, it does not use policy-specific texts, but the entire manifesto.

context of the manifestos. Monroe and Maeda (2004) suggest a multidimensional word scaling approach where the dimensions are inductively determined ex post. Proksch & Slapin (2006) and Slapin & Proksch (2008) have proposed subdividing the manifestos into broad policy categories and running a word scaling technique such as *Wordfish* or the *Wordscores* algorithm on these different text categories. Using this method, estimates on the different dimensions, regardless of the actual technique, no longer hinge on expert scores or post hoc interpretation. However, the process of deciding which sections of text belong to which policy dimension can be time consuming, and different coders may disagree about the topic assignment of each manifesto section. Using this method, it would be virtually impossible to obtain dimensionality scores that are any more refined than those obtained from expert surveys. In practice, assigning more than a few broad categories through human coding would be difficult, error-prone, and time consuming (Miller 1956; Mikhaylov et al. 2008). Indeed, this is precisely what the CMP project has done, and it has taken them years and vast numbers of research assistants to produce the data.

Thus, while computer-assisted quantitative content analysis promises reliability, it is still necessary to identify policy-relevant content in manifestos to ensure that position estimates are accurate for all portfolios of interest. The identification of such policy-relevant content in political texts should be automated and objective. This is precisely what our new method accomplishes.

A New Approach to Extracting Policy-Specific Language from Manifestos

Our approach can be summarized as follows. To estimate party positions on policy dimensions relevant in the legislative arena, we first identify policy keywords using bills found in a legislative decision-making database. We argue that words found in legislative proposals regarding a particular policy portfolio are of political relevance on that dimension, and their contextual use in election manifestos provides information about policy conflicts between parties. Keywords can easily be extracted from bills by policy area, as they are pre-classified in such databases according to policy portfolios. Those keywords are then identified in party manifesto sentences. For example, if we find that the word "tax" is relevant on a finance dimension because it appears frequently in summaries of financial bills, we could examine the content of manifesto sentences containing the word "tax".[11] Thus, we not only capture the keyword, but the remaining information in the sentence that qualifies the statement. A political party could talk about lowering corporate taxes or introducing an extra income tax for the rich. Both statements would fall into the finance portfolio, but

[11] In essence, we are interested in topic-coding manifestos. However, we differ from computer-based methods of topic-coding (e.g., Hopkins and King 2010; Quinn et al. 2010) in that we use keywords from bills to explicitly link policy-specific information in manifestos to policy portfolios.

emphasize different aspects of taxation. Hence, the relative frequencies of the words contained in sentences with finance keywords provide information about the placement of parties on a financial policy dimension (König and Luig 2009). Having automatically identified the policy-relevant statements in manifestos, we can then extract policy positions from those sentences by applying a text scaling algorithm on the selected subset of manifesto sentences. Here we choose to focus on the word counts and use the Wordfish technique (Slapin and Proksch 2008).

Using our approach, outlined in Fig. 4.1 and described in this section, we estimate positions along 14 portfolio-specific dimensions for German political parties in 1983, 1987, and 1990. We chose this time period because we wish to compare our results to the Laver and Hunt (1992) survey conducted in 1988–1989. We demonstrate that during this period there was party movement which could potentially affect empirical analysis of policy change and government formation, but which expert surveys cannot capture. This has consequences for the application of these data in empirical studies such as the one by Tsebelis (1999).

Step 1: Identifying Legislative Keywords

As shown in Fig. 4.1, we start by identifying legislative keywords. To identify keywords indicative of the context of a policy portfolio, we draw upon the corpus of legislative initiatives between 1983 and 1994 (10th to 12th legislative period). This includes all bills introduced in parliament, regardless of final passage and regardless of the type of initiator. The 'State of Federal Legislation' (GESTA) database documents all legislative proposals introduced to either chamber of the German parliament.[12] For each legislative proposal, the GESTA database contains the title, the

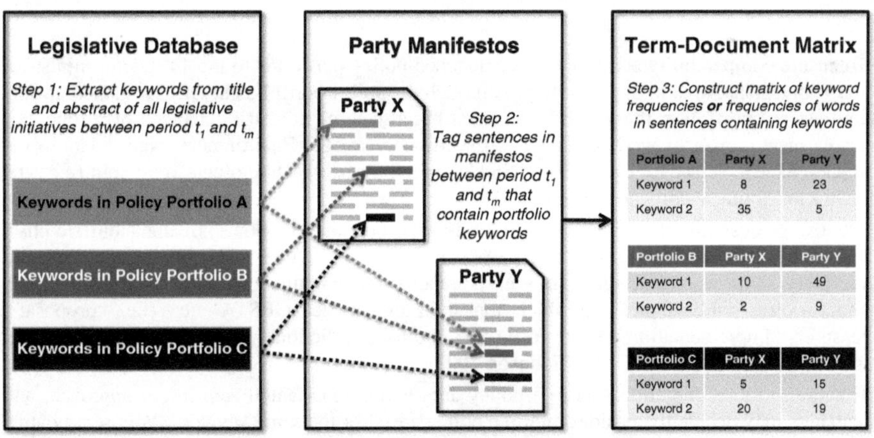

Fig. 4.1 Overview: tagging manifestos using legislative keywords

---

[12] GESTA is electronically available via the 'Documentation and Information System for Parliamentary Materials' (DIP) system (http://dip.bundestag.de).

policy portfolio to which the proposal belongs, its thematic classification, main and secondary keywords, a summary of the content, as well as additional procedural information (König and Bräuninger 2005). We extract the title, the main and secondary keywords, and the summary. These extracted text elements constitute the set of keywords. The extraction was performed for each government policy portfolio within each legislative period, allowing us to collect a set of keywords for each ministerial portfolio at a given point in time.[13]

At this point we have lists containing keywords for each ministerial portfolio during each legislative period.[14] The process described earlier allows the same keywords to appear in various policy portfolios. Prominent keywords do, in fact, appear in multiple policy areas. Although some words may be multidimensional in nature, we decided to assign each keyword to only one policy area for position estimation purposes. Specifically, we assign a keyword to the portfolio with the highest relative frequency of occurrences in legislative initiatives. While policy-specific words may have multiple uses, we argue that they most clearly belong to one policy area. The word "science", for example, appears in bills regarding labor policy, foreign policy, education, finances, health, interior policy, justice, agriculture, environment, transport and building, and economy and technology, but at its core it is an "education" word, appearing with the highest relative frequency in education bills. It is, therefore, a keyword indicative of education policy, and not the other policy areas.[15]

Step 2: Smart Tagging Political Texts Using Legislative Keywords

Once we have the lists of keywords compiled for each policy portfolio, we tag the sentences in party manifestos that contain those keywords (the second step depicted in Fig. 4.1).[16] We then count the frequencies of all words that appear in the sentences

[13] To ensure comparability across time, we matched policy portfolios to the 14 federal ministries in the 16th legislative term of Bundestag. Although the policy portfolios in GESTA closely mirror the ministerial portfolios, the match is not exact because some ministries changed over time. For example, new ministries were added (e.g., the Ministry for the Environment, Nature Conservation and Nuclear Safety following the 1986 Chernobyl disaster) while others were split (e.g., the Ministry for Youth, Family and Health in 1991).

[14] We also process the files by removing all numbers, punctuation, other nonalphanumeric characters, and checking for spelling errors. We furthermore exclude words with little semantic value (very short words, articles, pronouns, prepositions, conjunctions, etc.) as well as words without a clear political meaning which appear in almost each GESTA entry (i.e., "proposal", "measure", "implementation," etc.). To do this, we used a dictionary approach implemented in Simstat/WordStat (Davi et al. 2005; Johnson 2007).

[15] However, this unique allocation to a policy area is not an essential step in our approach, and researchers may decide to consider multiple policy areas for the same keyword. We use a relative frequency criterion rather than an absolute frequency criterion because the absolute frequency criterion would mean that policy areas in which more legislation is written would also have far more keywords than areas in which less legislation is produced.

[16] If a manifesto sentence contains keywords from two or more portfolios, the sentence counts for each of those portfolios. An alternative approach would be to assign each sentence exclusively to one portfolio.

with keywords.[17] When estimating positions, we assume that keywords are constant within policy areas over time. In other words, regardless of when a keyword is mentioned in a legislative initiative, we count its occurrences in all manifestos.[18] The underlying assumption is that the nature of the policy space does not change over time. This assumption is required if we wish to examine the shifts in positions within each portfolio across time. If the nature of the policy space were allowed to change in addition to the policy position, we would be unable to determine whether a party's policy shift was due to a change in policy position or the underlying nature of the policy space. At the end of this step, we have 14 word count matrices (also referred to as term-document matrices in the text mining and linguistics literature), one for each policy portfolio. The words from sentences containing keywords are listed in the rows and the party manifestos form the columns. Each element of the matrix is a count of the number of times a word was mentioned in a given manifesto for a given portfolio.

Step 3: Estimate Portfolio Positions

The word count matrices produced in step 2 provide the data for the estimation of policy positions in this final step. At this stage, any text scaling approach for extracting policy positions from word count matrices could be employed. Such approaches in political science include Wordscores (Laver et al. 2003), Wordfish (Slapin and Proksch 2008), and the Bayesian approach adopted by Monroe and Maeda (2004). In a naïve Bayes approach, a text is represented as a vector of word counts or occurrences and multiple document vectors are put together in a word count matrix (Eyheramendy et al. 2003; Lewis 1998). The order of words and grammatical structure of the original document is lost. In our case, we are not even preserving entire documents, but rather only counting the occurrences of words in sentences containing policy keywords. We estimate positions using the Wordfish technique (Slapin and Proksch 2008; Proksch and Slapin 2009, forthcoming). In doing so, we extract unidimensional policy positions for each portfolio.[19]

---

[17] We use keyword stems and stemmed manifesto sentences.

[18] For example, in some instances a keyword may only occur during one legislative period. Nevertheless, we examine how many times that word was mentioned in the manifestos drafted before and after this period.

[19] Wordfish assumes that the frequency with which words occur in documents is generated by a Poisson process, the simplest of the count distributions. The systematic component of this process contains four parameters: document (party) positions, document (party) fixed effects, word weights (discrimination parameters), and word fixed effects. Formally, $y_{ijt} \sim \text{Poisson}(\lambda_{ijt})$, where y_{ijt} is the count of word j in party i's manifesto at time t. The lambda parameter has the systematic component $\lambda_{ijt} = \exp(\alpha_{it} + \psi_j + \beta_j * \omega_{it})$, with α as a set of document (party-election year) fixed effects, ψ as a set of word fixed effects, β as estimates of word specific weights capturing the importance of word j in discriminating between manifestos, and ω as the estimate of party i's position in election year t (therefore *it* is indexing one specific manifesto). For a more detailed description of the estimation process, see Slapin and Proksch (2008).

Results

We now present the results from a systematic evaluation of our approach with data from the German legislative decision-making database and German election manifestos. First, we focus on labor policy, the area investigated by Tsebelis (1999). Second, we systematically examine all policy portfolios and demonstrate that keywords appear not only in government bills but also to a significant extent in bills proposed by the opposition. Furthermore, we show that the keywords appear both in manifestos written by coalition government parties and opposition parties. Finally, we present the estimated Wordfish position estimates for all portfolios and compare these estimates to those generated by the Laver-Hunt expert survey.

Labor Policy in Germany

Legislative Keyword Coverage in Manifestos

We first illustrate how the approach works. Relying on the labor legislation dataset created by Döring (1995), Tsebelis identified two significant labor laws passed during the 1980s in Germany (Tsebelis 1999). The first was the Employment Promotion Act of 1985 and the second was the Shop Closing Hours Amendment Act of 1989. Both bills were proposed by the government. Using those bills, our approach identifies several keywords in the labor policy area, including the terms "social" and "employment," but also "shop closing hours," "late night service day," and "employment promotion."[20] The latter keywords arguably provide the best indicator for these two pieces of legislation, and these keywords do in fact appear in election manifestos during the 1980s. Parties made a retrospective reference to the passage of the first law on employment promotion. The CDU–CSU cited the law in its 1987 manifesto as an example of its successful labor market policy. The government party wrote that "early retirement, the promotion of return policies for foreign workers, significant measures to expand job training, and Employment Promotion Act are all important examples" of its policy. During the same election campaign, the opposition party SPD also made a reference to the law, promising to "undo the erosion of workers' rights by the so-called Employment Promotion Act." Similarly, in the 1990 manifesto, the SPD repeated its demand to repeal the "unsocial so-called Employment Promotion Act." The issue of shop closing hours addressed in the second law was mentioned prior to the bill passage in 1989 by the government party FDP in its 1987 manifesto. In the manifesto, the Free Democrats argued in favor of relaxing the restrictions on shopping hours. It proposed to "relax restrictions on shop closing hours without extending the total opening times and to introduce one late night service day for banks and government agencies." These brief anecdotes make an

[20] In German, *Ladenschluss*, *Dienstleistungsabend*, and *Beschäftigungsförderung*, respectively.

important point. Legislative keywords provide a precise indicator for policy and parties pick up the terms in their election manifestos. The sentences in which these keywords appear provide information regarding the ideological position of the parties on the policy area of interest. Moreover, the references show that parties refer to legislation both before and after its passage.

Labor Policy Positions

Using all legislative proposals in the area of labor policy contained in the German law-making database, we were able to identify 402 legislative keywords unique to this policy portfolio. We then tagged all manifesto sentences containing these keywords and ran the text scaling algorithm Wordfish on the tagged sentences. This yielded labor policy position estimates for every legislative party and legislative period. Figure 4.2 compares the Wordfish party positions with the Laver-Hunt expert estimates on taxes vs. spending, since this was the policy dimension used by Tsebelis in his empirical analysis. The Laver and Hunt estimates place the Green

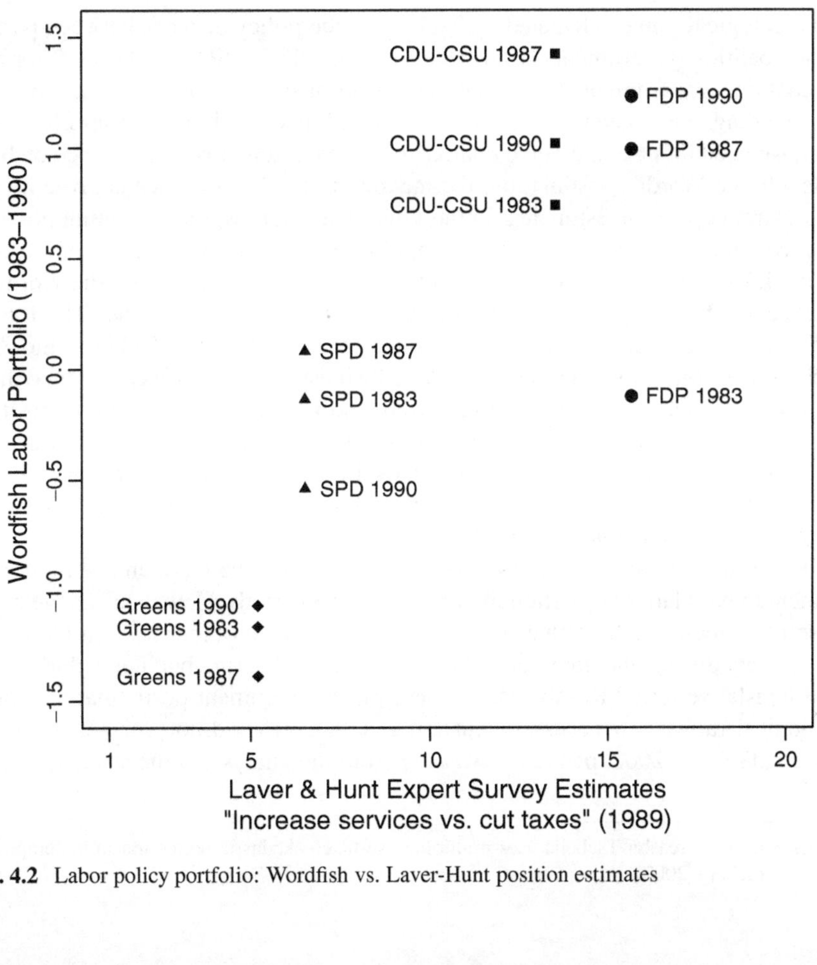

Fig. 4.2 Labor policy portfolio: Wordfish vs. Laver-Hunt position estimates

party on the left of the dimension and the FDP on the right. The SPD is estimated to be center-left and the CDU–CSU center-right. A slightly different picture of labor policy emerges when we examine the dynamic Wordfish estimates. Similarly to Laver and Hunt, the Greens are estimated to the left of the SPD. However, the position of the FDP reveals significant differences between the estimation approaches. Contrary to Laver & Hunt, we find the FDP to be centrist and close to the SPD in 1983. Only then does the FDP move to the right throughout the period – as does the CDU – , eventually taking a more right-wing stance than the CDU–CSU by 1990. This movement toward a more conservative position seems plausible because the Liberals became a coalition partner in a CDU–CSU/FDP government following the breakdown of the SPD/FDP coalition in 1982. Researchers using expert survey data would not be able to capture this party movement, potentially leading to increased measurement error compared with our positions. In the next section, we examine how the dynamic positions translate into a different estimate for one of the key variables in veto players analysis, the *ideological range between veto players*.

Ideological Range

The ideological range calculated by Tsebelis is the policy distance between parties in the coalition government. In our example, the CDU–CSU and the FDP formed the coalition government throughout the period of investigation. In order to compare the range calculated on the basis of our estimates with those from Laver and Hunt, we need to make the range relative to the maximum possible distance on both scales. In the Wordfish estimation, the maximum possible distance is given by the most extreme position estimates. In the Laver-Hunt survey, the maximum possible distance is the difference between the endpoints of the scale presented to the experts. Figure 4.3 shows both ranges on the same plot. The left y-axis shows the Wordfish distance scale, the right y-axis shows the Laver-Hunt distance scale. The Laver-Hunt ideological range is simply the distance between the CDU–CSU and the FDP on the issue of taxes vs. services. The Wordfish estimates, however, produce three range values, one for each legislative period, taking into account the party position shifts over time. It shows that the ideological differences between the coalition government actually decreased during the 1980s. Interestingly, the Laver-Hunt range – calculated from an expert survey in 1988/1989 – lies exactly between the Wordfish ranges for 1987 and 1990.

Our results would suggest that it becomes easier for the German coalition government to pass labor legislation in later legislative periods. How then can we make sense of Tsebelis' finding that there were two significant labor laws in Germany, one passed during the first, one during the second term, but none during the third legislative term? Recall that the veto players argument posits that a smaller ideological range is a necessary but not a sufficient condition for actual policy change (Tsebelis 2002, p. 172).[21] Missing from the analysis is the status quo, and

[21] This is also the reason Tsebelis uses multiplicative heteroskedastic regression in his empirical analysis (Tsebelis 2002).

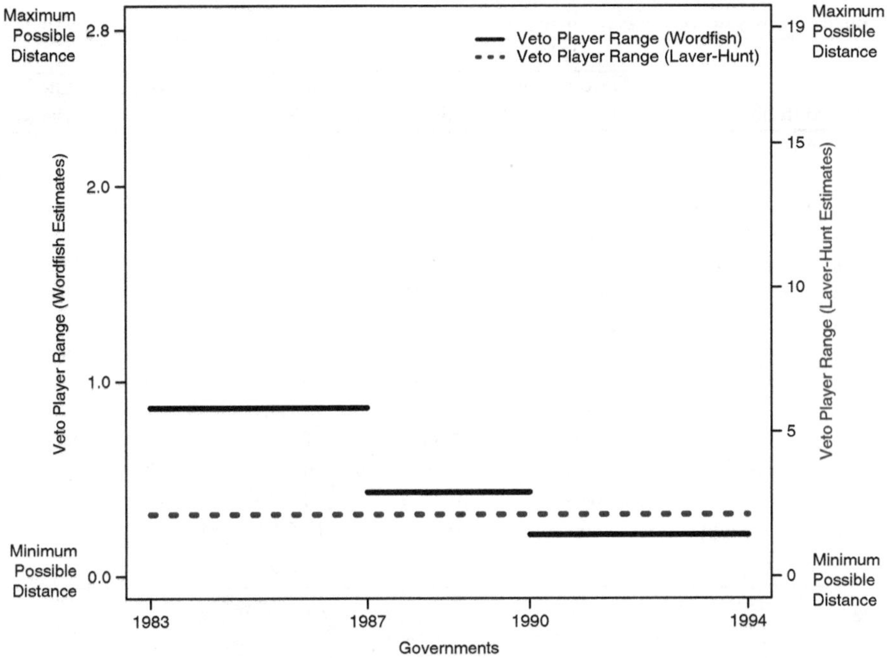

Fig. 4.3 Ideological range of veto players for labor policy in Germany

whether the coalition government *wants* to change it. Given the change in German government from a social-liberal to a conservative-liberal coalition in 1982, we would, in fact, expect that change is most likely during the initial phase, as the status quo should have been located far away from the new coalition's program. Once the policy changes have been made, the new status quo will be close to the positions of the veto players and no additional changes will be needed. This is likely to remain true even when the ideological range between the veto players decreases further, as is the case in our example.

Aggregate Analysis

Keyword Coverage in Bills and Manifestos

We now perform a systematic analysis of the extent to which legislative keywords appear in government and opposition bills across all ministerial portfolios. We also examine how many party manifesto sentences can be tagged as portfolio-specific using those keywords. It is well known that governments enjoy agenda-setting privileges in parliamentary democracies (Tsebelis 2002). Therefore, most bills introduced in the legislature are generated by cabinet ministers and government parties. This could mean that the selection of keywords may be unevenly

Table 4.1 Coverage of keywords in legislative proposals

	Legislative keywords				
Policy portfolio	Government bills	Opposition bills	State bills	Mixed bills	Total No. keywords
Agriculture	44.94%	2.83%	15.38%	36.84%	248
Defense	69.88%	7.23%	3.61%	19.28%	84
Development	56.10%	34.15%	0.00%	9.76%	41
Economy & technology	43.62%	16.11%	4.03%	36.24%	298
Education & research	49.14%	1.72%	12.93%	36.21%	117
Environment	47.64%	14.18%	6.18%	32.00%	276
Family	35.75%	21.72%	6.79%	35.75%	221
Finances	60.75%	4.44%	6.07%	28.74%	428
Foreign	91.37%	1.52%	0.00%	7.11%	197
Health	40.00%	2.86%	18.86%	38.29%	175
Interior	32.92%	12.87%	11.39%	42.82%	404
Justice	25.16%	14.50%	6.40%	53.95%	469
Labor	31.67%	10.97%	8.73%	48.63%	402
Transport & building	33.46%	10.29%	12.50%	43.75%	272
Average Portfolio	*47.31%*	*11.10%*	*8.06%*	*33.53%*	*259*

distributed between government bills and opposition bills. But if we select many more keywords from government bills, and if those keywords appear only in the manifestos from the very same governing parties then our results might be biased toward finding a conflict between governing and opposition parties. Thus, it is important to investigate both the distribution of keywords in bills and in manifestos. Table 4.1 lists the 14 policy portfolios, the number of legislative keywords assigned to each, and their coverage in the bills used to identify them.[22] The policy areas with the largest number of keywords are justice policy, finances, interior policy, labor policy, and economy and technology policy. On average, slightly less than half of the extracted keywords appear only in government bills (CDU–CSU/FDP), around 10% of keywords only in opposition bills (SPD/Greens/PDS), 8% of keywords only in federal state *(Länder)* bills, and around a third of keywords in at least two of these three sources.[23] This means that the majority of keywords do *not*, in fact, appear only in government bills. The policy areas with the strongest government keyword coverage (above 50%) are foreign policy, defense policy, financial policy, and development policy. With the exception of development, these are also the policy areas with the lowest opposition coverage. It is worth noting that, with the exception of the finance portfolio, these areas all address external relations and security, policies dominated by the executive. When we look at domestic policies, the proportion of keywords that appear only in government bills drops significantly. Areas with the

[22] The results are based on keyword stems. Only keywords that appear in at least one election manifesto are considered.

[23] The CDU–CSU and FDP formed the governing coalition throughout the period of investigation.

lowest proportion include justice policy, labor policy, interior policy, and transport and building policy. One of the highest proportion of keywords appearing only in those bills initiated by the federal states is in the area of education. However, this is not surprising given that education policies are to a large extent under the jurisdiction of the *Länder*. Finally, the analysis shows that a substantial number of keywords appear in multiple sources (mixed occurrence).

Next, we show that although government bills generate a substantial number of keywords, those keywords do not appear more frequently in government party manifestos than in opposition party manifestos. Table 4.2 lists the percentage of manifesto sentences that are tagged using the keywords for each policy area. Note that a sentence can be tagged a number of times if it contains keywords from more than one policy area. Therefore, the percentages do not add up to 100%. In addition, the table lists the proportion of keywords that appear in government party manifestos (CDU–CSU and FDP) and in opposition party manifestos (SPD, Greens, PDS). Finally, the last column lists the number of unique words identified using the tagged sentences in each policy area. The proportion of tagged sentences does vary significantly across policy areas. The area most frequently covered by manifestos is interior policy (37.5%), labor policy (35.2%), finances (29.2%), and foreign policy (28.4%). The large share of foreign policy shows that the proportion of tagged sentences cannot be explained by the number of keywords per policy area alone, as foreign policy has less than half the number of keywords than the other dominant areas. Areas with the fewest percentages of tagged sentences are defense policy, development policy, and education policy.

While the keyword coverage in government and opposition bills varies quite significantly, these differences disappear when we compare the keyword coverage in the manifestos from governing parties and opposition parties. First, the coverage

Table 4.2 Coverage of legislative keywords in election manifestos

	Party election manifestos			
Policy portfolio	Tagged sentences	Keywords Gov. manifestos	Keywords Opp. manifestos	Unique words in analysis
Agriculture	24.3%	74.6%	73.8%	6,570
Defense	8.7%	78.6%	75.0%	3,245
Development	11.3%	87.8%	80.5%	3,738
Economy & technology	23.8%	77.2%	72.5%	6,494
Education & research	10.8%	84.6%	72.7%	3,743
Environment	22.0%	71.4%	75.0%	6,214
Family	24.9%	71.5%	74.7%	6,102
Finances	29.9%	71.3%	66.8%	7,349
Foreign	28.4%	77.7%	72.6%	6,700
Health	24.6%	75.4%	74.9%	6,410
Interior	37.5%	72.0%	72.3%	8,464
Justice	26.6%	64.2%	72.7%	6,972
Labor	35.2%	69.4%	70.6%	7,700
Transport & building	24.4%	75.0%	72.4%	6,529

rate is high for almost all policy areas. Government party manifestos cover between 64% (justice policy) and 88% (development) of keywords that are mentioned at least once in a manifesto. Opposition party manifestos cover on average between 67% (finances) and 81% (development) of keywords. In sum, in almost all portfolios the average coverage in government manifestos is similar to the average coverage in opposition manifestos.[24]

Portfolio Positions for German Parties

Having collected the keywords and created the word count data sets, we estimate positions by running the Wordfish algorithm for all policy dimensions separately. Table A-1 in the Appendix lists the estimates for all 14 policy portfolios and parties. Figure 4.4 plots our results against the Laver and Hunt (1992) survey positions for two areas that are comparable. Of course, our method not only produces policy positions on more dimensions than expert surveys do, but also on dimensions that are more closely related to ministerial portfolios. This is certainly one advantage of our method as compared to existing approaches. Nevertheless, we wish to demonstrate

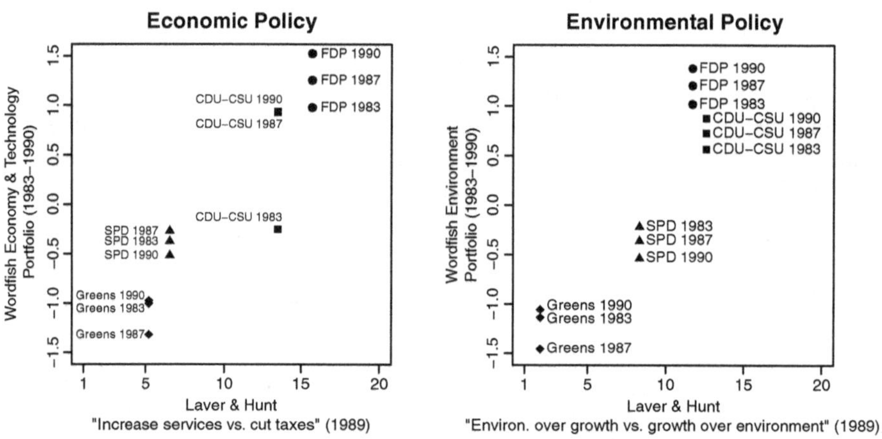

Fig. 4.4 Policy portfolio party positions in Germany: economy and environment

[24] Moreover, the keyword coverage in manifestos across legislative periods, which is not shown in the table, reveals that for almost all portfolios the majority of keywords appear in at least two legislative periods. In other words, we are not simply selecting keywords that are relevant in one legislative period only. The most stable keyword coverage is in the areas of development and defense, in which more than 70% and 60%, respectively, of keyword stems occur in more than one legislative period. The least stable keyword coverage is in the areas of finances and justice, in which slightly less than 50% occur in at least two periods. We consider this stability to be sufficient to use the keywords to construct a term-document matrix and estimate positions over all three periods simultaneously.

that our method recovers positions similar to those found in the expert survey, and, more importantly, we wish to demonstrate that our method captures variation over time that the expert survey data fails to capture.

The left plot shows our positions on economic policy against the Laver-Hunt "Taxes vs. Services" positions. Note that Tsebelis used this Laver-Hunt dimension to infer positions on labor policy. Here, we show that this dimension actually comes closer to the our economic policy dimension. The ranking of the parties is the same and the positions correlate highly. The Greens are the most left–wing party on this dimension while the liberal FDP is the most right-wing. Again, our positions reveal that there is movement over time. The range of CDU–CSU positions during this period is particularly large. On the environmental policy dimension shown in the right plot, our estimates place the FDP to the right of the CDU–CSU while the expert surveys place the FDP in the center, between the SPD and the CDU–CSU. Of course, because policy positions are a latent variable, it is impossible to say which of these rank orderings is correct. However, differences such as this may arise if experts believe the FDP to be a centrist party because of their positions on other dimensions, such as social policy. This may lead experts to place the FDP further to the center even when the party should be in fact more to the right.

In short, our method provides for more refined estimates, in part because we are able to estimate positions for more narrowly defined policy areas that match to ministerial portfolios, but also because we are able to examine change over time in ways that expert surveys cannot. The FDP, which quit the coalition with the SPD in 1982 and formed a coalition with the CDU–CSU, consistently moved to the right. This move is most notable in the labor policy area, where the FDP in fact positioned itself away from the SPD toward the right of CDU–CSU by 1990.

Towards New Policy-Making Analysis of Parliamentary Systems

Until now, human judgments have been the crucial link in determining the subject matter of policy dimensions, be it through the manual division of the manifestos or expert evaluations. We have demonstrated the feasibility of a new approach that replaces human judgment with automatic text selection using legislative keywords. The implications for empirical studies such as Tsebelis's are clear. More variation means that research designs can be significantly improved. There is more variation across policy areas and over time. This means that changes in the ideological distances between governmental parties can be measured with more precision than before. The increased variation across time and policies also means that more longitudinal studies are now feasible.

What does our approach mean for comparative studies that do try to explain institutional variation between countries in addition to testing general ideological polarization effects on policy making? We have provided an approach that is applicable in a variety of settings but that is country-specific at its core. To test policy-focused theories in parliamentary systems, we suggest researchers estimate the relative locations of parties on substantive dimensions of conflict using information generated by each country's legislative process as well as party election manifestos. Because each country has a different policy context, each country produces different legislative keywords. Therefore, conflict can only be estimated separately for each country. Since the resulting positions are on an arbitrary scale, we cannot directly compare party positions across countries. Statistical models would need to account for the fact that governing coalitions in two different countries may have the same distance measure generated by the scaling technique even though the conflict between the parties is greater in one country than in the other. Even though researchers should be wary of cross-sectional analysis using these data, we have compiled a list of electronic law-making databases in Table A-2 of the Appendix to demonstrate that our approach is easily applicable to parliamentary systems beyond Germany. The table shows the availability of electronic legislative databases for selected countries, the data with the earliest full text accessibility, as well as the internet address of the archive. All the legislative databases listed include summaries and titles of legislative initiatives which can be used as keywords and then linked to manifestos. Also, there might be instances in which a true comparison is possible. For example, we could compare positions of parties and governments in the European Union, using translated keywords from the common law-making database of the European Union. This may allow us to estimate and compare the positions of political parties in each country for the legislative context of the European Union.

Conclusion

Existing methods for estimating parties' positions suffer from drawbacks that hinder empirical work seeking to test legislative theories. First, policy spaces are often too broadly defined and do not correspond to the context required to test theoretical models of government formation and legislative decision making. While policy-focused theories assume political parties behave as if they are committed to implementing their policy preferences in the legislature, existing measures of political party preferences ignore the legislative agenda. Second, estimates are often incomplete and time invariant. Scholars therefore have to reduce their data sample according to available policy-specific dimensions, leaving open questions about selection bias and conflicts in the remaining portfolios. When data are only available for a limited period, variation is often induced by interacting position estimates generated by experts using other, less theoretically sound, institutional variables.

These problems combined mean that the existing estimates used by most scholars of comparative politics do not capture the full range of context and variation that they should have for testing policy-focused theories. We have demonstrated the restrictions under which scholars have evaluated their policy-focused theories. Until now, dynamic estimates for the positions of political parties on the issue-specific context of government portfolios are largely missing, meaning that empirical tests often had to rely on less than adequate measurements.

Our new automated method for identifying policy content in political texts tags election manifestos by using keywords from legislative databases. Positions can then be estimated on the tagged, policy-relevant subset of sentences. Our approach is the first that generates policy portfolio specific scores without researchers' subjective evaluation of what the policy space should consist of. Furthermore, all steps of our approach are replicable. Our application to the positions of political parties in the German parliament shows that these estimates cover a wider range of policy areas and vary over time and across portfolios. They produce similar results to expert surveys, but display greater variation, as we would expect. The method provides for more refined estimates, in part because we are able to estimate positions for more narrowly defined policy areas that match to ministerial portfolios, but also because we are able to examine change over time in ways that expert surveys cannot. This will facilitate tests of policy-focused theories.

Acknowledgements The authors' names appear in alphabetical order. All authors have contributed equally to all work. A previous version of this chapter was presented at the 67th Annual MPSA National Conference in Chicago, April 2009, and the Veto Players Workshop at the University of Mannheim in May 2009. We thank the participants for helpful comments and suggestions.

Table A-1 Party position estimates for 14 policy areas, Germany (1983–1990)

Manifesto	Labor	Foreign	Education	Development	Finances	Family	Health	Interior	Justice	Agriculture	Environment	Transport	Defense	Economy
1983														
FDP	−0.124	1.036	0.999	0.998	0.995	1.157	−0.279	1.075	1.042	1.069	1.017	1.070	−0.646	0.977
Greens	−1.164	−1.487	−1.324	−1.541	−1.099	−1.057	−1.085	−1.169	−1.130	−1.456	−1.136	−1.349	−0.725	−1.001
SPD	−0.137	−0.369	0.214	0.172	−0.544	−0.270	−0.390	−0.223	0.160	−0.213	−0.220	−0.350	−0.303	−0.375
CDU–CSU	0.740	0.513	−0.491	0.580	0.361	0.464	0.473	0.293	0.133	0.231	0.565	0.240	1.066	−0.254
1987														
FDP	0.992	1.206	1.138	1.088	1.213	1.499	1.080	1.143	1.103	1.190	1.205	1.174	0.794	1.252
Greens	−1.387	−1.261	−1.113	−1.122	−1.293	−1.382	−1.229	−1.405	−1.433	−1.264	−1.455	−1.215	−1.283	−1.314
SPD	0.082	−0.122	−0.547	−0.755	−0.570	−0.490	−0.488	−0.433	−0.321	−0.331	−0.361	−0.515	−0.509	−0.271
CDU–CSU	1.423	0.780	1.637	0.775	0.882	0.799	1.620	0.903	0.843	0.806	0.727	0.933	1.634	0.928
1990														
FDP	1.232	1.351	1.314	1.455	1.542	1.235	1.460	1.465	1.463	1.424	1.380	1.543	1.167	1.595
Greens	−1.069	−0.935	−0.749	−0.734	−0.990	−1.051	−0.947	−1.026	−1.029	−0.904	−1.056	−0.925	−0.960	−0.974
SPD	−0.540	−0.557	−0.657	−0.407	−0.537	−0.516	−0.388	−0.468	−0.669	−0.551	−0.536	−0.484	−0.473	−0.516
CDU–CSU	1.018	0.825	0.355	0.668	0.881	0.597	0.991	0.825	0.881	0.926	0.876	0.771	1.142	0.938
PDS	−1.066	−0.980	−0.776	−1.177	−0.841	−0.984	−0.817	−0.981	−1.043	−0.927	−1.006	−0.894	−0.903	−0.985

Table A-2 Overview of electronic lawmaking databases in selected European parliamentary democracies

		Legislative database	
Country	Chamber	Full text since	Internet address
Austria	LH & UH	1996	www.parlament.gv.at
Belgium	LH	1988	www.lachambre.be
	UH	1995	www.senate.be
Denmark	LH	1997	www.folketinget.dk
Finland	LH	1992	www.parliament.fi
France	LH & UH	1997	www.assemblee-nationale.fr
Germany	LH & UH	1976	dip.bundestag.de
Ireland	LH & UH	1997	www.oireachtas.ie
Italy	LH & UH	1996	www.senato.it
Luxembourg	LH	1976	www.chd.lu
Netherlands	LH & UH	1961	www.statengeneraaldigitaal.nl
Poland	LH & UH	1997	www.sejm.gov.pl/www.senat.gov.pl
Slovak republic	LH	2006	www.nrsr.sk
Spain	LH	1979	www.congreso.es/www.senado.es
Sweden	LH	1971	www.riksdagen.se
UK	LH & UH	2001	www.parliament.uk

Note: *LH* Lower House; *UH* Upper House. Coverage periods for legislative databases refer to the availability of searchable, full-text databases. Information regarding the legislative databases as of May 2009

References

Adams J, Somer-Topcu Z (2009) Do parties adjust their policies in response to rival parties' policy shifts? Br J Political Sci 39(4):825–846

Adams J, Clark M, Ezrow L, Glasgow G (2006) Are niche parties fundamentally different from mainstream parties? the causes and the electoral consequences of western european parties' policy shifts, 1976–1998. Am J Political Sci 50(3):513–529

Alt JE, Lassen DD (2006) Transparency, political polarization, and political budget cycles in oecd countries. Am J Political Sci 50(3):530–550

Bawn K, Rosenbluth F (2006) Short versus long coalitions: electoral accountability and the size of the public sector. Am J Political Sci 50(2):251–265

Benoit K, Laver M (2006) Party Policy in Modern Democracies. Routledge, London

Benoit K, Laver M, Mikhaylov S (2009) Treating words as data with error: uncertainty in text statements of policy positions. Am J Political Sci 53(2):495–513

Blanpain R (ed) (1995) International encyclopedia for labour law and industrial relations. Kluwer, Amsterdam

Browne EC, Gleiber DW, Mashoba CS (1984) Evaluating conflict of interest theory: Western European cabinet coalitions, 1945–1980. Br J Political Sci 14(1):1–32

Budge I (2000) Expert judgements of party policy positions: uses and limitations in political research. Eur J Political Res 37:103–113

Budge I, Robertson D, Hearl D (1987) Ideology, strategy, and party change: spatial analyses of post-war election programmes in 19 democracies. Cambridge University Press, Cambridge

Budge I, Klingemann HD, Volkens A, Bara J, Tanenbaum E (2001) Mapping policy preferences: estimates for parties, electors, and governments 1945–1998. Oxford University Press, Oxford

Castles FG, Mair P (1984) Left-right political scales: some expert judgements. Eur J Political Res 12(1):73–88
Crombez C (1996) Minority governments, minimal winning coalitions and surplus majorities in parliamentary systems. Eur J Political Res 29(1):1–29
Davi A, Haughton D, Nasr N, Shah G, Skaletsky M, Spack R (2005) A review of two text-mining packages: Sas textmining and wordstat. Am Statist 59(1):89–103
Dodd L (1976) Coalitions in parliamentary government. Princeton University Press, Princeton, NJ
Döring H (ed) (1995) Parliaments and majority rule in Western Europe. St. Martin's Press, New York, NY
Druckman JN, Thies MF (2002) The importance of concurrence: The impact of bicameralism on government formation and duration. Am J Political Sci 46(4):760–771
Eyheramendy S, Lewis D, Madigan D (2003) On the naive bayes model for text categorization. Proceedings of the 9th Workshop on Artificial Intelligence
Gabel MJ, Huber JD (2000) Putting parties in their place: inferring left-right ideological positions from party manifestos data. Am J Political Sci 44(1):94–103
Hooghe L, Bakker R, Brigevich A, de Vries C, Edwards E, Marks G, Rovny J, Steenbergen M (2010) Reliability and validity of measuring party positions: The Chapel Hill expert surveys of 2002 and 2006. Eur J Political Res
Hopkins D, King G (2010) A method of automated nonparametric content analysis for social science. Am J Political Sci 54(1):229–247
Huber JD, McCarty N (2001) Cabinet decision rules and political uncertainty in parliamentary bargaining. Am Political Sci Rev 95(2):345–360
Johnson T (2007) Review of wordstat 5.1, simstat 2.5 and qda miner 2.0. Political Methodol 15(1):11–14
Klingemann H-D, Volkens A, Bara J, Budge I, McDonald M (2006) Mapping policy preferences II: estimates for parties, electors and governments in Central and Eastern Europe, European Union and OECD 1990-2003. Oxford University Press, Oxford
König T, Bräuninger T (2005) Gesetzgebung im Föderalismus. Speyerer Forschungsberichte 237, Forschungsinstitut für Öffentliche Verwaltung, Speyer
König T, Luig B (2009) German 'lexiconspace': policy positions and their legislative context. German Politics 18(3):345–364
König T, Finke D, Daimer S (2005) Ignoring the non-ignorables?: missingness and missing positions. Eur Union Politics 6(3):269–290
Laver M, Garry J (2000) Estimating policy positions from political texts. Am J Political Sci 44(3):619–634
Laver M, Hunt WB (1992) Policy and party competition. Routledge, Chapman and Hall, New York
Laver M, Schofield N (1998) Multiparty government: the politics of coalition in Europe, 2nd edn. Oxford University Press, Oxford
Laver M, Shepsle KA (1996) Making and breaking governments: cabinets and legislatures in parliamentary democracies. Cambridge University Press, Cambridge
Laver M, Benoit K, Garry J (2003) Extracting policy positions from political texts using words as data. Am Political Sci Rev 97(2):311–332
Lewis DD (1998) Naive (bayes) at forty: the independence assumption in information retrieval. Proceedings of the 10th European Conference on Machine Learning pp. 4–15
Lijphart A (1999) Patterns of democracy: government forms and performance in thirty-six countries. Yale University Press, New Haven
Lowe W (2008) Understanding wordscores. Political Anal 16(4):356–371
Mair P (2001) Searching for positions of political actors: a review of approaches and a critical evaluation of expert surveys. In: Laver M (ed) Estimating the policy positions of political actors, pp. 10–30. Routledge, London
Martin LW, Stevenson RT (2001) Government formation in parliamentary democracies. Am J Political Sci 45(1):33–50
Martin LW, Vanberg G (2003) Wasting time? the impact of ideology and size on delay in coalition formation. Br J Political Sci 33(2):323–332

Martin LW, Vanberg G (2004) Policing the bargain: coalition government and parliamentary scrutiny. Am J Political Sci 48(1):13–27
Martin LW, Vanberg G (2005) Coalition policymaking and legislative review. Am Political Sci Rev 99(1):93–106
Mikhaylov S, Laver M, Benoit K (2008) Coder reliability and misclassification in comparative manifesto project codings. Paper presented at the 66th MPSA Conference, 3–6 April 2008
Miller G (1956) Magical number seven, plus or minus two. Psychol Rev 63(2):81–97
Monroe BL, Maeda K (2004) Talk's cheap: text-based estimation of rhetorical ideal-points. Paper presented at the 21st PolMeth Conference, 29–31 July 2004
Proksch SO, Slapin JB (2006) Institutions and coalition formation: the german election of 2005. West Eur Politics 29(3):540–559
Proksch SO, Slapin JB (2009) How to avoid pitfalls in statistical analysis of political texts: the case of germany. German Politics 18(3):323–344
Proksch SO, Slapin JB (2010) Position Taking in European Parliament Speeches. Br J Political Sci 40(3):587–611
Quinn KM, Monroe BL, Colaresi M, Crespin MH, Radev D (2010) How to analyze political attention with minimal assumptions and costs. Am J Political Sci 54(1):209–228
Rohrschneider R, Whitefield S (2007) Representation in new democracies: party stances on european integration in post-communist eastern europe. J Politics 69(4):1133–1146
Roozendaal PV (1992) The effect of dominant and central parties on cabinet composition and durability. Legis Stud Quart 17(1):5–36
Santoni M, Zucchini F (2004) Does policy stability increase the constitutional court's independence? the case of italy during the first republic (1956–1992). Public Choice 120(3/4):439–461
Scholtz E, Trantas G (1995) Legislation on benefits and on regulatory matters: social security and labor matters. In: Döring H (ed) Parliaments and majority rule in western Europe. St. Martin's Press, New York
Slapin JB, Proksch SO (2008) A scaling model for estimating time-series party positions from texts. Am J Political Sci 52(3):705–722
Steenbergen MR, Marks G (2007) Evaluating expert judgments. Eur J Political Res 46(3):347–366
Strøm K, Leipart JY (1993) Policy, institutions, and coalition avoidance: Norwegian governments, 1945–1990. Am Political Sci Rev 87(4):870–887
Tsebelis G (1995) Decision-making in political systems: Veto players in presidentialism, parliamentarism, multicameralism, and multipartyism. Br J Political Sci 25(3):289–325
Tsebelis G (1999) Veto players and law production in parliamentary democracies: an empirical analysis. Am Political Sci Rev 93(3):591–608
Tsebelis G (2002) Veto players: how political institutions work. Russell Sage/Princeton University Press, Princeton, NJ
Tsebelis G, Money J (1997) Bicameralism. Cambridge University Press, Cambridge
Volden C, Carrubba CJ (2004) The formation of oversized coalitions in parliamentary democracies. Am J Political Sci 48(3):521–537
Warwick P (1994) Government survival in west European parliamentary democracies. Cambridge University Press, New York
Warwick P (1996) Coalition government membership in west european parliamentary democracies. Br J Political Sci 26(4):471–499
Warwick P (1998) Policy distance and parliamentary government. Legis Stud Quart 23(3):319–345
Warwick P (2005) When far apart becomes too far apart: evidence for a threshold effect in coalition formation. Br J Political Sci 35(3):383–401

Part III
Interpretation of Veto Players

Chapter 5
Mutual Veto? How Coalitions Work

Wolfgang C. Müller and Thomas M. Meyer

Delegation in Coalition Governments

Multiparty elections in proportional representation systems rarely result in single-party majorities. In such minority situations (Strøm 1990), the most frequent outcome is a coalition government. But if two or more parties share government office, conflicts may arise due to the coalition partners' divergent interests. This chapter studies how coalitions cope with this problem by designing their governance structure.

Political science has long been interested in how coalition governments overcome diverging interests and decision-making problems. Laver and Shepsle (1990, 1996) have developed a powerful theory from the assumption that the executive privileges of departmental ministers make *joint* cabinet decision-making unfeasible. In their reasoning, departmental ministers are simply too strong in their respective fields to be bound to joint policy positions. If coalitions exist and prosper, it is because the parties adopt the solution of "dividing the cake": Each coalition party takes full decision power with regard to the portfolios held by its ministers (see also Austen-Smith and Banks 1990). Because each government party confines itself to the portfolios under its control, policy compromises are not necessary. Rather, government policies can be located at "lattice points," marking specific combinations of party jurisdictional ideal positions in the policy space.

As always, the parsimony and the beauty of this deductive approach raised criticism among more empirically oriented scholars (see the country chapters in Laver and Shepsle 1994; Dunleavy and Bastow 2001). They emphasize the existence of joint policymaking mechanisms, the prominence of inter-party policy negotiations and compromises in real world coalitions, and they highlight the constraining effects which crosscutting jurisdictions have on departmental ministers. Efforts at *coalition*

W.C. Müller (✉)
University of Vienna, Vienna, Austria
e-mail: wolfgang.mueller@univie.ac.at

T.M. Meyer
University of Mannheim (MZES, CDSS), Mannheim, Germany
e-mail: tmeyer@mail.uni-mannheim.de

T. König et al. (eds.), *Reform Processes and Policy Change: Veto Players and Decision-Making in Modern Democracies*, Studies in Public Choice 16,
DOI 10.1007/978-1-4419-5809-9_5, © Springer Science+Business Media, LLC 2010

policymaking may indeed be rewarding, as such policy compromises can (1) leave all government parties better off than the status quo of government policy and (2) provide them with better *overall* policy pay-offs from government participation than the combinations of individual party ideal point policies (Laver and Shepsle 1996: 63). George Tsebelis (2002: 96) has provided the most general and similarly parsimonious alternative to Laver and Shepsle's model of *ministerial party government*. In his account of coalition governance, each cabinet party is a veto player. Hence, a government coalition is characterized by mutual veto rights of the participating parties. We can, therefore, speak of a model of *cabinet party government*.[1]

The ministerial government model in its fully blown version does without coordination mechanisms beyond political parties directing their teams of ministers. If, however, coalition parties enjoy mutual veto rights, then questions of inter-party control and coordination arise. The possibility of each coalition party to veto government policy is only the means to motivate the individual parties to engage in checking their partner(s). Although Tsebelis (2002: 106–109) provides a brief discussion of a few instruments and related empirical research, this is clearly not his main concern. Building on the data and earlier work of the "Constitutional Change & Parliamentary Democracies" project (Müller and Strøm 2000; Strøm, Müller, and Bergman 2003, 2008) and other scholarship, we hope to take steps towards a better understanding of coalition governance in this chapter.

Of course, turning away from the portfolio allocation approach reintroduces problems such as government instability and (potential) policy cycles. A major concern for coalition parties hence is controlling each other and enforcing their deal. The literature on coalition governance considers a number of *specific* mechanisms employed by real world coalitions, including fixing compromises *ex ante* in policy agreements (Müller and Strøm 2008), excluding particularly divisive topics from the coalition agenda (Timmermans 2003, 2006), employing "watchdog" junior ministers (Thies 2001; Verzichelli 2008) and coalition committees (Andeweg and Timmermans 2008), and making use of parliamentary institutions for checking ministers and resolving coalition conflict (Martin 2004; Martin and Vanberg 2004, 2005). In this chapter, we develop a more general perspective, focussing on the architecture of the entire governance structure of coalitions. First, we ask which mechanisms allow parties to control their coalition partners' ministers. To answer this question, we apply concepts from the delegation literature to coalition governance. We discuss the micro-logic of specific mechanisms and how they may help to contain agency loss. Second, we ask which factors make the actual use of these control mechanisms more or less likely and how the specific mechanisms combine to the coalitions' governance structures.

Using multi-level models, we find that coalitions do not employ the entire arsenal of control mechanisms but aim at cost-efficiency. Specifically, coalition

[1] Our terms *ministerial party government* and *cabinet party government* resemble Strøm's (1994) *ministerial government* and *cabinet government* but express the concepts more clearly and keep the latter distinct from the classic understanding of cabinet government as formulated by authors such as Crossman (1972) and Mackintosh (1977).

governments choose control mechanisms that complement each other in predictable ways. Thus, coalition architects are more likely to establish coalition committees if they have written coalition agreements and have committed themselves to holding an election if the coalition breaks down, rather than allowing the formation of a new coalition in the sitting parliament. Parliamentary committee monitoring of the executive makes *ex ante* commitments to coalition discipline more likely and diminishes the use of "watchdog" junior ministers, who constitute an alternative *ex post* control mechanism. We find that the longer a cabinet's potential duration in office, the more likely is the use of control mechanisms. In addition, coalition architects are more likely to use specific control mechanisms when these have been employed by prior coalitions. Coalitions also tend to apply more *ex ante* control mechanisms in complex bargaining situations (whether indicated by the number of parties or ideological heterogeneity). Conversely, veto points external to the coalition (such as powerful second chambers or strong presidents) lead parties to rely less on *ex ante* controls. However, such veto points encourage mutual *ex post* control if the coalition partners, notwithstanding their presence, have made the investment of working out policy compromises *ex ante*.

In this chapter, we first present the menu of control mechanisms from which coalition governments may choose. Drawing on the delegation literature, we treat the specific mechanisms of coalition governance using contract design, screening procedures, monitoring devices, and institutional checks, respectively (Kiewiet and McCubbins 1991). We then formulate hypotheses on the choice of these control mechanisms. We argue that some control mechanisms are engrained in the institutional rules or country-specific histories and traditions. Although both, in principle, are subject to changes, in the short run they are mostly not at the discretion of coalition architects or it would be too costly to introduce changes. Building on this heritage, coalitions choose further control mechanisms to create the most efficient governance structure. They take into account the following factors: the timing of coalition formation, the bargaining environment, the actors' policy preferences, and political institutions. We then describe the data and methods employed. Next, we present our results and conclusions, and suggest avenues for future research.

How Delegation Works in Coalition Governments

Government coalitions bring together two or more parties with more or less diverging policy preferences. At the same time, these parties may continue to compete for government office and votes. However, in systems of parliamentary government, the cabinet remains collectively responsible for government policy and hence needs to agree. *All* coalitions do agree on a programme of government policies. In Laver and Shepsle's portfolio allocation model, they do so *implicitly*. Their assumption is that the office of cabinet minister is that of a policy dictator who cannot be checked, so that parties use ministries and their jurisdictions as the currency of their deals. Ministers, in turn, are loyal party agents. Once in office, they carry out their parties' ideal policies. Being aware of the powers of ministerial office and knowing the other parties' policy positions, party leaders form the coalition promising what is the best overall policy result from their partisan perspective.

Contrary to this powerful assumption, we contend that *joint* policy positions of the coalition partners are feasible. Parties may agree on compromises over the substance of individual issues, logroll some *specific* issues (rather than entire portfolios), or exclude specific topics from the coalition's agenda (and thus uphold the status quo even if disliked by the minister's party). Hence, coalitions have specific policy programmes that differ from any collection of party ideal positions.

Compared to parties, coalitions face greater problems in controlling their ministers' performance. They have a very limited time horizon as they may cease to exist after the next election or, indeed, at any day before that event. In contrast, political parties are long-lasting institutions (Aldrich 1995; Müller 2000). As such, they provide the ministers with office and policy incentives for sticking to the party line. Ministers crucially depend on their party's good will for re-election to parliament, reappointment to cabinet, and promotion to more important positions. And they may get intrinsic rewards from implementing their own party's policy ideals. Coalitions typically cannot offer such incentives. As heterogeneous actors with a short-term perspective, coalitions face the dilemma that ministers have strong incentives for sticking to their respective party's policy preferences. The incentive structure outlined here is in line with the assumptions of the "portfolio allocation" approach (Laver and Shepsle 1990, 1996). Yet, its solution concept – ministerial government – neglects the feasibility of Pareto-superior policies that in the aggregate would make all coalition parties better off (Laver and Shepsle 1996: 63; Müller and Meyer 2010; Thies 2001). Once we consider coalition policy compromises feasible and cost-efficient, we should not expect ministerial government but something closer to mutual veto.

In the parlance of the principal–agent approach, coalitions and parties (as principals) delegate competences to their ministerial agents. These agents therefore have two principals and a priori they are more likely to pursue the policy goals of the one (party) rather than the other (coalition). The question is, therefore, how coalitions as collective principals can strengthen their control over the cabinet. Although employing the principal–agent approach in coalition research is not novel (see Martin and Vanberg 2004; Thies 2001), this chapter constitutes the first attempt to go beyond the analysis of individual control mechanisms and to address the entire governance structure in comparative and empirically rigorous form. We group the more concrete control devices employed by coalitions under the governance mechanisms identified by the delegation literature: contract design, screening, monitoring, and institutional checks (see Kiewiet and McCubbins 1991: Chap. 2).

Contract Design

One way to address coalition problems is by writing a contract before delegating specific tasks to individual agents. Such coalition agreements lay down the rules of the game and define the common goals to be pursued in the government term. Although sometimes vague and incomplete, in other cases these contracts are considered "holy agreements." Consequently, ministers consult them regularly and observe them closely (see Timmermans and Andeweg 2000: 382). Most often, the contracts contain *policy agreements* (Müller and Strøm 2008: 174). By fixing policy compromises comprehensively, coalitions aim at limiting the ministers' room for manoeuvre.

Coalition agreements suffer from two deficiencies – they remain necessarily incomplete and there is no external enforcement agency to which the contract parties can appeal (Müller and Strøm 2008). So why would political parties invest in making such agreements? According to Luebbert (1986: 52), the answer is intra-party politics. Inter-party negotiations in this perspective are hardly more than a play performed for intra-party audiences. A few symbolic issues are chosen to demonstrate to the party's rank-and-file that their leaders are not willing to compromise the party's core beliefs, but not much is actually negotiated between the parties. Timmermans (2003: 17) therefore speaks of a "ritual dance." Recent work supports earlier judgments of country experts (in Müller and Strøm 2000) that coalition agreements are not mere by-products of ritual acts party leaders perform for the purpose of remaining party leaders, as suggested by Luebbert (1986). Accordingly, Timmermans (2003, 2006) and Moury (2010) show that coalition agreements reduce cabinet conflict, improve the chances that policy compromises are indeed turned into legislation, and help avoiding conflict in office. In a similar vein, Saalfeld (2008) shows that coalition agreements have a positive effect on coalition survival.

How is it then that policy agreements, although incomplete and not externally enforced, involve agency loss? First, policy agreements are an informational device: From reading the contract, ministers can estimate what is acceptable to their partners. Ministers who participated in working out the coalition agreement typically also understand what the politically most critical issues are and what solutions would be acceptable to their partners (Timmermans 2006: 273–274). Second, policy agreements provide yardsticks (in terms of policy prescriptions) against which ministerial proposals can be measured. This allows the partners to the coalition deal to pinpoint deviations from the agreement and demand their correction. Although each party may interpret the coalition contract differently, it serves as a "reference point" that is anchoring entitlements and thereby limiting disagreement (Hart and Moore 2008). When the agreement is public, as is the case with the majority of such documents, third parties can observe how faithful the coalition partners are to their deal. Not observing the agreement may thus involve credibility costs and cut into the political capital of parties (Groseclose and McCarty 2001).

Thus far, we have only discussed the policy content of coalition agreements. Yet, such contracts may also contain *procedural rules*. The two most important ones are the commitment to coalition discipline and the election rule. If the parties commit to *coalition discipline in legislation*, they oblige themselves to joint legislative behaviour and rule out building legislative alliances against the government partner(s). When observed, this rule prevents changes to the status quo against the will of one coalition party. Yet, by itself it is not helpful to enforcing *policy change* that had been agreed at the coalition formation stage.

In agreeing to the *election rule*, the parties commit to calling early elections if the coalition terminates.[2] This commitment increases the stakes of the game as elections always introduce uncertainty. The voters may punish some parties and reward others and government parties are more often among the former than the latter.[3] Moreover, the election result may change the set of viable coalitions in unpredicted ways. In short, such a clause raises the stakes in the game and provides parties with incentives for avoiding action that might bring down the coalition. Being unfaithful to policy commitments contained in the coalition deal is an example of such potentially dangerous behaviour, particularly if the issue is important to one partner and the deviation from the original agreement substantial.

Agreeing on an election rule is at the discretion of the coalition parties where the constitution does not preclude such commitments. Yet, the empirical patterns in Western Europe reveal that the election rule is used in only three countries: Austria, France, and the Netherlands. In Austria (in all minority situations) and France (in the entire Fifth Republic), all coalitions agreed on the election rule. Even the Netherlands changed their pattern only once: while no coalition worked under the election rule before 1967, all cabinets did from that year onwards. Hence, except for the Netherlands the election rule is a country-specific phenomenon. Coalition parties seem unable or unwilling to change these rules. And it is easy to see why election rules once established are difficult to get rid of. Any such attempt by one party would suggest to its partner(s) that their government cooperation is not really valued and may be terminated for opportunistic reasons at any time.

The procedural rules discussed here are straightforward and easy to verify. By taking out ambiguity and noise from inter-party deals, they give more weight to the reputational concerns of the coalitions partners. To the extent that this is true, procedural rules may be self-enforcing. For many reasons, this is not the case with regard to policy agreements. They are always in the danger of falling victim of contending interpretations, as the devil may be in the detail not contained in the contract. It thus requires political actors who follow up on the original policy agreement and make sure that it is processed according to plan. They can be helped by the mechanisms to which we turn now.

Screening

Screening helps principals to select agents willing and able to perform a task on the principal's behalf. Checking an agent's record, for example, can reveal his attitudes and preferences. Screening thus helps to avoid the costs resulting from a "hiring and

[2] The election rule is technically the most difficult to enforce, as the dissolution of parliament in most cases requires the agreement of individuals who may be outside the coalition deal (the head of state) or who may have strong personal interests against such an act (the sitting prime minister).

[3] Rose and Mackie (1983), Narud and Valen (2008), see also Adams and Somer-Topcu (2009) and Tavits (2007).

firing" policy (Kiewiet and McCubbins 1991: 30–32). Although it is highly useful in other delegation relationships, coalitions as collective actors do not rely much on this mechanism. Rather than selecting ministers jointly, coalitions either grant selection rights to individual parties or allow for the vetoing of ministerial candidates (Müller and Strøm 2000: 574). In both cases, the party holding the portfolio proposes candidates and hence still sets the agenda. Even under mutual veto rights, ministers still represent their own party's policy preferences. In practice, under mutual veto rules coalition parties' can prevent only truly unacceptable candidates and they rarely use the veto. Nevertheless, the veto constrains the nominating party and provides ministers with incentives to show behaviour acceptable to the coalition partners. This mechanism works via the law of anticipated reaction (Friedrich 1941: 589–591). Parties refrain from nominating particularly controversial ministerial candidates and ministers who expect the current coalition to continue avoid alienating actors who may be veto players in their reappointment process. Constraining the parties' freedom of appointment thus strengthens the link between the coalition as a whole and its agents.

In Western Europe, veto rights of government parties against ministerial candidates from their partners are common in German and French coalitions. Coalitions in Finland and Norway have mixed records and in all other countries, cabinet parties do not allow the mutual vetoing of ministerial candidates. Given the value party leaders attach to high public office, this may not be too surprising. Note also that veto rights are not always symmetric. The changing patterns in Finland and Norway result from varying prime minister leadership styles: Whereas most Norwegian chief executives accepted an appointment procedure governed exclusively by the individual parties, prime ministers Willoch and Bondevik claimed strong control over that process (Narud and Strøm 2000: 181). And for Finland, Nousiainen notes that "only an experienced and strong *formateur* can use a veto to block the candidacy of an unsuitable person" (Nousiainen 2000: 282). In contrast, institutional factors impact on the use of the veto in France and Germany. In both cases, the veto rights are allocated unequally as it is mainly the prime minister (and in the French case also the president) who commands these in the ministerial selection process (Saalfeld 2000: 36; Thiébault 2000: 521). The institutional rules supporting the chief executives probably result from the experience of unstable governments in the Weimar Republic and the French Fourth Republic. Saalfeld (2000: 58) suggests that veto abilities depend on a party's bargaining power and the minister's intra-party backing. Strong parties with positive "walk-away" values (Lupia and Strøm 2008: 63) are more likely to veto their partners' ministerial candidates. Moreover, parties differ in their backing of (potential) ministers. If the successful completion of negotiations is at risk, parties may sacrifice some individuals but back others.

Institutional rules resulting from past experience, individual leadership styles, party bargaining power, and the intra-party support of (potential) ministers may account for the use of the screening mechanism. Yet, we lack a comprehensive theory explaining the empirical patterns in Western Europe. Although an institutional factor (prime ministerial power) seems to play a role in Germany, screening also occurs when prime ministers do not have much institutional power, as is the case in Finland.

And although different prime ministerial styles of leadership are likely to play a role in Norway and Finland, we do not observe such differences in other countries. While the bargaining power of individual parties seems to impact on the use of screening mechanisms, in some countries coalitions do not rely on this mechanism although strong parties exist (e.g. the CDA in the Netherlands). Therefore, we believe that these factors do not fully explain screening. Although we cannot offer a new theory here, interacting patterns of country-specific institutions resulting from historic experience, individual prime ministerial leadership styles, the bargaining power of parties, and the intra-party backing of ministers are likely to impact on the coalitions' rules for making ministerial appointments.

Reporting and Monitoring

The most obvious way in which principals check their agents is by requiring them "to report whatever relevant information they have obtained and whatever action they have taken" (Kiewiet and McCubbins 1991: 31). At the same time, principals are well advised to collect information on their own not to fall victim to self-serving reports of the agents. All coalitions employ these control mechanisms, which is most obvious in cabinet and parliamentary plenary and committee sessions. These allow for the discussion of the ministers' policy proposals and executive behaviour. Martin and Vanberg (2004, 2005) show that the process of *parliamentary scrutiny* works as an intra-coalition monitoring device. This can be inferred from more time being devoted at committee stage to draft legislation that is potentially controversial between the coalition partners. Although we agree with their indicators and substantive interpretation, it is worth pointing out that the unobserved part of the process is often more complex and less straightforward than these indicators may suggest.

As Martin and Vanberg (2005: 97) point out, parliamentary committees are well suited for checking government policy proposals. Permanent committees comprise considerable policy expertise, have access to information, and often occupy a gate-keeper function, that is the committee's consent is required (legally and/or politically) for passing legislation. We could add that MPs are more likely to be motivated to intervene on behalf of their party than cabinet members. This is so because the proposals will fall in their own area of expertise[4] and they do not need to fear their own policies being taken hostage in return. Martin and Vanberg also highlight the fact that "the work of committees typically proceeds behind closed doors, further reducing the costs of challenging and amending the drafts of ministers from within the coalition" (2005: 97). Yet, the committee doors are typically closed on assorted government and opposition MPs and although the public is excluded, revealing internal differences before the opposition may be unattractive. In many cases, the

[4] Clearly, this is much less likely with regard to ministers. Although ministers command departmental resources, these will be better qualified for checking the proposals from other ministries from a *departmental* rather than *party* perspective (see, e.g., Andeweg 2000).

committee stage is therefore used to generate opportunities for conducting another round of *intra-coalition* negotiations, this time involving specialized MPs. Such negotiations can take place in sub-committees, if suitable, or informal meetings of the coalition parties. Keeping the issue on the committee agenda allows buying time until the intra-coalition negotiations are concluded and can be formalized by the passage of the bills in the full committee, often in amended form. In that way, the opposition can only infer the nature of coalition conflict from the changes in draft legislation. The parliamentary committee stage can thus be critical for enforcing the coalition deal without revealing too much about the government's internal affairs.

Coalition parties may also draw on information from outside actors such as experts, think tanks, journalists, and opposition parties for assessing ministerial behaviour. If these sources are trustworthy, the information provided by them can enhance mutual control in the coalition (Lupia and McCubbins 1998).

All these devices, however, are at the coalitions' disposal only to a limited extent. Cabinets can rarely change the relevant institutional features (such as the power of committees), or affect the provision of information by third parties. Even if the coalition can introduce institutional reforms in parliament, these may take time to become effective (Shepsle 2001). Hence, coalition builders will plan the coalition's governance structure with existing monitoring devices in mind,[5] but only rarely rely on their ability to manipulate external factors that may impact on mutual control and ministerial behaviour.

Institutional Checks

Putting institutional checks in place means delegating tasks to two or more agents, who control each other's performance. This introduces additional veto players. Coalitions make use of this mechanism in two ways. First, they may install coalition committees usually consisting of party leaders, parliamentary leaders, and ministers in various compositions (see country chapters in Müller and Strøm 2000). Such committees are extra-constitutional bodies but they are powerful in bringing together the heavyweights of all coalition parties who can issue commands along the party line. Coalition committees are created for governing the coalition and resolving conflicts, preferably before they cause damage to the coalition. They thus constitute an arena so that where ministers drift from the coalition policies the cases can be tabled and resolved (Andeweg and Timmermans 2008).

Second, coalitions may agree on installing "watchdog" junior ministers (i.e. non-cabinet executive politicians who serve in departments headed by a minister from a different party). They have access to the pre-cabinet policy process and

[5] Although it might be argued that the effects of institutions may differ from their actual use, we see no argument why coalitions should refrain from using existing opportunities for the mutual checking of the partners. This is certainly true if the daily costs of control are borne by MPs rather than party leaders and cabinet ministers.

early information on possible deviations from the coalition line. To be sure, junior ministers cannot directly prevent ministerial actions. They are therefore "watchdogs," who can only bark a warning. In coalition politics, this can be enough to cause their party to activate the coalition committee or threaten sanctions such as exposing the minister's behaviour to parliamentary scrutiny or issuing a veto against the enactment of the policy under discussion. To the extent that ministers anticipate such moves, the presence of "watchdog" junior ministers should smooth coalition work.

How Coalitions Choose Control Mechanisms

As we have seen, coalitions are not always free to choose from the full range of control devices as some are engrained in institutional rules (the power of parliamentary committees) or country-specific traditions (election rules and screening). Coalition parties in practice thus decide on the use of the remaining control mechanisms only: policy agreements, coalition discipline, coalition committees, and "watchdog" junior ministers.[6]

Controlling agents always involves costs for the principal. In the case of coalition governments, perhaps the most valuable resource is time. Writing agreements, listening to junior minister reports, and attending coalition committee meetings take up time.[7] Whether coalition parties accept the costs will depend on the potential benefits of such control devices. We identify two clusters of factors affecting the benefits of individual control mechanisms: the internal logic of the coalition's governance architecture and environmental factors.

Internal Logic of the Coalition's Governance Architecture

Some control mechanisms increase the benefits of others (see Müller and Meyer 2010). For example, policy agreements offer a guideline for judging ministerial behaviour. All else being equal, policy agreements should therefore increase the likelihood of installing "watchdog" junior ministers and coalition committees. Using similar arguments for other control mechanisms, we identify specific patterns of coalition governance.

---

[6] Nevertheless, the fixed control mechanisms affect their application and hence are used as independent variables.

[7] For coalition discipline, the costs rather consist of policy costs due to the voting restrictions.

Environmental Factors

Different coalition environments make the use of control mechanisms more or less likely. The time until the next scheduled election, for example, indicates the potential benefit of control mechanisms: The more time remains, the greater the potential benefits of policy agreements, coalition discipline, coalition committees, or "watchdog" junior ministers. Controlling for such potential benefits is crucial for the estimates in the first cluster.

Patterns of Coalition Governance

How do the control mechanisms reinforce the benefits of mutual control? Explicit *policy agreements* commit the coalition partners to policy compromises formulated at formation stage. A written document reduces the uncertainty of what the coalition actually stands for and serves as a yardstick for judging ministerial behaviour. We argue that the existence of such yardsticks increases the likelihood of coalitions also employing other control mechanisms: First, the benefit of coalition discipline increases. A commitment to coalition discipline reduces the bargaining complexity as it binds together the coalition partners in legislative voting. Without having a substantive policy agreement, however, the consequences of such a behavioural restriction (i.e. not voting with the opposition) remain unclear. It can mean both the joint passing of legislation (containing the agreed policies) by the government parties or involuntary policy immobility, resulting from the coalition partners' inability or unwillingness to enact their earlier agreements. Having detailed policy agreements thus increases the benefits of coalition discipline.

Second, a policy agreement also increases the benefits resulting from coalition committees. As bodies of joint decision-making and conflict resolution such committees benefit from being able to draw on written policy agreements in judging ministerial behaviour. Clearly, no policy agreement is precise enough to resolve each and every conflict and with regard to many details coalition parties may have their own interpretation of some policy compromise contained in the agreement. Nevertheless, policy agreements are very precise in other cases. They narrow the ministers' discretion and leave little room for interpretation.

Finally, policy agreements also increase the likelihood of installing "watchdog" junior ministers. Such executive appointees from a party other than the minister's observe the minister's (mis)behaviour from within the respective ministry and report to their own party. Without any guidelines, however, judging the ministers' behaviour is not an easy task. Policy agreements offer such a guideline, telling "watchdog" junior ministers when to "bark."

Agreeing on *coalition discipline* commits the coalition parties to abstain from entering into legislative alliances with opposition parties. The coalition discipline rule should make policy agreements containing substantive policy concessions and package deals more likely. Without this rule, coalition parties have incentives to seek legislative cooperation with opposition parties to blackmail or outvote their coalition partner(s). Once the coalition discipline rule is in place, such behaviour is no longer an option for actors concerned about their reputation. Consequently, detailed policy agreements become more valuable for all coalition partners. Commitment to coalition discipline also makes coalition committees more likely. Without "outside" options for legislative majority building, coalition parties have to resolve their differences in internal negotiations. And coalition committees constitute a particularly suitable arena for coalition-internal discussion and conflict resolution. Finally, we do not have any expectations for the impact of coalition discipline on the likelihood of "watchdog" junior ministers.

Committing to the *election rule* (i.e. the agreement to call early elections if the coalition fails) increases the uncertainty of the coalition parties. Future election results are less predictable than alternative government coalitions in the sitting parliament. Under the election rule, parties are thus less likely to terminate coalitions. Even if a specific coalition party hopes to benefit from early elections, its partners may expect electoral punishment and therefore make concessions to save the current coalition (Lupia and Strøm 1995). The election rule creates a "joint fate" of the coalition parties and that has consequences for the value attached to other control mechanisms. Specifically, under this rule parties should invest more in writing policy agreements and they should be more likely to agree on coalition discipline and employing coalition committees and "watchdog" junior ministers.

Provided coalition governments selected ministers jointly they would pick candidates with policy preferences close to the coalition's policy compromise. As a result, the ministers' policy proposals would approximate the coalition's ideal position and there would be less need for control devices. As we have seen, coalition parties in fact do not jointly select ministers but rather maintain the right to *veto ministerial appointments*. Hence, the ministers continue to hold the policy preferences of their nominating parties. The veto right vis-à-vis other parties' ministerial candidates nevertheless eliminates the "worst" candidates and hence reduces the benefits of policy agreements, coalition discipline, coalition committees, and "watchdog" junior ministers.

The work of *parliamentary committees* generates information about the ministers' actions and policy proposals. Stronger committees mean more and better information. Strong parliamentary committees reduce the benefit of other *ex post* mechanisms but increase that of *ex ante* devices of coalition governance. First, such committees enable coalition partners to evaluate the minister's actions against the policy goals mentioned in the coalition agreement. This should increase the benefit of coalition agreements. Second, strong parliamentary committees should also increase the likelihood of agreeing on coalition discipline. Such committees also empower opposition parties who may aim at driving a wedge into the coalition by offering attractive policy deals to some government parties (and their committee members in particular). Coalitions may thus find it useful to safeguard against such challenges by agreeing on coalition discipline. Third, strong parliamentary committees can also partially substitute for the work of coalition committees. To the extent that this is true, they thus decrease the benefit, and hence the likelihood of coalition committees. Fourth, the same holds for "watchdog" junior ministers: reading documents and hearing witnesses in parliamentary committees serve the same purpose as "watchdogs." Hence, strong parliamentary committees reduce the (additional) benefit of "watchdog" junior ministers and therefore make their appointment less likely (see also Kim and Loewenberg 2005: 1123).

As policy agreements and coalition discipline affect the use of *coalition committees*, the latter in turn also impacts on the application of the *ex ante* control mechanisms. In fact, *ex ante* and *ex post* mechanisms complement each other, reinforcing their respective benefit. Policy agreements are more likely if coalition committees supervise their implementation. Without such supervision, the policies agreed upon *ex ante*, may not be implemented at all and hence coalitions may save the costs of writing them down. Moreover, employing coalition committees also affects the likelihood of agreeing on coalition discipline. Coalition committees offer an arena for solving conflicts between coalition partners. As mentioned earlier, coalition discipline increases the likelihood of observing these policy conflicts. Therefore, coalition committees reduce the risks resulting from coalition discipline (e.g. a policy deadlock) and positively affect their application.[8] Finally, "watchdog" junior ministers and coalition committees complement each other. By providing an arena for resolving policy conflicts, coalition committees increase the benefit of the junior ministers' reports. Hence, a positive relationship exists.

Like coalition committees, *"watchdog" junior ministers* constitute checks on ministerial behaviour. Once parties agree on installing "watchdog" junior ministers, this increases the likelihood of also hammering out detailed policy agreements. This is so because these two mechanisms complement each other. The same is true for "watchdog" junior ministers and coalition committees. In contrast, we do not expect any relationship between "watchdog" junior ministers and coalition discipline.

Environmental Factors

A number of environmental factors impact on coalitions' use of control mechanisms. Here we consider familiarity, parliamentary bargaining complexity, parliamentary polarization, policy preference divergence, time, and the institutional environment.

Familiarity

Coalitions learn from the past (Müller and Strøm 2008). Employing control mechanisms for the first time involves costs (because the mechanisms have to be designed

---

[8] This is the same argument as the one for the positive impact of coalition discipline on the installation of coalition committees. In fact, we do not argue that a causal relationship exists. Rather, the mechanisms complement each other and hence no causal direction is required. The same holds for the relationship between other control mechanisms.

and negotiated between the partners) and risks (because they may not work as expected). Employing mechanisms that have proved effective in previous coalitions (even of other parties) is thus always cheaper than developing new ones. Hence, we expect increasing use of control mechanisms over time.

Bargaining Complexity in Parliament

This factor ought to exercise influence on the use of control mechanisms. However, the direction of the effect is not clear. If alternative governing coalitions are feasible, strengthening the ties between the current coalition parties may be a good investment. Yet, precisely the availability of alternative coalitions may provide some government parties with incentives to keep commitment to the current coalition at low key only and steer clear of mutual controls. Hence, bargaining complexity may lead to more or less use of control mechanisms.

Parliamentary Polarization

The more polarized a parliament, the smaller the number of feasible cabinet alternatives. On the one hand, more cabinet alternatives should make control mechanisms worthwhile (because alternative coalitions are always at hand). On the other hand, parties may have fewer incentives to commit themselves to serving in a coalition, as other options may appear more attractive (e.g. minority government). As with parliamentary bargaining complexity, the effect of polarization on the use of control mechanisms is not clear.

Policy Preference Divergence

Coalitions are more likely to employ the control mechanisms outlined here if the potential gains are high. In policy terms, *coalitions with divergent policy preferences* are more likely to negotiate contracts, agree on coalition discipline and employ "watchdog" junior ministers and coalition committees. If, however, the coalition parties largely share policy preferences, applying these controls is probably not worth the effort.

Time

Whether coalition partners apply control mechanisms hinges on the time remaining until the regular election. Simply, the longer the coalition's potential lifetime, the higher the benefits from establishing control mechanisms. Coalitions will not waste their time on negotiating policy agreements, restricting themselves to coalition discipline, or installing coalition committees and "watchdog" junior ministers if the next general election is close.

Institutions

In addition to the cabinet-specific factors discussed so far, the institutional environment affects a coalition's choice of governance mechanisms. Such formal rules may impact on the individual coalition parties' bargaining power, which, in turn, may raise the demand for private agreement to offset the resulting advantages for individual cabinet parties. If constitutions provide prime ministers with strong powers – making the head of government a primus supra pares (Sartori 1997) – the coalition partners may aim at balancing such individual gains by putting control mechanisms in place. Hence, the greater the *prime minister's institutional powers*, the greater the incentives for establishing control mechanisms. Additional veto players such as strong presidents or not "absorbed" second chambers also impact on coalition governance. If they can exercise considerable influence on policy decisions, they may force coalition parties to adjust their mechanisms of mutual control. Similar to prime ministerial prerogatives, the existence of *additional veto players* is likely to impact on the individual coalition parties' bargaining power. If, for instance, the president is a member of one coalition party or if the second chamber is strongly leaning to support the policy position of one particular cabinet party, the relevant party may try to capitalize on its advantage. With the help of the additional actors, it may shift the coalition policy in its preferred direction. In the first place, coalition governments should spend *less* effort codifying their compromises. The fact that third actors can veto these agreements may make it ineffective to use elaborate *ex ante* mechanisms (policy agreements and coalition discipline). If, however, a coalition facing additional veto players has nevertheless invested into front-loading its cooperation by working out policy agreements, it will follow the generally predicted pattern of bolstering these by also establishing *ex post* controls. We can thus expect "watchdog" junior ministers and coalition committees to be in place in such cases.

Table 5.1 summarizes the factors expected to impact on the use of control mechanisms and their expected direction. As mentioned earlier, some of these control devices (commitment to an election rule, the mutual veto against ministerial candidates, and parliamentary committee monitoring) are institutionally fixed or do not vary within countries for other reasons. Hence, coalition cabinets choose whether or not to write policy agreements, commit to coalition discipline in legislation, and install coalition committees and "watchdog" junior ministers. These four control mechanisms are the dependent variables in our analysis.

In Table 5.1, we show the factors impacting on the use of these control mechanisms (rows). The covariates cover *ex ante* and *ex post* mechanisms, as well as environmental variables that affect the potential benefits of control mechanisms. Plus and minus indicate the expected direction of the effect (e.g. the use of control mechanisms will increase over time). We do not have clear expectations for parliamentary bargaining complexity and parliamentary polarization. Both factors increase (decrease) the benefits of control mechanisms while simultaneously increasing (decreasing) their costs. Note that the number of additional veto players such as strong presidents or second chambers is expected to have different effects on the four dependent variables: additional veto players should reduce *ex ante* controls

Table 5.1 Expected effects on control mechanisms

Independent variables		Dependent variables: Policy agreement	Coalition discipline	Coalition committees	Watchdog junior ministers
Ex ante mechanisms	Policy agreement		+	+	+
	Coalition discipline	+		+	0
	Election rule	+	+	+	+
	Screening	−	−	−	−
Ex post mechanisms	Monitoring: parliamentary committees	+	+	−	−
	Coalition committees	+	+		+
	Watchdog junior ministers	+	0	+	
Environmental factors	Familiarity	+	+	+	+
	Bargaining complexity	+/−	+/−	+/−	+/−
	Parliamentary polarization	+/−	+/−	+/−	+/−
	Cabinet preference divergence	+	+	+	+
	Time until next election	+	+	+	+
	Prime ministerial powers	+	+	+	+
	Additional veto players	−	−	Interaction: + if *ex ante* mechanisms used	Interaction: + if *ex ante* mechanisms used

(i.e. policy agreements and coalition discipline). Yet, they encourage parties to use institutional checks *if* coalition parties have invested in working out policy contracts despite the presence of additional veto players. Hence, additional veto players interact with *ex ante* mechanisms, impacting on the existence of "watchdog" junior ministers and coalition committees.

Data and Methods

To test the hypotheses developed earlier, we rely on the data set on coalition governments in Western Europe, which provides comprehensive data on coalition governance based on the work of country experts (Müller and Strøm 2000;

Strøm et al. 2003, 2008).[9] The data set contains the cabinets of 17 West European countries beginning with the first post-war (or current regime) cabinet until 1999. Out of the 424 cabinets covered in the sample, 260 cabinets are coalition governments. To test the hypotheses mentioned earlier, we only consider those countries where coalitions can choose among all the control mechanisms discussed. Hence, we do not include countries where junior ministers do not exist (Denmark, Finland, and Iceland) or where an election rule is not feasible (Norway) or is unattractive (Sweden).[10] Consequently, the number of cases drops to 161 coalition cabinets in ten countries[11] in the multivariate analyses.

Policy agreement is a dichotomous variable indicating whether parties fixed their compromises in a comprehensive policy agreement. The second dependent variable, *coalition discipline*, takes values ranging from 0 (no coalition discipline required) over 1 (commitment to coalition discipline only for a few selected issues) and 2 (coalition discipline in most policy areas) to its maximum value 3 (commitment to coalition discipline in all policy areas). For *coalition committees*, we count the number of those committees resulting in a variable ranging from 0 to 4. Simply, more committees mean a greater amount of specialization and thus more control. Finally, the presence of "*watchdog*" *junior ministers* is measured as the share of ministries with junior ministers from parties different from the minister's party.

Turning to the independent variables, we use a dummy variable for the parties' commitment to the *election rule*. The *screening* variable is a simple dichotomous variable, indicating whether coalition parties can veto their coalition partners' ministerial appointments. It is coded 1 if the government parties agree on mutual veto rights with regard to their ministerial appointments and 0 if the individual parties can freely choose their cabinet members. As a crude measure for *monitoring*, we rely on Mattson and Strøm (1995), who provide scores for the committees' drafting authority and agenda control.[12] The higher the respective country's scores on both dimensions, the more powerful are the parliamentary committees. And the more powerful the committees (giving equal weight to both dimensions), the greater is the coalition's ability to monitor ministerial behaviour.

To measure the effects of *familiarity*, we include the lagged value of the dependent variable as an independent variable. The theoretical concept behind this variable is "system learning" (i.e. learning from experience with coalition governance mechanisms is not confined to the directly involved politicians and

[9] The data set is available from http://www.pol.umu.se/ccpd/.

[10] We also estimated models including cabinets in countries where an election rule is unfeasible or unattractive (Norway and Sweden) and where junior ministers are not the rule (Denmark, Finland, and Iceland). Excluding the respective variables for watchdog junior ministers and the election rule, the results are similar to those reported here ($n = 242$).

[11] The countries are Austria, Belgium, France, Germany, Greece, Ireland, Italy, Luxembourg, the Netherlands, and Portugal.

[12] According to Mattson and Strøm's analysis, "drafting authority' includes the committees' abilities to initiate legislation, to rewrite bills, and to summon documents. The second factor "agenda control' comprises the committees' control of the own timetable and the right to summon witnesses.

parties). Including this variable also controls for serial correlation (see Beck and Katz 1995, 1996). We measure *bargaining complexity* in parliament by the effective number of parliamentary parties (Laakso and Taagepera 1979). As an indicator of the number of feasible cabinet alternatives, *parliamentary polarization* is a measure of the spread of the parliamentary parties' policy positions. For that purpose, we use squared distances of the parties' policy positions from the mean policy position of all parties. Weighted by the party's respective bargaining power (the Banzhaf index), these differences are then summed up and the square root is taken. Data on the *cabinet preference range* comes from the Comparative Manifestos Project (Budge et al. 2001). The variable indicates the maximum distance in terms of left–right positions between the government parties. *Time until the next scheduled election* is measured in the days remaining until the end of the constitutional inter-election period. Turning to the country-specific covariates, the prime minister's right to appoint and dismiss ministers, to control the cabinet agenda and similar factors are summed up to a scale ranging from 1 to 7 capturing the *prime minister's institutional powers*. Finally, strong second chambers and/or strong presidents indicate the number of *additional veto players* ranging from 0 to 2.

Our data structure is multi-level and our hypotheses cover cabinet-specific and institutional variables. Therefore, we use multi-level analysis as our statistical tool. Specifically, we calculate random intercept models, expressing the model's intercept as a function of institutional variables. In case these macro-level rules changed over time, we split the countries in different time periods.[13] We use logistic regression to explain policy agreements, and ordered logistic regression to predict the different forms of coalition discipline. We estimate linear regression models to explain the number of coalition committees and the share of "watchdog" junior ministers.

Results

Table 5.2 show the results of multi-level regressions predicting when coalitions turn to policy agreements, coalition discipline, coalition committees, and "watchdog" junior ministers. Note that writing policy agreements positively affects the installation of coalition committees. As hypothesized earlier, policy agreements serve as a guideline for judging the ministers' behaviour and hence contribute to the solution of policy conflicts by coalition committees. The impact of policy agreements on coalition discipline and the appointment of "watchdog" junior ministers, however, are not statistically significant. Although the commitment to coalition discipline does not affect the use of control mechanisms, agreeing to the election rule makes it more likely that parties also install coalition committees. The election rule creates a common fate among the coalition parties and hence provides them with incentives to use control mechanisms. For coalition committees, this effect is statistically significant and in the expected direction.

[13] Specifically, we distinguished three time periods for Italy (before 1948, between 1948 and 1988, and after 1988). If institutional regimes only covered one cabinet, we dropped these cases from the analysis. In our sample this only affects one cabinet in Portugal (Soares I).

Table 5.2 The use of control mechanisms in coalition governance

	Policy agreements	Commitment to coalition discipline	Number of coalition committees	Share of watchdog junior ministers
Comprehensive policy agreement		−1.976	0.265$^+$	−0.0110
Coalition discipline in legislation	1.760		−0.0470	0.00566
Election rule	−1.190	0.754	0.387$^+$	0.0397
Screening	−3.602	0.645	−0.155	0.0245
Monitoring: drafting authority	0.305	2.408$^+$	−0.0298	−0.0609$^+$
Monitoring: agenda control	4.044	−1.248	−0.0224	−0.0258
Number of coalition committees	2.468*	0.0463		0.0178
Share of watchdog junior ministers	−3.237	1.189	0.0880	
Comprehensive policy agreement (lag)	4.650**			
Coalition discipline in legislation (lag)		7.333**		
No. of coalition committees (lag)			0.605**	
Share of watchdog junior ministers (lag)				0.501**
Effective no. of parties	0.976$^+$	0.594	−0.0171	0.0238
Polarization in parliament (weighted)	−0.101	−0.198*	0.00887	0.00334
Policy distance in cabinet	−0.0528	−0.0244	−0.00319	0.000979
Maximal time in office (days)	0.00507**	0.00193$^+$	−0.000113	0.0000698*
PM powers	0.176	0.753	0.0186	−0.0257
No. of additional veto points	−12.41*	0.902	−0.0109	0.0195
Constant	−7.865		0.866	−0.0614
Observations	161	161	161	161
Correctly predicted/explained variance[14] (%)	95 (baseline: 67)	95 (baseline: 71)	20	66

$^+p < 0.1$
$^*p < 0.05$
$^{**}p < 0.01$

For the *ex post* mechanisms, Table 5.2 shows that the power of parliamentary committees affects the likelihood that coalitions agree on coalition discipline and the appointment of "watchdog" junior ministers. As expected, the effects

[14] Compared to a variance-components model.

point in different directions. Strong parliamentary committees which empower the opposition provide coalitions with incentives to shore up their cooperation by committing to coalition discipline in legislation. Yet, the more powerful parliamentary committees are, the lower the share of "watchdog" junior ministers. With such committees in place, the additional benefits of "watchdog" junior ministers diminish. Coalition committees are our next *ex post* mechanism. They have a positive impact on working out policy agreements. As argued earlier, the two mechanisms complement each other: policy agreements are more likely to be translated into government policy if coalition committees are in place. Discussing and resolving policy conflicts in coalition committees is easier if policy agreements exist which provide yardsticks for measuring ministerial behaviour. Finally, we expected that "watchdog" junior ministers have a positive impact on the use of policy agreements and coalition committees. However, both expectations do not hold empirically.

Turning to the environmental factors, note that the lagged value of the dependent variable has a statistically significant positive impact. For each of the four mechanisms, its use by one coalition increases the likelihood that the subsequent coalition also relies on it. Coalitions learn from their predecessors and tend to apply familiar control mechanisms. We did not generate specific expectations as to how the complexity of the bargaining environment will impact on the use of control devices. More complex bargaining situations simultaneously increase the costs and the benefits of control mechanisms. Hence, we have no clear expectation of how bargaining complexity affects the use of control mechanisms. It turns out that coalitions are more likely to use *ex ante* control mechanisms if the complexity of the bargaining situation is high. Policy agreements are more likely to occur if the effective number of parties in parliament is high. Table 5.2 also reveals that the higher the polarization (i.e. the fewer cabinet alternatives there are), the less the cabinet parties require commitment to coalition discipline. For the remaining mechanisms, both effects are insignificant.

The time until the next scheduled election impacts on three of the four control mechanisms. The longer their potential time in office, the more coalitions will invest in elaborating policy agreements, commit to coalition discipline, and appoint "watchdog" junior ministers. Again, these findings conform to the expectations formulated earlier. In contrast, the parliamentary preference range has no significant impact for any of the four models. The prime minister's institutional powers do not affect the use of control mechanisms. Although three out of four effects point in the expected direction, the positive coefficients do not reach conventional levels of statistical significance. However, as expected, additional veto players reduce the likelihood of investment in policy agreements. As argued earlier, the presence of additional veto players exercises a strong negative effect on the making of *ex ante* agreements.

We hypothesized that the effect of additional veto players on *ex post* mechanisms interacts with the *ex ante* mechanisms employed by coalitions. In the presence of strong presidents or second chambers, coalitions use fewer *ex ante* controls. However, *if* they do employ *ex ante* control mechanisms, additional veto players lead coalition parties to make extra efforts to enforcing the deals *ex post*. To test these expectations, we estimated modified regressions for the two *ex post* control mechanisms: the number of coalition committees and the share of "watchdog" junior ministers. The modified models employ two new variables. First, instead of including three separate contract mechanisms, policy agreement, coalition discipline, and the election rule, we create an aggregate index of contract mechanisms. Second, the models also contain an interaction term so that the effect of additional veto players interacts with the contract mechanisms. If our hypothesis is correct, the marginal effect of additional veto players is indifferent from zero if the government coalition does not rely on policy agreements, coalition discipline, and an election rule. In contrast, the effect is positive if coalitions rely on contract mechanisms.

Because graphs allow for an easy interpretation of interaction effects, Fig. 5.1 plots the effect of one additional veto player (a president, a second chamber) on the coefficient of the use of coalition committees (upper graph) and "watchdog" junior ministers (lower graph) depending on the contract mechanisms employed. The graphs clearly show the expected positive interaction. Without contract mechanisms, additional veto players do not impact on the use of both institutional checks. The more coalitions decide to front-load their cooperation by means of contract design, however, the more do additional veto players lead coalitions to establish coalition committees and "watchdog" junior ministers. The positive interaction is, however, only significant for the use of coalition committees (see upper graph in Fig. 5.1). For "watchdog" junior ministers, the confidence intervals cut across the zero line (see lower graph in Fig. 5.1). Independent of the use of contract mechanisms, the effect of additional veto players on the appointment of "watchdog" junior ministers is statistically insignificant.

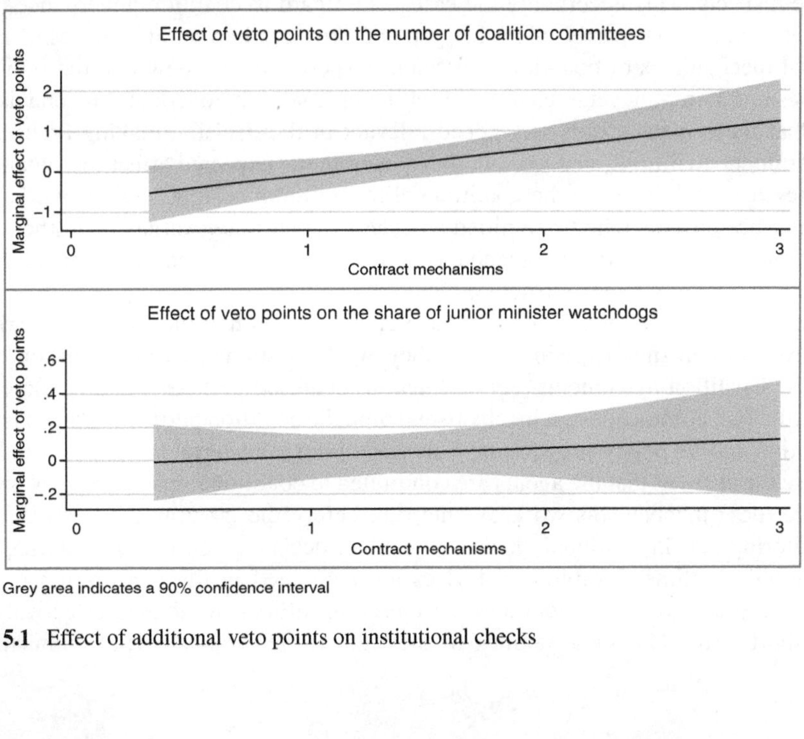

Fig. 5.1 Effect of additional veto points on institutional checks

Conclusion: Mutual Veto?

In this chapter, we have asked how coalition governments contain agency loss resulting from individual ministers serving their respective parties rather than the coalition as a whole. The radical solution to this problem, as proposed by Laver and Shepsle (1990, 1996), is to abandon the idea of *coalition* policies. Rather, coalition partners agree on "dividing the cake" and allow for ministerial policy dictators who in their own jurisdictions implement party ideal policies. Coalition policy is then the combination of pure party policies resulting from the specific allocation of ministerial portfolios among the cabinet parties. As rational actors, parties choose the coalition partners that allow the best overall policy result from their partisan perspective. Their choice is restricted to selecting the best combination of party ideal points.

The Laver and Shepsle model of coalition governance is attractive to government builders because they do not need to be concerned about the governance structure of the coalition and potential agency loss from ministerial drift. But it poses the question whether the search for Pareto-optimum alternatives in form of a joint coalition policy in each ministry is really a fruitless task. Even if non-perfect (i.e. with some agency loss remaining), such joint policies may well be worth their price and result in overall policy gains for all government parties compared to any combination of party ideal points. This consideration seems to guide the behaviour of real world coalition builders and it is behind Tsebelis' claim of the mutual veto. Like Laver and Shepsle's work, Tsebelis' study is primarily a theoretical contribution. Given its broad scope, it is only natural that its empirical support is illustrative only in some respects. This is certainly the case with regard to coalition governance. The recent literature has partly filled that gap and provides important analyses of individual mechanisms of coalition governance. These studies show (1) that political parties invest in policy agreement and setting up coalition governance mechanisms, (2) that these mechanisms are indeed relevant in the decision-making process of government coalitions, and (3) that they generate the expected effect of containing agency loss and enduring the coalitions' life. Building on that body of work, this chapter has provided the first unified analysis of coalition governance. Rather than addressing individual control mechanisms we have focussed on the architecture of the coalitions' governance structures.

In our theoretical discussion, we have elaborated on the micro-logic of various control mechanisms, explaining *how* they work to strengthen the coalition as a whole. Coalition agreements, commitment to coalition discipline and to the election rule (i.e. contract design mechanisms) bind the coalition partners to the existing coalition and its policy programme. Likewise, joint ministerial selection would increase the chances that the agents are committed to coalition rather than party goals. While these mechanisms work ex ante (i.e. before the government is sworn in), monitoring and institutional checks on cabinet decisions are effective during the coalition's lifetime. Monitoring devices are contained in the constitution or the standing orders of parliament and are therefore difficult to change effectively in the short term. The same applies to the right to veto other parties' ministerial candidates and the commitment to the election rule. These features hardly vary within countries. Their prior use (or non-use) determines whether the current coalition employs these tools. In contrast to these path-dependent control devices, the use of policy agreements, coalition discipline, coalition committees, and "watchdog" junior ministers is indeed at the discretion of individual coalitions.

As control involves costs, coalition governments are careful in employing control mechanisms. More control is not always better. Rather, control is useful only when the expected benefits outweigh the costs. From this cost–benefit imperative, we have derived more specific expectations about the use of control devises in government coalitions.

The multi-level regression analyses presented here support most of our hypotheses and none of the statistically significant effects contradicts our theoretical predictions. We show that coalitions choose control mechanisms which complement each other. Specifically, coalition parties that write policy agreements also tend to establish coalition committees, as these are more useful once a "reference point" for their work has been established. Conversely, coalition committees make substantive policy agreements more likely. Moreover, an election rule shows the expected positive impact on the use of coalition committees. The power of parliamentary committees has a positive impact on coalitions' reliance on *ex ante* mechanisms and a negative impact on *ex post* mechanisms. For the use of coalition discipline and the share of "watchdog" junior ministers, the results support our hypothesis. Turning to the environmental factors, we find strong familiarity effects: coalitions tend to adopt control mechanisms used in prior multi-party cabinets. For bargaining complexity and polarization in parliament, our theory did not suggest specific expectations. The empirical results indicate that complex bargaining situations increase the likelihood of policy agreements. Moreover, coalitions are more likely to agree on coalition discipline if the number of feasible cabinet alternatives is high. In sum then, bargaining complexity (whether indicated by the number of parties or ideological heterogeneity) increases the coalitions' turning towards *ex ante* controls. Furthermore, a cabinet's potential time in office affects the coalition partners' willingness to work out a regime of mutual control. Finally, the empirical results also support our expectations for the effect of additional veto players. Coalition parties facing strong presidents and second chambers with policymaking powers rely less on *ex ante* control mechanisms. However, those coalition parties that still negotiate coalition contracts make greater use of coalition committees to see their policy compromises implemented.

Coalition governments can draw on a large toolkit of control mechanisms. Studying the micro-logic of *how* these control mechanisms are used, we show that some of these mechanisms complement each other whereas others tend to serve as substitutes. Our empirical results support these theoretical expectations. Future studies of coalition governance should take these interacting patterns into account. Rather than analyzing single control mechanisms in isolation, researchers should study how these devices place themselves in the governance architecture of coalitions. Otherwise, the results may be severely biased.

Acknowledgements An earlier version of this chapter was presented at the conference "Reform processes and policy change: How do veto players determine decision-making in modern democracies" at the University of Mannheim/MZES, 14–16 May 2009. The authors thank the participants for helpful comments and criticism.

References

Adams J, Somer-Topcu Z (2009) Moderate now, win votes later: the electoral consequences of parties' policy shifts in twenty-five postwar democracies. J Polit 71(2):678–692

Aldrich JH (1995) Why parties? University of Chicago Press, Chicago, IL

Andeweg RB (2000) Ministers as double agents? The delegation process between cabinet and ministers. Eur J Polit Res 37(3):377–395

Andeweg RB, Timmermans A (2008) Conflict management in coalition government. In: Strøm K, Müller WC, Bergman T (eds) *Cabinets* and coalition bargaining: the democratic life cycle in western Europe. Oxford University Press, Oxford, pp 269–300

Austen-Smith D, Banks J (1990) Stable governments and the allocation of policy portfolios. Am Polit Sci Rev 84(3):891–906

Beck N, Katz JN (1995) What to do (and not to do) with time-series cross-section data. Am Polit Sci Rev 89(3):634–647

Beck N, Katz JN (1996) Nuisance vs. substance: specifying and estimating time-series-cross-section models. Polit Anal 6(1):1–36

Budge I, Klingemann H-D, Volkens A et al (eds) (2001) Mapping policy preferences: estimates for parties, electors, and governments 1945–1998. Oxford University Press, Oxford

Crossman RHS (1972) The myths of cabinet government. Harvard University Press, Cambridge, MA

Dunleavy P, Bastow S (2001) Modelling coalitions that cannot coalesce: a critique of the Laver-Shepsle approach. West Eur Polit 24(1):1–26

Friedrich CJ (1941) Constitutional government and democracy. Little, Brown and Company, Boston, MA

Groseclose T, McCarty N (2001) The politics of blame: bargaining before an audience. Am J Polit Sci 45(1):100–119

Hart O, Moore J (2008). Contracts as reference points. Q J Econ 123(1):1–48

Kiewiet DR, McCubbins MD (1991). The logic of delegation: congressional parties and the appropriations process. The University of Chicago Press, Chicago

Kim D-H, Loewenberg G (2005) The role of parliamentary committees in coalition governments. Keeping tabs on coalition partners in the German Bundestag. Comp Polit Stud 38(9): 1104–1129

Laakso M, Taagepera R (1979) "Effective" number of parties: a measure with application to West Europe. Comp Polit Stud 12(1):3–27

Laver M, Shepsle KA (1990) Coalitions and cabinet government. Am Polit Sci Rev 84(3):873–890

Laver M, Shepsle KA (eds) (1994). Cabinet ministers and parliamentary government. Cambridge University Press, Cambridge

Laver M, Shepsle KA (1996) Making and breaking governments: cabinets and legislatures in parliamentary democracies. Cambridge University Press, Cambridge/New York

Luebbert GM (1986) Comparative democracy. Policymaking and governing coalitions in Europe and Israel. Columbia University Press, New York

Lupia A, McCubbins MD (1998) The democratic dilemma: can citizens learn what they need to know? Cambridge University Press, Cambridge

Lupia A, Strøm K (1995) Coalition termination and the strategic timing of parliamentary elections. Am Polit Sci Rev 89(3):648–665

Lupia A, Strøm K (2008) Bargaining, transaction costs, and coalition governance. In: Strøm K, Müller WC, Bergman T (eds) Cabinets and coalition bargaining: the democratic life cycle in western Europe. Oxford University Press, Oxford, pp 51–83

Mackintosh JP (1977) The British cabinet. Stevens and Sons, London

Martin LW (2004) The government agenda in parliamentary democracies. Am J Polit Sci 48(3):445–461

Martin LW, Vanberg G (2004) Policing the bargain: coalition government and parliamentary scrutiny. Am J Polit Sci 48(1):13–27

Martin LW, Vanberg G (2005) Coalition policymaking and legislative review. Am Polit Sci Rev 99(1):93–106

Mattson I, Strøm K (1995) Parliamentary committees. In: Döring H (ed) Parliaments and majority rule in Western Europe. Campus/St. Martin's Press, Frankfurt/New York, pp 249–307

Moury C (2010) Coalition agreement and party mandate: how coalition agreement constrain the ministers Party Polit

Müller WC (2000) Political parties in parliamentary democracies: making delegation and accountability work. Eur J Polit Res 37(3):309–333

Müller WC, Meyer TM (2010) Meeting the challenges of representation and accountability in multi-party governments. West Eur Polit 33(5)

Müller WC, Strøm K (eds) (2000) Coalition governments in western Europe. Oxford University Press, Oxford/New York

Müller WC, Strøm K (2008) Coalition agreements and cabinet governance. In: Strøm K, Müller WC, Bergman T (eds) Cabinets and coalition bargaining: the democratic life cycle in western Europe. Oxford University Press, Oxford, pp 159–199

Narud HM, Strøm K (2000) Norway: a fragile coalitional order. In: Müller WC, Strøm K (eds) Coalition governments in western Europe. Oxford University Press, Oxford, pp 158–191

Narud HM, Valen H (2008) Coalition membership and electoral performance. In: Strøm K, Müller WC, Bergman T (eds) Cabinets and coalition bargaining: the democratic life cycle in western Europe. Oxford University Press, Oxford, pp 369–402

Nousiainen J (2000) Finland: the consolidation of parliamentary governance. In: Müller WC, Strøm K (eds) Coalition governments in western Europe. Oxford University Press, Oxford, pp 264–299

Rose R, Mackie TT (1983) Incumbency in government: asset or liability? In: Daalder H, Mair P (eds) Western European party systems. Sage, London, pp 115–138

Saalfeld T (2000) Germany: stable parties, chancellor democracy, and the art of informal settlement. In: Müller WC, Strøm K (eds) Coalition governments in western Europe. Oxford University Press, Oxford, pp 32–85

Saalfeld T (2008) Institutions, change, and choices: the dynamics of cabinet survival. In: Strøm K, Müller WC, Bergman T (eds) Cabinets and coalition bargaining: the democratic life cycle in western Europe. Oxford University Press, Oxford, pp 327–368

Sartori G (1997) Comparative constitutional engineering. Macmillan, Houndmills

Shepsle KA (2001) A comment on institutional change. J Theor Polit 13(3):321–325

Strøm K (1990) Minority government and majority rule. Cambridge University Press, Cambridge

Strøm K (1994) The political role of Norwegian cabinet ministers. In: Laver M, Shepsle KA (eds) Cabinet ministers and parliamentary government. Cambridge University Press, Cambridge, pp 35–55

Strøm K, Müller WC, Bergman T (eds) (2003) Delegation and accountability in parliamentary democracies. Oxford University Press, Oxford

Strøm K, Müller WC, Bergman T (eds) (2008) Cabinets and coalition bargaining: the democratic life cycle in Western Europe. Oxford University Press, Oxford

Tavits M (2007) Principle vs. pragmatism: policy shifts and political competition. Am J Polit Sci 51(1):151–165

Thiébault J-L (2000) France: forming and maintaining government coalitions in the fifth republic. In: Müller WC, Strøm K (eds) Coalition governments in western Europe. Oxford University Press, Oxford, pp 498–528

Thies MF (2001) Keeping tabs on partners: the logic of delegation in coalition governments. Am J Polit Sci 45(3):580–598
Timmermans A (2003) High politics in the low countries: an empirical study of coalition agreements in Belgium and The Netherlands. Ashgate: Aldershot
Timmermans A (2006) Standing apart and sitting together: enforcing coalition agreements in multiparty systems. Eur J Polit Res 45(2):263–283
Timmermans A, Andeweg RB (2000) The Netherlands: still the politics of accommodation? In: Müller WC, Strøm K (eds) Coalition governments in western Europe. Oxford University Press, Oxford, pp 356–398
Timmermans A, Moury C (2006) Coalition governance in Belgium and the Netherlands: rising government stability against all electoral odds. Acta Polit 41(4):389–497
Tsebelis G (2002) Veto players. How political institutions work. Princeton University Press, Princeton, NJ
Verzichelli L (2008) Portfolio allocation. In: Strøm K, Müller WC, Bergman T (eds) Cabinets and coalition bargaining: the democratic life cycle in western Europe. Oxford University Press, Oxford, pp 237–267

Chapter 6
Veto Players, Agenda Control and Cabinet Stability in 17 European Parliaments, 1945–1999

Thomas Saalfeld

Introduction

Throughout the post-war period, the parliamentary and semi-presidential systems in Europe have experienced significant cross-national and diachronic variations in cabinet duration (Müller 2008: 206–207). Many authors have emphasized the importance of cabinet duration as a crucial condition of the executive branch's dominance over parliament (Lijphart 1999: 132–133) and the political regime's policy performance (Dodd 1976: 5; Huber 1998). Therefore, understanding the sources of cabinet durability and the dynamics of cabinet termination in such systems of government is "a very important substantive concern for political science" (Laver 2003: 23). Given the practical and normative importance of cabinet stability, it not surprising to find a long tradition of scholarship seeking to identify important institutional sources of such variations (for a survey, see Saalfeld 2008), including relevant properties of party systems such as their fractionalization and polarity (Laver and Schofield 1990: 147–162) or particular institutions such as the prime minister's parliamentary dissolution powers (e.g. Strøm and Swindle 2002). Despite considerable progress in the statistical modelling of cabinet durability (e.g. King et al. 1990; Warwick 1994; Diermeier and Stevenson 1999, 2000; Saalfeld 2008; Schleiter and Morgan-Jones 2009; Ferris and Voia 2009) there is still a shortage of deductive and testable models of cabinet durability. In some cases, models have been criticized for being based on implausible assumptions (e.g. Laver and Shepsle 1996); in other instances the gap between game-theoretic models and indicators available for rigorous empirical testing has been a major stumbling block (e.g. Lupia and Strøm 1995); finally, many empirical research designs raise serious questions of causal inference (cf. Diermeier 2006). In a recent review of the state of the art, Michael Laver concluded therefore "the essential research task has been seen as one of fitting data, refining descriptions of by now rather well-known empirical regularities rather than evaluating some model that has been carefully developed on an a priori theoretical basis".

T. Saalfeld (✉)
University of Bamberg, Bamberg, Germany
e-mail: thomas.saalfeld@uni-bamberg.de

T. König et al. (eds.), *Reform Processes and Policy Change: Veto Players and Decision-Making in Modern Democracies*, Studies in Public Choice 16,
DOI 10.1007/978-1-4419-5809-9_6,

Although not specifically designed for this purpose, George Tsebelis' (2002) veto player theory is such a model and could potentially provide a deductive game-theoretic model of cabinet durability which is sufficiently parsimonious to lend itself to rigorous empirical testing across time and space, while avoiding some of the pitfalls of existing explanations.

Cabinet Stability in Cross-national Comparison: Data and Description of the Dependent Variable

What institutional variables might explain the considerable variations in cabinet longevity observed in Europe's democracies? This is the empirical research puzzle that the present chapter seeks to address. The data on cabinet duration used in this chapter were collected by country experts participating in the research project on "Constitutional Change in Parliamentary Democracy" directed by Wolfgang C. Müller, Kaare Strøm and Torbjörn Bergman (for a description, see Bergman et al. 2005). The dataset includes detailed information about 424 cabinets in 17 parliamentary and semi-presidential European democracies, covering the period between the end of the Second World War (1945) and the end of 1999. The operationalization of a cabinet's longevity follows a widely accepted (if not entirely undisputed) definition according to which cabinets begin when they are appointed by a head of state. A cabinet is considered to be terminated with any change in the set of parties holding cabinet membership; any change in the identity of the head of government; and any general election, whether mandated by the end of the "constitutional inter-election period" (CIEP) or precipitated by a premature dissolution of parliament (Müller and Strøm 2000: 12).

Table 6.1 identifies the 17 European democracies included in the present study and provides information on the mean relative cabinet duration in these countries in the window of observation. "Relative" duration is defined as the number of days between a cabinet's appointment and its termination expressed as a percentage of the remaining CIEP, that is, a cabinet's maximum feasible duration according to the definition of cabinet terminations used in this study (see above). If a cabinet is formed at the beginning of a four-year legislative term, its "life expectancy" is four years; if it is formed six months before the next scheduled election, its maximum feasible period would only be six months. If we rank the countries by their mean relative cabinet duration, the average cabinet in The Netherlands exhibits the highest life expectancy as it survived for approximately 84% of its maximum feasible period (0.84). The most short-lived cabinets can be observed for Italy, where the average cabinet lasted for approximately one-third of its maximum period (0.33). The standard deviations reported in the final column (which are relatively large for some countries) suggest that there was considerable "within-country" variation as well as clear cross-national differences in cabinet duration. In other words, the cross-national variations observed in Table 6.1 cannot be explained by country-specific

Table 6.1 Mean relative cabinet duration in 17 European democracies, 1945–1999

Country	Period	Number of cabinets with complete (uncensored) records	Mean relative cabinet duration	Standard deviation
Netherlands	1945–1998	21	0.84	0.27
Luxembourg	1945–1995	15	0.83	0.26
Greece	1977–1996	9	0.81	0.23
Sweden	1945–1998	25	0.80	0.30
Spain	1977–1996	6	0.77	0.17
Norway	1945–1997	25	0.73	0.33
Austria	1945–1997	20	0.68	0.27
United Kingdom	1945–1997	19	0.64	0.30
Iceland	1944–1999	25	0.63	0.36
Germany	1949–1998	25	0.60	0.37
Finland	1945–1995	36	0.57	0.34
Ireland	1944–1997	21	0.57	0.22
France (V Rep.)	1959–1997	22	0.56	0.29
Denmark	1945–1998	30	0.51	0.25
Portugal	1976–1995	10	0.48	0.34
Belgium	1946–1995	32	0.41	0.34
Italy	1945–1998	47	0.33	0.30
Mean/Total	1945–1999	388	0.59	0.34

Source: Dataset of the project Constitutional Change in Parliamentary Democracy (http://www.pol.umu.se/ccpd/index.html)

factors such as political culture or unique path-dependent developments. Other analyses (Saalfeld 2008) show that the within-country variation is generally not due to period effects.

Explaining Cabinet Stability: The Story So Far

The first attempts at explaining variations in cabinet duration – whether in the "European politics tradition" (Laver and Schofield 1990: 7–11) or the tradition of formal game-theoretic modelling – focused on the effects of so-called structural attributes of the relevant political systems, party systems and cabinets. This included variables such as the size and polarization of the party system or the number of parties in the cabinet (for a summary of the most important findings, see Grofman and van Roozendaal 1997; Laver 2003; Laver and Schofield 1990: 147–155; Warwick 1994: 1–14; Saalfeld 2008). Despite the discovery of a number of empirical regularities, the work on the structural-attributes tradition was criticized for the static nature of its explanations. Although at least the game-theoretic work in the structural-attributes tradition specified causal mechanisms, it did so in a peculiar way: Cabinet terminations were effectively seen as the theoretical "flip side" of cabinet formation – the same causal variables favouring the formation of certain types of equilibrium cabinets (for example, minimal-winning coalitions) were also taken to be responsible for such cabinets' longevity. The main empirical problem is that such explanations typically "reference government or parliamentary attributes whose values are fixed or set at the time a government takes office; none takes account of the (subsequent) events that actually bring governments down" (Warwick 1994: 8). Moreover, many cabinet-specific structural attributes may not be as exogenous to the explanatory model as they seem at first glance. For example, Diermeier and Merlo (2000) argue that minimal-winning coalitions may be chosen during coalition bargaining precisely because they promise to be more durable. If this is the case, the structural attribute of being a minimal-winning coalition cannot be used as a causal factor [as, for example, in Dodd (1976)].

Advocates of the "critical-events" perspective did not offer any answers to these theoretical issues. They attacked the very causal determinism of the structural-attributes approach, arguing that the vast majority of cabinets were terminated in response to unpredictable events such as deaths or ill-health of prime ministers, scandals, dramatic downturns in the economy, sudden shifts in public opinion and the like (Frendreis et al. 1986: 621, 623). Strøm challenged the non-strategic nature of random-effects models based on this position from a theoretical vantage point, taking issue with the assumption that the events causing cabinets to fall are exogenous and random. In reality, he asserts, "such events ... are frequently engineered, or at least affected, by players in the game (i.e. parties inside or outside the government)" (Strøm 1988: 929). The most powerful empirical critique of the random-events perspective arose from Warwick's (1994) work, who found for a sample of West European cabinets that the hazard rate of discretionary cabinet terminations is not constant (as randomness would imply), but tends to rise with cabinet age. The obvious next step was to tie the destructive potential of such events to the parties' changing electoral incentives across an electoral cycle (e.g. Lupia and Strøm 1995). Despite their theoretical and empirical shortcomings, works in the random-events tradition made one lasting contribution to the debate about cabinet durability: They replaced the traditional cross-sectional regression-analytic approach with the longitudinal approach of event-history analysis, which is a far more appropriate statistical technique to model the processes between cabinet formation and termination – and they expanded the focus of coalition studies to include the process of governing in coalitions after cabinet formation and portfolio allocation.

This methodological lead was taken up by the authors of a number of "unified" models combining the causal reasoning of the structural-attributes approach with the sort of stochastic environment suggested by random-events theorists. King et al. (1990) presented a stochastic process model, which – unlike the early work of Browne and his associates – makes the hazard rate of cabinet survival a function of a range of covariates. Whilst this unified perspective represented a major improvement in the statistical theory and methods used to analyse cabinet durability, it still did not go much beyond existing theoretical work in specifying the causal mechanisms that were thought to drive the dynamics of cabinet survival in the interval between cabinet formation and termination. Lupia and Strøm (1995) were the first authors to develop a dynamic game-theoretic model of discretionary coalition dissolutions accounting for the rising hazard rates for cabinet terminations towards the end of the CIEP. This model is capable of integrating structural and other variables (see below) and combining them with a dynamic perspective including the possibility of random shocks subsequent to cabinet formation. Diermeier and Merlo (2000) and Diermeier and Stevenson (1999, 2000) later built on this model. Nevertheless, Laver (2003: 38) criticized this literature:

> Neither the Lupia–Strom nor the Laver–Shepsle approaches, for example, can be properly operationalized in terms of current datasets. ... The empirical tradition [of coalition research] has developed a powerful methodological tool, but, with the exception of Diermeier and Stevenson (2000), this has been applied to at best quarter-baked theoretical propositions using recycled data. The tradition of a priori theoretical modelling is at last beginning to tackle the problem of government termination, but so far with very little empirical underpinning.

Veto Players, Agenda Control and Cabinet Duration

Although the emphasis of veto player theory is on policy stability rather than cabinet stability, it is an example of "a priori modelling" in Laver's sense and does allow the generation of a number of original and potentially fruitful hypotheses about the conditions under which cabinets form in equilibrium – and, more importantly for the purposes of this chapter, on the conditions under which their risk of subsequent failure increases (Tsebelis 2006, 2002: 215–218). The purpose of this section is not to assess the extent to which veto player theory offers a more "complete" explanation of variations in cabinet duration than other models [e.g. the Lupia–Strom (1995), Laver–Shepsle (1996) or Diermeier–Merlo (2000) models], but to identify its potential to illuminate interesting dynamics in the process of cabinet termination and longevity – and whether this can be done in such a way that Laver's (2003: 38) call for "closer integration of theoretical and empirical work" can be met.

Nevertheless, the particular contribution of the veto player model necessitates a few observations on the main similarities and differences between veto player theory and other influential models of cabinet durability. The most exhaustive attempt at explaining variations in cabinet survival has been produced by Warwick (1994) whose magisterial empirical study discusses a very large array of possible explanations. Ultimately, his conclusion is that ideological variables are of particular explanatory power: For majority cabinets, Warwick finds the ideological diversity within the cabinet to be the most convincing explanation for the variations found. For minority cabinets, the ideological polarization of the parliament as a whole is more important. Warwick's emphasis on ideological explanations is highly compatible with the theoretical expectations which Tsebelis generates on the basis of a veto player framework.

Laver and Shepsle's (1996) portfolio allocation model is more strongly deductive than Warwick's work and shares some common ground with a veto player framework: Firstly, similar to veto player theory the actors in the portfolio allocation model are assumed to be largely driven by policy motivations. Secondly, like in the veto player theory, cabinets in the portfolio allocation model are formed in equilibrium but are subsequently exposed to exogenous shocks that can destroy the initial equilibrium. Thirdly, for both models centrist parties are particularly influential in cabinet formation and maintenance. The fundamental difference between the portfolio allocation model on the one hand and veto player theory on the other is the strong emphasis on ministerial autonomy in Laver and Shepsle's model. Cabinets are assumed to be in equilibrium – and therefore likely to remain stable – "if the government portfolio with jurisdiction over each relevant policy dimension is allocated to the party with the median legislator on that dimension" (Laver and Shepsle 1996: 66). In Laver and Shepsle's theory, ministers are virtually policy dictators within their jurisdiction, whereas in Tsebelis' model all veto players need to agree to a change of the policy status quo. The assumptions underpinning the portfolio allocation model are unrealistic and have attracted criticisms from empirical scholars (e.g. Warwick 1999).

Like veto player theory and the portfolio allocation model, Lupia and Strøm's (1995) model of strategic cabinet termination is a game-theoretic model in which the original equilibrium that led to the formation of a coalition is constantly threatened by actor opportunism and exogenous shocks. However, Lupia and Strøm's party leaders are not only motivated by policy considerations but also by electoral incentives. For example, Lupia and Strøm argue that the benefits party leaders derive from a coalition vary across the electoral cycle. The value of a coalition to party leaders declines as the next election approaches. This explains the rising risk of a cabinet termination in the second half of a parliamentary term found by Warwick (1994) and others. In addition, Lupia and Strøm model party leaders as people who consider policy, electoral and transaction costs when making decisions about the termination of a coalition. Diermeier and Stevenson (1999, 2000) have built on this model and extended it.

The distinctive theoretical arguments of veto player theory could be summarized as follows: political parties are predominantly regarded as policy seekers. They strive to be in government, because (and insofar as) inclusion in the cabinet allows them to achieve their preferred policy outcomes. Being in the cabinet turns political parties into "partisan veto players" whose agreement is required to change the policy status quo (Tsebelis 2002: 2). The parties' scope to do so is constrained by the number of other veto players, the ideological distance between the party and other veto players in relation to the status quo, and the cohesiveness of all partisan veto players. When the number of veto players and the ideological distance between them increases (in relevant dimensions of the policy space), the size of the winset of bargaining solutions that are jointly preferred to the status quo cannot increase (provided the partisan veto players are cohesive and operate as if they were unitary actors). On the contrary, the winset is likely to shrink in such situations.

Why should a cabinet, once it is formed in equilibrium, fail after some time? Veto player theory offers several possible answers. Firstly, certain veto players may enjoy positional advantages over others, which can be exploited. These advantages typically arise from a veto player's ideological location at the centre of the policy space. Such a party is "a very expensive partner to be included in a coalition, and a coalition without it has very little chance of policy success" (Tsebelis 2006: 22). Such a privileged position may create incentives to renegotiate an existing coalition agreement, or to look for a partner who offers a better deal (Lupia and Strøm 1995). The reason for the positional advantage of centrality is as follows: "if a minority government is centrally located in space, it can be part of most possible parliamentary majorities and, consequently, move the status quo inside its own winset. In fact, most of the time it might not have to compromise at all, and it can locate the final outcome on its own ideal point" (Tsebelis 2002: 98). The effect of a veto player being able to exploit positional advantages is complex, however. For majority coalitions, the costs of governing with, and without, a centrally located player may be very high and create temptations for non-centrist parties to explore alternative coalition arrangements. For a minority government, in contrast, the positional advantage of centrality may be a stabilizing factor, especially if strategic election timing is not available as an option for non-centrist majority parties to dislodge the centrist party in power (such as in Norway with fixed-term parliaments).

Secondly, minority cabinets, in particular, may be stabilized by institutional advantages arising from the parliament's standing orders or from the constitution. This notion of "institutional advantages" is closely related to theories of legislative agenda control. In many parliaments, for example, heads of government are entitled to attach a confidence motion to a substantive motion on the passage of a bill. If this power is combined with the right to dissolve the parliament unilaterally and call early elections, the incentives for opposition parties to topple a minority government will depend on non-policy factors such as their electoral prospects as well as the policy question at hand. The mere threat of a confidence motion (whether it is made explicit is irrelevant) can also persuade veto players inside a government to defer to the prime minister or their party's policy preferences (essentially because a further highly salient dimension – fall of the government and/or early elections – is added to the decision space). Below the level of confidence votes as the "nuclear option" at the hands of a prime minister, Tsebelis (2002, 2006) explicitly builds on Döring's (1995) conceptualization of agenda powers in legislation, capturing the government's powers to determine the plenary agenda in the parliament; to treat the introduction of "money bills" as a government prerogative; to limit the scope of legislative deliberations at the committee stage of a bill through a preceding plenary decision; to grant or deny committees the right to rewrite draft government bills; to control the timetable of legislative committees; to curtail debate before the final vote of a bill in the plenary (e.g. by imposing time limits) and to deny the parliament the possibility to deliberate on a bill beyond a legislative term. Döring (1995) used a principal-component analysis of data on these seven types of agenda powers from 17 European democracies to create an index, which shows very high levels of governmental agenda control in the United Kingdom, Ireland, France and Greece. By contrast, parliaments in The Netherlands, Sweden and Italy were less dominated by the government. How is this related to cabinet longevity? According to Tsebelis' (2002), minority cabinets can compensate for a lack of parliamentary voting strength if the parliamentary institutions allow them to control the legislative agenda.

Thirdly, as in most dynamic theories of cabinet survival, veto player theory allows the equilibrium prevailing at the time of cabinet formation to be perturbed – or even destroyed – by subsequent "exogenous shocks" (Tsebelis 2002: 217). Such a shock, which is essentially random from a modelling perspective (as suggested by the random-events theorists), could be an economic crisis, a scandal, the severe illness or death of a head of government, a dramatic and/or sustained deterioration of government popularity or a series of severe government defeats in mid-term or regional elections. One of the most innovative ideas of Tsebelis' veto player theory is the conceptualization of such exogenous random shocks as (more or less abrupt) changes to the location of the status quo.

One effect of such shocks is that existing policies, which may have been adequate at the time of legislation, are no longer sufficient. He argues that government ministers are not generally interested in the wording of a particular piece of legislation, but in the bill's effect once it becomes law and has been implemented. However, politicians do not have complete information on the link between the wording of a particular legislative measure and its effect after its implementation. Tsebelis' argument is based on a standard model used in policy analysis, which could be described as follows: The median legislator in a parliament passes a policy, p, and delegates its implementation to an executive agency with a certain amount of discretion. The executive agency makes use of its leeway and decides to implement the policy, p, with an adjustment, a. It does so either in order to adapt the law to local conditions, to respond to unforeseen events that have occurred since the passage of the law or to bring the policy closer to the agency's own ideal point in the policy outcome space. Thus, the effect of a measure could be expressed by the equation $x = p + a + \omega$, where ω represents an external shock, which the legislator did not anticipate when passing the bill, but which may have been considered by the executive agency when making adjustment a (cf. Epstein and O'Halloran 1994; Volden 2002: 111–112). From the perspective of Tsebelis' partisan veto player, the consequence is as follows:

> ... actors are located on the basis of their preferences in an outcome space, but they cannot select outcomes directly. They have to select policies, which include a random element in them. Only some experts have specific knowledge of the exact correspondence between policies and outcomes, and as a result decision-makers have to extract this information from them (I say "extract" because experts may not want to reveal it and act strategically)
>
> Tsebelis (2002: 216)

This problem is likely to be aggravated further by a severe exogenous shock, which may have significant implications for the equilibrium in which a cabinet was formed:

> ... such outside events modify the position of the status quo in the outcome space even if the policy does not change. For example, when there is an oil crisis, the government budget (which could have been a perfect compromise at the time it was voted) appears completely inadequate because the price of energy increases dramatically. Such variations of outcomes (while policy remains constant) are additional sources of uncertainty. The uncertainty between policies and outcomes was dealt with at the time of the vote of the budget, but now the same policy produces very different outcomes than before
>
> Tsebelis (2002: 216)

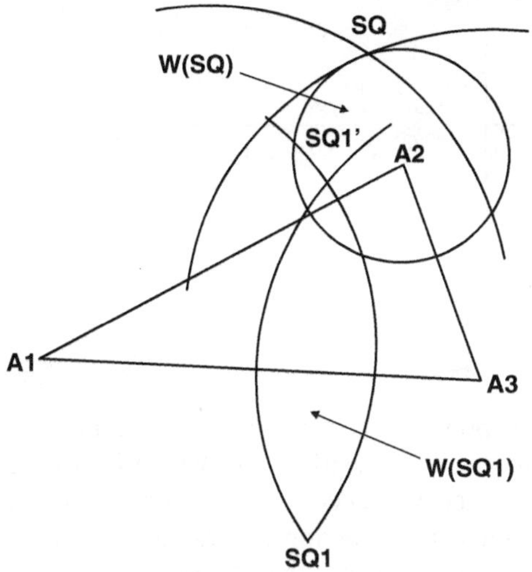

Fig. 6.1 Effect of an external shock on the status quo

It is likely that policy-seeking actors will be sensitive to such shifts. But do all exogenous shocks have a destructive impact on the equilibrium between the partisan veto players? The answer is "no". Tsebelis' (2002: 217) argument can be summarized and illustrated intuitively using Fig. 6.1, where three potential partisan veto players, A1, A2 and A3, agree on a policy located within the winset W(SQ). This solution entails an improvement over the status quo (SQ) for all three parties. Based on the fundamental propositions of veto player theory, the winset should increase as the ideological distance between the three veto players decreases. The occurrence of an unexpected exogenous shock is modelled as a shift of the status quo. Such a shift could be from SQ to SQ1′. If this is the case, the shock would still be "manageable", although the winset is changed dramatically to W(SQ1). The reason is that SQ1′ remains within the original winset W(SQ). By contrast, a shock of exactly the same size that shifts the status quo to SQ1 would be unmanageable. In this case, the coalition would be likely to fail (Tsebelis 2002: 217–218). Whilst this is a convincing theoretical argument, it has been notoriously difficult to observe the location of the status quo ante, let alone any shifts of the status quo as the result of an exogenous shock. This continues to pose problems for empirical studies.

Figure 6.2 summarizes Tsebelis' propositions about the link between the number of, and ideological distance between, veto players and government agenda powers on the one hand, and cabinet stability on the other. The ideological distance between cabinet parties and the number of cabinet parties has been part of many traditional models of cabinet survival. Like these models, veto player theory predicts these variables to have a direct (and negative) effect on cabinet survival: the higher the number of partisan veto players in the cabinet and the greater the ideological distance between them, the more difficult it will be to change the policy status quo, the less likely it is that a shift in the status quo will be "manageable", the more likely will be increasing tensions within the coalition and, hence, the lower will be the survival chances of the cabinet.

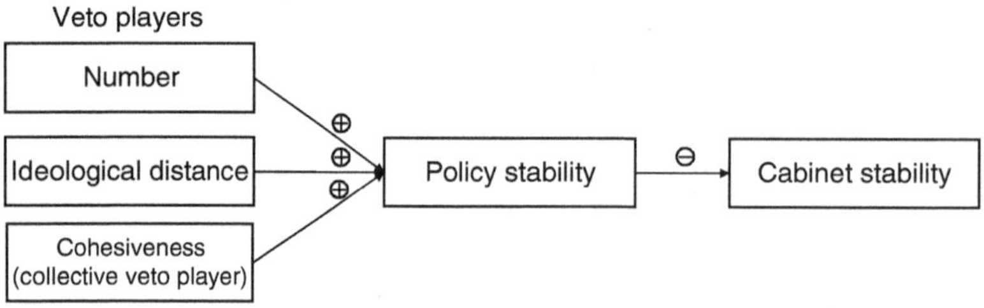

Fig. 6.2 Veto players and cabinet stability

Government agenda powers are predicted to have a direct and positive influence on executive dominance over the parliament (which is not the focus of this chapter and will therefore not be estimated). Veto player theory goes beyond traditional models of cabinet stability by predicting that variables capturing variations in government agenda powers and, in particular, the interaction of such powers with the variable "majority status" (as a variable capturing a crucial veto-player characteristic) will have a systematic effect on cabinet survival time. The interactive nature of these predictions will have to be accounted for in the statistical modelling strategy.

Based on the theoretical arguments briefly outlined above, veto player theory promises to offer a theoretical framework for the analysis of variations in cabinet duration that focuses strictly on the key characteristics of partisan veto players, at least for majority cabinets. The number of veto players, their ideological distance from one another and their cohesiveness are the key predictors of cabinet stability. The theory provides reasons why features of the cabinet's bargaining environment should not be expected to play a crucial role in the explanation of variations in the duration of majority cabinets. The theory also incorporates important institutional features of parliamentary government through propositions about the effect of agenda powers, which are predicted to be of particular importance when partisan veto players operate in a parliamentary minority situation. A survey of minority cabinets across all parliamentary systems of government between 1945 and 2002 demonstrates that the category of minority cabinets is far from negligible, that is, over 45% of all cabinets in parliamentary systems did not have majority status during this period (Cheibub et al. 2004: 573–575). In empirical terms, the most interesting and at the same time problematic aspect connected with veto player theory is the conceptualization of exogenous shocks as sudden shifts of the status quo, whose precise location is notoriously difficult to establish empirically. Nevertheless, it is possible to derive observable implications for five types of independent variables – and to test five hypotheses from veto player theory:

1. Ceteris paribus, the smaller the ideological distance between partisan veto players, the larger the winset in the outcome space and the more likely a cabinet is to manage an exogenous shock. Hence the smaller the ideological distance, the greater a cabinet's survival chances.
2. The ideological polarization of parties in the parliament overall will not have a significant effect on the survival of majority cabinets.

3. The size of the winset will not increase with an increase in the number of partisan veto players in the cabinet (rather, it is likely to shrink). The larger the number of partisan veto players, the smaller is the cabinet's chance to successfully manage an exogenous shock, and the greater the risk of an early termination.
4. The fractionalization of parliament will not have a significant impact on cabinet duration.
5. If a cabinet does not control a parliamentary majority, its survival chances will increase with the fractionalization of the parliament overall, with the inclusion of the median party in the cabinet (positional advantages) and the government's control of the parliamentary agenda (institutional advantages).

Testing the Hypotheses

In the following section, three survival models will be estimated to test the five hypotheses formulated above. In each model, the dependent variable is the conditional probability for a discretionary cabinet termination to occur at any particular point in time (rather than a technical termination, for example, due to a regular election), given that the cabinet has survived up to that point (hazard rate). Changes in hazard rates are taken to indicate the presence of causal effects. The models presented in this chapter are specified as Cox proportional hazard models, which assume the existence of a baseline hazard rate $[\lambda_0(t_i)]$. This baseline hazard indicates the underlying probability of cabinet termination over time when the vector of all covariates is zero. However, no assumptions are made about the distribution of probabilities of the occurrence of such "failures" over time. Box-Steffensmeier and Jones (2004: 88) consider this to be a great advantage vis-à-vis alternatives:

> The primary advantage of the Cox model is simple: the relationship between covariates and the hazard rate can be estimated without having to make any assumptions whatsoever about the nature and shape of the baseline hazard rate. This advantage makes the Cox model the first choice among modeling strategies for many applied problems.

The covariates may lead to shifts in the hazard rate from this baseline, assuming that the impact of the covariates is the same across the entire life course of a cabinet (proportionality assumption).

A key issue in event-history models is the "censoring" of certain records. While event-history models have always used censoring to deal with incomplete information about the start and/or end dates of records in a dataset, theoretical censoring has played an important role in the study of cabinet survival. In the present study, for example, the records of all cabinets terminated for technical reasons (e.g. termination as the result of a regular election or the death of a prime minister) were right-censored as were all cabinets that were still in office on 31 December 1999 (the endpoint of our "window of observation"). The advantage of censoring is that selection bias is avoided. The record remains in the dataset and is included in the estimation of termination risks. It is treated as a case whose termination date is not known. All we know is that the cabinet survived *at least* to the day it was terminated for technical reasons and right-censored.

Model 1 in Table 6.2 reports the estimates for a Cox proportional hazard model. The "hazard ratios" reported for the various covariates are the exponents of the estimated β coefficients. Ratios equal to 1 indicate that as a covariate's value changes by 1 unit, the marginal change in the hazard is zero. Ratios greater than 1 imply that the hazard is increasing as the value of the covariate increases by 1 unit. In contrast, ratios less than 1 imply the hazard is decreasing as the value of the covariate increases by 1 unit. Model 2 accounts for the possibility of country-specific unobserved heterogeneity. Unlike model 1, the estimates of the Cox model are based on a shared frailty design. A shared frailty model allows testing for the existence of time-constant unobserved heterogeneity resulting from specific contextual factors in some or all of the 17 countries (for a discussion of the problem, see Grofman 1989). It is worth noting that country-specific "frailties" are not estimated as fixed "country effects". Rather estimates of theta show whether the frailty component (i.e. possible differences in the frailty of different countries resulting from unobserved country-specific heterogeneity) is significantly different from zero. The highly significant theta of 0.390 (Table 6.2, model 2) demonstrates the need to control for country-specific effects and highlights that the variables in the model do not completely capture all country-specific information.

Both model 1 and model 2 are based on the assumption that the risk of failure is distributed proportionally across the life span of a cabinet. A violation of this assumption would lead to biased parameter estimates in proportional hazard models (especially with regard to the standard errors). Violations of the proportionality assumption in Cox models were tested by analysing the Schoenfeld residuals for models 1 and 2 in their entirety, and by examining the scaled Schoenfeld residuals for possible time dependence of the effect of the individual covariates. The detailed results of these tests are reported in Saalfeld (2009: 18–19). At this point it suffices to say that both the entire model and a number of covariates violate the proportionality assumption. The bias resulting from such duration dependence can be corrected by using a so-called extended Cox model, which explicitly controls for the impact of covariates whose impact varies over time. The most frequently used correction is to multiply the value of the time-constant covariate with the natural log of analysis time. Model 3 includes these newly created covariates for all variables that violated the proportionality assumption (for a general description of such a strategy, see Box-Steffensmeier et al. 2003). They will not be interpreted in detail, although it is interesting to note that most of the estimated coefficients for these variable's are above 1, which means that the destructive effect of these institutional arrangements becomes more severe over time (see Saalfeld 2009: 19–22 for further interpretations).

The data for the composition of cabinets, the ideological distance between partisan veto players and the longevity of cabinets were extracted from the "Constitutional Change in Parliamentary Democracy" (CCPD) database. The data on agenda control were provided by the group of researchers collaborating in the Döring (1995) project. The data on the power of last amendments were taken from Heller (2001).

Table 6.2 Determinants of behavioural cabinet terminations in 17 European democracies, 1945–1999 (hazard ratios, standard errors in parentheses)

Covariate	Model 1: Cox proportional hazards	Model 2: Shared frailty	Model 3: Non-proportional hazards (lnt)
Majority cabinet	0.164* (0.058)	0.064* (0.026)	0.010* (0.013)
Cabinet ideological range	0.997 (0.004)	0.999 (0.004)	0.997 (0.004)
Number of cabinet parties	1.483* (0.127)	1.297* (0.115)	1.467* (0.122)
Parliament fractionalization (effective number of parties)	0.954 (0.076)	0.909 (0.073)	0.952 (0.075)
Parliamentary seat share of extreme parties	1.030* (0.009)	1.028** (0.014)	1.068 (0.057)
Median party (most important dimension) in cabinet	1.200 (0.340)	1.656 (0.530)	1.200 (0.340)
Prime minister has right to dissolve parliament	0.777 (0.178)	0.839 (0.354)	0.771 (0.177)
Government legislative agenda control (Döring)	1.508 (0.509)	1.217 (0.800)	0.059 (0.139)
Government right to table last amendment (Heller)	1.013 (0.219)	0.915 (0.366)	0.370 (0.518)
Interaction minority cabinet × seat share of extreme parties	1.045* (0.014)	1.009 (0.018)	1.032 (0.071)
Interaction minority cabinet × median party in cabinet	0.653 (0.240)	0.546 (0.216)	0.600 (0.220)
Interaction minority cabinet × prime minister dissolution powers	3.516* (1.432)	2.381*** (1.241)	1.588 (2.591)
Interaction minority cabinet × government legislative agenda control	0.482 (0.277)	0.112* (0.085)	0.005 (0.018)
Interaction minority cabinet × government right to table last amendment	0.270* (0.110)	0.221* (0.094)	0.031*** (0.057)
Interaction time × majority cabinet			1.662** (0.366)
Interaction time × seat share of extreme parties			0.994 (0.009)
Interaction time × government agenda control			1.664 (0.611)
Interaction time × government right to table last amendment			1.182 (0.268)
Interaction time × minority cabinet × seat share of extreme parties			1.000 (0.012)
Interaction time × minority cabinet × prime minister dissolution powers			1.106 (0.311)
Interaction time × minority cabinet × government agenda control			2.451 (1.497)

(continued)

Table 6.2 (continued)

Covariate	Model 1: Cox proportional hazards	Model 2: Shared frailty	Model 3: Non-proportional hazards (ln t)
Interaction time × minority cabinet × government right to table last amendment			1.584 (0.508)
Log-likelihood	−1,410.69	−1,398.11	−1,398.95
Chi^2	188.73*	127.68*	212.21*
Number of failed cabinets	244	244	244
Theta	–	0.390* (0.175)	–

$^{*}p < 0.01$; $^{**}p < 0.05$; $^{***}p < 0.1$ (two-tailed test)

Discussion of Results

The five hypotheses formulated above are only partially confirmed by the analyses. The first covariate in the three models in Table 6.2, a dummy variable (0,1) indicating whether the parties represented in a cabinet control an overall parliamentary majority, serves as a control variable representing the fundamental institutional property of parliamentary and semi-presidential systems: cabinets can only survive in office as long as there is no parliamentary majority willing to topple them. As expected, majority status reduces the risk of a behavioural cabinet termination significantly in all the three models.

Hypothesis 1 predicts a growing risk of behavioural cabinet terminations as the ideological distance between partisan veto players increases, because this is likely to reduce the size of the winset and the cabinets' ability to manage exogenous shocks. The ideological diversity within cabinets was operationalized as the range of the cabinet parties' ideological positions on a one-dimensional left-right continuum. The relevant data in the CCPD dataset are estimates extracted from the Comparative Manifesto Project (Budge et al. 2001). Based on these left–right scores it was possible to calculate the range (absolute difference between the most left-wing and the most right-wing party in the cabinet). Operationalized this way, the cabinets' ideological heterogeneity did *not* have a statistically significant impact on the risk of a behavioural cabinet termination. This is true for all the three models estimated. This surprising result is stable in all model specifications chosen, including models that drop the covariate "number of parties in the government" (coefficients not reported). This finding challenges one of the core predictions derived from veto player theory with regard to cabinet stability. It also contradicts the findings of Warwick (1994), who used slightly different indicators to measure cabinet ideological range. Warwick's strongest results are based on a left–right index that weighs the parties' ideological positions with their parliamentary seat share. Although this strategy may be generally plausible, it was not adopted here, because it is inconsistent with veto player theory: veto player status does not depend on a party's strength in parliamentary seats per se.

As predicted in *hypothesis 2*, the ideological polarization of a cabinet's bargaining environment (the parliament) *does not* generally and significantly increase the risk of behavioural terminations. Following the standard literature, this covariate was operationalized as the seat share of ideologically extreme political parties (mainly Communists and parties of the extreme Right). This indicator of parliamentary ideological polarization increases the risk of behavioural terminations significantly in models 1 and 2. Yet this effect loses its statistical significance (at the conventional 5% level) when violations of the proportional hazards assumption are corrected for (model 3).

In line with Warwick's (1994) findings, the ideological polarization of parliament increases the risk of behavioural terminations for minority cabinets. In the models presented in Table 6.2, this possibility was captured through an interaction effect multiplying the dummy variable "cabinet minority status" with the seat share of ideologically extreme parties. Increasing values for this interaction term do increase the risk of a behavioural termination in all the three models, but estimates only reach conventional levels of statistical significance in model 1. When unobserved country-specific variation and non-proportionality are controlled for, the estimated coefficients lose their statistical significance. Thus, *hypothesis 2* cannot be rejected on the basis of the analyses carried out here.

Hypothesis 3 cannot be rejected either. The findings are clearly in line with predictions based on the veto player theory. In all the three models estimated here, the risk of a behavioural cabinet termination is increased by at least 29% (model 2), if one further partisan veto player is added to a cabinet.

Hypothesis 4 predicts that the fractionalization of the parliament as a whole should not increase the risk of behavioural cabinet terminations. This hypothesis can also not be rejected. Operationalized as the effective number of parties in the parliament (following Laakso and Taagepera 1979), this covariate does not attain a statistically significant influence on the risk of behavioural cabinet terminations in any of the models presented here.

While the findings presented here do not lend much credence to theories focusing on the cabinets' bargaining environment, and while tests of hypotheses 2, 3 and 4 lend at least some support to a theoretical model of cabinet survival based on veto player characteristics, the rejection of hypothesis 1 – encapsulating the most important, preference-based prediction – is not encouraging from the theory's perspective. The findings open up possibilities for alternative interpretations, which are largely unrelated to veto player theory that is based on the assumption of policy-seeking actors. If the number of partisan veto players (holding all other covariates constant) has a strong, significant and robust influence whereas the ideological range amongst partisan veto players does not (even if other crucial variables are controlled for), it is at least plausible that a different type of mechanism might be better suited to explain the variations in cabinet survival, namely the *transaction costs of governing in coalitions*.

In order to test *hypothesis 5*, which relates to the importance of institutional and positional advantages of partisan veto players, a number of further covariates had to be included in the three models in Table 6.2. Positional advantage (centrality) was operationalized as a dummy variable with a value of 1, if a cabinet included the party controlling the median legislator in the most important policy dimension. The most important policy dimension was identified on the basis of the expert interviews conducted by Laver and Hunt (1992); the parties' positions in relation to these issues were again extracted from the CCPD database. The estimates show that the inclusion of the median legislator in the most important policy dimension does not have a statistically significant impact on the risk of behavioural termination in any of the three models. The theoretical arguments suggesting that centrally located parties have better chances to join the government and become a veto player (Laver and Shepsle 1996; Tsebelis 2006; van Roozendaal 1992) do not seem to play the same role when it comes to cabinet survival.

However, the most interesting proposition based on Tsebelis' veto player theory in this context is the prediction that *minority* cabinets should be able to compensate for their lack of parliamentary strength by exploiting positional advantages. In order to capture this effect, an interaction effect of "minority status" and inclusion of the median party on the most important dimension was introduced. Based on the logic outlined above, the interaction effect of veto player properties (minority status) and positional advantages should reduce the risk of a behavioural termination. This proposition is confirmed in all the three models, although the estimated coefficients are not statistically significant at conventional levels.

Institutional advantages as such do not seem to influence the survival chances of cabinets. None of the institutional covariates introduced in models 1, 2 and 3 (prime minister's dissolution powers, agenda control in the legislative process, right to table the last amendment) have a statistically significant effect on the risk of behavioural cabinet terminations. Based on a veto player model, such institutional advantages should, however, improve the survival chances of minority cabinets. In this case, governments should be able to exploit institutional resources to compensate for a lack of parliamentary support. Models 1 and 2 support these predictions at least in part. In all three models, the interaction effect of the right to table the last amendment and cabinet minority status reduces the risk of behavioural terminations clearly and significantly. If a minority cabinet has a high degree of agenda control in the legislative process, its risk of failing prematurely is reduced in all the three models, although the effect is only significant in model 2, that is, in the model which controls for unobserved country-specific heterogeneity. In contrast, the prime minister's right unilaterally to dissolve the parliament does not increase the survival chances of minority cabinets in European democracies. In contrast, the interaction effect of minority status and dissolution powers does increase the risk of behavioural terminations, and this effect is statistically significant at conventional levels in models 1 and 2. This suggests that this particular instrument of agenda control is not used predominantly and successfully as a deterrent against recalcitrant government backbenchers, but as a lever for the head of a minority government to overcome the problems of governing without a parliamentary majority by calling for early elections.

In short, hypothesis 5 cannot be rejected. In contrast, there is considerable evidence that minority cabinets can reduce the risk of an early termination if they have powers to control the legislative agenda.

Conclusion

Tsebelis' veto player theory was developed as a deductive model seeking to explain policy stability. Yet, it can also be extended to analyse the dynamics of cabinet survival. The present chapter, firstly, sought to identify the extent to which, and in what way, veto player theory helps to illuminate interesting and hitherto unresolved research questions about the dynamics of cabinet survival and termination. Secondly, the chapter sought to utilize data produced for the CCPD project and test a number of predictions derived from veto player theory. In particular, the chapter aimed to examine the impact of a number of institutional variables on the survivability of minority cabinets.

In seeking to explain cabinet durability, veto player theory is distinctive in emphasizing properties of the partisan veto players (number, preference diversity and cohesion) rather than the parliamentary bargaining environment they operate in. It also incorporates particular institutional variables, which have so far been neglected in neo-institutionalist accounts of cabinet stability. The theory predicts that minority cabinets can be relatively stable if the partisan veto players are able to employ positional and institutional advantages as well as the government's agenda powers vis-à-vis parliament in order to compensate for their lack of parliamentary strength. In addition, veto player theory provides a particularly interesting way of modelling exogenous shocks, which are conceptualized as sudden shifts in the status quo, whose manageability depends on the size of the winset of the existing partisan veto players.

It was possible to derive five hypotheses from veto player theory, which were tested using the CCPD data and multivariate survival models controlling for unobserved country-specific heterogeneity and violations of the distributional assumptions of the Cox proportional hazards model, which is widely used in studies of cabinet survival. Based on the core veto player model, it was hypothesized that the number of parties in the cabinet and their ideological heterogeneity will be inversely related to the size of the winset and the veto players' ability to respond to sudden changes in the policy status quo. The number of parties in the parliament and the parliament's ideological polarization was hypothesized to be irrelevant in explanations of cabinet durability. Finally, it was hypothesized that if a cabinet does not control a parliamentary majority its survival chances will increase with decreases in the fractionalization of the parliament overall, with the inclusion of the median party in the cabinet (positional advantages) and the government's control of the parliamentary agenda (institutional advantages).

The statistical tests performed to test these hypotheses were ambiguous. The location of the status quo ante could not be determined with available data. The most important explanatory variable, the ideological differences between partisan veto players, did not have the expected effect on cabinet durability. However, there was relatively strong support for the interaction of minority status and a number of institutional variables capturing the government's agenda power. Strong government agenda powers in the legislative process and the right to table the final amendment are examples of tools that may prolong the lives of minority cabinets, if they are available to them.

Acknowledgements I owe thanks to Simona Bevern, Simon Fink and the participants of the George Tsebelis Conference: Reform processes and policy change: How do veto players determine decisionmaking in modern democracies? (Mannheim Centre for European Social Research, May 14–16, 2009) for their helpful comments, which have improved this chapter. All remaining opacities and errors are mine.

References

Bergman T, Müller WC, Strøm K (2005) Comparative parliamentary democracy: a project report. Eur Polit Sci 4(1):42–54

Box-Steffensmeier JM, Jones BS (2004) Event history modeling: a guide for social scientists. Cambridge University Press, Cambridge

Box-Steffensmeier JM, Reiter D, Zorn C (2003) Nonproportional hazards and event history analysis in international relations. J Conflict Resolut 47(1):33–53

Budge I et al (2001). Mapping policy preferences: estimates for parties, electors, and governments 1945–1998. Oxford University Press, Oxford

Cheibub JA, Przeworski A, Saiegh SM (2004) Government coalitions and legislative success under presidentialism and parliamentarism. Br J Polit Sci 34:565–587

Diermeier D (2006) Coalition government. In: Weingast BR, Wittman D (eds) The Oxford handbook of political economy. Oxford University Press, Oxford, pp 162–179

Diermeier D, Merlo A (2000) Government turnover in parliamentary democracies. J Econ Theory 94:46–79

Diermeier D, Stevenson RT (1999) Cabinet survival and competing risks. Am J Polit Sci 43: 1051–1068

Diermeier D, Stevenson RT (2000) Cabinet terminations and critical events. Am Polit Sci Rev 94:627–640

Dodd LC (1976) Coalitions in parliamentary government. Princeton University Press, Princeton

Döring H (1995) Time as a scarce resource: government control of the agenda. In: Döring H (ed) Parliaments and majority rule in Western Europe. St. Martin's Press, Frankfurt am Main: Campus/New York, pp 223–246

Epstein D, O'Halloran S (1994). Divided government and the design of administrative procedures, information and agency discretion. Am J Polit Sci 38(3):697–722

Ferris JS, Voia M-C (2009) What determines the length of a typical Canadian parliamentary government? Can J Polit Sci 42(2):881–910

Frendreis JP, Gleiber DW, Browne EC (1986) The study of cabinet dissolutions in parliamentary democracies. Legis Stud Q 11:619–628

Grofman B (1989) The comparative analysis of coalition formation and duration: distinguishing between-country and within-county effects. Br J Polit Sci 19(2):291–302

Grofman B, van Roozendaal P (1997) Review article: modelling cabinet durability and termination. Br J Polit Sci 27(3):419–451

Heller WB (2001) Making policy stick: why the government gets what it wants in multi-party parliaments. Am J Polit Sci 45(4):780–798

Huber JD (1998) How does cabinet instability affect political performance? Portfolio volatility and health care cost containment in parliamentary democracies. Am Polit Sci Rev 92:577–591
King G, Alt JE, Burns NE et al (1990) A unified model of cabinet dissolution in parliamentary democracies. Am J Polit Sci 34(3):846–871
Laakso M, Taagepera R (1979) Effective number of parties: a measure with applications to Western Europe. Comp Polit Stud 12:3–27
Laver M (2003) Government termination. Annu Rev Polit Sci 6:23–40
Laver M, Hunt WB (1992) Policy and party competition. Routledge, New York
Laver M, Schofield N (1990) Multiparty government: the politics of coalition in Europe. Oxford University Press, Oxford
Laver M, Shepsle KA (1996) Making and breaking governments: cabinets and legislatures in parliamentary democracies. Cambridge University Press, Cambridge
Lijphart A (1999) Patterns of democracy: government forms and performance in thirty-six countries. Yale University Press, New Haven
Lupia A, Strøm K (1995). Coalition termination and the strategic timing of parliamentary elections. Am Polit Sci Rev 89(3):648–665
Müller WC (2008) Governments and bureaucracies. In: Caramani D (ed) Comparative politics. Oxford University Press, Oxford, pp 189–216
Müller WC, Strøm K (2000) Coalition governance in Western Europe: an introduction. In: Müller WC, Strøm K (eds) Coalition government in Western Europe. Oxford University Press, Oxford, pp 1–31
Saalfeld T (2008) Institutions, chance and choices: the dynamics of cabinet survival in the parliamentary democracies of Western Europe (1945–1999). In: Strøm K, Müller WC, Bergman T (eds) Cabinets and coalition bargaining: the democratic life cycle in Western Europe. Oxford University Press, Oxford, pp 327–368
Saalfeld T (2009) Vetospieler, Agendakontrolle und Kabinettsstabilität in 17 europäischen Parlamenten. In: Ganghof S, Hönnige C, Stecker C (eds) Parlamente, Agendasetzung und Vetospieler: Festschrift für Herbert Döring. VS Verlag für Sozialwissenschaften, Wiesbaden, pp 93–115
Schleiter P, Morgan-Jones E (2009) Constitutional power and competing risks: monarchs, presidents, prime ministers, and the termination of east and west European cabinets. Am Polit Sci Rev 103(3):496–512
Strøm K (1988) Contribution to "contending models of cabinet stability." Am Polit Sci Rev 82:923–930
Strøm K, Swindle SM (2002) Strategic parliamentary dissolution. Am Polit Sci Rev 96:575–591
Tsebelis G (2002) Veto players: how political institutions work. Russell Sage Foundation, New York and Princeton University Press, Princeton, NJ
Tsebelis G (2006) Coalition theory: a veto player approach. Unpublished manuscript, UCLA, Los Angeles, CA
van Roozendaal P (1992) Cabinets in multi-party democracies: the effect of dominant and central parties on cabinet composition and durability. Thesis Publishers, Amsterdam
Volden C (2002) A formal model of the politics of delegation in a separation of powers system. Am J Polit Sci 46(1):111–133
Warwick PV (1994) Government survival in parliamentary democracies. Cambridge University Press, Cambridge
Warwick PV (1999) Ministerial autonomy or ministerial accommodation? Contested bases of government survival in parliamentary democracies. Br J Polit Sci 29:369–394

Chapter 7
The Sources of Bipartisan Politics in Parliamentary Democracies

Thomas Bräuninger and Marc Debus

Introduction

The ability to effectively legislate is largely correlated with the capacity to set the parliamentary agenda. Veto player theory provides a brief but impressive argument of who is provided with agenda-setting powers and to what effect (Tsebelis 2002: 82). In presidential systems, as a general rule, the Congress makes law proposals while the president can just accept or veto them. In parliamentary systems, the government drafts bills that the parliament can accept or reject, suggesting that parliaments are rather strong in presidential but weak in parliamentary systems. U.S. president Barack Obama's efforts to keep control over his health reform package after losing the 2010 U.S. Senate special election in Massachusetts is just one example. It was the job of Senate Majority Leader Harry Reid and House Speaker Nancy Pelosi to consider changes to the reform bill in the hope to make it acceptable to liberal Congress members even though the president still wanted to sign a major healthcare reform bill (Politico, 23 Jan 2010). While Democrats controlled both Houses at that point in time, members of Congress often work together even across party lines (Mayhew 1974; Krehbiel 1991; Wilson and Young 1997; Epstein 1998). In fact, in political systems with rather weakly organized and less cohesive political parties and executives not elected by the legislature but with their own source of legitimacy, bipartisan legislative activities are a normal feature of the policy-making process.

Such legislative behaviour is rather uncommon in parliamentary systems, where the success or even the investiture of government usually depends on the support of a majority of votes in parliament. In order to assure stable majorities, (government) parties have to be strongly organized, more cohesive and disciplined. Multiparty governments likewise have to employ means to deal with the divergence

T. Bräuninger (✉)
Department of Political Science, CDSS and MZES, University of Mannheim, Mannheim, Germany
e-mail: thomas.braeuninger@uni-mannheim.de

M. Debus
MZES, University of Mannheim, Mannheim, Germany
e-mail: marc.debus@mzes.uni-mannheim.de

T. König et al. (eds.), *Reform Processes and Policy Change: Veto Players and Decision-Making in Modern Democracies*, Studies in Public Choice 16,
DOI 10.1007/978-1-4419-5809-9_7, © Springer Science+Business Media, LLC 2010

of preferences within the coalition. Individual MPs who are potential or actual defectors risk their re-nomination for the next election; and in coalition agreements the possibilities for activities with opposition parties are explicitly settled (see Timmermans 1998, 2006; Müller and Strøm 2000, 2008; Müller 2005: 74). As each party in a coalition government is a veto player (Tsebelis 1995, 2002) it seems that there is little room for bipartisan activities in parliamentary systems. Nor would we expect to see *successful* law proposals that are sponsored by parliamentary actors from both the government *and* the opposition camp.

Bipartisan agenda-setting seems to be an anomaly in parliamentary systems, in particular in situations when minimal winning coalitions offer straightforward strategic options. With minimal winning coalitions, each party in government is a veto player and no outside support is required so that the policy outcome expected is identical to the government reform proposal. Yet, the degree of institutional agenda-setting power varies within parliamentary democracies qualifying any overly simplistic government-as-agenda-setter argument (Tsebelis 2002: 99–104). And there is also widespread anecdotic evidence that major policy reforms in parliamentary democracies result from the activity of politicians who belong to government and opposition parties, e.g. the abortion law reforms in Belgium and Germany (De Winter and Dumont 2003: 274; Fitzmaurice 1992: 179; Poguntke 1993: 438), which are reported to have been successful because the moral issues involved finally outweighed partisan politics. Apart from these renowned reforms, not much is known about the reform potential that stems from bipartisan bills.

In fact, most of what we know about bipartisan activities across the government–opposition divide comes from the analysis of (dissenting) legislative voting behaviour (Saalfeld 1995; Cowley 2002). Cases of dissenting voting behaviour are not too frequent but they are sometimes consequential (Bowler et al. 1999). There are numerous factors that affect faction and coalition (voting) discipline, ranging from institutional contexts (intra-party organization, legislative rules, party and electoral system) to individual incentives (ideological preferences, re-election and office motivations) (for an overview, see Bergman et al. 2003; Saalfeld 2005). Dissenting voting behaviour, however, is a high cost situation that is likely to underrate conflictual patterns in policy-making. In contrast, dissenting behaviour at the agenda-setting stage is less consequential and should therefore yield additional insights into the complex relationships within the triangle of cabinets, government parties and opposition parties in parliament, regardless whether such a bipartisan bill is finally successful or is voted down in the legislative process.

In this paper, we thus focus on bipartisan legislative agenda-setting. We argue that despite the zero-sum competition between government and opposition there are indeed incentives for MPs to cooperate across the government–opposition divide. Our argument is based on the distinction of party cohesion and party discipline as two sources of party unity. In parliamentary systems, party unity in legislative voting is large in general as failure to follow the government risks the collapse of the government itself with all its consequences from loss of office, policy and the imponderability of early elections (e.g. Sieberer 2006: 151). On the other hand, individual legislators often have policy preferences that differ quite substantially from those of their core party or party leaders (e.g. Bäck et al. 2009; Giannetti and

Laver 2009). When these programmatic differences are grounded in distinct constituency interests, legislators have clear incentives to signal their deviating position to the public. We argue that the initiation of bipartisan bills (and private members' bills, more generally) can be used as a position-taking strategy (Huber 1996), even though at the final voting stage, legislators are regularly forced into the party line.

Analysing legislative activity in Belgium and Germany between 1986 and 2003, we find that there is cooperation between legislators from government and opposition parties. Moreover, bipartisan legislative activity is sometimes successful and such *mixed bills* get adopted by a parliamentary majority. In line with what to expect from the theoretical argument, we find that at the *agenda-setting stage*, bipartisan bills are more likely the larger the policy conflict is within the government coalition (the so-called *veto player distance*), and the smaller the policy conflict is between the government and the opposition camp in parliament. In contrast, at the *final voting stage*, the government–opposition divide prevails. Bipartisan bills are voted down more often than not, and more specifically, the larger the policy distance between governmental veto players, the less likely the bills are to receive final approval.

We also find that weak coalition cabinets (narrow majorities in parliament) are more often confronted with bipartisan bills than stronger ones. In terms of the success of a bipartisan bill, one major and decisive restraint is the proportion of governing party representatives who support a bipartisan law proposal. In general, bipartisan bills are more likely to be successful when supported by large parts of the government coalition.

In the next section, we develop a simple two-stage model that covers potential mechanisms at the institutional and the individual level that are likely to have an influence on the emergence and/or the success of bipartisan bills in parliamentary democracies. From this, we derive our hypotheses about which factors should influence bipartisan legislative activity and which variables should affect the fate of bipartisan bills. The third section provides a description of the data for the empirical analysis. In the fourth section, we present multivariate regression analyses based on a Heckman selection model on legislative agenda-setting as well as on the success of bipartisan bills.

Bipartisan Legislative Activity and Success in Parliamentary Democracies

Most of what we know about the origins and fate of bipartisan bills stems from the U.S. Congress system (Gilligan and Krehbiel 1989; Epstein 1998). To be sure, presidential systems differ from parliamentary systems in terms of the role the executive and the legislature play in the legislative game. In presidential systems, legislative agenda-setting often rests with the Congress while in parliamentary democracies the executive takes the lead (Tsebelis 1999, 2002). Whenever a parliamentary government is endowed with the resources of a huge ministerial bureaucracy and can threaten to call for a vote of confidence, significant and successful private members' bills should be rare.

In this paper, we focus on bipartisan bills and inquire about their sources and fate. In a first step, therefore, we look at the determinants of legislative agenda-setting. We pay specific attention to the question "What factors favour the introduction of bipartisan bills in comparison with bills introduced by the government, government supporting parties, or law proposals introduced by the parliamentary opposition?" This is also but not exclusively a question of a single strategic choice. MPs may deliberately choose to introduce a private members' (oppositional) bill but if they decide, for whatever reason, to introduce a bipartisan bill, they will have to find a government party or MP who is willing to cosponsor the bill.

Given our focus on parliamentary systems and the sharp divide between government majority and parliamentary minority, we distinguish between three types of actors and, accordingly, four types of bills: (1) In virtually every parliamentary system, governments have the right to introduce bills. Notably, this is a one-by-one relationship. First, the government *as a whole* introduces bills even though the proposal may be drafted and presented by a single minister (belonging to one of possibly several coalition parties). Secondly, government bills usually cannot be co-sponsored by members of parliament. (2) All other bills are sponsored by members of the legislature either from the first or the second chamber. *Government party bills* are those introduced by MPs (or parliamentary groups) belonging to parties supporting the government. (3) Opposition bills are bills that have been presented by MPs not belonging to parties supporting the government. (4) Bipartisan bills are sponsored by at least two MPs, one from the government, one from the opposition camp (see Bräuninger and Debus 2009).

It seems pertinent to note that this classification is based on formal roles. It reveals nothing about the origin of the draft. Government ministers may draft a bill but hand it to a member of parliament in order to save time in the legislative process or to avoid being associated with it directly. Disguised government bills in Germany and so-called handout bills in the UK are examples in this respect. Also, government party bills may be sponsored by members of one government party only, but have the backing (or not) of all government parties. Here, the formal rules of who is entitled to present a bill may make a difference. In most parliaments individual MPs are allowed to introduce a bill, whereas in the German Bundestag, for instance, only party factions (at least 5% of all MPs) or sizable groups of MPs are allowed to submit a bill.

Here, we speculate about situations and circumstances that support the tabling of bipartisan bills mentioned above. Notably, bipartisan bills in parliamentary democracies are hardly ever successful. In our sample of legislative bills in two parliamentary democracies – Belgium and Germany – over a 25-year period, we observe a total of 996 bipartisan bills making only 8.4% of all government or private members' bills introduced in either the first or second chamber. From these 996 bills, a total of 344 have been approved, making for a success rate of 34.5%.

Even though the average success rate of bipartisan bills in the two parliamentary systems under study is considerably smaller than that of bipartisan bills in the U.S. presidential system (see e.g. Patterson and Caldeira 1988), the mere existence of successful bills calls into question the dominant view of agenda-controlling governments and thus demands an inquiry into the reasons for their success. Building on the above arguments on push and pull factors that shift the power balance in the triangle of government, supporting parties and opposition parties in parliament, we discuss their possible impact on the fate of bipartisan bills.

A Model of Bipartisan Politics

In multiparty systems, governments that contain more than one party are the norm. Generally speaking, party leaders of coalition governments face three (related) problems resulting from the divergence of the coalition partners' policy preferences: the formulation of a joint government policy, the delegation of government authority in a way that actual policy outcomes match with the agreed government policy, and, finally, guaranteeing that all MPs vote for the government policy agenda even when their policy preferences differ significantly from what was agreed or what the coalition partner stands for (for an overview, see Strøm et al. 2003; Müller and Strøm 2008). As a result of these problems, coalition governments plagued with divergent interests are less likely to induce policy change. Indeed, there is ample evidence that the heterogeneity of coalitional veto players makes significant policy changes unlikely (Tsebelis 1999, 2002). Ignoring incentives to implement changes resulting from exogenous events or shocks, the *veto player distance* argument implies that changes or reforms should be more likely the closer the policy positions of political actors are on the policy dimension to which the respective reform efforts belongs.

In this paper, we seek to build on the veto player argument when studying legislative activity of parliamentary actors. Specifically, we argue that preference divergence has two seemingly opposing effects on bipartisan politics. While coalition heterogeneity makes policy change less likely (no matter whether governmental, government party and/or oppositional actors took the initiative), in the same vein, it renders bipartisan agenda-setting more likely (i.e. cooperation across the government–opposition divide). The reason is that policy-making is not the only goal parliamentary actors pursue. Intra-party actors may use legislative activity to raise their profile and garner support from their constituents to enhance their chances of re-election or to capture more influence within their political party (e.g. Bowler et al. 1999: 9–11). When this is the case and policy positions within a coalition government diverge significantly, there are clear incentives for government and opposition actors to cooperate in the submission of bills.

To clarify our argument we use a simple two-stage legislative model where bills are introduced at a proposal stage and approved or disapproved at a voting stage (say, the final voting on a bill in parliament). We make two assumptions which we feel are reasonable: First, there is intra-party heterogeneity of preferences, second, party leaders are more eager to enforce party discipline in the voting stage than the proposal stage. Figure 7.1 shows the time line of our model. At the agenda-setting stage, an individual legislator g of a government party G_1, has two options – to draft

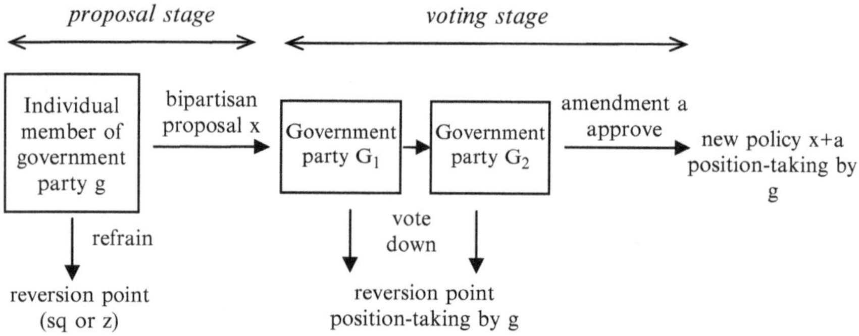

Fig. 7.1 Two-stage legislative model

and submit a bipartisan bill in cooperation with an oppositional actor, or to refrain from doing so, so that the issue on the agenda might be picked up (or not) by other actors (including the government or the government parties). At the voting stage, government parties G_1 and G_2 either approve of g's proposal, possibly including some amendment, or they disapprove. More specifically, we can think of G_1 and G_2 as the party leaders that have the final say over the vote of the parties.

There are three types of outcome. First, if there is no submission by g, the status quo (sq) will prevail or another actor will pick up the issue and set the agenda, possibly resulting in a policy change with some outcome z. Second, if g submits a bipartisan bill x which is then voted down, status quo or policy z will result but g's policy preferences have been signalled to the electorate. Thirdly, if g's party leaders and those of the coalition partner(s) support the bipartisan bill or an amended version, the outcome is a new policy x (if the government coalition accepted the policy proposal) or an amended policy proposal x+a.

What is to be expected in this setup? If we employ the standard assumption in spatial models that legislators are exclusively motivated by policies, the result is straightforward. Individual legislators will most often refrain from proposing anything. They anticipate that unless their proposal is tailor-made to get the approval of their party leaders and other coalition parties (i.e. party leaders), bill submission is not worth the effort. They would also know that making amendments in such a world has no political costs. What counts are policy outcomes, not who set the agenda, or who picked that up. They could anticipate that G_1 and G_2 might amend the proposal in a way that for g, the outcome x+a is even worse than the status quo, or, more generally, the expected reversion point.

In a model of intra-party politics, the standard assumption is better regarded as a special case. There are clear incentives for individual MPs to engage in position-taking to communicate information to voters about their issue positions (Huber 1996). This is even more so when governments are formed of coalitions of parties so that voters have difficulties to assess and assign responsibility for policy change to individual coalition parties (Powell 2000). We therefore follow a broad strand of literature on legislator motivations in parliamentary systems (Harmel and Janda 1994; Lupia and Strøm 1995) and assume that legislators are concerned with both final policy outcomes and the electoral implications of their legislative behaviour. Thus, if legislators have incentives to signal their positions, bipartisan proposals become more likely, regardless of whether they finally get passed or not. Note that we do not explicitly model the behaviour of opposition actors. Opposition parties likewise have incentives to signal their positions on issues but also to drive a wedge between the members of the coalition government. Bipartisan legislative initiatives serve both purposes.

Things are more complex for the leaders of G_1. Legislative voting unity may be considered a precondition for responsible party government, giving party leaders strong incentives to uphold a sufficient level of unified party voting (Depauw and Martin 2009: 109). Moreover, without party discipline, party labels are of no use for voters (Strøm and Müller 2009: 29). Of course, the actual level of party unity also hinges on the rewards party leaders can offer to party members willing to follow the party line. But dissension at the proposal stage is hardly critical for government survival. It may even serve the purpose of communicating the general position of the party on a particular issue when the party is bound to a coalition partner with quite different policy positions. In the end, party leaders have to weigh up the costs and benefits from tolerating dissenting behaviour of their file and rank. In any case, they should be more willing to tolerate dissension at the proposal stage than the voting stage. And they should also have more incentives to tolerate dissension in the form of bipartisan bills when the conflict with their coalition partner is large and the proposal more closely reflects the party position.

The cost–benefit considerations of intra-party actors are influenced by numerous conditions. The incentives of individual legislators to express their dissent with the party line or to submit to the party discipline vary with the electoral system, party organization and the institutional setting. The same can be said about the willingness, need and ability of party leaders to enforce party discipline (Müller 2000). In this study, we shall take a closer look at how policy preferences and different types and levels of policy conflict between parties affect the emergence and success of bipartisan bills.

To clarify the relevance of the programmatic positions of political actors when it comes to the introduction and, finally, the potential success of a bipartisan bill, consider Fig. 7.2. As above, we consider a majority coalition government of two parties G_1 and G_2, and an opposition party O occupying policy positions on a single

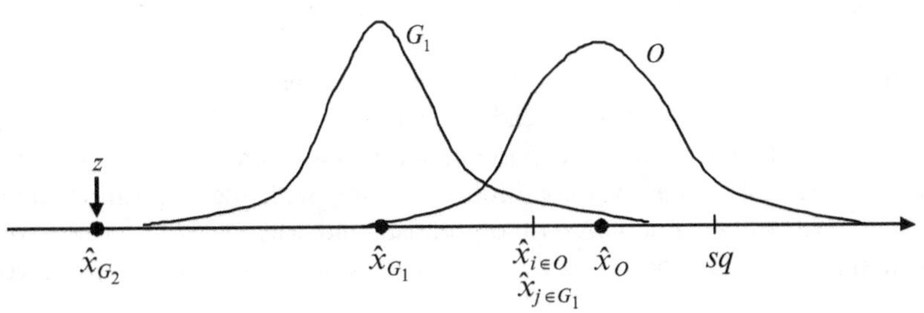

Fig. 7.2 Party cohesion and bipartisan politics

issue dimension. We allow for intra-party heterogeneity of policy preferences so that the policy positions of individual legislators are distributed around the position of the party leadership reflecting the preferences of *core* party members or those of the median party member. Generally, a number of party members from two parties will then have similar preferences or even share the same position on the issue on the agenda. The actual level of overlap depends on the parties' cohesion (or, more generally, the shape of the distributions) and the distance between the party leader positions.[1]

Consider a situation where the status quo is located to the right of the party leader position of O so that all parties prefer a new policy to the left of the status quo (sq). Because G_1 and O have quite similar preferences, a number of individual members from G_1 and O share a common policy position, giving them incentives to submit a bipartisan bill – even though they certainly have diverging interests with respect to the electoral game. Consider a right-wing member i of G_1 with policy position x_i. On the one hand, if i does nothing, sq prevails or the government might pick up the issue. The outcome then can be anywhere in the range between G_1 and G_2, and – from i's point of view – at worst at z which is not unreasonable when ministerial discretion is high and G_2 occupies the relevant ministry (Laver and Shepsle 1996). In that event, depending on the exact location of the government bill, i might be forced to follow the party line when voting on the bill. On the other hand, if $i \in G_1$ and $j \in$ O submit a draft proposal that reflects their policy position $x_i = x_j$ on that issue, they are able to communicate their position to their constituents while the final policy outcome (sq or some z) may be the same.

Because the actual incentives to pursue such a strategy depend on the distribution of ideal points, we can derive general expectations about the likelihood that bipartisan bills are submitted involving the distances between the governmental veto players (i.e. the party leaders) and between the government and the opposition camp. When there is no conflict between G_1 and G_2 (or G_1 and G_2 collapse into a single-party government), then the incentives of i depend on the extent of the disagreement with the party leader position. If the distance between the veto players G_1 and G_2 increases, the more likely becomes a government or government coalition bill that differs from *i's* position. Thus with increasing veto player distance, we would expect bipartisan bills to become more likely. With the same logic, we would also expect that bipartisan bills become more likely the more the distributions of G_1 and O overlap, other things being equal. This is the case when party cohesion is small or the distance between G_1 and O is small.

With regard to the chances of a bipartisan bill to be adopted, the argument is simple. Because government party leaders have strong incentives to uphold a sufficient level of unified party voting in parliamentary systems, we should hardly expect parties to create divisions in a coalition by voting with the opposition unilaterally. Therefore, whoever submitted the proposal and whatever the position of the opposition party is, G_1 and G_2 as the veto players have the final say in the voting

[1] For the ease of presentation we display G_2 as if it had perfect cohesion.

stage. Of course, if the proposal is tailor-made to accommodate the preferences of G_1 and G_2, or if the bill is amended accordingly, the proposal is likely to be adopted. We would therefore expect that the likelihood that a bipartisan bill gets adopted increases when the distance between governmental veto players decreases. We summarize this as follows:

Conjecture 1: Bipartisan bills become more likely (as compared to other types of bills), when the policy range within a coalition government is large, or the distance between government and opposition parties is small.

Conjecture 2: Bipartisan bills are more likely to be approved when the policy range of a coalition government is small.

Unfortunately, we lack systematic data about party cohesion for our empirical analysis so we are unable to study further conjectures on the impact of intra-party heterogeneity on bipartisan politics (for Germany see, however, Bernauer and Bräuninger 2009). Policy preferences are of course not the only factors that have an impact on legislative decision-making in general and the fate of bipartisan legislative activity in particular. It may make a difference if the parties supporting the government in the lower chamber do not have a majority in the upper chamber. Whilst this is presumably less of a problem in unicameral or weak bicameral legislation, cooperation is necessary between government and opposition actors if a bill has to be adopted by both chambers. This is the case, for instance, in German mandatory legislation or for all Belgian bills before the constitutional reform of 1993, which became effective in 1995 (Bräuninger and König 1999; De Winter et al. 2000: 307–310). We therefore expect bipartisan bills to be more frequent and more often successful under strong bicameralism.

Above, we argued that setting the legislative agenda to demonstrate one's views on a policy or to blame the government's failure on an issue is a key instrument used by parliamentary actors (Groseclose and McCarty 2001). Not all times and not all issues are equally suitable for attracting electoral support. Competition for votes is intense before elections, when we would expect to see an extra effort to impress voters with more elaborate and partisan bill proposals. More specifically, we would expect to see fewer bipartisan bills in the pre-election period, but more bills from the opposition and governing parties. Secondly, issue area salience is likely to make a difference. We know that the importance of policy areas varies between countries and parties (see, e.g. Mair and Mudde 1998; Gallagher et al. 2006: 230–254). Generally speaking, socialist and social democratic parties are more interested in economic issues, while political actors from the Christian party family often focus more on social policy and education (Budge and Keman 1990: 97). Furthermore, legislative bills can range from highly conflictual redistributive welfare reforms to technical or *hodgepodge* bills that are not suited for political contests (Müller and Jenny 2004: 313). One aspect we consider here is the electoral salience of an issue area. Given scarce resources and time constraints, MPs focus on bills that they *own*, i.e. that are salient for themselves (and their parties and electorate) but not their opponents, so that they can gain support and votes in the electoral game. We would therefore expect bipartisan bills to be successful when an issue area is not particularly salient for any of the legislative actors involved. Otherwise, there are clear incentives to use the legislative arena to score in the electoral game.

Research Design and Measures

We test our expectations on the determinants of the introduction and the success of bipartisan bills on the basis of law initiatives and bills submitted to the upper or lower chamber of the Belgium and the German legislature between 1986 and 2003.[2] This in mainly because coalition governments are typical in both countries and a significant share of bipartisan bills finally become enacted (see Bräuninger and Debus 2009: 819–820). In terms of party competition patterns, both countries represent the so-called *Benelux* type of party constellation, with three ideological poles – a Christian democratic, a socialist and a liberal pole (Laver and Hunt 1992: 56). While liberal parties in both countries share policy positions with the Christian Democrats on economic issues, they adopt quite similar positions in societal affairs. This makes legislative activity and decision-making in Belgium and Germany an ideal test for our model. In contrast to other studies (e.g. Döring 1995, Huber and Shipan 2002; Döring and Hallerberg 2004) that focus on economic and labour policy issues, we seek to substantiate our results by considering legislative policy-making in all policy areas. This allows us to incorporate policy-area specific conflict not only between coalition parties, but also between governments and parliaments.

Our dependent variables are, first, the *initiator of a bill*, and, secondly, the legislative approval or *success of bipartisan bills*. As mentioned above, we distinguish between four types of initiator. Government bills are law proposals formally presented by the government as a whole. Bills introduced by MPs belonging to a party that holds government offices are coded as *government party bills*. Thirdly, we consider bills that were introduced by members of opposition parties. Fourthly, we coded bipartisan bills if members of at least one government and one opposition party introduced the bill into the legislative process.[3]

Contrary to what one might read about party discipline and the dualism of government and opposition in parliamentary systems, there is a significant proportion of bills where at least one governing party legislator worked together with legislators from the opposition (see Bräuninger and Debus 2009: 819). When comparing Belgium and Germany, the largest share of bipartisan bills can be found in Germany (10.5%; see Table 7.1). This is no surprise because of the role of German Laender in federal policy-making. Yet, the share of bills introduced by members of government and opposition parties in Belgium is also quite remarkable (7.5%).

---

[2] We treat the terms law initiatives and bills as synonyms even though, strictly speaking, law initiatives by Länder delegates in the German Bundesrat become bills only by majority vote.

[3] We use the term "private members' bills" although in the German Bundestag only groups of MPs can initiate bills.

Table 7.1 Number of legislative bills introduced in the Belgian and German lower and upper chamber by initiator (in %)

Country	Government	Governing parties	Opposition parties	Government and opposition	Total
Belgium	1,658 (19.8)	2,845 (33.9)	3,254 (38.8)	625 (7.5)	8,382 (100)
Germany	1,573 (44.6)	630 (17.8)	957 (27.1)	371 (10.5)	3,531 (100)

Table 7.2 Total number and percentage share of passed and failed bills in Belgium and Germany by initiator

	Government		Governing parties		Opposition parties		Government and opposition	
Country	Passed	Failed	Passed	Failed	Passed	Failed	Passed	Failed
Belgium	1,542 (93.0)	116 (7.0)	281 (9.9)	2,564 (90.1)	75 (2.3)	3,179 (97.7)	206 (33.0)	419 (67.0)
Germany	1,418 (90.2)	155 (9.9)	378 (60.0)	252 (40.0)	38 (4.0)	919 (96.0)	138 (37.2)	233 (62.8)

Table 7.2 shows the absolute number and the share of successful and unsuccessful bills by the four types of initiators in both countries. The figures show that the dominant actor in legislative agenda-setting is indeed the government. If the cabinet introduces a law proposal, then more than nine out of ten bills will pass. In contrast, when bills are introduced by parliamentary groups that support the government, 60% will be enacted in Germany, while only 10% of government party bills in Belgium will finally pass. More interestingly, a small, but significant share of successful bills is initiated by members of opposition parties. Between 2% and 4% of bills written solely by opposition parties survive the legislative process, respectively. With regard to the bills initiated by members of both camps, the share of successful bills is quite similar in both countries. In Belgium and Germany most of the bipartisan bills fail, but an appreciable share of bipartisan proposals are finally successful. In sum, while the government certainly dominates law-making, it is not the sole agenda-setter, and parliamentary actors are sometimes able to introduce bills that are ultimately successful. The question then concerns the conditions that favour (successful) agenda-setting by parliamentary actors.

As outlined above, two variables that may explain agenda-setting and bill success are the *policy conflict within government* and the *policy conflict within parliament*. The question of how to measure differences in the ideological and/or policy positions of parties and voters has recently attracted extensive attention in the literature (Budge 2001; Mair 2001; Volkens 2007). Expert surveys (e.g. Castles and Mair 1984; Huber and Inglehart 1995) have frequently been used to locate parties on an ideological-programmatic left–right scale and then to analyse their impact on policies and policy outcomes. This uni-dimensional model, however, does not account for differences in the policy conflict when one is interested in specific policy areas.

Table 7.3 Assignment of policy areas to policy dimensions

Policy areas in legislation dataset	Economic affairs and energy, finance	Interior, justice, social affairs, education, science and research, health	Foreign affairs, defence	Traffic, mobility, construction, consumer protection, environment, animal protection, agriculture	European integration, regionalization
Policy dimensions covered by Laver and Hunt (1992)	Economic policy (increase services vs. cut taxes)	Social policy (promote permissive social policy vs. not)	Foreign policy (pro vs. anti friendly relations with USSR)	Environmental policy (environment over growth vs. growth over environment)	Decentralization policy (pro vs. anti decentralization of decisions)

In this study, we therefore use data from the Laver and Hunt (1992) expert survey, which reports the positions of parties on eight common policy dimensions for 25 Western democracies (Laver and Hunt 1992: 49–53).[4] To define not only comparable but also exhaustive policy categories, we took the typical cabinet structure in each country as a base and came up with a list of 12 ministries. A bill's policy area was identified by coding titles and short descriptions of bills in the official legislative databases. Table 7.3 summarizes how policy fields were matched to five of the policy dimensions covered by the Laver and Hunt (1992) expert survey.

Based on these party positions, we use the policy-area-specific veto player distance between governmental parties (Tsebelis 2002; see also Schulz and König 2000: 658) as a measure of intra-governmental policy conflict. For the policy conflict between government and opposition parties in parliament, we follow the literature on polarization in party systems (Taylor and Herman 1971: 34) and use the distance between the centres of gravity of the government and opposition camp. The centre of gravity is the weighted average of the ideological positions of the parties in government (opposition), where the weight is the vote share among all coalition (opposition) parties (Cusack 2001). This follows the "classic" assumption that the strength of a coalition party or its impact on the policy agenda is associated with its strength in the cabinet (Gamson 1961; Browne and Franklin 1973; Browne and Frendreis 1980; Schofield and Laver 1985; Warwick and Druckman 2001). Note that, strictly speaking, our index measures the conflict between the executive and the legislative opposition rather than the whole legislature. The conflict between the government (as a unitary actor) and the parties in the legislative coalition is, however, already captured by the veto player distance.

[4] We refer to the Laver and Hunt (1992) data rather than the more recent Benoit and Laver (2006) expert survey because the time of data collection of the Laver and Hunt study falls approximately in the middle of our observation period. Policy positions on the original 20-point scale were recoded to range from -1 (far left) to $+1$ (far right).

Another set of hypotheses refers to issue ownership and the role of the electoral cycle. We expect that MPs from the governing parties and the opposition camp have higher incentives to introduce bills before elections rather than in the middle of the legislative term. We therefore use a dummy variable that takes on a value of one if the bill is introduced in the 365-day period prior to the next election and zero otherwise. Because party-specific information on the dimension saliency is also provided by the Laver and Hunt (1992) expert survey, we can assign a measure for issue ownership to each law proposal. For example, the *issue area saliency* of an economic policy bill is the weighted average economic policy saliency of all government parties less than the same weighted average for all opposition parties. Positive values then indicate the respective issue is more important for the government, while negative scores imply that the opposition attaches more weight to the policy area a bill belongs to.[5]

To account for the *size of the government majority* in parliament, we use the government parties' seat share of all seats in the lower house at a point in time. With regard to the fact that a number of law proposals are introduced towards the end of a legislative period, we include a variable that measures the *remaining time* in the respective legislation period until the end of the term. Finally, we also control for *divided government* between two chambers and for the effect of required approval by the second chamber by including a dummy for strong *bicameral settings*.

One may argue that the closeness of the coalition government, i.e. the number of government parties that participated in the writing and introduction of a *bipartisan* bill, is an important factor when it comes to the legislative voting stage. According to our data, in 339 of 996 identified bipartisan bills (34%) all governing parties participated in the drafting of those law proposals. The degree of support of all government bills should have a decisive impact on the success of a bill introduced by governing and opposition parties. Table 7.4 shows the total number and percentage of bipartisan bills by the support of governing parties. In the left column, the number as well as the share of passed and failed bipartisan bills are reported that were introduced by (MPs of) all governing and at least one opposition party. We see that in Belgium and Germany at least 60% of these bills are finally successful. Comparing these figures to the ones for bills without the support of all governing parties, the picture clearly changes. Only 15.6% of bills with bipartisan initiators in Germany

Table 7.4 Success of bipartisan bills by degree of government party support (absolute numbers and percentages)

	Support by all government parties		Support by some government parties	
Country	Passed	Failed	Passed	Failed
Belgium	107 (61.9)	66 (38.2)	99 (21.9)	353 (78.1)
Germany	106 (63.9)	60 (36.1)	32 (15.6)	173 (84.4)

[5] We use the weighted average of government party saliencies for a government initiator, and the weighted average of all parliamentary parties for initiators belonging to both camps.

and 21.9% of the same type of law proposals in Belgium are successful. In sum, the table provides clear evidence that the *share of governing parties that support a bipartisan bill*, as expected, correlates to the success of the bill.

Analysis

To test the above hypotheses, we specify a Heckman selection model (Heckman 1976, 1979). This procedure not only captures our theory appropriately, it is also more efficient and robust than other procedures and – most importantly – the only consistent estimator given the truncated distribution of the sample in the second stage (see Plümper et al. 2006: 24). As we described in the theoretical section of the paper, the first stage of analysis is whether MPs from the government manage to work with oppositional members of parliament, so that a bipartisan bill is proposed. Once a bipartisan law proposal is introduced, the second stage of its fate is whether it finds support among the government or at least some government parties (and their intra-party groups) on the one hand and (parts of) the parliamentary opposition on the other hand. Since an MP can have different motives for introducing a bill, e.g. signalling policy preferences or showing individual legislative activity to gain attention before an election, the question is whether the bill's intention is attractive to a majority from the government and opposition camp. Thus, different incentives and mechanisms motivate MPs to introduce bipartisan bills and, finally, to decide whether these bills become enacted or not.

We run a dynamic Heckman selection model to deal with these problems (see Table 7.5). In this statistical model, the estimated mean function in the second stage is conditioned on the selection process of the first stage. The econometric logic behind the Heckman model fits our theoretical problem. It reflects the self-selection process in the first stage and also assumes that the probability of the introduction of a bipartisan bill influences the likelihood of acceptance of a bill with bipartisan initiators in the second stage.

The statistical analysis includes all Belgian and German law proposals in the first step, that is, bills introduced by the government, government parties, oppositional actors and members from both government and opposition camps. This results in 11,914 observations in the statistical analysis. In the second stage, we exclude all but bipartisan law proposals from the dataset leading to a sample of 996 bills from both countries. The period under observation spans from 1988 to 2003 in the Belgian case and from 1987 to 2002 in the case of German law proposals.

We start with analysing the factors that have an impact on the introduction of a bipartisan bill. The results are mostly in line with our expectations. We find that, as compared to the government bills, government party bills and law proposal introduced solely by the opposition, bipartisan bills are less likely when the seat share of a majority government is large and when the difference in issue area saliency between government and opposition camps is large. The results also suggest that bipartisan bills are more likely when policy conflict within the government

Table 7.5 Heckman probit selection model for the likelihood of the introduction and adoption of bipartisan law proposals

	(1)	(2)
Second stage: Voting stage		
Intra-governmental policy conflict	−0.549** (0.205)	−0.578* (0.235)
Share of government parties supporting the bills	2.126** (0.300)	2.118** (0.315)
Divided government/strong bicameralism	−0.151 (0.129)	−0.218 (0.285)
Urgency procedure	0.627** (0.183)	0.661** (0.191)
Germany	−0.158 (0.126)	0.843** (0.212)
Constant	−0.630 (0.645)	−0.859 (0.761)
First stage: Proposal and initiation stage		
Seat share	−1.209** (0.311)	−1.308** (0.339)
Intra-governmental policy conflict	0.314** (0.121)	0.310* (0.138)
Policy conflict between government and opposition camp	−0.289+ (0.154)	−0.337* (0.171)
Pre-election period	−0.137* (0.057)	−0.241** (0.065)
Issue area saliency (difference between government and opposition camp)	−1.226* (0.526)	−1.577* (0.615)
Finance policy	−0.179** (0.059)	−0.271** (0.071)
Foreign and defence policy	−0.974** (0.103)	−0.802** (0.113)
European policy	−0.864** (0.156)	−0.808** (0.215)
Divided government/strong bicameralism	0.102+ (0.059)	−0.070 (0.093)
Germany	0.247** (0.055)	−0.206** (0.070)
Remaining time in legislative term	−0.008** (0.002)	−0.014** (0.002)
Constant	−0.504* (0.204)	−0.260 (0.218)
argtanh(ρ)	−0.591* (0.281)	−0.435 (0.318)
Observations (uncensored observations)	11,914 (996)	11,150 (735)
Wald χ^2	84.58	97.74
$[p \geq \chi^2]$ whole model	0.0000	0.0000
LR Chi-square	274.78	239.57
$[p > \chi^2]$ first stage	0.0000	0.0000
Pseudo R^2 first stage	0.040	0.044

Standard errors in parentheses; $^{+}p < 0.1$, *<0.05, $^{**}p < 0.01$

coalitions (operationalized by the veto player distance) is large. This is in line with the expectations derived from our two-stage legislative model. Divided government in a bicameral setting does also have the expected positive effect, but only at a 10% significance level. With respect to our control variables, we note that in finance, foreign, defence and European affairs, bipartisan bills are less likely than any other bills with different types of initiator. This is quite reasonable as the government has an agenda-setting prerogative in these policy areas dealing with government budgets, international treaties and the transposition of European law. We also note that bipartisan bills are generally more likely in Germany than in Belgium. Finally, the significant impact of the issue saliency variable once more shows that party competition is important. The negative coefficient suggests that bipartisan bills are more likely in policy areas that are of lesser importance for MPs from the government camp, but that are rather of relevance for members belonging to the parliamentary opposition. This makes sense since bipartisan activity in policy areas that are of relatively low importance for the government should result in only small conflicts and discussion inside the coalition government.

Our second bloc of hypotheses deals with the determinants of the success of the 996 bipartisan bills included in the Heckman selection model. We first look at institutional settings. First, divided government under strong bicameralism has no significant effect. Second, when the government invokes an urgency procedure, bipartisan bills are more likely to get passed by the parliament. This is the purpose of the urgency procedure as a means of governmental agenda control (Döring 1995).

The results for the measures of policy conflict are also in line with our expectations. The regression model shows that the veto player distance of government parties has a negative effect on the success of bipartisan bills. Finally, we note that the share of government parties supporting the bill has a positive and substantial effect on bill success which is in line with the expectations above.

One might object that bill initiatives introduced in Germany by Laender governments through the upper chamber (Bundesrat) should not be pooled with bills presented in the lower chamber. We tested for a possible distortion of our analysis by running our statistical model again without bill initiatives of German Laender. The second column of Table 7.5 shows the results. The effects are robust, suggesting that bill submission through the German Bundesrat largely follows the same logic that we find in the rest of our sample.

Conclusion

We have focused on two aspects of legislative activity. Firstly, we argued that the government is not the sole agenda-setter. According to the two-stage model presented, there are incentives for MPs from the government parties to introduce bills which have been co-authored by opposition members of parliament. As the descriptive results have shown, there is even a share of successful law proposals of bipartisan bills that is worth being studied when analysing legislative activity and political reforms more generally. Secondly, we looked at the determinants that influence the success of bipartisan bills in two parliamentary systems, Belgium and Germany. The results show that ideological conflict between government veto players and between government majority and opposition in parliament have a decisive impact on the success of bipartisan bills, but the share of governing parties that supports the respective bipartisan law proposal is also decisive.

The findings suggest that a more detailed analysis of the relationship between government and MPs supporting the government would be worthwhile. One goal for future research would be to study and actually measure the assumed ideological gap between the government (or cabinet members) and each MP who supports it (cf. Kam et al. 2007; Kam 2009; Bernauer and Bräuninger 2009; Bäck et al. 2009). By doing so we would be in a better position to consider whether, for instance, a backbencher introduces a bill because of a distinct policy stance or simply to achieve an enhanced profile before an imminent election campaign. Furthermore, if the positions of MPs were known, we could map them on (salient) policy dimensions and identify those who are more or less likely to work with the parliamentary opposition. A second goal would be to incorporate individual characteristics of MPs such as their functional position in the parliamentary party and the socio-economic structure of the MP's constituency. On that basis, we would like to know whether it is only backbenchers or even members of the party elite who tend to work across the government–opposition divide (cf. Bishin 2000). In the case of major policy reforms resulting from exogenous events or policy shocks, it would be surprising if leading politicians did not pick up on such issues, missing the chance to win medial attraction and thus the chance to get in a stronger position inside the parliamentary party.

In addition, data on the economic and social structures of constituencies would allow us to analyse whether MPs from similar constituencies work together. The inclusion of such information would offer more detailed insights into the emergence and success of the government and parliamentary bills identified here. Finally, a detailed analysis of the characteristics and content of each bill seems to be worthwhile. On that basis, one could, first, analyse whether the bill proposes a major change of the status quo. Various techniques exist to measure the substance of each law proposal (see, e.g. König and Mäder 2009; see also the contribution by König et al. in Chap. 4). Secondly, one incentive for further research is whether political actors use their legislative activity to react to public opinion or the mass media on specific policy issues (e.g. Petrocik 1996; Riker 1996; Walgrave et al. 2008). This would enable us to analyse whether parliamentary parties not only use questions to government officials to clarify their issue competence (Green-Pedersen and Krogstrup 2008), but also use the stage of legislative agenda-setting to signal their positions and capabilities for solving problems in such policy areas that are seen as relevant by a significant share of the electorate.

References

Bäck H, Debus M, Müller WC (2009) The ideological cohesion of political parties. An analysis of parliamentary speeches in Austria and Germany. Paper presented at the ECPR General Conference, Potsdam, Germany, 10–12 September 2009

Benoit K, Laver M (2006) Party policy in modern democracies. Routledge, London

Bergman T, Müller WC, Strøm K, Blomgren M (2003) Democratic delegation and accountability: cross-national patterns. In: Strøm K, Müller WC, Bergman T (eds) Delegation and accountability in parliamentary democracies. Oxford University Press, Oxford, pp 109–220

Bernauer J, Bräuninger T (2009) Intra-party preference heterogeneity and faction membership in the 15th German Bundestag. A computational text analysis of parliamentary speeches. Ger Polit 18(3):385–402

Bishin BG (2000) Constituency influence in congress: does subconstituency matter? Legis Stud Q 25(3):389–415
Bowler S, Farrell DM, Katz RS (1999) Party cohesion, party discipline, and parliaments. In: Bowler S, Farrell DM, Katz RS (eds) Party discipline and parliamentary government. Ohio State University Press, Columbus, pp 3–22
Bräuninger T, Debus M (2009) Legislative agenda-setting in parliamentary democracies. Eur J Polit Res 48(6):804–839
Bräuninger T, König T (1999) The checks and balances of party federalism: German federal government in a divided legislature. Eur J Polit Res 36(2):207–234
Browne EC, Franklin MN (1973) Aspects of coalition payoffs in European parliamentary democracies. Am Polit Sci Rev 67(2):453–469
Browne EC, Frendreis JP (1980) Allocating coalition payoffs by conventional norm: an assessment of evidence for cabinet coalition situations. Am J Polit Sci 24(4):753–768
Budge I (2001) Theory and measurement of party policy positions. In: Budge I, Klingemann H-D, Volkens A, Bara J, Tannenbaum E (eds) Mapping policy preferences. Oxford University Press, Oxford, pp 75–90
Budge I, Keman H (1990) Parties and democracy. coalition formation and government functioning in twenty states. Oxford University Press, Oxford
Castles F, Mair P (1984) Left–right political scales: some expert judgements. Eur J Polit Res 12(1):73–88
Cowley P (2002) Revolts and rebellions: parliamentary voting under Blair. Politicos, London
Cusack TR (2001) Partisanship in the setting and coordination of fiscal and monetary policies. Eur J Polit Res 40(1):93–115
Depauw S, Martin S (2009) Legislative party discipline and cohesion in comparative perspective. In: Giannetti D, Benoit K (eds) Intra-party politics and coalition governments in parliamentary democracies. Routledge, London, pp 103–120
De Winter L, Dumont P (2003) Belgium: delegation and accountability under partitocratic rule. In: Strøm K, Müller WC, Bergman T (eds) Delegation and accountability in parliamentary democracies. Oxford University Press, Oxford, pp 253–280
De Winter L, Timmermans A, Dumont P (2000) Belgium: on government agreements, evangelists, followers, and heretics. In: Müller WC, Strøm K (eds) Coalition governments in Western Europe. Oxford University Press, Oxford, pp 300–355
Döring H (ed) (1995) Parliaments and majority rule in Western Europe. Campus/St. Martin's Press, Frankfurt
Döring H, Hallerberg M (eds) (2004) Patterns of parliamentary behaviour. passage of legislation across Western Europe. Ashgate, Aldershot
Epstein D (1998) Partisan and bipartisan signaling in congress. J Law Econ Organ 14(2):183–204
Fitzmaurice J (1992) Belgian paradoxes: the November 1991 election. West Eur Pol 15(4):178–182
Gallagher M, Laver M, Mair P (2006) Representative government in modern Europe: Institutions, parties, and governments. McGraw-Hill, New York
Gamson W (1961) A theory of coalition formation. Am Sociol Rev 26(3):373–382
Giannetti D, Laver M (2009) Party cohesion, party discipline, and party factions in Italy. In: Giannetti D, Benoit K (eds) Intra-party politics and coalition governments in parliamentary democracies. Routledge, London, pp 146–168
Gilligan T, Krehbiel K (1989) Asymmetric information and legislative rules with a heterogeneous government. Am J Polit Sci 33(2):459–490
Green-Pedersen C, Krogstrup J (2008) Immigration as a political issue in Denmark and Sweden. Eur J Polit Res 47(5):610–634
Groseclose T, McCarty N (2001) The politics of blame: bargaining before an audience. Am J Polit Sci 45(1):100–119
Harmel R, Janda K (1994) An integrated theory of party goals and party change. J Theor Polit 6(3):259–287

Heckman JJ (1976) The common structure of statistical models of truncation, sample selection, and limited dependent variables and a simple estimator for such models. Ann Econ Social Meas 5(4):475–492
Heckman JJ (1979) Sample selection bias as a specification error. Econometrica 47(1):153–161
Huber JD (1996) Rationalizing parliament: legislative institutions and party politics in France. Cambridge University Press, Cambridge
Huber JD, Inglehart R (1995) Expert interpretations of party space and party locations in 42 societies. Party Pol 1(1):73–111
Huber JD, Shipan CR (2002) Deliberate discretion: the institutional foundations of bureaucratic autonomy. Cambridge University Press, Cambridge
Kam C (2009) Party discipline and parliamentary government. Cambridge University Press, Cambridge
Kam C, Bianco W, Smyth R, Sened I (2007) Parliaments, cabinets, and uncovered sets. Paper presented at the ECPR General Conference, Pisa, Italy
König T, Mäder L (2009) Antwort auf die Replik von Daniel Göler zum Beitrag "Das Regieren jenseits des Nationalstaates und der Mythos einer 80-Prozent-Europäisierung in Deutschland". Polit Vierteljahresschr 50(1):80–85
Krehbiel K (1991) Information and legislative organization. University of Michigan Press, Ann Arbor
Laver M, Hunt WB (1992) Policy and party competition. Routledge, New York
Laver M, Shepsle KA (1996) Making and breaking governments. Cambridge University Press, Cambridge
Lupia A, Strøm K (1995) Coalition termination and the strategic timing of parliamentary elections. Am Polit Sci Rev 89(3):648–665
Mair P (2001) Searching for the positions of political actors: a review of approaches and an evaluation of expert surveys in particular. In: Laver M (ed) Estimating the policy positions of political actors. Routledge, London, pp 10–30
Mair P, Mudde C (1998) The party family and its study. Annu Rev Polit Sci 1:211–229
Mayhew DR (1974) Congress: the electoral connection. Yale University Press, New Haven
Müller WC (2000) Political parties in parliamentary democracies: making delegation and accountability work. Eur J Polit Res 37(3):309–333
Müller WC (2005) Die Relevanz von Institutionen für Koalitionstreue: Theoretische Überlegungen und Beobachtungen zur Bundesrepublik Deutschland. In: Ganghof S, Manow P (eds) Mechanismen der Politik. Campus, Frankfurt, pp 73–107
Müller WC, Jenny M (2004) Business as usual mit getauschten Rollen oder Konflikt- statt Konsensdemokratie? Parlamentarische Beziehungen unter der ÖVP-FPÖ-Koalition. Österreichische Zeitschrift für Politikwissenschaft 33(3):309–326
Müller WC, Strøm K (eds) (2000) Coalition governments in Western Europe. Oxford University Press, Oxford
Müller WC, Strøm K (2008) Coalition agreements and cabinet governance. In Strøm K, Müller WC, Bergman T (eds) Cabinets and coalition bargaining: the democratic life cycle in Western Europe. Oxford University Press, Oxford, pp 159–199
Patterson SC, Caldeira GA (1988) Party voting in the US congress. Br J Polit Sci 18(1):111–131
Petrocik JR (1996) Issue ownership in presidential elections, with a 1980 case study. Am J Polit Sci 40(3):825–850
Plümper T, Schneider CJ, Troeger V (2006) The politics of EU eastern enlargement: evidence from a Heckman selection model. Br J Polit Sci 36(1):17–38
Poguntke T (1993) Germany. Eur J Polit Res 24(4):435–440
Powell GB (2000) Elections as instruments of democracy: majoritarian and proportional visions. Yale University Press, New Haven
Riker W (1996) The strategy of rhetoric: campaigning for the American constitution. Yale University Press, New Haven
Saalfeld T (1995) Parteisoldaten und Rebellen: Fraktionen im Deutschen Bundestag 1949–1990. Leske und Budrich, Opladen

Saalfeld T (2005) Determinanten der Fraktionsdisziplin: Deutschland im internationalen Vergleich. In: Ganghof S, Manow P (eds) Mechanismen der Politik. Campus, Frankfurt, pp 35–71
Schofield N, Laver M (1985) Bargaining theory and portfolio payoffs in European government coalitions. Br J Polit Sci 15(1):143–164
Schulz H, König T (2000) Institutional reform and decision-making efficiency in the European Union. Am J Polit Sci 44(4):653–666
Sieberer U (2006) Party unity in parliamentary democracies. J Legis Stud 12(2):150–178
Strøm K, Müller WC (2009) Parliamentary democracy, agency problems, and party politics. In: Giannetti D, Benoit K (eds) Intra-party politics and coalition governments in parliamentary democracies. Routledge, London, pp 25–49
Strøm K, Müller WC, Bergman T (eds) (2003) Delegation and accountability in parliamentary democracies. Oxford University Press, Oxford
Taylor M, Herman VM (1971) Party systems and government stability. Am Polit Sci Rev 65(1): 28–37
Timmermans A (1998) Conflicts, agreements, and coalition governance. Acta Pol 33(4):409–432
Timmermans A (2006) Standing apart and sitting together: enforcing coalition agreements in multiparty systems. Eur J Polit Res 45(2):263–283
Tsebelis G (1995) Decision making in political systems: veto players in presidentialism, parliamentarism, multicameralism and multipartyism. Br J Polit Sci 25(3):289–325
Tsebelis G (1999) Veto players and law production in parliamentary democracies: an empirical analysis. Am Polit Sci Rev 93(3):591–608
Tsebelis G (2002) Veto players. how political institutions work. Princeton University Press, Princeton
Volkens A (2007) Strengths and weaknesses of approaches to measuring policy positions of parties. Elect Stud 26(1):108–120
Walgrave S, Soroka S, Nuytemans M (2008) A longitudinal analysis of media, parliament, and government in Belgium (1993 to 2000). Comp Polit Stud 41(6):814–836
Warwick PV, Druckman JN (2001) Portfolio salience and the proportionality of payoffs in coalition governments. Br J Polit Sci 31(4):627–649
Wilson RK, Young CD (1997) Cosponsorship in the U.S. Congress. Legis Stud Q 22(1):25–43

Chapter 8
Why Don't Veto Players Use Their Power?

Thomas König and Dirk Junge

Veto Players and Voting in the Council: The Empirical Puzzle

Among the striking features of European Union (EU) legislation is the culture of consensus among an increasing number of member states with veto rights and varying interests in European integration and Commission initiatives. This has aroused criticism of analytical approaches to EU legislative decision making that focus on the voting preferences and power of the member states (e.g. Heisenberg 2005; Achen 2006). On closer inspection of their empirical voting behaviour, it remains extremely puzzling that member states almost always support Commission proposals, thereby refraining from exercising their veto power and trying to bring about policy change in the Council. One hypothesis would be that they adhere to a norm of consensus (Lewis 2003). Even scholars who sympathize with this line of argument on consensus voting behaviour in the Council must nonetheless concede that the same member states constantly make attempts to reform the EU's legislative framework and, in particular, the voting rules in the Council, as they have been doing at the most recent Intergovernmental Conferences (IGCs) in Amsterdam (1997) and Nice (2000) and with the current Lisbon treaty. Why do these member states repeatedly attempt to reform the Council's voting rules when they are always in favour of the Commission's initiatives? Why do they repeatedly refer to the need to improve the EU's obsolete legislative procedures, hence officially requesting an increase in the EU's legitimacy, transparency and capacity to act in legislative decision-making? Apart from these official justifications, the need to reform the Council's legislative rules is also suggested by several politico-economic indicators pointing to a substantial variation in, and a great (and expanding) distance between, the interests of the member states, which increases the danger of a legislative blockage in the Council.

1. The number of member states rose from 12 in the mid-1980s to 15 in 1995, 25 in 2004 and 27 in 2007 (Sutter 2000; Napel and Widgren 2004).

T. König (✉) and D. Junge
Mannheim University, Mannheim, Germany
e-mail: t.koenig@uni-mannheim.de; djunge@mail.uni-mannheim.de

T. König et al. (eds.), *Reform Processes and Policy Change: Veto Players and Decision-Making in Modern Democracies*, Studies in Public Choice 16,
DOI 10.1007/978-1-4419-5809-9_8, © Springer Science+Business Media, LLC 2010

2. The macroeconomic indicators for their national economic and welfare systems reveal increasing structural differences between the member states, mostly owing to enlargement and other 'external shocks' (Baldwin et al. 1997; Sapir 2004)
3. The variation in the programmatic positions of the political parties in the member states is also increasing, even with respect to the EU's core policy domains, owing to national elections and different public demands (Franklin and Wlezien 1997; Franchino 2007).

From an analytical perspective, this higher number of member states with veto power, in combination with this increasing diversity of interests (of a larger number of member states), would lead us to expect an increase in the likelihood of a No vote in the Council rather than the promotion of consensus across Commission proposals (Romer and Rosenthal 1978; Tsebelis 2002; Scharpf 2006). According to Tsebelis's analytical veto player perspective (2008), member states therefore have good reasons for being concerned about the EU's legislative framework although the aggregated legislative statistics of the EU suggest evidence of a culture of consensus in the Council: the numbers reveal that, over recent decades, the adoption rate of Commission proposals has continuously exceeded 90%. Thus, pending Commission initiatives have been adopted even after treaty revisions that have changed the rules of the legislative procedures. Commission initiatives also found support after several enlargement rounds that have increased the number of member states (Hagemann and de Clerck-Sachsse 2007; König 2007). On closer inspection of the voting behaviour of the member states, several authors provide further evidence for this empirical regularity of Council consensus, drawing attention to the Council's statistical voting records according to which only few member states eventually cast No votes if a qualified Council majority guarantees the final adoption of a Commission proposal (Mattila and Lane 2001; Mattila 2004; Heisenberg 2005; Hayes-Renshaw et al. 2006).

Although these statistics suggest evidence of a consensus culture in the Council, it still remains an open question whether member states support Commission initiatives owing to a specific strategy or to a norm among the actors involved that prevents member states from using their veto power. From an analytical perspective, another question that arises is which actor is able to prevent member states from using their veto power in the Council – is it the Commission or are the member states themselves able to resolve their conflicts? Compared with the strong assumption about the decisive impact of norms, which may transform member states' interests, a simple analytical explanation would be that a well-informed Commission avoids proposing initiatives that would lead to a divided Council. In the extreme, if the Commission is able to exclude contested proposals from the agenda, member states have no incentive to make use of their veto power and can always support the Commission's initiatives. Another analytical explanation could be that the member states themselves seek consensus in the Council when their interests in a particular Commission proposal arouse only some disagreement. When several member states are in favour of policy change, they have an incentive to reach a compromise and are perhaps willing to make concessions to those member states in favour of the status quo. Independently of the explanatory power of a particular analytical or normative explanation, we believe that understanding the empirical puzzle of the Council's culture of consensus and the simultaneous attempt by the member states to reform the voting provisions of the Council by treaty revision requires consideration of their empirical voting preferences.[1] In other words, the empirical question is whether the interests of the member states are already compatible and harmonious when the Commission initiates proposals, or whether there is actually some level of contestation and dispute between the member states, foreshadowing the rejection of a Commission proposal by the Council, which is, however, finally adopted by the member states.

Currently, the common wisdom is that strong norms can affect member states' voting behaviour and prevent them from using their veto power even when their interests are not in harmony. Apart from the normative consensus literature, which draws inferences about the strong impact of norms from legislative statistics (e.g. Heisenberg 2005; Hayes-Renshaw et al. 2006), Thomson et al. (2006) analyse contested Commission proposals in the period from 1999 to 2001 from an empirical–analytical perspective and observe a high error rate of proposal-specific models in their prediction of the outcome location of adopted legislation (Schneider et al. 2006). Their analyses show that these predictions significantly underestimate member states' support for Commission initiatives and too often forecast vetoes and the maintenance of the status quo. Achen (2006) therefore points to the important role of informal norms for Council support of these contested proposals in EU legislative decision making. Although this research also concludes that the procedural provision of veto power is less important for EU legislative decision-making, Junge and König (2007) draw attention to the empirical specification of voting preferences. This specification may also have an important impact on the models' predictive power regarding legislative outcomes and their prediction error, respectively. On closer inspection of the sources of error, they find that the specification of the policy space – by either (un)weighting the issues of a proposal regarding the actors' saliencies or (un)restricting the number of issues – affects the predictions of these analytical models more than do the correct identification of the voting weights and the legalistic interpretation of the procedures.

In brief, the empirical literature finds disagreements in the Council, but the proposal-specific study of their solution from an analytical perspective does not provide sufficient insight into the empirical puzzle of consensus in the Council. It therefore remains an open question whether member states follow a general norm or whether they apply a specific strategy for reaching compromise and adopting Commission proposals by consensus in a contested Council – and, if the latter, how this strategy works in practice. More specifically, the question is whether current

[1] The data set for the empirical analysis in this article can be found at http://eup.sagepub.com/supplemental. By voting preferences, we mean the relative distance between the status quo and an actor's ideal position and between the proposed change and his/her ideal position. This preference is measured by the actor's position in multidimensional policy spaces weighted by his/her relative saliency across dimensions. If the difference between the two distances is negative, the actor is predicted to vote in favour of the status quo; otherwise, he/she supports the proposed change.

analytical models can explain Council consensus or whether they have to consider the strong impact of norms for predicting the voting behaviour of the member states.

This study therefore departs from prior work by investigating more closely the voting preferences and strategies of the member states in the Council. For this purpose, we start by calculating the predictive error of proposal-specific models that derive the voting preferences of the member states separately for each initiative before we examine the potential of various kinds of logrolling across Commission proposals to explain Council consensus. Thus, instead of developing and testing a new voting model and comparing the predictive power of rival approaches to the outcome of Commission proposals, we are interested in the empirical voting behaviour of the member states and, more specifically, in logrolling strategies that can explain the culture of consensus in the Council. Our research design also diverges from previous Council studies on contested Commission proposals (e.g. Selck 2004; Steunenberg and Selck 2006; Bailer and Schneider 2006; Thomson and Hosli 2006) by additionally including data on voting behaviour in the Council that we gathered from the minutes of the final meeting of the Council on each proposal. This allows us to determine the predictive power of proposal-specific analytical models and to distinguish between actors' voting preferences on the one hand and the actual strategies they employ to pursue their interests on the other.

Furthermore, we avoid selecting a particular strategy from the set of all available strategies in order to verify the explanatory power of analytical models. Rather, inspection of the institutional organization of the Council suggests distinguishing between two strategies that member states can apply to reach consensus in the Council. These 'institutional' logrolling strategies may affect their voting preferences, namely by linking (a) domain-specific and (b) intertemporally contested Commission proposals. In brief, the institutional organization of the Council entails a coordinating presidency and a three-level committee system with a working group level that helps to coordinate contested proposal-specific interests (König and Pöter 2001; Hage 2007, 2008), while the Committee of the Permanent Representatives (Coreper) promotes logrolling across the ministerial level within policy domains. Our results finally reveal that these logrolling strategies within and across policy domains can indeed offer a powerful explanation for consensus in a contested Council. This suggests that it is the institutional organization of the Council that promotes logrolling opportunities for the member states and their continuous support of Commission proposals.

Veto Power, Voting Preferences and Consensus: Why Bother?

In the literature on European integration, veto player theory plays a prominent role in understanding the inter-institutional distribution of power between the Commission, the Council and the European Parliament; whether the institutional provisions are themselves subject to change by means of treaty reforms, i.e. by the treaty of Amsterdam in 1999 (Tsebelis and Garrett 2001; Slapin 2006), the Nice treaty in 2003 (Yataganas and Tsebelis 2005) and the most recent treaty reforms in 2007 (Tsebelis and Proksch 2007); whether the membership size of the EU expands in 1995, 2004 and 2007 (König and Bräuninger 2004); whether the legislative procedures include the European Parliament as an additional veto player since 1993 and 1999 (Steunenberg 1994, 1997; Tsebelis 1994; Crombez 1996, 1997, 2000; König and Pöter 2001; Tsebelis and Garrett 2000, 2001); or whether the adopted bills are correctly implemented on time (Mastenbroek 2003; König and Luetgert 2009). Tsebelis (2002: 248–282) himself devotes a large part of his book *Veto Players: How Political Institutions Work* to the study of EU institutions, and, most recently, Scharpf (2006) renewed his joint decision-making trap approach, shifting it closer towards veto player theory and arguing that both approaches were based on similar theoretical considerations relevant for the analysis of EU decision making.

In the analytical tradition of studying EU legislative decision making, the institutional veto players are the Commission, the member states and sometimes the European Parliament – all these players interacting in a legislative procedure, with actors having both the interest and the power to change the status quo. In brief, analytical models share the assumption that actors have an ideal notion of the eventual legislative outcome and exercise power by voting on behalf of their interest in a proposed outcome (Hotelling 1929; Enelow and Hinich 1984; Poole 2005). In most applications of this perspective, an actor's voting preference is identified by his/her individual distance from a Commission proposal in relation to the status quo: if the distance from the status quo is larger, the actor will vote in support of the proposal; otherwise, he/she will vote against its adoption (Enelow and Hinich 1984; Tsebelis 1995, 2002; Poole 2005).

Inferring voting preferences from an actor's individual distance from a proposal relative to the status quo is, however, not an easy empirical task. Often, a proposal raises more than one controversial issue and thus allows for an eventual trading of interests in a multidimensional policy space. This possibility of trading creates additional opportunities for finding compromise and compensation by increasing the incentives for an actor to vote in support of a proposal (Tollison and Willett 1979). Furthermore, member states usually attach actor-specific saliencies to those issues of a multidimensional proposal that might ultimately shape their voting preferences. The final votes may also differ in their impact on the outcome prediction whenever the member states have weighted votes under the procedure of qualified majority voting[2] and whenever the European Parliament performs as an additional veto player in the co-decision procedure. Figure 8.1 shows how these elements determine the voting preferences of the actors as well as the consequences predicted by analytical models for the outcome of the proposal.

[2] In the period under study, 62 out of 87 total votes are needed for the adoption of a Commission proposal under the qualified majority rule in the Council. The Treaty of Amsterdam provided Germany, Italy, France and the United Kingdom with ten votes, Spain with eight votes, Austria, Belgium, Greece, the Netherlands, Portugal and Sweden with four votes and Denmark, Ireland and Finland with three votes, while Luxembourg has only two votes.

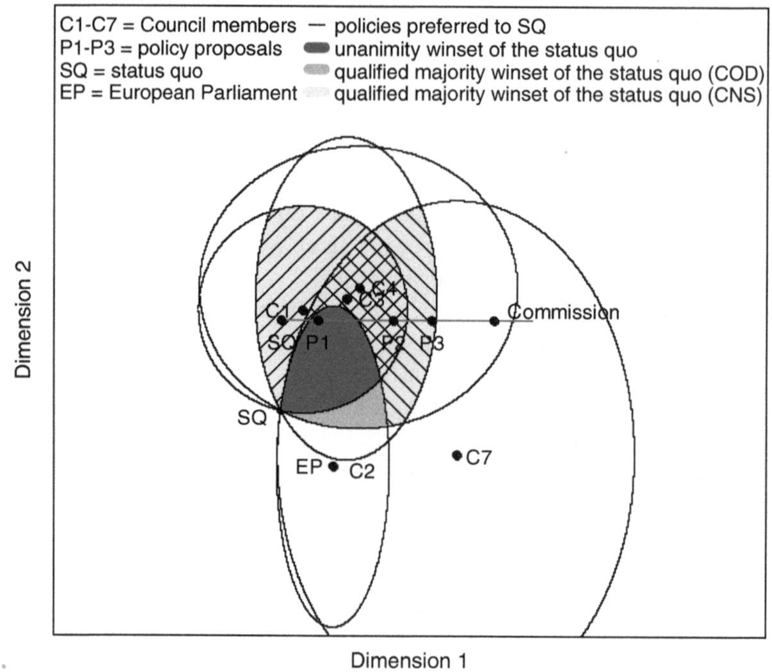

Fig. 8.1 A spatial model of legislative decision making in the EU decisive players in a two-dimensional policy space

As shown in Fig. 8.1, all member states C1 to C7 plus the European Parliament and the Commission have ideal points (referring to their position on a policy) in a two-dimensional policy space that allows for trading between their interests. They may also attach different saliencies to the two issues of the proposal, a fact that is expressed by indifference curves with an elliptical form. According to the analytical perspective, member states prefer all proposals P inside these ellipses to the status quo and should therefore vote for their adoption. Hence, all actors are predicted to vote in favour of proposal P1. However, C2 is expected to reject P2 and P3, and the former might be rejected by C1 as well. Furthermore, analytical models can also consider their voting weights and further procedural provisions – such as the qualified majority rule in the Council and/or the veto right of the European Parliament (EP) in the co-decision procedure – to predict the final outcome. Hence, the evaluation of an analytical model's predictive power for legislative outcomes and of the voting behaviour of member states depends on the (accurate) specification of their voting preferences. Therefore, the following empirical analysis applies a fully specified model that takes into account the saliencies and the voting weights of the member states on all dimensions of a proposal.

As can be seen from Fig. 8.1, it also follows that it is difficult to make inferences from outcome predictions about the voting behaviour of the member states. In particular, the distance between an observed and a predicted outcome does not provide sufficient information on the sources of error, i.e. to what extent the voting preference of a single or more actors is wrongly specified and/or whether the error is caused by a wrong identification of agenda-setting, amendment power, etc. Nor can legislative statistics – whether they report the adoption rate of proposals or the voting behaviour of the member states – provide sufficient information on this error rate because it is impossible to draw inferences about the reasons for consensus without considering the empirical voting preferences of the member states. In order to specify these empirical voting preferences, we need data on the actors' interests in each proposal, which we propose to combine with the information on their observed voting behaviour.

The DEU Data: Actors' Interests in Contested Commission Proposals

For the specification of the member states' empirical voting preferences, the DEU (decision making in the European Union) study provides quantitative estimates for actors' interests with respect to contested Commission proposals initiated between 1999 and 2001 (Thomson et al. 2006). We propose to combine the DEU data with the voting records of the Council in order to closely examine the voting behaviour of each member state. In the DEU study, key informants first identified the controversial issues raised by each Commission proposal. Second, these experts worked out the policy position initially favoured by each of the 15 member states, the Commission and the EP, and the levels of salience they attached to those 174 issues from 66 Commission proposals, respectively. For the selection of a proposal, each case had to attract some public awareness in the period under study[3] A second selection criterion was that some controversy had to have arisen during the decision-making process of the proposal.

Both criteria suggest a selection bias of the DEU data towards contested proposals. For a closer assessment of the representativeness of the DEU data for EU legislative decision making, Table 8.1 shows the comparison of the DEU and CELEX *(Communitatis Europeae Lex)* sample distribution with respect to the Council voting rule, the involvement of the EP, policy domains and other characteristics of EU legislative decision making. In this period, CELEX was the official database for Commission initiatives containing major characteristics of the legislative process.[4]

[3] To guarantee some public awareness and controversy, proposals have been selected for the study only if they had been mentioned in the Agence Europe, a news service for EU affairs, and revealed at least a minimum level of conflict in the interviews (Thomson et al. 2006).

[4] In a recent study, König et al. (2006) checked the reliability of CELEX data using PreLex – another EU legislative database PreLex – and found that more than 90% of all cases correspond across these different sources of information, although PreLex documents the legislative process, CELEX contains legislative events.

Table 8.1 Representativeness of the DEU study

	Domain	DEU 1999–2000 (%)	CELEX 1984–2004 (%)	CELEX 1999–2000 (%)
Procedure	Consultation	40 (60.6)	8644 (78.1)	2405 (67.30)
	Co-decision	26 (39.4)	1529 (13.8)	1043 (29.21)
Voting rule	Unanimity	23 (34.8)	4341 (39.24)	1883 (52.73)
	QMV	43 (65.2)	6721 (60.75)	1563 (43.77)
Type	Decision	7 (10.6)	2942 (25.93)	1225 (34.30)
	Regulation	33 (50)	6393 (56.35)	1280 (35.84)
	Directive	26 (39.4)	2011 (17.72)	1066 (29.85)
Domain	Agriculture	14 (21.21)	2553 (22.5)	262 (7.34)
	Internal market	13 (19.69)	174 (1.53)	73 (2.04)
	Fisheries	7 (10.6)	865 (7.62)	105 (2.94)
	ECOFIN	6 (9.09)	112 (0.99)	27 (0.76)
	JHA	5 (7.57)	118 (1.04)	33 (0.92)
	General	6 (9.09)	63 (0.55)	21 (0.59)
	Others	15 (22.72)	7177 (64.89)	3050 (85.41)
Total		66 (100)	11062 (100)	3571 (100)

As shown in Table 8.1, most of the DEU cases were decided under the consultation procedure and about 65% by the qualified majority voting (QMV) rule in the Council, the latter applying voting weights of the member states. With respect to the distribution of all Commission proposals from 1984 to 2004, especially for the period of study from 1999 to 2000, we find that the DEU sample approximately reflects the overall distribution of the cases by procedures. Moreover, half of the DEU proposals are regulations, followed by a large number of directives, although the proportion of decisions is lower in the DEU data than in the overall legislation according to CELEX, which is unsurprising because decisions often address technical – and thus non-controversial – issues. Furthermore, the DEU sample pays tribute to the dominant role of agriculture, even though legislative activity in the agricultural domain greatly decreased in the second half of the 1990s. Proposals regarding the Internal Market, Economic and Financial Affairs (ECOFIN) and Justice and Home Affairs (JHA) are over-represented in the DEU sample owing to their important political activities, arousing more disagreement among the member states. None of the proposals is still pending, and only one has been rejected.

On closer inspection of the DEU data, each proposal contains one or more contested issues with estimates of the actors' interests (policy positions and saliencies), including the location of the status quo and legislative outcomes. For each issue, the interviewees were asked to assign the extreme values on a scale from 0 to 100 to those actors with the most extreme policy positions. They subsequently located the actors with intermediate positions (Thomson et al. 2006). A cross-validation of the data revealed that the DEU estimates are highly reliable as well as independent from the institutional affiliation of the experts (König et al. 2007).[5] More specifi-

[5] Comparing the DEU with data on seven cases negotiated in the conciliation committee, they find a surprisingly high similarity regarding the point locations of the EP, the Commission, the status

cally, 21% of all proposals are one-dimensional, 38% are two-dimensional and 41% have higher dimensional policy spaces with between three and six issues. For all cases, the actors have different saliencies and, since 79% of these cases are multidimensional, this should be reflected in the shape of the actors' utility functions by a fully specified analytical model.

Like all empirical studies, the DEU data are limited in that they lack specified values for more than half of the contested 162 issues, i.e. for the status quo and the policy position of at least one actor. In some cases, such missing values can pose a significant problem for the evaluation of analytical theories because the models usually assume complete information on the variables of the game (König et al. 2005). Research on missing values emphasizes the superiority of multiple imputation techniques against listwise deletion, but the question is which imputation method should be applied. In the following, we employ AMELIA, currently the most prominent imputation algorithm, for the imputation of missing actor positions (King et al. 2001). However, if proposals lack values for the status quo, we have to drop them from our analysis because we can hardly assume that the status quo location of one proposal is determined by that of other proposals. Table 8.2 shows whether this reduction of 18 proposals affects the representative nature of our study.

Table 8.2 Procedures and voting rules in the reduced DEU data set

		Number of proposals	Percentage	Number of issues	Percentage
Co-decision	QMV	14	29.17	35	33.02
	Unanimity	5	10.42	12	11.32
Consultation	QMV	18	37.5	42	39.62
	Unanimity	11	22.92	17	16.04
Type	Directive	20	41.67	47	44.34
	Regulation	23	47.92	50	47.17
	Decision	5	10.42	9	8.49
Domain	Agriculture	11	22.92	29	27.36
	Internal market	11	22.92	28	26.42
	Fishery	6	12.5	11	10.38
	ECOFIN	5	10.42	8	7.55
	JHA	2	4.17	3	2.83
	Common	2	4.17	4	3.77
	Other	11	22.92	23	21.7
Total		48	100	106	100

quo, the outcome and the Council pivot. Although most experts were rapporteurs, the DEU experts came primarily from the Council, and although these experts were asked at different points in time, the point location of 15 positions is the same (deviation of 0–5 on a scale ranging from 0 to 100), 13 positions are very close (deviation of 6–25), 4 positions are not comparable owing to missing values and only 3 measures indicate a large deviation (50, 50 and 70). Closer inspection of these three deviating cases reveals that two of them list a slight Council qualified majority position and the minority position is again almost identical with the Council estimate. This suggests that the Council may have introduced the minority position in the bargaining of the conciliation process (König et al. 2007).

In spite of the sample reduction to 48 cases, the relative proportion of cases in each subcategory remains approximately unaltered. Furthermore, we deal with a sufficiently large number of cases in most subcategories to estimate the effects for each group and to control for a possible bias in the overall estimation. Combining our data with the voting records of the Council, we determine the actor-specific error rate for predicting the voting behaviour of the member states on each of the 48 Commission proposals. Furthermore, the data allow us to examine alternative analyses of actors' voting preferences that identify domain-specific and inter-temporal logrolling across Commission proposals.

Voting Preferences, Selection Bias and Strategies for Consensus

Our combination of the DEU data with the voting records of the Council reveals that member states voted against a proposal on only 14 occasions taken from the total sample of 719 votes on the 48 proposals.[6] Note that all 48 proposals were finally adopted, which implies that the No votes did not in effect change the legislative outcome.[7] The few No votes were cast only under qualified majority voting.

In the lower rows of Table 8.3, we provide a prediction of member states' voting behaviour as determined by a fully specified analytical model that considers the multidimensionality of all proposals as well as the saliencies of the actors involved. Accordingly, some member states prefer the status quo and are thus predicted to reject proposals under legislative procedures requiring unanimity.

A closer inspection of these results shows that the percentage of rejections is higher for proposals under qualified majority procedures than under the unanimity rule, and we find a slightly higher rejection rate for proposals submitted under the

Table 8.3 Observed and predicted voting preference by procedure

		Consultation		Co-decision		
		QMV (%)	Unanimity (%)	QMV (%)	Unanimity (%)	Sum (%)
Observation	Support	260 (96.3)	164 (100)	206 (98)	75 (100)	705 (98)
	Rejection	10 (3.7)	0 (0)	4 (2)	0 (0)	14 (2)
	Total	270 (100)	164 (100)	210 (100)	75 (100)	719 (100)
Prediction	Support	173 (64.1)	137 (83)	178 (84.8)	56 (74.6)	544 (75.5)
	Rejection	97 (35.9)	28 (17)	32 (15.2)	19 (25.4)	176 (24.5)
	Total	270 (100)	165 (100)	210 (100)	75 (100)	720 (100)
Error		95 (35.1)	28 (17)	28 (13.3)	19 (25.4)	170 (23.6)

[6] Note that voting predictions are not affected by voting weights (in contrast to outcome predictions); we therefore do not distinguish between predictions with and without voting weights with respect to voting predictions in the table.

[7] In EU legislation, under QMV abstention is de facto a vote against a proposal, whereas under the unanimity rule it supports adoption.

consultation procedure. This – and the different number of proposals under each procedure – suggests that institutional rules matter, and a strong impact by norms is hardly likely to reveal different numbers.

One striking result is that the proposal-specific analytical model correctly predicts more than 75% of the member states' voting behaviour. Compared with roll-call analysis (Mattila and Lane 2001; Mattila 2004; Heisenberg 2005; Hayes-Renshaw et al. 2006), this model indeed has a higher explanatory power when correctly deriving the high adoption rate in the Council in at least 75% of the cases from proposal-specific interests. However, it is a demanding methodological task to explain the remaining cases in which some member states voted for the adoption of a proposal in spite of their favouring the status quo and their power to maintain it. A simple explanation for this limited set of incorrectly predicted cases would be that the preferences of a few member states have been measured inaccurately, but a more complex theoretical approach draws our attention to the countervailing role of the Commission and eventually to a strategy that is applied in the Council by actors in the legislative process who seek to obtain consensus.

In the analytical literature, the Council is usually conceived of as a voting platform in which member states cast their votes under closed rule and the Commission initiates proposals in order to promote European integration. From this perspective of the so-called supranational scenario, the crucial question on the role of the Commission is whether it fully knows the voting preferences of the member states, anticipates their voting behaviour and, taking all the available information into consideration, consequently only initiates proposals related to the process of European integration on which the member states generally agree. This preference-related analytical explanation for an integrationist selection of proposals undertaken by the Commission prior to the voting procedures could indeed explain the high adoption rate of initiatives and would let us expect to observe conflict in the Council only when the Commission has imperfect information about the process and incomplete information about the voting preferences of the member states.

Although postulating the availability of complete and perfect information makes the formal analysis more tractable, it is, however, more realistic to assume that the Commission cannot entirely foresee the whole legislative process as well as the voting preferences of the member states since this process includes several stages and lasts sometimes for more than 1 year. Moreover, the proposals often contain multiple issues on which a large number of member states hold different positions. Empirically, we observe a large number of controversial cases with some member states located close to or even at the status quo. This configuration clearly rejects the notion that the Commission can perfectly preselect proposals with regard to the voting preferences of the member states. However, this does not mean that the Commission is not trying to identify proposals according to the member states' attitudes on European integration. A closer inspection of the DEU data shows that about 46% (or two-thirds when missing values are excluded) of the member states indeed prefer a policy change towards more European integration, and only about 5.5% clearly reject a move in this direction and favour a change towards less European integration (Table 8.4).

Table 8.4 Integration preferences of the EU 15 for the DEU data

	Number of positions	Percentage
Preference for more integration (ideal position compared to status quo)	1,109	45.6
Preference for less integration (ideal position compared to status quo)	131	5.5
Preference for status quo (ideal position is status quo)	484	19.9
Missing values (status quo or position)	706	29
Total	2,430	100

As shown in Table 8.4, there is a considerable level of contestation between the majority of member states preferring more European integration and a small opposition that either supports the maintenance of the status quo or even opts for less European integration. Particularly under Council unanimity, this configuration implies disagreement between the vast majority of member states favouring more European integration and a smaller number of member states opposed to this change. But if these opposing member states disagree only with a specific proposal and support change towards European integration by other proposals, it is likely that logrolling across proposals can lead to the bundling of a package that is consensually supported by all member states in an otherwise contested Council. In this regard, we examine which logrolling strategies are actually promoted by the Council.

A closer inspection of the Council's organization reveals that two strategies seem to be promoted by the Council's committee system, which organizes decision-making on three levels. At the lowest working group level, the so-called 'dossier' contains the contested issues of a Commission proposal. The working groups attempt to coordinate these proposal-specific interests and report to Coreper whether and which controversial issues have been settled. Coreper receives the working group reports on all dossiers and discusses only the unresolved controversial issues. The outcome of its discussion is then again classified into remaining open and settled questions, which are finally sent to the ministerial level according to their portfolios. This is, officially, the last stage of Council decision-making where the ministers meet and attempt to resolve on their own account the 5–10% of remaining controversial issues. According to Tallberg (2004), the Council presidency has brokerage resources owing to privileged information provided by the Council's secretariat. Moreover, the Council controls the process in terms of determining the negotiation pace and the possibility of shifting meetings into restricted sessions and of presenting a presidency's compromise formula.

Following the institutional organization of the Council, we can assert that, whenever the working groups have solved many controversies at the first level, the Coreper stage offers the possibility of exchange across proposals from various domains in a timely restricted fashion, and the portfolio responsibility of ministers finally promotes domain-specific exchanges across proposals within a specific policy field (König and Proksch 2006). These different logrolling strategies may increase the likelihood of adoption and consensus by providing member states with more opportunities to accommodate their interests when linking proposals. Obviously, the two strategies are not mutually exclusive but complementary explanations for consensus in the Council. This raises the question of which strategy might ultimately be better suited for explaining consensus in the Council.

Logrolling Across Proposals Within a Period and Within a Domain

The empirical identification of logrolling strategies is not a trivial task because minimal benefits from exchange do readily occur and can be sufficient for predicting consensus.[8] In order to control for this trivial effect, we consider two criteria: the transaction costs of logrolling and the institutional opportunities for logrolling strategies. The transaction costs of logrolling basically prevent trades across a larger number of proposals in legislatures. In other words, the smaller the number of linked proposals necessary for achieving consensus, the more convincing is the logrolling argument. Thus, the larger the number of proposals that must be linked for a successful promotion of beneficial logrolling trades, the less likely is the application of a logrolling strategy by the member states, owing to the higher transaction costs involved in linking these proposals in the Council.

When an institutional characteristic constrains the number of proposals to be linked, the specific features of these proposals will matter much more for the success of a logrolling strategy because actors' preferences must better match to produce consensus. With respect to the Council's institutional organization, we evaluate two kinds of institutional characteristics, In our domain-specific analysis, logrolling is possible only between proposals drawn from the same policy domain. This type of analysis follows the idea that the Council facilitates logrolling within the portfolio responsibility of the ministers. In our second intertemporal analysis, we allow logrolling across all policy domains but with respect to proposals that have been negotiated in the same period. This type of analysis is based on the view that contestation is resolved at the Coreper level in the same period. Hence, we interpret these institutional characteristics of the Council's organization as a promotion of logrolling. However, logrolling can plausibly solve contestation in the Council only when the member states' voting preferences appropriately match within either a specific policy domain or a particular time period. This, too, should make it more difficult for the logrolling argument to succeed in empirical tests.

Although we can use the DEU data to examine these two logrolling strategies, we must acknowledge that we can scarcely presume that only the DEU proposals were an integral part of the logrolling trades for finding Council consensus. Hence, we have to consider the DEU sample as a sub-sample of all proposals and assume

[8] This particularly applies in the framework of deterministic models.

that logrolling takes place only between proposals *of the kind* described by the DEU data. We might thus on occasion predict a *single decision* in an incorrect way, but we should be able to draw correct conclusions about the potential effect of logrolling in the Council *on average*. Note that the DEU sample is biased in favour of contested proposals that produce a higher level of conflict and involve more divergent interests than does the total sample of EU legislative initiatives. This means that we carry out a conservative evaluation of the two logrolling strategies because the available subsample of more contested cases is likely to reduce the probability of consensus in the Council.

Finally, we take into account that member states do not always cooperate completely and trade votes entirely by logrolling, but that some degree of defection can still be consistent with rational behaviour because it still outperforms complete defection. Theoretically, when the member states are aware of the benefits from trade and thus apply logrolling strategies in the Council, the resulting logrolling patterns of trade imply that member states support proposals that they would otherwise reject. On the other hand, a member state with a voting preference for the status quo asserts that logrolling trades have not been sufficiently agreed upon and that issues have not been sufficiently linked. Hence, whenever a logrolling strategy is applied, the level of consensus observed should be expected to correspond to the logrolling potential in the relevant policy domain or period. For example, we should observe a higher rate of consensus in policy domains that entail a high potential for mutually beneficial logrolling trades, this likelihood being based on the characteristics of the proposals in these domains (and a comparatively low rate of consensus in domains where this potential is low).

For our empirical evaluation, we begin by assessing the logrolling potential for the various domains and time periods by linking each proposal with up to nine other proposals that have been negotiated within the same policy domain or time period. If logrolling is a plausible explanation for consensus in the Council, this should be achieved by a very limited number of proposals taking into consideration transaction costs. We furthermore assume that proposals are more likely to be linked the more typical they are and the more often similar proposals therefore occur in our sample. We can thus gather a set of linked proposals by randomly drawing combinations from the respective subsamples of the DEU data, a method guaranteeing that each proposal in the subsample has the same chance of being selected and even of being chosen more than once for any combination of proposals.

On the basis of our analysis on the combinations of different proposals, we are able to predict the voting behaviour of the member states by referring to their voting preferences – by applying our empirical knowledge on their ideal position, their saliencies, their relative distance from the legislative status quo and on every proposal they have linked in the multidimensional policy space. For each size of the logroll, we take 1,000 different decision-making situations into account, which have been chosen from the DEU data set by the random procedure described above. This will thus provide an account of the average rate of consensus across actors and decision-making situations.

To show the effect of each logrolling strategy, we evaluate whether and to what extent logrolling benefits that result from the combination of a limited number of proposals (maximum ten) can explain consensus in the Council and whether the different logrolling potentials in the various policy domains and time periods correspond to the level of consensus actually observed. We then compare our results with linkages made in completely arbitrarily assigned decision-making situations where the interests of the member states and the locations of the outcome and status quo have been drawn from a uniform preference distribution. This approach allows us to control for variation in the scope of consensus that might artificially be produced by a higher dimensionality of the aggregated policy space. To adequately assess the voting preferences of the member states, we need to ask whether their interests and outcomes have been aligned not in a random but a systematic way.

Figures 8.2 and 8.3 show the information about the effect of both logrolling strategies across different policy domains and time periods and about how the strategies may affect member states' voting behaviour in the Council. The x-axis lists the number of linked proposals and the y-axis presents the average level of consensus across 1,000 decision-making situations in which up to ten proposals were linked

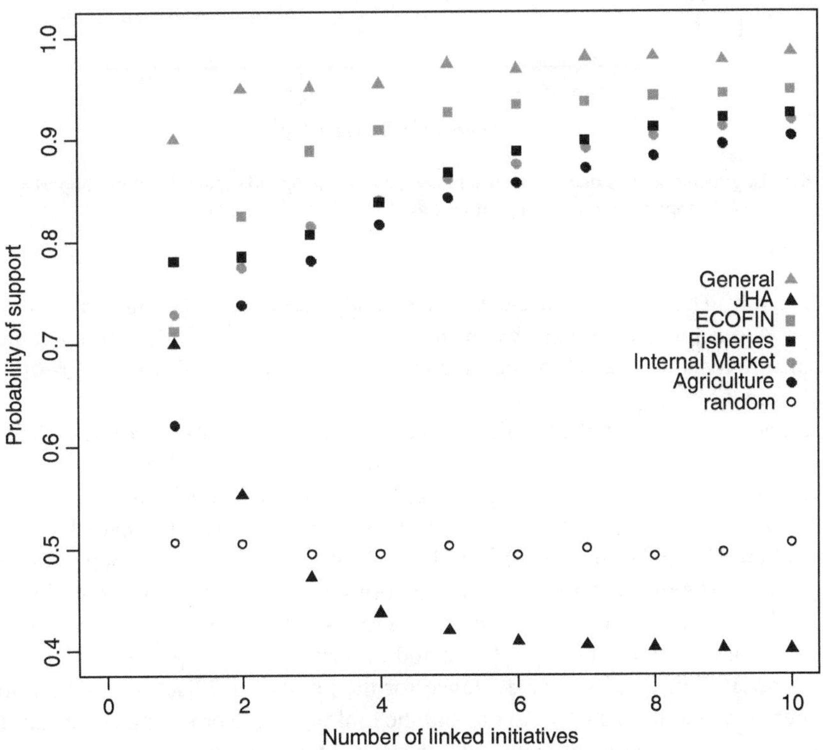

Fig. 8.2 Logrolling across decisions in the same policy domain: mean level of support in empirical versus random decision-making situations

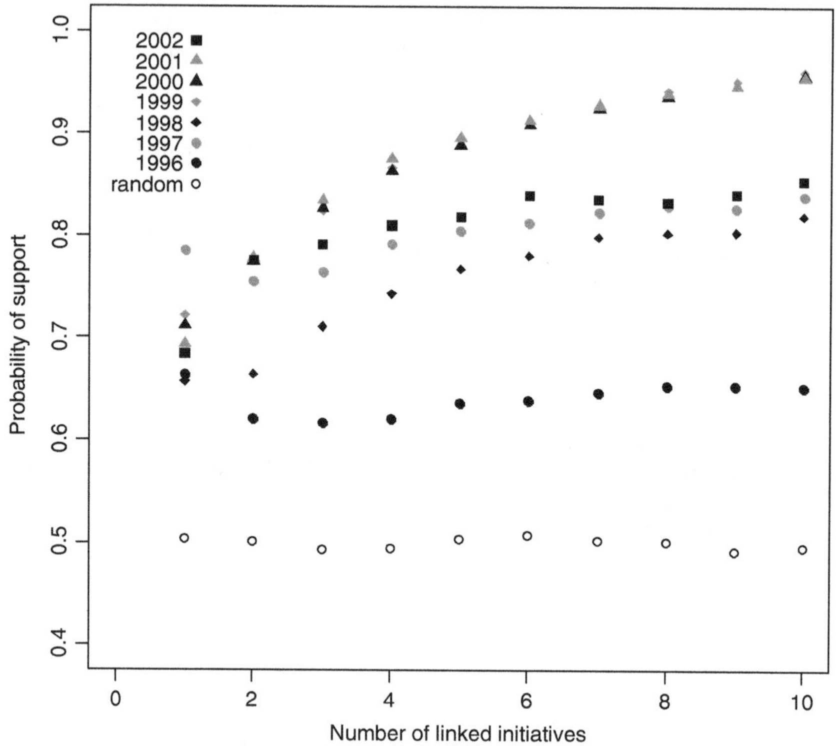

Fig. 8.3 Logrolling across decisions simultaneously on the agenda mean level of support in empirical versus random decision-making situations

respectively. The level of consensus in this analytical model is an indicator of how easy it is to achieve consensus by means of the application of a logrolling strategy and also reflects the ways in which the member states can profit from logrolling in the different settings.

As shown in Fig. 8.2, the predicted level of consensus rapidly increases when we presume that member states link a small number of proposals from the same policy domain. This logrolling strategy mainly increases the average rate of consensus in the General and ECOFIN domains, followed by Fisheries, Internal Market and Agriculture. Table 8.5 displays the predicted level of consensus for each policy domain and shows the comparison with the voting pattern actually observed in these areas. To simplify the complex statistics, we ranked all policy domains according to the scope of consensus, both predicted and observed. With respect to the observed voting behaviour, we also give evidence for the number of rejections and the total number of decisions in each domain, and the ranking of the predicted consensus has been based on the whole curvature of consensus rates from Fig. 8.2.

Table 8.5 shows that the logrolling model correctly predicts the highest levels of consensus in the General and ECOFIN domains.

Table 8.5 Observed and predicted level of consensus by policy domain (rank order)

	Observed level of consensus (rejections)	Predicted level of consensus (rank order)
ECOFIN	1 (0/75)	2
General	2 (0/30)	1
Justice and home affairs	3 (0/29)	6
Agriculture	4 (2/165)	5
Fisheries	5 (3/90)	3
Internal market	6 (6/165)	4

A more modest level is indicated in the table for the policy domain of Justice and Home Affairs. The latter would have been expected to exhibit the lowest level of consensus but the actual voting patterns show evidence of consensus. A possible explanation for the incorrect expectation is that only two proposals in this policy domain were under consideration, and a small number of proposals cannot be linked in a mutually beneficial way. Here, the comparison with the simulated decision-making situations established by means of random distribution suggests that the likelihood of individual support for Commission proposals does not automatically increase with the number of combined proposals.

Theoretically, the combination of several proposals usually increases the likelihood of support by the member states, and the total number of possible solutions in the policy space increases as well. In this regard, the likelihood of incidentally finding a proposal that fosters the support of the member states does not increase in the simulation but remains approximately constant. We interpret this result as that the member states take the distribution of interests in other proposals into account. Although the configuration of the voting preferences and outcomes follows the systematic pattern described by the analytical model, the combination of random decision-making situations does not work in the same way and produce the same effect. Figure 8.3 shows the expected average rate of both predicted and observed consensus when logrolling takes place across proposals that have been negotiated in the same period.

Again, the likelihood of Council consensus rapidly increases with the number of linked proposals. Moreover, we can observe that the logrolling effect does not depend on the number of different proposals in each period in the data set. With the combination of only a few proposals, the likelihood of consensus approaches the maximum of ten. The simulation clearly shows that logrolling between proposals that were negotiated between 1999 and 2001 was able to achieve Council consensus most easily, followed by logrolling in 2002, 1997, 1998 and 1996. Table 8.6 shows the level of Council consensus per year. With regard to the voting behaviour of the member states, we also report the number of rejections and the total number of proposals in each period, and the ranking of the predictions is again based on the whole curvature of Council consensus shown in Fig. 8.3, for which no single value can be calculated.

As shown in Table 8.6, logrolling across proposals in periods that were predicted to entail the highest, second-highest and third-highest logrolling potentials led to

Table 8.6 Observed and predicted level of consensus by time on agenda (rank order)

	Observed level of consensus (rejections)	Predicted level of consensus (rank order)
2002	1 (0/15)	4
2000	2 (10/509)	1
1999	3 (10/449)	2
1998	4 (5/150)	6
2001	5 (10/225)	3
1997	6 (5/90)	5
1996	7 (5/60)	7

the second-, third- and fifth-highest levels of Council consensus. The highest level of Council consensus occurs for proposals negotiated in 2002, but there is only one proposal that fulfils this criterion and has been adopted by the member states. Finally, the order for the years 1998, 1997 and 1996 is confirmed with the fourth-, sixth- and seventh-lowest level of consensus in the Council.

We note for the interpretation of these results that they cannot be produced by the combinations of randomly drawn decision-making situations. This suggests a systematic selection of proposals that takes into account the patterns of interests in other decision-making situations as approximated by our sampling procedure. Hence, our results should provide a particularly robust explanation for consensus in the Council because it relies on particularly contested legislative initiatives and preferences from the DEU project, which limits the potential for mutually beneficial logrolling by design.

Discussion

This study aimed at investigating why member states with veto power usually support policy change proposed by Commission initiatives even in cases where they have different interests and are located closer to the status quo. This culture of consensus has been observed by statistical analyses of the adoption rate of Commission proposals and the voting records of the member states, which reveal consensus in the Council even after additional veto players, such as new member states or the European Parliament, have joined EU legislative decision-making. This observation stands in contrast to the attempts to reform the EU's legislative framework launched by those member states complaining about the voting rules of the Council. To solve this empirical puzzle of making reform attempts and voting consensually in the Council, we have investigated the voting preferences of the member states with respect to 48 Commission proposals.

Our analysis has revealed that proposal-specific models cannot sufficiently and adequately explain consensus in the Council. However, the limitations of these analytical models have drawn our attention to the countervailing role of the Commission and the committee system of the Council in the legislative process, since they both have the power and the institutional means to promote strategies that may explain

Council consensus; while the Commission can preselect legislative proposals and then only initiate legislation if a sufficient level of Council support can be expected, the Council promotes logrolling by trading votes across a limited number of initiatives to facilitate support.

A closer inspection of the data on the 48 Commission proposals indicates that the Commission indeed preselects proposals according to the configuration of interests of the member states. For the 48 proposals, most of the member states prefer policy change that is favourable to further European integration and only a few of them prefer the status quo or a change towards less European integration. Although preselection may to some extent explain the high adoption rate of Commission proposals, several proposals still remain contested with some actors preferring the status quo or even opposing a more drastic policy change towards more European integration, a configuration that should lead to a rejection of the proposal under the procedure of unanimity. According to this proposal-specific analytical view, these actors have both the incentives and the actual possibility to maintain the status quo by their veto power, but, the voting records of the Council reveal that they ultimately support the policy change proposed by the Commission in the Council.

In order to explain this Council consensus, our analysis has drawn attention to another and more specific explanation based on logrolling strategies in the Council. On closer inspection of the Council's institutional organization, logrolling opportunities across proposals within either a policy domain or a common period of time point to the potential of this analytical explanation. If many member states strongly favour the adoption of Commission proposals, they have a sufficient incentive to find solutions for their desired policy change and thus offer concessions and possibilities of compromise to the few member states that have a good reason to vote against the adoption of a particular proposal. The crucial question, however, has been whether the Council can promote these logrolling opportunities in an efficient way. In our view, the Council's use of a logrolling strategy is more likely to occur when it is possible to reach consensus by linking only a few proposals, because linking a larger number would increase the transaction costs and diminish the benefits from mutual exchange.

Therefore, our empirical investigation has focused on the assessment of the preconditions for logrolling and we have observed that these conditions are met in the Council in the following ways. First, consensus can easily be achieved by means of logrolling because vote trades produce the required benefits very rapidly. Second, the preference configurations within policy domains and across time periods are sufficiently diverse to allow for such beneficial deals. This suggests that logrolling is a plausible and powerful explanation of consensus in the Council. We can thus believe that rational member states exploit these logrolling opportunities in the Council to increase their overall benefits. However, although we have demonstrated that the conditions for such logrolling strategies are actually met in the Council, we do not attempt to develop a complete theoretical model that can predict member states' decisions with respect to each single initiative. Rather, our analysis is limited to the potential of these strategies and offers only a promising starting point for future attempts to model decision-making in the EU in a more accurate manner.

Apart from their relevance for decision-making and consensus in the Council, our findings may also have important implications for the study of the EU and the application of analytical models in the future because they challenge the currently dominant proposal-specific concept of actors' preferences. The first generation of analytical models focused almost exclusively on the interpretation of the power-distributional effects of institutions for the adoption of a single Commission proposal, whereas a second generation may draw attention to the accurate specification of the preference component in decision-making, thus allowing for a reinterpretation of the theory's decision-making argument. In this respect, our analysis suggests that member states have established an effective committee system that might even help them to avoid a legislative blockage after treaty changes and enlargements have increased the risk of legislative gridlock. However, our findings also reveal that a limited number of proposals is necessary for finding compromise and consensus. This suggests that member states have good reasons to complain about the actual legislative framework of the EU while supporting Commission initiatives when logrolling across Commission proposals can provide mutual benefits.

Acknowledgement This chapter is a reprint of an article entitled 'Why Don't Veto Players Use Their Power?' by Thomas König and Dirk Junge, which originally appeared in *European Union Politics* (2009) 10:507–534.

References

Achen CH (2006) Institutional realism and bargaining models. In: Thomson R, Stokman FN, Achen CH, König T (eds). The European Union decides. Cambridge University Press, Cambridge, pp 86–123

Bailer S, Schneider G (2006) Nash versus Schelling? The importance of constraints in legislative bargaining. In: Thomson R, Stokman FN, Achen CH, König T (eds). The European Union decides. Cambridge University Press, Cambridge. pp 153–177

Baldwin RE, Francois JF, Portes R, Rodrik D, Szekely IP (1997) The costs and benefits of eastern enlargement: the impact on the EU and Central Europe. Econ Policy 12(24):125–176

Crombez C (1996) Legislative procedures in the European Community. Br J Polit Sci 26(2): 199–228

Crombez C (1997) The co-decision procedure in the European Union Legis Stud. Q 22(1):97–119

Crombez C (2000) Institutional reform and co-decision in the European Union. Const Polit Econ 11(1):41–57

Enelow JM, Hinich MJ (1984) The spatial theory of voting: an introduction. Cambridge University Press, Cambridge

Franchino F (2007) The powers of the union: delegation in the EU. Cambridge University Press, Cambridge

Franklin MN, Wlezien C (1997) The responsive public – issue salience, policy change, and preferences for European unification. J Theor Polit 9(3):347–363

Hage F (2007) Committee decision-making in the council of the European Union. Eur Union Polit 8(3):299–328

Hage F (2008) Who decides in the council of the European Union? J Common Mark Stud 46(3):533–558

Hagemann S, de Clerck-Sachsse J (2007) Old rules, new game: decision-making in the council of ministers after the 2004 enlargement. Special Report, Centre for European Policy Studies

Hayes-Renshaw F, Aken WV, Wallace H (2006) When and why the EU Council of ministers votes explicitly. J Common Mark Stud 44(1):161–194

Heisenberg D (2005) The institution of "consensus" in the European Union: formal versus informal decision-making in the Council. Eur J Polit Res 44(1):65–90

Hotelling H (1929) Stability in competition. Econ J 39 (153):41–57

Junge D, König T (2007) What's wrong with EU spatial analysis? The accuracy and robustness of empirical applications to the interpretation of the legislative process and the specification of preferences. J Theor Polit 19(4):465–487

King G, Honaker J, Joseph A, Scheve K (2001) Analyzing incomplete political science data: an alternative algorithm for multiple imputation. Am Polit Sci Rev 95(1):49–69

König T (2007) Divergence or convergence? From ever-growing to ever-slowing European legislative decision making. Eur J Polit Res 46(3):417–444

König T, Bräuninger T (2004) Accession and reform of the European Union – a game-theoretical analysis of eastern enlargement and the constitutional reform. Eur Union Polit 5(4):419–439

König T, Luetgert B (2009) Troubles with transposition? Explaining trends in member-state notification and the delayed transposition of EU directives Br J Polit Sci 39(1):163–194

König T, Pöter M (2001) Examining the EU legislative process. The relative importance of agenda and veto power. Eur Union Polit 2(3):329–351

König T, Proksch S-O (2006) A procedural exchange model of EU legislative politics. In: Thomson R, Stokman FN, Achen CH, König T (eds). The European Union decides. Cambridge University Press, Cambridge, pp 211–238

König T, Finke D, Daimer S (2005) Ignoring the non-ignorables? Missingness and missing positions. Eur Union Polit 6(3):269–290

König T, Luetgert B, Dannwolf T (2006) Quantifying European legislative research. Using CELEX and PRELEX in EU legislative studies. Eur Union Polit 7(4):553–574

König T, Lindberg B, Lechner S, Pohlmeier W (2007) Bicameral conflict resolution in the European Union: an empirical analysis of conciliation committee bargains. Br J Polit Sci 37(2):281–312

Lewis J (2003) Institutional environments and everyday EU decision making: rationalist or constructivist? Comp Polit Stud 36(1/2):97–124

Mastenbroek E (2003) Surviving the deadline – the transposition of EU directives in the Netherlands. Eur Union Polit 4(4):371–395

Mattila M (2004) Contested decisions – empirical analysis of voting in the EU council of ministers. Eur J Polit Res 43(1):29–50

Mattila M, Lane J-E (2001) Why unanimity in the council? A roll call analysis of council voting. Eur Union Polit 2(1):31–52

Napel S, Widgren M (2004) Power measurement as sensitivity analysis. A unified approach. J Theor Polit 16(4):517–538

Poole KT (2005) Spatial models of parliamentary voting. Cambridge University Press, Cambridge

Romer T, Rosenthal H (1978) Political resource allocation, controlled agendas, and the status quo. Public Choice 33(4):27–43

Sapir A (2004) An agenda for a growing Europe: the Sapir report. Oxford University Press, Oxford

Scharpf FW (2006) The joint-decision trap revisited. J Common Mark Stud 44(4):845–864

Schneider G, Steunenberg B, Widgren M (2006) Evidence with insight: what models contribute to EU research. In: Thomson R, Stokman FN, Achen CH, König T (eds). The European Union decides. Cambridge University Press, Cambridge, pp 299–316

Selck TJ (2004) The impact of procedure: analyzing European Union legislative decision-making Cuvillier, Gottingen

Slapin JB (2006) Who is powerful? Examining preferences and testing sources of bargaining strength at European intergovernmental conferences. Eur Union Polit 7(1):51–76

Steunenberg B (1994) Decision making under different institutional arrangements: legislation by the European community. J Inst Theor Econ 150(4):642–669

Steunenberg B (1997) Codecision and its reform: a comparative analysis of decision-making rules in the European Union. In: Steunenberg B, van Vught F (eds). Political institutions and public policy: perspectives on European decision making. Kluwer Academic Publisher, Dortrecht, pp 205–229

Steunenberg B, Selck TJ (2006) Testing procedural models of EU legislative decision-making. In: Thomson R, Stokman FN, Achen CH, König T (eds). The European Union decides. Cambridge University Press, Cambridge, pp 54–85

Sutter M (2000) Fair allocation and re-weighting of votes and voting power in the EU before and after the next enlargement. J Theor Polit 12(4):433–449

Tallberg J (2004) The power of the presidency: brokerage, efficiency and distribution in EU negotiations. J Common Mark Stud 42(5):999–1022

Thomson R, Hosli M (2006) Who has power in the EU? The commission, council and parliament in legislative decision-making. J Common Mark Stud 44(2):391–417

Thomson R, Stokman F, Achen C König T (eds) (2006) The European Union decides. Cambridge University Press, Cambridge

Tollison RD, Willett TD (1979) An economic theory of mutually advantageous issue linkage in international negotiations. Int Organ 33(4):425–449

Tsebelis G (1994) The power of the European Parliament as a conditional agenda setter. Am Polit Sci Rev 88(1):128–142

Tsebelis G (1995) Decision making in political systems: veto players in presidentialism, parliamentarism, multicameralism und multipartyism. Br J Polit Sci 25(3):289–325

Tsebelis G (2002) Veto players: how political institutions work. Princeton University Press, Princeton

Tsebelis G (2008) Thinking about the recent past and the future of the EU. J Common Mark Stud 46(2):265–292

Tsebelis G, Garrett G (2000) Legislative politics in the European Union. Eur Union. Polit 1(1): 9–36

Tsebelis G, Garrett G (2001) The institutional foundations of intergovernmentalism and supranationalism in the European Union. Int Organ 55(2):357–390

Tsebelis G, Proksch S-O (2007) The art of political manipulation in the European Convention. J Common Mark Stud 45(1):157–186

Yataganas X, Tsebelis G (2005) The treaty of nice, the convention draft and the constitution for Europe under a veto players analysis. Eur Const Law Rev 1(3):429–451

Part IV
Modelling of Veto Players

Chapter 9
Testing the Law-Making Theories in a Parliamentary Democracy: A Roll Call Analysis of the Italian Chamber of Deputies (1988–2008)

Luigi Curini and Francesco Zucchini

Introduction

The theoretical efforts in the rational choice approach to explain the law-making process in United States Congress has been increasingly matched by attempts to test the explanatory power of different theories (Cox and McCubbins 2005; Krehbiel et al. 2005). No such effort has so far been made by the scholars of parliamentary democracy[1]. There are various reasons for this gap. "Positive" explanations for law making in parliamentary democracy are recent and they are yet to trigger the same debate among the scientific community of Congress scholars. Besides, given the centrality of the cabinet in the parliamentary system, most of the theoretical and empirical efforts have been focused on studies of government formation and dissolution. This led to the collection of data, such as expert survey data required for testing coalition theories (Laver and Hunt 1992; Benoit and Laver 2006). Further, it ignored other data, such as roll call data, which, though less useful for testing government formation models, are potentially helpful for other research goals.

Using the roll calls of 10th to 15th Italian legislatures, we aim to test the explanatory power of some law-making theories in a parliamentary system. The long period of Italian history (1988–2008) considered for this study is characterized by two different party systems (pivotal party system in the 10th and 11th Legislatures and alternational party system in the succeeding parliaments); and by all possible types of government (oversized in the 10th and 14th Legislatures, non-partisan caretaker in the 12th legislature, minority and minimal winning governments in the 13th and 15th Legislatures). Therefore we can evaluate the explicative strength of each law-making model under a large variety of political circumstances.

In the first section we present a typology of law-making models in parliamentary democracies based on the agenda-setting and veto power in the legislative arena. In

[1]A partial exception are the papers published on the Cox and McCubbins website: www.settingtheagenda.com.

L. Curini (✉) and F. Zucchini
Dipartimento di Studi Sociali e Politiche, Università degli Studi di Milano
e-mail: luigi.curini@unimi.it

T. König et al. (eds.), *Reform Processes and Policy Change: Veto Players and Decision-Making in Modern Democracies*, Studies in Public Choice 16,
DOI 10.1007/978-1-4419-5809-9_9, © Springer Science+Business Media, LLC 2010

this typology we contrast a version of the procedural cartel model with two different versions of the veto player theory (according to the agenda setting power enjoyed by the government). In the following two sections we then explain how the cut points method is used to assess the empirical validity of each model, and the roll call analysis to create the legislative space. The ideal points of the crucial political actors are then inferred from the roll call analysis and their meaning and nature are discussed. In the last two sections the test results are presented, followed by discussion of the broad implications. The veto player theory appears to explain in a very consistent way the patterns of the Italian law-making. However our analysis reveals also under which conditions it works better and which adaptations are necessary to improve its performance.

Theories of Law Making in Parliamentary Democracy: A Typology

Empirical research of recent developments of the positive theory of American Congress shows two competing theoretical models of law making: the so called pivotal politics model and the procedural cartel model (Krehbiel 2006).

In the pivotal politics model, Krehbiel (1998) contends that either of the two agents – a veto pivot or a filibuster pivot – can prevent any change of status quo if the outcome of such a change proves worse for them than the status quo. The nature and identity of these two actors are crucially determined by the following: (a) the majorities stipulated by the standing orders and practices that control both the activity in the Senate (filibustering) and the interaction between the Congress and the President (veto over-riding); (b) the position of the political actors in the legislative one-dimensional space.

In the procedural cartel model, on the other hand, Cox and McCubbins (2005) contend that the majority party leadership, located in party median position, can prevent any change in the status quo that the majority of the majority party dislikes. Both theories insist therefore on the negative powers of some political actors but they differ very much about the identity of these political actors, and their role when there is no veto.

In the procedural cartel model, once the party leadership has "opened the gate", it cannot prevent the parliament from legislating what the floor median voter desires. In contrast, in the pivotal politics model, the pivotal actors have the last say. In this case, if a change is considered positively by both pivots, then the outcome will be the alternative closest to the floor median voter among the alternatives still considered an improvement by the pivot closest to the status quo. If the status quo is "far enough", both models will predict that the floor median position is the final outcome. Otherwise, the predictions will differ.

The two models cannot be immediately and unconditionally transferred to a parliamentary democracy. Procedural cartel model can be directly applied only to a one party government. For multiparty government, however, the coalition of parties can by itself be considered a party. In this case, only the government median party should exercise the veto power.

The pivotal politics model depends, on the other hand, crucially on the special majorities of the U.S. system. Therefore, it seems even harder to export than the procedural cartel model. Fortunately we do not have to transplant models from the Congressional studies. The veto player theory (Tsebelis 2002), supplies the most suitable framework to study law making in a parliamentary democracy, and shares with the pivotal politics model an important aspect: according to Tsebelis all government parties in the parliamentary systems, as the pivots in the Congress according to Krehbiel, have "practically" the last say. In this sense, when the policy change is a Pareto improvement for all government party leaders, the government party leaders can arrive at an agreement and this becomes the new law. In order to infer precise models to test, some clarifications and modifications of the theory of veto players are however necessary:

1. The Veto Players theory is considered in a multidimensional space where no accurate prediction about the legislative outcome is possible. Therefore, if we want to test models inferred from such a theory we have to use a one-dimensional version of it.
2. Pivotal politics and Procedural cartel models make precise assumptions about the agenda setting power enjoyed by the political actors who can veto the policy change. On the contrary, Veto Players theory is less clear cut in this regard. On one hand, according to Tsebelis, different parliamentary governments enjoy different levels of agenda setting power. On the other hand, the area in the political space usually chosen to indicate the set of potential policies that cannot be changed (i.e. the unanimity core) is compatible only with a strong agenda setting power of the government.
3. In the Pivotal politics model the floor median voter can be considered as a policy change promoter but is not a "proper" veto player as his/her position in the policy space is always "absorbed" by the two pivots who are individuals representing qualified majorities. On the contrary, the floor median voter of a parliamentary system, *even* when the government is not a minority government, can be located outside the line that separates the two most extreme government parties. When this happens, the median voter is not absorbed and is in the position to effectively put a veto. Such a phenomenon depends critically on the way one identifies the parties in the relevant political space. In the literature that employs roll-call data, a common solution to this problem is to represent the positions of parties by their respective mean or, more often, median voters (Myagkov and Kiewiet 1996; Han 2007; Hug and Schulz 2007; Schonhardt-Bailey 2003). The ideological range of the government can then be estimated as a function of those median (or mean) party positions.

Note, however, that according to the above procedure, for any party there will almost always be MPs on the left and on the right of its median (mean) voter, including the party viewed as extreme on the government range and centrally located in the whole political space. The theoretical consequences of this last point are more than trivial.

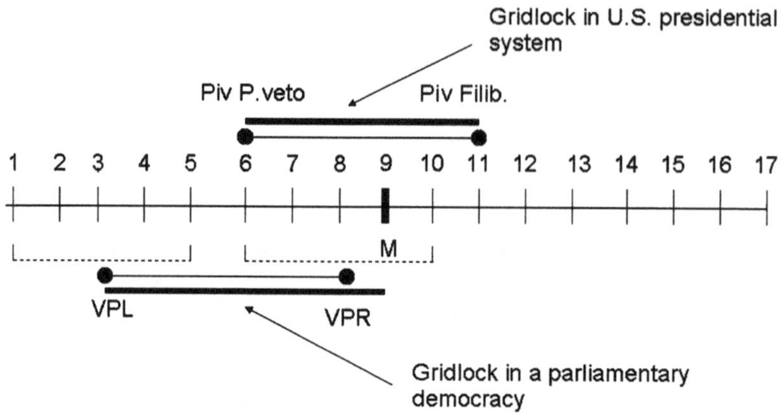

Fig. 9.1 Pivotal players in a Presidential system and Veto Players in a Parliamentary democracy. *Note*: Parliament/Congress has 17MPs. The Parliamentary Government is composed of MPs (1–5) belonging to VP_L and MPs (6–10) belonging to VP_R, and it has the closed rule. U.S. Presidential government has a leftist president. The party position of VP_L and VP_R is inferred by their respective median voters. In the Congress the median voter M is absorbed by the two pivots, while in the Parliament case M lies outside the ideological range of the government

Figure 9.1 shows in this regard a hypothetical scenario that we suspect being quite common in the empirical world of Parliamentary Democracies. Let us assume a centre-left non-minority government with strong agenda setting power. In this case, if the government is not very "oversized" and/or if the cohesion of the extreme right party is not very high, then the parliamentary median voter can belong to the extreme right of the government and still be outside the government range. Therefore, in all the real situations shown in Fig. 9.1, we should consider the parliamentary median voter rather than the median voter of the rightist government party as the proper rightist veto player. Of course, when we have a centre-right non-minority government, the situation is reversed.

To clarify and summarize the possible law-making models of parliamentary democracy previously illustrated, we propose a typology (Table 9.1) based on two simple criteria: (1) the actors who have the veto power; (2) the government agenda setting power (i.e. strong whenever a closed rule applies, or weak whenever an open rule applies).

The government median party is supposed to be the first mover in all the models considered here (the formal solutions of each game are available on request from the authors). When the government median party is assumed to be the only veto player *and* the agenda setting power is weak we have called the model "Procedural Cartel Theory" (PCT) due to its similarity with the model proposed by Cox and McCubbins to explain U.S. legislative process. Whenever the government agenda setting power is strong, we have the Government median party supremacy (GMPS) model. The veto players theory, on the other hand, generates two different models according to the law making rule effectively in force (VPM1 when the government agenda setting power is strong and VPM2 when it is weak).

Table 9.1 Typology of law-making models

	Government Agenda Setting Power	
Distribution of veto power	Open Rule	Closed Rule
Government Median agent	Procedural Cartel Theory PCT 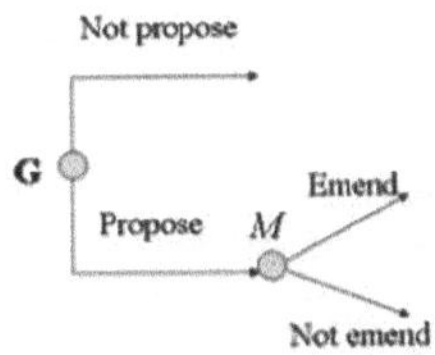	Government Median Party supremacy – GMPS 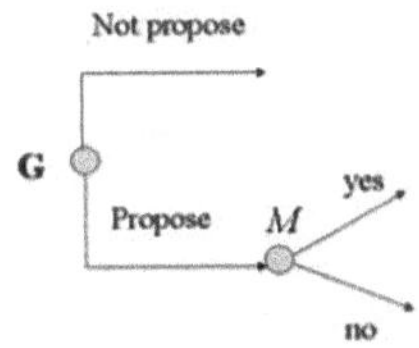
All Government Parties	Veto Players Model 2 VPM 2 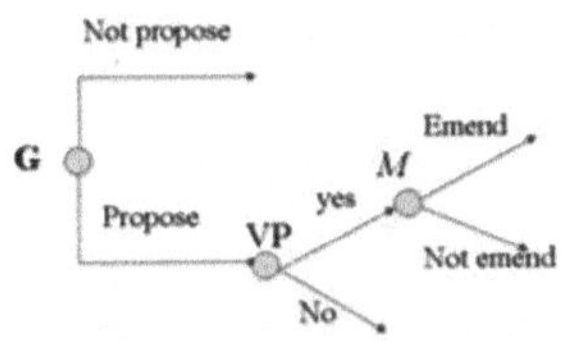	Veto Players Model 1 VPM 1 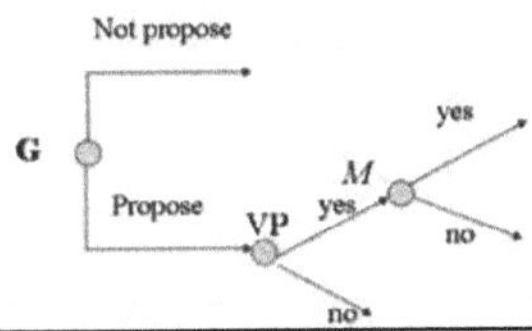

Note: *M* Floor median voter; *G* Government median party; *VP* Veto Player.

In a one-dimensional world, each model helps in identifying both the gridlock (in other words the set of policies that cannot be changed) and the legislative outcome when the legislative decision is possible. In the following graphs (see Fig. 9.2) the solid lines depict the outcome location in one-dimension for all possible positions of the status quo in horizontal axis. According to what is stressed above, it is assumed that the parliamentary median voter M is on the left of the government range (the line between the two extreme government parties: VP_L and VP_R)[2].

In this situation, when the outcome perfectly replicates the status quo, then there is no legislative change. This is possible if the change should prove worse than the status quo for at least one crucial actor who can prevent it according to the legislative game. For instance, with respect to the model VPM2, M and VP_R cannot agree to change a status quo when it falls in the interval (M; $2VP_R$–M), where ($2VP_R$–M) and M is equidistant from VP_R. As the government does not enjoy a strong agenda setting power in this model when a bill is proposed in parliament, its final outcome will be M.

Such an example shows that the extent of the "gridlock line" depends on two factors: the distance between the two most distant "crucial" actors (in this example M and VP_R) and the location of the final outcome in the policy dimension when

[2] The situation is perfectly specular when M is on the right side of the government range. On the contrary, when M is on the government range, the gridlock area is delimited by the two extreme government parties VP_L and VP_R.

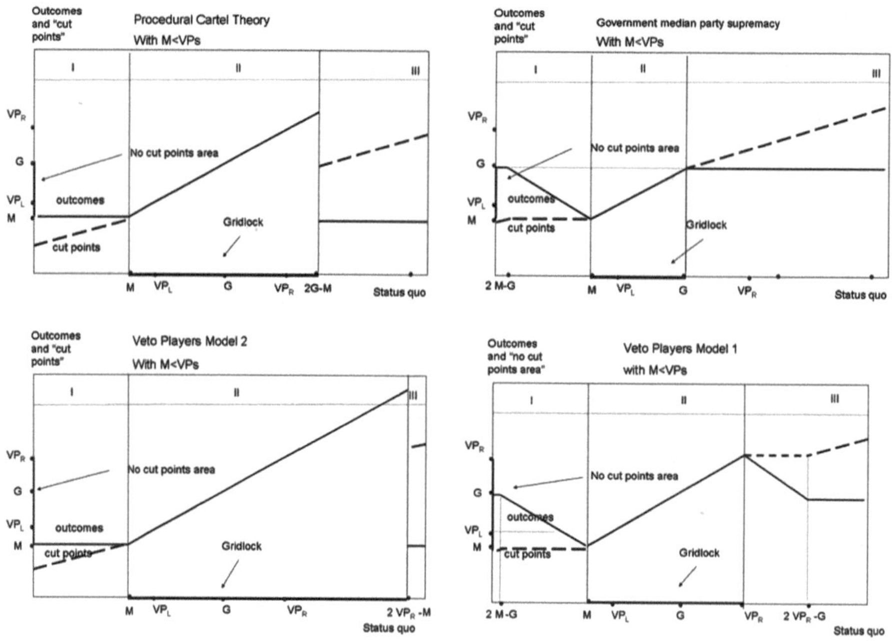

Fig. 9.2 Law-making models: legislative space, outcomes and cut points distribution

there is no veto. This feature depends, in turn, on the government agenda-setting power: a weak agenda-setting power (i.e. open rule), as hypothesized in both the PCT and the VPM2 models, will imply more policy stability and a larger gridlock. On the contrary, the closed rule should increase the probability of legislative change.

Along the horizontal axis of all models, the change of status quo creates different legislative outcomes. Therefore, if one knows the position of the status quo for each policy issue, the position of the bill as predicted by each model can be compared with the position inferred by data analysis, and thus the model that fits the empirical observation better can be selected. Unfortunately, no statistical method using roll call data allows identification of a reliable position of the approved bill. The next paragraph deals with this problem, while the following two paragraphs are devoted to showing the Italian legislative space and its parties and to discussing its origin and meaning.

Status Quo and Cut Points

A roll call data analysis does not allow identification of the reliable positions of the legislative outcome in the legislative space. However, it generates another measure, namely the cut point, which can indirectly help in testing different models. The cut point is a roll call specific midpoint between the estimated bill and the status quo

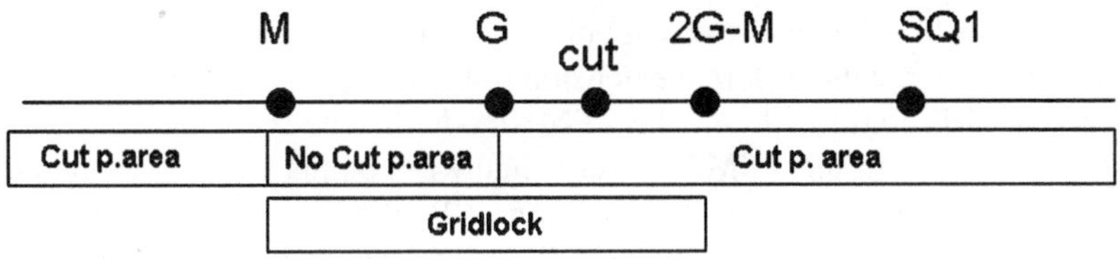

Fig. 9.3 Gridlock and Cut Points line

location (Krehbiel et al. 2005). The case of a vote on the final passage of a bill b is considered here. In this vote, b is implicitly paired against the status quo SQ. If the legislators have symmetric single-peaked preferences, then the cut point for such a vote is $c = [(b + \mathrm{SQ})/2]$.

Therefore, the same analytical model that predicts a certain distribution of the legislative outcomes for every possible status quo will also predict a certain distribution of cut points. As the last estimates are made available by the method employed here to analyse roll-calls (see below), one can indirectly test the models previously presented.

Take PCT (see Fig. 9.3) as example. When the status quo SQ is in the (M; 2G-M) range, any legislative change will be vetoed: the final outcome would be M and the status quo SQ is better than M for G. On the contrary, when the status quo is SQ1, G should welcome any legislative change, given that M is now better than SQ1 for G. What about the locations of the cut points? In the first case, by definition, no cut point is expected in the data. In the second case, a cut point must be found between G and 2G-M (if the status quo is SQ $>$ 2G-M). As a result, by looking at the partition of the policy space in which, according to PCT, no cut points are expected (i.e. between M and G), there is a way to test the validity of the theory. It is worth noting that in this case, the gridlock line is longer than the "no cut point line". The same happens with VPM2, but not with the other two models in which the two lines overlap perfectly.

The models of our typology sharing the same distribution of veto power (PCT and GMPS vs. VPM1 and VPM2) also share the same "no cut" line. However, as it is pretty clear by going back to Fig. 9.2, the expected distributions of the cut points on the whole legislative space are quite different from one model to the other, even when the "no cut points line" is the same.

Therefore, the cut points analysis helps to assess the lawmaking models of the typology in two steps. First, one looks at the presence/absence of the cut points inside the "no cut line". Through this one can evaluate which sets of models fit the data better: PCT and GMPS, or VPM1 and VPM2. Second, one observes the distribution of the cut points close to the crucial actors of the group of models that has fared better in the previous selection's stage. Our expectations can be summarized by a set of nested conditional propositions:

P1: if the VPM1/VPM2 models fit better the real legislative decision making than the PCT/GMPS models then we should observe fewer cut points in their common no cut points line than in the no cut points line of the other group of models (after having considered the different extension of the two lines, see below).

P2(a): if P1 is confirmed then the VPM1 model fits the real legislative decision making better than the VPM2 model if many cut points are next to the crucial actors who delimit the gridlock line (M and VP_R if $M < VP_L < VP_R$)[3].

P2(b): if P1 is not confirmed then GMPS fits the real legislative decision making better than PCT if many cut points are on the left (or on the right) of M.

Building the Space and Mapping the Parties: A Roll-Call Analysis

The dataset of this study comprises all the roll-calls in the Italian Chamber of Deputies beginning with the 10th Legislature (1987–1992) and ending with the 15th Legislature (2006–2008). To analyse them, the most commonly used method, namely W-Nominate methodology (Poole 2005)[4], was applied.

Following Poole and Rosenthal (1997), only roll calls with at least 2.5% in the minority are included in the computations. Also, MPs with fewer than 20 votes have been excluded. Further, the focus has been on the final passage votes in the Chamber of Deputies.[5]

It is worth noting that W-Nominate allows only dichotomous behaviour: for and against. But real voting includes at least two other options: absence and abstention. According to the rules in the Italian Lower House, all the MPs who abstain are counted for the quorum, but not counted for establishing the majority of votes necessary to win. Therefore, abstention is never neutral with respect to the final outcome. If there is a majority of ayes, then abstentions, by making up the quorum that validates voting, have positive valence; if there is a majority of nays, what happens would be exactly the opposite. However, in this last case, the bill will be rejected. As the proposed bill was approved in practically every roll call of the data set, the abstentions were counted as yes.

Similarly, in some circumstances being absent has a "negative" valence, in particular when a coalition of parliamentary groups tries to boycott voting by preventing

[3] If $M > VP_R > VP_L$, then according to the VPM2 model, the remarkable density of cut points should be observed around VP_L and M and if $VP_L < M < VP_R$, around VP_L and VP_R.

[4] To check the robustness of the results, we replied the analysis using a Bayesian Markov Chain Monte Carlo Method (see Clinton 2007). The ideal points estimations in the two case are highly correlated (R-Pearson's: 90%). On the relationship between the Nominate and the Bayesian method, see Carroll et al. (2009).

[5] Italian Senate does not record the voting activity electronically. Therefore, the last step of the legislative process was not necessarily taken into consideration. Because of the Italian bicameralism and the so called shuttle system ("navette"), not all bills that have been passed in the Chamber of Deputies become laws and a bill about the same issue can reach the floor voting stage more than once.

the quorum that validates the vote or when a group wants to publicly signal its complete refusal of the bill. Both actions require collective coordination and group discipline. Therefore, absence of an MP can be considered as a nay when all or almost all members of their parliamentary group[6] are absent and the few taking part in voting vote nay. Otherwise, it is considered a missing value[7].

Note, moreover, that the present analysis is based mainly on the assumption that each MP belongs to the parliamentary group of the last parliamentary session, and holds his/her ideal point constant during the whole legislature, *regardless* of any party switching. The only exceptions made to this rule were the MPs who switched sides during a Legislature from being government's members (or at least supporters) to being opposition members. In this case, the parties were labelled with different names according to their relationship with the government, and their median point was calculated for each label as if the legislature was characterized by more than one party, only officially with the same name. As will be shown more clearly below, this distinction matters.

Finally, as the discussion deals with Parliamentary democracy, where the government affiliation explains much of the legislative behaviour, we carried out different analyses in the same legislature for each government that differs from the other in terms of party composition.

The one-dimensional space, correctly fitted by W-Nominate, classified at least 93% of the votes in our sample. The APRE is remarkable as well, with the partial exception of the 11th and 12th Legislatures (where it still reaches almost 70%). Fitting a second dimension resulted in an improvement in classification accuracy of <2% in each legislature[8]. Therefore, using a one-dimensional world seems to us a reasonable choice.

After estimating the spatial location of each MP, the party positions are identified with the position of their respective median voter[9]. Figure 9.4 summarizes both results.

---

[6] The authors recoded the absence as negative vote only for MPs belonging to parliamentary groups with at least 30 members and only when at least 90% of them were absent and the remaining MPs voted "nay" or abstained. The absence of MPs belonging to smaller groups was recoded only when at least a group of 30 members respected the previous conditions.

[7] According to the rules of the Italian Chamber of deputies, MPs who were absent because of their involvement in an institutional mission were not considered, unlike the other MPs, in counting the quorum that validates the vote. As their behaviour was completely "neutral" to the vote outcome, they were considered missing.

[8] The data are available on request from the authors.

[9] By estimating the MPs ideal points and using them to find the position of a party, the party is not treated as a unitary actor. On the contrary, any possible divergence in the voting pattern of its members, as well as its degree and nature, is allowed to affect the estimate of party's position. Cox et al. (2008) use a different strategy in their study of the Italian case. First, they consider a party to have voted Yea or Nay to a given bill if the majority of its members voted Yea or Nay to it. Second, they apply a roll-call analysis, similar to the one employed here, directly to parties' voting patterns, instead of to MPs voting pattern'. However, by so doing, they run the risk of underestimating any possible conflict – even if marginally – within a given party. This is a typical ecological fallacy.

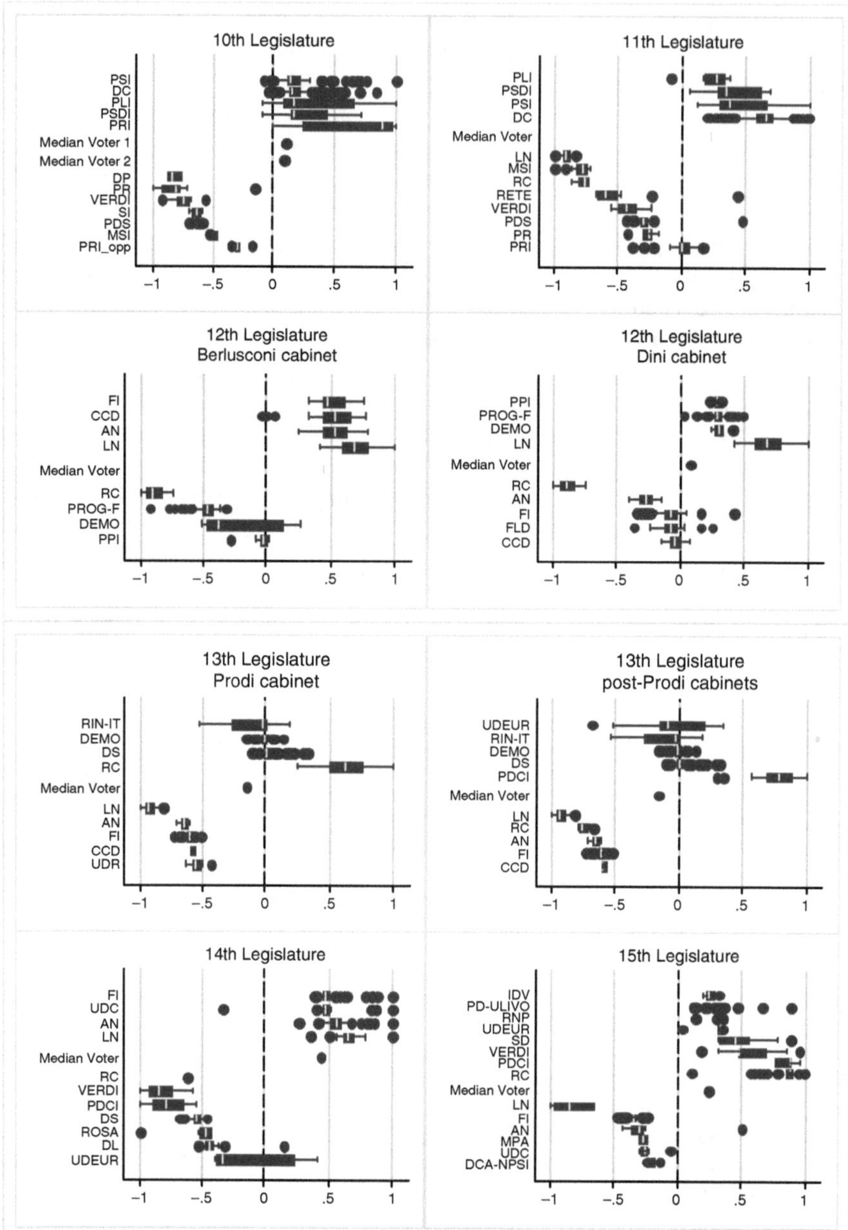

Fig. 9.4 Median positions and box plots of the main Italian parties: W-Nominate analysis*. *Note*. In the 10th Legislature, Median Voter 1 refers to the Median Voter during the first three cabinets; Median Voter 2 refers to the Median Voter after the exit of the PRI from the government. In the same 10th Legislature, PRI refers to the position of the Republican party when it was a member of the government, and PRI_opp to the position after it left the government. The parliamentary groups or subgroups are considered here parties. See Appendix for translation of the labels

The Quandaries of the Legislative Space

The box-plots in Fig. 9.4 deserve a comment for two reasons. First, some party positions appear at odds with the conventional knowledge and with the positions reported in expert surveys data on Italian politics (Laver and Hunt 1992; Benoit and Laver 2006). For instance, the position of the neo-fascist party (MSI) on the left of the government's parties and near the communists. Second, the estimated positions of the parties that during the same legislature withdraw their support from the government change radically (see PRI in 10th Legislature and RC in 13th Legislature).

Both phenomena should not, however, be much of a surprise. Indeed, by scaling roll-calls one directly measures the structure of the "revealed behavioural space" (Hix and Noury 2008; Rosenthal and Voeten 2004). The "dimension" revealed by the voting behaviour in the parliament is linked only indirectly with the underlying ideological dimension of conflict in a polity. The difference between an "exogenous preference space" and the "revealed behavioural space", as measured by scaling recorded votes in a parliament, is the outcome of two related factors: (a) the government's gate-keeping power (and the fact that in a parliamentary system most of the legislation is proposed by the government); (b) the strategic or instrumental nature of the opposition party's voting behaviour in a parliamentary setting.

As regards the first factor, all the models being tested here hypothesize that some government actors enjoy de facto gate-keeping power. If these models are valid from this point of view, it is also safe to assume that the proposals that actually reach the floor will be the least controversial, that is less likely to divide the government or the government's parties[10]. And it is precisely on these roll-calls that we run our analysis. Therefore it is not surprising that the dimension extracted by the roll call data represents mostly the conflict between government and opposition. For the same reason, the actors who control the agenda are expected to appear spatially close to each other (as they actually do). The only exception in this regard, is represented by those parties not always loyal to their government.

The "revealed behavioural space" retrieved from the roll-call analysis relies also on the (contrasting) motivations of the opposition parties' behaviour. Indeed, the opposition parties may risk their reputation and reliability before their electorate if they vote for a proposal supported by the government parties. So, they always have to balance between the policy effect of a bill and the effect of their voting behaviour on their reputation. If the government parties are cohesive enough to allow a proposal to pass (and the government is not a minority government), the opposition parties could paradoxically find it convenient to vote against the same proposal

[10] This fact, under plausible assumptions, will clearly under-estimate the "truth" level of intra-cabinet policy conflict as it appears from the NOMINATE analysis. We therefore explicitly accept the possibility of a selection bias when using roll call votes (see Carrubba et al. 2006, 2008; Hug 2006; Roberts 2007). However, we also recognize that this possibility, while hampering the utility of roll-call analysis as an exogenous source for measuring policy preferences of legislators, does not create an insurmountable obstacle for our analysis.

even when they evaluate it as an improvement of the current status quo. They will see such an improvement, preserving at the same time their reputation as opposition parties. The frequency of this behaviour is variable and depends on which aspect of voting will prevail in the party communication strategy (and consequently in the party utility function): the policy content of the bill or the political identity of its supporters (Spirling and McLean 2007).

After this discussion, the reader may doubt the utility of roll-calls in testing the law-making theories in a parliamentary setting, but such uncertainty is misplaced. The above theories are largely based on two common ingredients: (1) the distance in one dimension between the crucial actors (government parties and floor median voter) is based on sincere preferences; (2) whoever the crucial actors are, they are able to anticipate the final outcome of the decision-making process of any alternative move described in the specific legislative game.

In this regard, if the distance inferred from the voting behaviour is not calculated de facto on all political issues, but only on those issues which the same actors agree to consider in the government pact, then it means that the same actors consider the other issues less important than the government agreement. Far from being a "false" distance based on insincere preferences, such a distance can therefore be considered even more accurate, as it weighs indirectly the relative salience of different issues for the government actors.

Furthermore, the roll call analysis produces a location of the MPs that internalizes all possible motivations (and not only the policy content) of the opposition's voting behaviour. But, again, far from being a problem, such a feature seems to fit the scope of this study nicely. When the government actors try to anticipate the final outcome of each "branch of the game", they have no reason to overlook the instrumental and symbolic roots of the opposition's voting behaviour. For example, PRI after leaving the cabinet starts voting Nay (strategically and/or symbolically) very often to any bill sponsored or allowed by the government. Consequently, it moves to the left of the legislative space. This information is known and discounted by government parties who act accordingly. Nothing, in this reasoning, renders the estimations from the Nominate analysis unusable for this study. What the analyst must consider are the different roles played by PRI, subdividing the analysis into two periods (see below).

The Test Results

As has already been mentioned, any model of the typology under consideration here is falsifiable via the cut-point distribution in two steps. Two intertwined research questions must have an answer.

Do the Veto Player Models Fit the Real Legislative Decision Making Better than Other Models?

It is worth noting that the theories differ substantially in the degree of their exposition to refutation, because the no cut points line of one set of theories (VPM2 and VPM1) is usually longer than that of the other set of theories (PCT and GMPS). Indeed, given the data of this study, the rejection line for the "government median party models" (PCT and GMPS) is, on average, less than one-third the length of the VPM1 and VPM2 rejection line[11]. This implies that for most of the plausible distributions of the cut points, the first set of models (PCT and GMPS) are expected to perform much better than the other set of models (VPM1 and VPM2), simply because the latter are much more exposed to refutation.

To deal with this "differential exposure to confutation" of the two sets of models, the method proposed by Krehbiel et al. (2005) is followed. Three different cut point-generating processes are compared: the two theoretical sets of models, (PCT and GMPS), (VPM1/VPM2), and a null-theoretic generating process[12], that is an atheoretic random draw from a normal distribution[13]. This procedure, besides allowing direct comparison of the empirical support for the two sets of models in "neutralizing" the difference in the size of their rejection regions, also captures the idea that the fit of a theoretical model is very poor if the same model does not explain the data appreciably better than a simple naïve a-theoretical model.

As there was a remarkable change in the membership of the governments of the 10th, 12th and 13th legislatures, our unit of analysis in these three cases is not the single legislature. On the contrary, we focus on the "government sub-period", i.e. on the period within a legislature characterized by the same party cabinet membership. Moreover, during the 13th Legislature, when we consider the Prodi I government sub-period, we applied the analysis twice, by including (excluding) the RC position (i.e. the party that voted the investiture of the Prodi Cabinet without taking any ministerial role) to define the gridlock line (and consequently the no cut points line).

Table 9.2 presents the results for each government sub-period and the whole. The first three columns give the actual observed percentages of roll calls whose cut points would be consistent with the respective theory. On average, both sets of models perform very well[14]. The models that give a veto power to all government parties (VPM1/VPM2) seem however to work slightly worse than the "government

[11] Data available upon request.

[12] For each Parliament analysed, the cut points are drawn from a normal distribution where the mean and variance parameters correspond to the estimated sample mean and variance of that real Parliament's cutpoints. In particular, a Montecarlo simulation was run in which 500 "virtual" cut points were drawn a thousand times from the same normal underlying distribution.

[13] The normal distribution was utilized, because of an a priori affinity which is reinforced by the actual distribution of cutpoints. Employing a uniform distribution just strengthens the results of this study.

[14] Similar efforts to test the lawmaking models in the American Congress show lower performance levels. See Stiglitz and Weingast (2009).

Table 9.2 Law-making models performance: percentage of cut points consistent with theoretical models

Leg	Government sub-periods	PCT-GMPS Observed	VPM2-VPM1 Observed	PCT-GMPS Null	VPM2-VPM1 Null	PCT-GMPS Improvement (obs-null)/(null)	VPM2-VPM1 Improvement (obs-null)/(null)	Roll calls considered in the analysis
10	Pentapartito (Goria, De Mita, Andreotti VI)	100.00	99.17	99.43	98.18	0.58	1.02	122
	Quadripartito (Andreotti VII)	100.00	100.00	98.73	98.39	1.29	1.64	51
11	Amato, Ciampi	98.62	98.62	97.49	97.49	1.16	1.16	145
12	Berlusconi I	100.00	95.35	96.58	92.44	3.54	3.15	43
	Dini	100.00	86.44	89.55	77.79	11.66	11.12	59
13	Prodi I without RC	100.00	100.00	90.16	90.16	10.91	10.91	178
	Prodi I with RC	99.44	96.61	90.16	73.41	10.28	31.61	178
	Post Prodi (D'Alema I, D'Alema II, Amato II)	100.00	97.39	90.09	69.81	11.00	39.51	153
14	Berlusconi II and III	100.00	96.98	99.17	95.08	0.84	2.00	265
15	Prodi II	100.00	94.44	97.39	93.65	2.68	0.85	54
	Weighted average[a] without RC in Prodi I	99.83	97.38	95.68	90.35	4.49	9.10	
	Weighted average with RC in Prodi I	99.93	96.82	95.67	87.57	4.61	12.53	

[a]Overall average of the percentage of roll calls whose cut points would be consistent with the respective theory weighted for the number of roll calls considered in each government sub-period

median party" models (PCT/GMPS) according to their overall average performance (weighted according to the number of roll-calls considered in the analysis): 97.4% vs. 99.8%.

As the groups of models vary greatly in the length of the rejection line, the difference found in the empirical data between the two groups of models is not really impressive. In the columns under the label "Null", therefore, the percentage of roll calls whose cut points would be consistent with the respective set of models is reported if the cut points were indeed distributed normally. Finally, the last three columns indicate the percentage improvement in prediction over these null or baseline values. Both "theoretical" models improve the so called "null models". The overall difference, among the two sets of theoretical models now becomes meaningful and is in the opposite direction to the previous direct-test finding. In other words, on average, the models (VPM2/VPM1) seem to outperform the "government median party" models (PCT/GMPS).

Besides this general result, an investigation of the sub-periods reveals more variability:

1. In all the legislatures of the First Republic and the transition towards the Second one (10th, 11th and 12th Legislatures), the performance of the "government median party" models (PCT/GMPS) is close to the performance of the concurrent model (VPM2/VPM1) and is sometimes better. On the other hand, during the legislatures of the Second Republic (from the 13th up to the 15th) the "all government parties" models outperform the "government median party" models. In this sense, the general competitive environment and the dynamics of the party system seem to affect the explanatory strength of every group of the models. In particular, the models that assign a crucial role to the parties delimiting the ideological range of the government (i.e. both "all government parties" models) can be hypothesized to perform relatively better when the alternation in government is perceived as a real possibility. In this case, indeed, the threats by an extreme government party to trigger the collapse of the government, and new elections resulting in a different government majority, become more credible. The fact that a complete alternation in government appears as a political reality in the Italian party system only since the 13th Legislature is consistent with the above reasoning (and with our empirical findings).
2. When the Prodi Cabinet is considered, the models VPM2/VPM1 show the same explanatory power (10.91% of improvement) as the government median party models (PCT/GMPS). Note, however, that the Prodi government was a minority government (the only one among the cabinets considered in our analysis). The assumption behind VPM2/VPM1 models is that each government party exercises veto power as it can ensure the government's survival. Still, in the case of minority government, the agreement of the government parties is a necessary but not sufficient condition for government's survival. In theory, the centrally located government parties of a minority government could look for a support to their proposals alternatively on left and right of their ideal points, in terms of policy preferences (Tsebelis 2002). By doing so, the government could at the same time promote the desired legislative change and survive. However, as already mentioned in the previous sections, the opposition parties may consider not only the policy content of the bills, but also the symbolic (and instrumental) valence of their voting behaviour. They could deny their support even if they agree with the legislative change. Therefore, at least in the Italian institutional setting, most of the minority governments survive because they are firmly and systematically supported in the parliament by one or more parties that opt to remain outside the Cabinet. These parties are in fact "quasi veto players" as they allow the survival of the minority government as well as the government parties and by so doing they share their gate-keeping power. If the Prodi government is re-analysed by including the RC position to define the gridlock line, the model VPM2/VPM1 improves dramatically (reaching 31.61%). This choice increases the general improvement difference between the two sets of theories in favour of the VPM2/VPM1 models (from 9.10% to 12.53%).

3. The Dini Cabinet also deserves short consideration. As this was a non-partisan cabinet we do not have any precise hypothesis derived from a theoretical model to test. Nevertheless we have designated as government parties those parties that in fact supported it explicitly during the investiture voting. The VPM2/VPM1 models built upon such a fiction work slightly worse than the "Government median party models" (PCT/GMPS) and much better than a null model. Therefore it seems that in the case of non-partisan governments, information about the parties that strongly supported the creation of the government can help to predict reasonably well the subsequent legislative behaviour.

Strong or Weak Agenda Setting Power?

Figure 9.5 presents for each period, the kernel density plots of the cut points located on the legislative dimension (–1; +1) produced by the Nominate method. The corresponding normal distribution for each set of cut points is superimposed on the figures; the area delimited by the dashed line passing through M, and the solid line passing through the farthest VP corresponds to the (VPM2/VPM1) rejection area; the dashed vertical lines define the (PCT/GMPS) rejection area. The visual inspection of these figures offers some unique insights to decide between models assuming strong or weak agenda-setting power of government. Given the answer to our previous research question, we have to compare in particular VPM1 and VPM2 models.

As already reported, according to the VPM1 model, a high density of cut points should be expected around the position of the two political actors defining the gridlock area (i.e. VP_R and M, assuming M on the left side of the government) For any localization of status quo within (2M-G, M) and ($2VP_R$-G,VP_R), the final cut point position, according to this model should be, respectively, M and VP_R (see Fig. 9.2). In other words, for a more or less extended segment of possible status quos, the cut points should coincide or localize nearby the position of one of the two extreme government parties or the parliamentary median voter M if the latter is outside the government range (as we have hypothesized here). On the other hand, if VPM2 were to prevail, the distribution of the cut points should not concentrate around the same points. As can be seen from the figures on 13th and 14th Legislatures, when the models (VPM2/VPM1) clearly win against any other model, there are no peaks around these critical points. Therefore, the model that seems to correctly represent, on average, law making in the Italian Chamber of Deputies during the past two decades is the VPM2 model, which does not assume a strong government agenda-setting power. Of course, these expectations critically depend on the questionable assumption that potential status quo in different policy areas is not far from being uniformly distributed on the legislative space. Still, for any other reasonable (i.e. not that eccentric) distribution, our conclusion still holds.

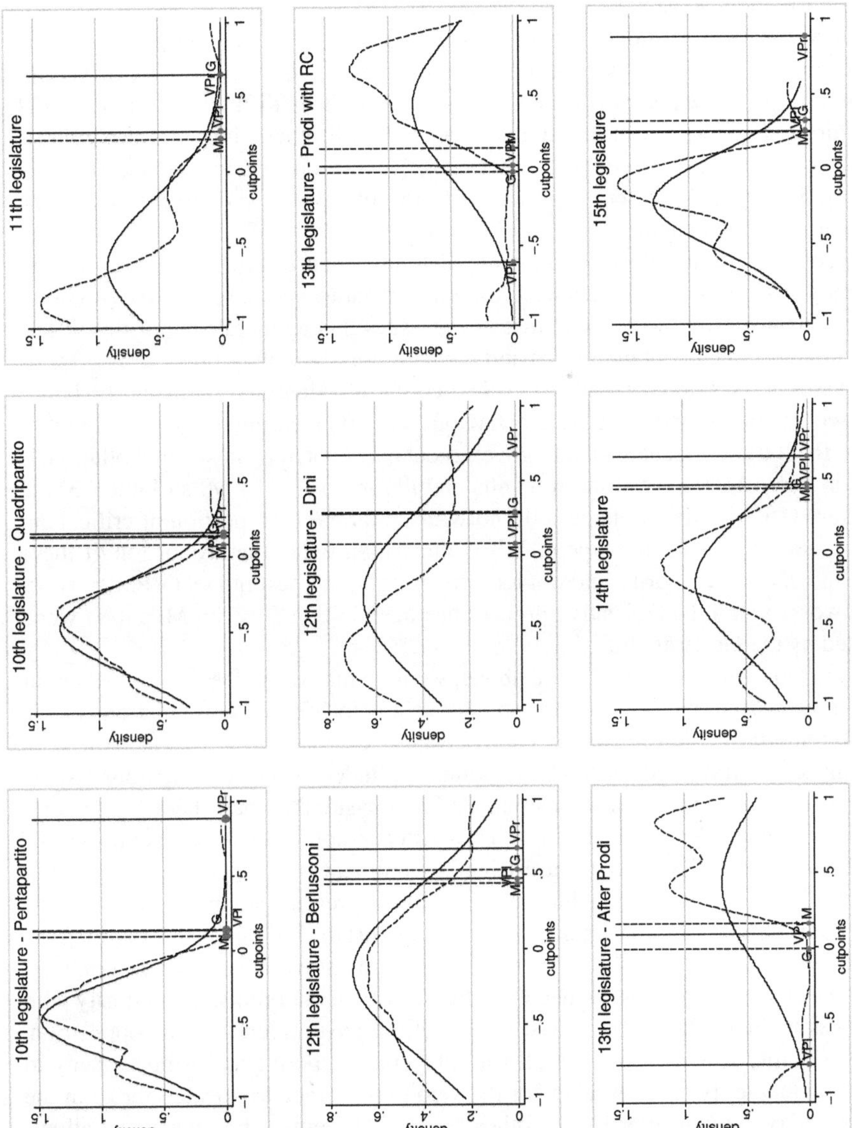

Fig. 9.5 Kernel density plot, cut points and normal distribution

When the Model "Fails"

The actors of the VPM2-model (which seems to account better for the empirical data in the Italian case) belong to the government area (given that the median voter of the Parliament always belongs to a government party). For a change of status quo, according to this model, all the actors must agree. When a cut point is in the no cut point line of the model (called here the "critical cut point"), the behaviour of some of the crucial actors of the model must have been different from the model predictions: some actors of the model disagreed with others, but their preferences were not taken into consideration. Moreover, if the change took place (the bill passed), a majority, different from the majority referable to the government, must have voted for the change.

These critical cut points were inspected to ascertain the following: (1) the explanatory strength of the model according to the nature of the legislative promoter (Government vs. MPs); (2) the nature of the issues that aggregate majorities different from the government majorities and the nature of these majorities[15].

Regarding the first issue, all the critical cut points identified by using the Nominate scores correspond to unusual behaviour of some government parties. In other words, in all the cases, at least one government party voted against some other government party. Moreover, if the roll calls on bills sponsored by MPs (Table 9.3) are quite rare (15% in the whole period), notwithstanding the proportion of critical cut points associated with this type of bill is more than twice the proportion of these bills (38%). In other words, and not too surprisingly, our best model (VPM2) works much worse when the legislative process has been initiated by the MPs than when initiated by the Government.

With respect to the second issue above, we note that while the voting behaviour in the macroeconomic and welfare policies seems to follow the predictions of the model, important policy sectors become a regular cause of division inside the government area. Almost all critical cut points are indeed connected to four issues: "Foreign policy" and "Institutions and Political system", when there is a centre-left government, "Distribution of resources and exemptions between South-North" and "Law and order" when a Centre-Right government is in office. These results fit perfectly into the conventional interpretation of the present Italian politics.

Moreover, the government parties that vote against the bills are usually among the extreme groups (in terms of policy-preferences) in the government. On the contrary, in almost all circumstances connected with the critical cut points, the majority who voted yes includes the most centrist parties of the government and the opposition. Such a situation suggests that not all veto players are "born equal": the capacity to veto is undoubtedly much weaker for the veto players that are located far from the parliamentary median voter. On the other hand, what seems to be a weakness allows the same extreme parties in the government to occasionally take positions which are very much in tune with their original policy preferences and without taking the risk of losing permanently a general influence on the main legislative agenda setter.

---

[15] As mentioned in the previous section, the Prodi govment is considered with RC included.

Table 9.3 Features of the critical cut points

Leg.	Government sub-periods	Sponsorship Gov.	Sponsorship MPs	% Roll calls on bills sponsored by MPs	% critical cut points referred to bills sponsored by MPs	Roll calls referred to critical point where the following parties vote largely or unanimously nay: Communist parties	Northern League	Post-fascist parties	Other government parties	No party pattern	Bill's Issue referred to critical cut points: Law and order	North and South	Institutions and Political System	Foreign Policy	Other
10th	Pentapartito	0	1	9	100	–	–	1	1	–	1	–	–	–	–
	Quadripartito	–	–	15	0	–	–	–	–	–	–	–	–	–	–
11th	Amato and Ciampi Governments	2	0	10	0	–	–	–	1	1	–	–	1	–	1
12th	Berlusconi I	2	0	0	0	–	1	–	–	1	–	1	–	1	–
	Dini	6	2	17	25	1	7	–	–	–	1	3	2	–	2
13th	Prodi (With Rif. Com.)	4	2	14	43	6	1	–	–	–	–	–	2	4	–
	Post-Prodi Governments	0	4	31	100	4	–	1	1	–	–	–	2	–	2
14th	Berlusconi II and III	4	4	17	38	–	6	5	–	–	3	2	–	2	1
15th	Prodi II	3	0	6	0	3	–	–	–	–	–	–	–	3	–
	Overall	21	13	15	38	14	15	7	3	2	5	6	7	10	6

Conclusions

This attempt to test the explanatory power of some general law-making models in a parliamentary system shows that the model that gives veto power to all the government parties, but with no strong agenda setting power to the government (VPM2) works better. However, this generalization does not apply equally well for all the periods considered.

Therefore, the most important and enduring results of this study cannot be summarized as a victory of one model over the others (albeit limited to one country). In fact, the empirical test carried out shows that the explanatory strength of different law-making models is variable and conditional. Other features of the political system, for example the party system dynamics, seem to play an important role in this regard.

The statement that all government parties play a crucial role in law making is not a surprising or path breaking assertion. However, we think that the present effort allowed us to specify better some features of the veto players theory (Tsebelis 2002) and to asses its performance in very different circumstances:

1. The government agenda setting power not only affects the location in the space of the final outcome but also the probability of the policy change. The area of policy stability is restricted to the unanimity core only when the government enjoys a strong agenda setting power, otherwise it is larger. Therefore in order to test the explanatory power of the theory of veto players one has to distinguish among different models according to different levels of government's agenda setting power.
2. In partial deviation from the theory of veto players, the government parties' role sometimes can be insufficient. Consider for example the case of the minority cabinet of Prodi during the 13th Legislature. As long as the opposition parties prefer to consolidate their image in the minds of the electorate, regardless of the policy content of the bills, then the non-government party that supports the formation of the government in parliament (in the above case: RC) can be reasonably considered to play a veto player role. This happens because in this situation the cabinet cannot rely on the existing consensus on some policy preferences of the opposition parties as they are symbolically and instrumentally intransigent. Consequently, it is constrained by the preferences of the non-government party that had supported its investiture, as if it was a proper government party. Such an amendment to the theoretical model dramatically improves the model's explanatory power, as is clearly shown in Table 9.2.
3. The nature of the legislative sponsor can also be important. When one considers the bills sponsored by MPs, the veto power of the government actors is less strong. Vetoing in the government arena indeed not only prevents policy change, but also prevents the veto players from being considered responsible for the policy change. This last reason for vetoing is much less compelling if the government does not sponsor the legislative proposal. In this case, for the government party against the bill, the advantages of being considered a credible

opponent to the new legislative status quo by the public can outweigh the cost of accepting the policy change. Under this condition the same government party may decide not to exercise a veto in the government.

It should be rewarding to extend the findings and ideas of this study to other countries. Such a research programme can take advantage of the methodological insight emerging from the present analysis. When focusing on roll-call analysis to test spatial theories of law making in parliamentary democracy, one should always avoid selecting automatically the single legislature as the unit of analysis. On the contrary, different analyses should be carried out in the same legislature when one government differs from the other in terms of party composition. When a party switches sides from the government to the opposition, its preferences as revealed by legislative voting change radically. If this simple fact is ignored, the party and median voter positions in the legislative space will be a misleading mixture of contrasting circumstances. If one wants to test the hypotheses about the role played by the government parties, their positions in the legislative space will have to be understood when they are really in the cabinet. This subtlety cannot be inferred from the previous roll call analysis of the US Congress. What matters, therefore, are institutions and this should be the guiding factor in all future analytical and empirical studies.

Acknowledgments We thank Stefano Iacus, Fabio Franchino, Marco Giuliani,Ulrich Sieberer and all participants to the conference "Reform Processes and Policy Change" for helpful comments and discussions. We also gratefully acknowledge the financial assistance of the Italian Ministry for Research and Higher Education, Prin 2007 prot. scrwt4 "Legislative process and policy arenas. Games, vetoes and networks in the age of the Italian political alternation". All data to replicate this study, as well as tables omitted because of space limitations, are available at: http://www.sociol.unimi.it/ricerca/parlamento/index.html.

Appendix: Italian Party Labels

	Communist parties	Ecological parties	Centre left parties	Liberal-non confessional parties (left and right)	Catholic parties (left and right)	Centre right parties	Right parties	Regional parties	Others
First Republic (1987–1994)	DP= Proletarian Democracy	Verdi = Greens	SI = Independent leftist	PRI = Italian Republican Party	DC = Christian Democracy		MSI = Italian social Movement (neo-fascist)	LN = Northern League	Rete = Network Party
	RC = Communist Refoundation		PDS = Democratic Party of the Left	PLI = Italian Liberal Party					
			PSI = Italian Socialist Party	PR = Radical Party					
			PSDI = Italian Social Democratic Party						
Second Republic (1994–2008)	RC = Communist Refoundation	Verdi = Greens	Prog-F = Federative Progressist	RNP = Rose in the fist	PPI = Italian Popular Party	AN = National Alliance		LN = Northern League	DCA-NPSI = New Christian Democrats and Socialist
	PDCI = Italian Communist People Party		DS = Democrats of the Left		CCD = Christian Democratic Centre	FI = Forward Italy		MPA = Autonomist Movement	IDV = Italy of Values
			PD-Ulivo = Democrats-Olive Tree		UDC = Union of Christian and Centre Democrats				RIN-IT = Italian Renewal
			DEMO = Democrats		DL = Liberal democrats				
			SD = Democratic Left		UDEUR = Union of European Democrats				

References

Benoit K, Laver M (2006) Party policy in modern democracies. Routledge, London

Carroll R, Lewis JB, Lo J, Poole K, Rosenthal H (2009) Comparing NOMINATE and IDEAL: Points of difference and Monte Carlo tests. Legis Stud Quart, forthcoming

Carrubba CJ, Gabel M, Murrah L, Clough R, Montgomery E, Schambach R (2006) Off the record: unrecorded legislative votes, selection bias and roll-call vote analysis. Br J Polit Sci 36:691–704

Carrubba CJ, Gabel M, Hug S (2008) Legislative voting behavior, seen and unseen: a theory of roll-call vote selection. Legis Stud Quart 33:543–572

Clinton JD (2007) Lawmaking and roll calls. J Polit 69(2):457–469

Cox GW, McCubbins MD (2005). Setting the agenda: responsible party government in the US house of representatives. Cambridge University Press, Cambridge

Cox GW, Heller WB, McCubbins MD (2008) Agenda power in the Italian Chamber of Deputies, 1988–2000. Legis Stud Quart, forthcoming

Han HJ (2007) Analysing roll calls of the European parliament: a Bayesian application. Eur Union Polit 8: 479–507

Hix S, Noury A (2008) Government-opposition or left-right? The institutional determinants of voting in fourteen parliaments, research paper

Hug S (2006) Selection effects in roll call voting. University of California, Berkeley: Working Paper 21

Hug S, Schulz T (2007) Left-right positions of political parties in Switzerland. Party Polit 13(3):305–330

Krehbiel K (1998) Pivotal politics: a theory of U.S. lawmaking. University of Chicago Press, Chicago

Krehbiel K (2006) Pivots. In: Wittman D, Weingast B (eds) Oxford handbook of political economy. Oxford University Press, New York

Krehbiel K, Meirowitz A, Woon J (2005) Testing theories of lawmaking. In: Smith DA, Duggan J (eds) Social choice and strategic decisions: essays in honor of Jeffrey S. Banks. Springer, New York

Laver M, Hunt B (1992) Party and policy competition. Routledge, London

Myagkov MG, Kiewiet DR (1996) Czar rule in the Russian Congress of people's deputies? Legis Stud Q XXI(1):5–40

Poole K (2005) Spatial models of parliamentary voting. Cambridge University Press, New York

Poole K, Rosenthal H (1997) Congress: a political-economic history of roll call voting. Oxford University Press, New York

Roberts JM (2007) The statistical analysis of roll-call data: a cautionary tale. Legis Stud Q XXXII(3), 341:60

Rosenthal H, Voeten E (2004) Analyzing roll calls with perfect spatial voting: France 1946–1958. Am J Polit Sci 48(3):620–632

Schonhardt-Bailey C (2003) Ideology, party and interests in the British Parliament of 1841–47. Br J Polit Sci 33:581–605

Spirling A, McLean I (2007). UK OC OK? Interpreting optimal classification scores for the U.K. house of commons. Polit Anal 15: 85–96

Stiglitz EH, Weingast BR (2009) Agenda control in congress: evidence from cutpoint estimates and ideal point uncertainty, research paper

Tsebelis G (2002) Veto players. How political institutions work. Princeton University Press, New Jeresy

Chapter 10
Domestic Veto Players, Commission Monitoring and the Implementation of European Policy

Bernard Steunenberg

Introduction

Once the European Union has adopted a new legislative policy, the member states are individually responsible for its implementation. This requires the formal transposition of the measure into the national legal order in the case of a directive, and the subsequent implementation of the policy. At each step, different configurations of political and administrative actors discuss how to deal with this policy. These actors may not be fully informed about discussions and agreements among other groups of actors at previous stages of the process. National actors who participated in the legislative negotiations are often not responsible for the subsequent transposition and implementation once the agreement has been reached (Mastenbroek 2003). Furthermore, national actors may have different views about a policy, partly shaped by their past experience about what works and what does not.

In this chapter, I focus on how national actors shape implementation after a European policy has been adopted. Departing from the formal adoption of a directive, which I call the legislative status quo, national actors need to agree on how this policy will be implemented. This process is overseen by the European Commission, which has formal responsibility for monitoring the application of European law. Because the provisions of a directive may not always be sufficiently clear or may require some adaptation towards existing domestic policy practices, national actors must interpret the directive. In this process of interpretation, the question arises as to how much the implementing policy may deviate from the policy as specified in a directive.

To explore this leeway, I develop a formal model of the interactions between domestic actors and the Commission. This model is based on a number of factors. First, implementation is approached as a process in which national players decide on an implementing policy that can be challenged by the Commission and ultimately

B. Steunenberg (✉)
Institute of Public Administration, Leiden University, P.O. Box 9555,
2300 RB Leiden, The Netherlands
e-mail: steunenberg@fsw.leidenuniv.nl

T. König et al. (eds.), *Reform Processes and Policy Change: Veto Players and Decision-Making in Modern Democracies*, Studies in Public Choice 16,
DOI 10.1007/978-1-4419-5809-9_10,

reversed. Secondly, players have different views on policy, which is reflected in their preferences. Thirdly, national players do not know exactly how much variation the Commission is willing to accept. Although Commission officials make statements about the policy, they may communicate different interpretations. Moreover, the views vary regarding the proper European policy and can be based on the intentions discussed at the time of negotiating the policy, existing case law, recent experience, or prevailing views of existing policy communities (e.g. European networks of national policymakers). National actors therefore have incomplete information and must determine what the Commission's true preferences are in making their decision. In particular, the national actor who takes the lead in formulating the implementing policy has to determine what the Commission's position is before successfully concluding the domestic implementation process.

On the basis of analysis I show that an implementing policy deviates from the legislative status quo the moment national actors as well as the Commission prefer such a shift. Uncertainty about the Commission's willingness to accept some deviations does not generally provide the Commission with additional strategic power. National actors are mostly able to infer the Commission's preferences. However, if uncertainty is combined with rather moderate preferences on the part of the Commission, the leading national implementing actor may not be able to estimate the Commission's preferences and will need to rely on prior beliefs. The domestic actor may adopt a too limited interpretation for the implementing policy, or a more ambitious one that risks a Commission challenge.

Despite the complexity of European policymaking, the current literature on the EU tends to put a strong emphasis on the EU legislative stage at which policy is shaped by the interactions between the Council of Ministers and the European Parliament.[1] From a policy perspective, however, this view is insufficient and does not show how the ambitions formulated in Brussels are transformed by the administrations in the member states. Recently, several empirical studies have shed more light on how member states transpose European directives.[2] One of the explanatory factors used in these studies is domestic veto players, which may hinder a smooth transformation of European obligations into national law. However, most studies focused on legislative veto players and found positive, negative, and insignificant correlations (Mbaye 2001; Giuliani 2003; Kaeding 2006; Linos 2007; Romeijn 2008). One reason for this inconclusive outcome is that most parliaments play a rather limited role in transposition due to generous existing delegation clauses in national law.[3] A second reason is that having the position of veto player does not sufficiently reveal an actor's influence on transposition or implementation. The

[1] For example, Crombez (1996), Tsebelis (1994), Tsebelis and Garrett (2000), and Steunenberg (1994). See Dowding (2002) for an excellent overview.

[2] For example, Mastenbroek (2003), König and Luetgert (2009), Falkner et al. (2005), and Thomson et al. (2007).

[3] See Steunenberg and Rhinard (2005) and Steunenberg and Kaeding (2009) for a different conceptualization of a veto player index to address this problem. The empirical findings using this new index are consistent with veto player theory.

preferences of these players also play a role, which complicates this relationship further (Steunenberg 2007). Veto player theory may help but requires further theorizing on how veto players affect outcomes in this context.

This chapter aims to contribute to this literature by analyzing the complex interactions between actors at the European and national levels in implementing European policy. In developing my argument, I move away from a perspective that defines players on an institutional (or constitutional) or partisan basis. Political or administrative actors become players, the moment they are in a position to shape the outcome of a decision-making process. This can be based on various resources, including information and expertise. Players are not restricted to institutional or "formal" players as proposed by Tsebelis (2002: 19), but include players with informal power. This notion relates to the concept of "factual veto points," as developed by Héritier (2001: 12), which refers to players with de facto decision-making power.

The extent to which political and administrative actors have power, and are therefore players in a game, can be represented with different decision-making rights. These rights provide a crude indication of what players can or cannot do as part of a game, and are the authority rules in Ostrom's terminology (1986: 19). For the purpose of this chapter, I make a distinction between the right to draft a proposal (agenda-setting power), the right not to be excluded, individually or collectively, from the approval of a proposal (veto power) (Tsebelis 1995, 2002), and the right to challenge a decision leading to a reversal (gate keeping and reversal power) (Steunenberg 1996: 314–316).

After discussing implementation as a process of interpretation, I present an incomplete information model on national implementation. In this model, the initial interpretation suggested by the Commission is regarded as a signal of its preferences. On the basis of the equilibria of this model, I show how domestic actors as well as the Commission affect implementation.

Implementation as a Process of Interpretation

In implementing European policy, domestic actors as well as the Commission must interpret the "legislative contract" as specified in a directive. The extent to which interpretation is needed depends on the contents of a directive. A directive may provide certain choice options or leave open how specific targets have to be achieved. In addition, it may contain ambiguous provisions which are a result of intergovernmental bargaining at the EU level. Franchino (2004: 286–291) studied the various degrees of specificity of directives and found that directives sometimes provide domestic actors with substantial discretion, especially when implementation requires specialized and technical knowledge (see also Franchino 2007). The discretion provided by a directive allows domestic actors to choose from a range of policies that could be implemented domestically. This raises several questions. What are the boundaries to making these choices? Which implementing policies can still be regarded as reasonable interpretations of a common policy's basic principles?

The Commission plays an important role in deciding on these issues. The Commission regularly answers questions about the interpretation of specific requirements in a directive from individual member states. In addition, the Commission actively addresses problems related to a new directive by organizing meetings with national officials. In selecting its interpretation, the Commission often seeks support from committees of policy experts in the field (e.g. comitology committees). In this way, the interpretation stated by the Commission is, to some extent, shared by a number of member states.

In its work, the Commission is backed by several enforcement mechanisms. The classical and still rather powerful method is enforcement through the European Court of Justice. Of course, the Commission needs to defend its claim that a member state is too liberal or too restrictive in its interpretation of EU law. But member states often do not want to be challenged, either because of possible damage to their reputation or because of the risk of losing a case that reverses their policy interpretation. In addition, the Commission has various "softer" enforcement mechanisms (Börzel 2003). These include inspections (e.g. in agriculture and fisheries), reviews, a systematic registration of complaints from private individuals and firms, independent internet-based sweeps of current practices (e.g. in the field of consumer rights), and auditing protocols. In combination with the "naming and shaming" of laggards, these mechanisms can be rather effective in limiting the range of policy alternatives.

The Commission's dominant role in the enforcement of European policy will be used in the model. To keep this model as simple as possible, the other actors at the European level are not explicitly incorporated. Their preferences are, to some extent, reflected in the views stated by the Commission.

At the national level, various political and administrative actors are also involved. Depending on the national legal system, directives are transposed by using legal instruments including statutory law, government decrees, and ministerial orders.[4] Naturally, a statutory law or act needs to be approved by parliament. Sometimes, parliament adopts a general authorization law, which allows the government to transpose all (like the *European Communities Act* in the UK) or a list of directives (like, for instance, the *lois d'habilitation* in France). In this context, often a "call back" procedure is used in which parliament has to approve the adopted measure, either by explicit or implicit approval.

Other member states, such as Denmark, Germany, and the Netherlands, generously employ specific delegation clauses, which give non-parliamentary actors the authority to adopt implementing measures in some area. These measures, which include government decrees and ministerial orders, are typically prepared by administrative actors within national ministries or implementing agencies. Parliamentary acts regulating the delegation to these actors are often very general covering a wide range of issues (Steunenberg and Voermans 2006: 43–45), providing administrative actors with substantial power. Sometimes the delegation clause

[4] See Asser Instituut (2004: 24–25) and Steunenberg and Voermans (2006) for overviews of different national legal instruments in several EU member states.

includes the possibility to transpose any directive in a field, long before a directive is passed. In those circumstances, governments or parliaments have little choice over the procedure that applies to the transposition of a directive in a given field.

Implementation Under Uncertainty: A Model

To demonstrate how domestic players implement a European policy while they do not know for sure whether their interpretation will stand, I use a signalling model with three types of players.

The first type is the unit responsible for a specific policy within the European Commission, which is assumed to be a single player (a desk officer or a director of a unit). The Commission is a rather decentralized administration in which these units often have a semi-autonomous position based on their information and expertise. Furthermore, the Commission is assumed to be the gatekeeper in the enforcement process. If challenged by the Commission the domestic actors may have to reverse their implementing policy and bring it into line with the legislative status quo. To simplify this enforcement process, and to focus on the interactions between the domestic players and the Commission, I assume that a challenge is sufficient for a reversal of the domestic policy.[5]

The second type are *domestic players*, $i \in D = \{1, 2, \ldots, d\}$, who participate in the implementation process. As indicated, the national policy arena is not uniformly organized, but consists of different patterns of transposition and subsequent implementation. The domestic players may include political parties, ministers, specific ministerial units, and administrative agencies. The implementing policy is the result of the interplay of these domestic actors. Their interdependency can be represented in terms of veto power for each of these participating national players.

Thirdly, there is the one national player who has the lead in the national implementation process. I will label this player the *national authority*. This player $a \in D$ has agenda power and shapes the implementing policy proposed to the other national players. Depending on the context, this player could be the only player involved in the decision-making process on implementation. In that case, the authority's proposed policy is equal to the policy that will be implemented.

The national players have to decide on some issue (e.g. the minimum value of works of art for which the directive on resale rights applies), which can be represented with a one-dimensional outcome space $X = R$.[6] In addition, the na-

[5] The dynamics of the enforcement process could be a further extension of the model presented here. The enforcement process is, for instance, modelled by Steunenberg (2010), using a different model in which the Commission has to decide whether or not to open its gates and accept that an enforcing player – the European Court of Justice, or a large number of member states – determines a new interpretation of the European policy.

[6] Although the model is specified for a one-dimensional outcome space, the main results may also apply to a multi-dimensional space. The only difference is that in a multi-dimensional outcome

tional players are uncertain about how the European policy should be implemented. To simplify the argument, the way the Commission interprets the policy can be of two types, $t \in \{1, 2\}$. These types can be associated with interpretations supported by existing case law or about how this policy will be further developed.[7] In other words, these two types illustrate a possible discrepancy in views about the interpretation of the European policy. The Commission's preference over X is given by a utility function $u_C(., t)$, which has a single-peak at C_t and satisfies the single-crossing property $\partial^2 u_C/\partial x \partial t > 0$. Furthermore, the preferences of the two types differ in terms of ideal positions. One type prefers a relatively "high" value of the outcome dimension, whereas the other type prefers a "low" value, that is, $C_1 > C_2$. The preferences of a national player i are described with a utility function $u_i(.)$ on X that is single peaked at V_i, which satisfies $\mathrm{d}u_i/\mathrm{d}x < \mathrm{d}u_j/\mathrm{d}x$ for $i, j \in N$ and $V_i < V_j$.

Implementation is modelled as a sequential process with three stages, which reflects, in a stylized way, the more complex interactions between the domestic players and the Commission.

In the first stage, which can be called the *transposition stage*, the Commission clarifies how a policy should be implemented and announces the interpretation $x \in X$ to the domestic players. This announcement can be made in the relevant standing committee or is part of the Commission's response to a request for information from the national authority. The Commission may also re-emphasize the legislative status quo. After receiving the Commission interpretation, the national authority makes the second move. However, this player is uncertain about what the Commission really wants and thus does not know the Commission's type.[8] This uncertainty is reflected in the authority's beliefs. Prior to the legislative process, these beliefs are defined by a probability function p, which assigns a strictly positive probability to each of the possible types of the Commission. Let p denote the probability that the Commission is of type 1, so $(1 - p)$ gives the probability that the Commission is of type 2. The Commission's interpretation x can be regarded as a signal of its preference. So, given this interpretation, the authority will update its beliefs; $\mu(C_t|x)$ denotes the conditional probability of the Commission having an ideal

---

space more instances of compromising and accommodating Commission types exist, making a straightforward objection against a policy shift during implementation, as the guardian type does, less frequent. Because using a multi-dimensional space will make the presentation of the main argument more complex, I prefer the simpler presentation.

[7] See Schmidt (2000) for examples of how the Commission may present different interpretations of the status quo. Note that Schmidt's analysis is about legislative decision making at the European level.

[8] Before the game begins, the other national players are also uncertain about the preferences of the Commission but know the views of the other domestic players including the national authority. The other players will make the same conjectures as the national authority and follow this player assessing the position of the Commission. Collecting information independently about the Commission preferences might be costly to these players because they are not well linked to existing formal or informal policy networks.

point C_t given some initial interpretation x. The authority considers the Commission interpretation and may select an alternative implementing policy $y \in X$ $(y \neq q)$.

In the second stage, which I call the *national approval stage*, the national authority seeks support for its implementing policy. Because the national authority may act as the (internal) agenda setter and make a take-it-or-leave-it offer to the other domestic players, this vote is modelled as a veto. The actions of the players are restricted to $v \in \{0, 1\}$; if they veto y (i.e. choose $v = 1$), the domestic players require the national authority to stick to the status quo policy q by presenting a literal interpretation. The joint-win set of these players, denoted as W, is the intersection of their win sets (i.e. $W = \cap_i \{x|u_i(x) > u_i(q)\}$ for all $i \in D$). The left-most or right-most domestic player closest to the status quo effectively determines this intersection, assuming that all others prefer a policy change. The ideal point of the left-most or right-most domestic player will be denoted as V_l and V_r, respectively. A player's point of indifference to the legislative status quo q – that is, a point for which $u_i(x) = u_i(q)$ – will be denoted as $i(q)$. Without loss of generality, I assume $q \geq V_l$, so that the status quo is either in the veto players' Pareto set (i.e. $V_l \leq q \leq V_r$) or to right of the right-most domestic member (i.e. $q > V_r$), indicating that all domestic players want to have less regulation than the legislative status quo.

The last stage is the *enforcement stage* in which the Commission is allowed to challenge the national policy y, which is given by $w \in \{0, 1\}$. If the Commission challenges the national policy (i.e. it chooses $w = 1$), it is assumed to be able to enforce the legislative *status*. In fact, this authority provides the Commission with some kind of veto power over national implementation. The win set of the Commission, that is the set of proposals the Commission will not challenge, is defined as $W_C(t) = \{x|u_C(x, t) > u_C(q, t)\}$. If $y \notin W_C(t)$ the Commission challenges y. This action is eventually assumed to lead to the reversal of policy y to q. So, a Commission type indicates whether the Commission is willing to accept the national authority's policy.

Taking the last two stages together, the implementing policy has to be selected from $W \cap W_C(t)$, otherwise it will be rejected by at least one of the domestic players or the Commission. The payoffs to the players in this game can be characterized by

$$U_i(x, y, v, w, t) = \begin{cases} u_i(y) \text{ if } y \in [j, q), j = \min\{l(q), c(q)\}, \text{ and } C, V_r < q \\ u_i(q) \text{ else,} \end{cases}$$

for $i = C, V_k$, with $k \in D$.

If the Commission or one of domestic players has an ideal position to the right of the status quo (i.e. if C or $V_r \geq q$), the intersection of their win sets will be the empty set avoiding any movement away from the status quo. A divide among the domestic players or between these players and the Commission implies that a deviation from the status quo will be blocked. So, regardless of what the Commission proposes and reveals about its preferences, the domestic response is one that induces the outcome q. This outcome indicates that the domestic players take a literal inter-

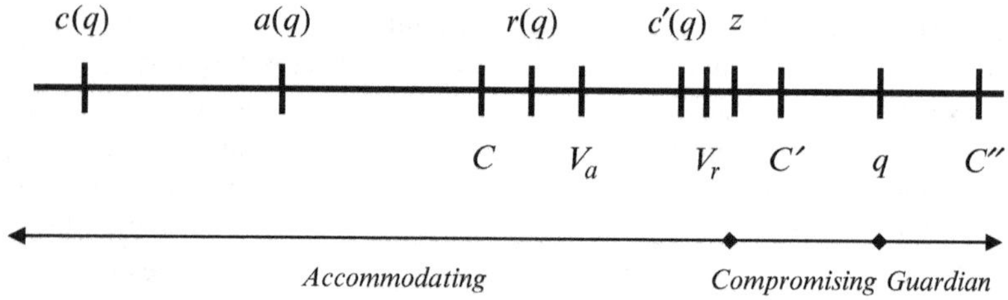

Fig. 10.1 Preferences of the different types of the Commission

pretation of the European policy (Dimitrova and Steunenberg 2000). I will therefore focus on the less trivial case of C and $V_r < q$.

If $V_r < q$, the domestic players will no longer block a deviation from the European legislative policy. Different Commission types may affect the response of the national authority. If $V_a \geq r(q)$, the authority may select its own ideal point as response to a Commission proposal. If $V_a < r(q)$, such a response will be vetoed by the other domestic players. Given this threat, the national authority is restricted to select a proposal from $[r(q), q)$ of which $r(q)$ is as close as possible to V_a. To describe the national authority's response to different Commission types, define the policy $P = \max\{V_a, r(q)\}$.

If $c(q) \leq P$, the Commission prefers interpretation P to the status quo. This type of Commission can be called *accommodating* (Matthews 1989: 351). An example is the Commission with the ideal point C in Fig. 10.1. If the national authority knows the Commission is of an accommodating type, it will implement a deviating policy $y = P$. The Commission will not challenge this policy, thus leading to reversal. If $P > c(q) > q$, the Commission type is *compromising*.[9] This is, for example, the Commission with the ideal point C'. If the national authority knows this preference of the Commission, it will formulate a policy $y = c'(q)$. This proposal reduces the Commission's utility, because it will be left indifferent between the status quo and the proposed outcome. Finally, if $C \geq q$ (and thus $c(q) \geq q$), the type of the Commission's type can be called *guardian*. This type is illustrated with the ideal point C'' in the figure. The Commission objects to any movement away from the legislative status quo towards the ideal outcome of the national authority.

On the basis of these three Commission types, six different combinations of types may occur, as described in Table 10.1. For each combination one or more equilibria exist, which consist of an optimal signal of the Commission (x), beliefs of the national authority about the Commission's type (μ), a proposal for an implementing policy by the national authority (y), a veto or not of the domestic players (v), and a decision whether or not to challenge the national policy by the Commission (w). In this chapter, I will only explore equilibria in pure strategies.

[9] More specifically, compromising Commission types have an ideal point between z and q, with $z = P + 1/2(q - P)$.

Table 10.1 Possible combinations of Commission types for $C_1 > C_2$ and $q \geq V_l$

C_1:C_2	Guardian	Compromising	Accommodating
Guardian	I	–	–
Compromising	II	IV	–
Accommodating	III	V	VI

Different Outcomes of the Game

Guardian Types

A guardian type of Commission will maintain the existing, literal understanding of the current policy as embedded in the directive. In addition, it will object to any interpretation that may lead to a deviating implementing policy in $[P, q)$.[10] Accommodating and compromising types, on the other hand, (slightly) prefer some alternative implementing policies other than the status quo outcome and will suggest different interpretations. So, if one of the Commission types is guardian, it will lead to equilibria in which both types reveal their preference.

For instance, if C_1 is the ideal point of a guardian Commission and C_2 represents a compromising type, C_2 will propose the interpretation $x = c_2(q)$. The national authority will update its beliefs such that $\mu(C_1|c_2(q)) = 0$ and $\mu(C_2|c_2(q)) = 1$, and the optimal response is a measure $y = c_2(q)$. An interpretation $x = q$ causes the national authority to infer that the Commission is indeed guardian.

If C_2 is an accommodating type of Commission, the interpretation will be $x = P$. Putting zero conditional probability on the Commission having an ideal point of a guardian type (i.e. being C_1), the national authority will propose to implement a deviating national policy.[11]

Compromising Types

A more interesting case occurs when C_1 is the ideal point of a compromising type of Commission.[12] Then C_2 may be the ideal point of a compromising (combination

[10] If both types are guardian (combination I in Table 10.1), there will be no separation since the domestic players cannot distinguish between both types. In equilibrium, the Commission signals $x = q$, the national authority proposes $y = q$, which will not be vetoed ($v = 0$) or challenged ($w = 0$) leading to q as the outcome.

[11] For the combinations II and III in Table 10.1, there are equilibria in which national authority correctly identifies the Commission as guardian and one in which the Commission is identified as compromising (combination II) or accommodating (combination III).

[12] As indicated, a guardian type of Commission will not deviate from the status quo. So, given some interpretation $x. \neq q$, the Council knows that the Commission (weakly) prefers some outcome to

IV in Table 10.1) or an accommodating type of Commission (combination V). The second possibility is the most interesting one, because it allows for a wider range of equilibria.[13] If C_2 is associated with an accommodating type of Commission, a separating equilibrium may exist. An accommodating type of Commission will then reveal its preference, which leads to a measure $y = P$. In the case of a compromising type, the legislative outcome will be $y = c_1(q)$. Thus, a necessary condition for a separating equilibrium is

Condition 1 (*separation*) : $u_{C_2}(P) \geq u_{C_2}(c_1(q))$.

If condition 1 is satisfied, the Commission with an ideal point at C_2 will propose $x = P$. The national authority will infer that the Commission is an accommodating type when it observes the Commission interpretation. Its beliefs will be updated such that $\mu(C_2|P) = 1$, putting zero conditional probability on type C_1. Given this, the optimum response to the Commission proposal is a measure $y = P$. If the Commission has an ideal point C_1, it will propose $x = c_1(q)$. Now the national authority infers that the Commission's type is compromising and updates its prior beliefs such that $\mu(C_1|c_1(q)) = 1$. To avoid a challenge and ultimate reversal, the national authority will propose $y = c_1(q)$. Clearly, these strategies and beliefs form a sequential equilibrium, so condition 1 is also sufficient for separation.

If condition 1 is not satisfied, a Commission with an ideal point C_2 does not have an incentive to reveal its true preference as the proposal $c_1(q)$ is strictly preferred to P. See for example, the preference configuration in Fig. 10.2. The Commission of type C_2 prefers $c_1(q)$ to $P = V_a$. Now, both types will formulate a "compromise" proposal $x = c_1(q)$, which does not provide the national authority any information about their type. So, the national authority's posterior belief is the same as the prior one. If

$$pu_a(P) + (1 - p)u_a(q) < u_a(c_1(q)),$$

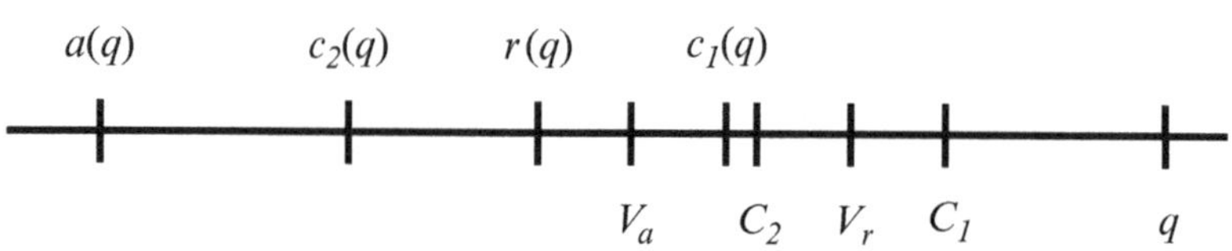

Fig. 10.2 A compromising (C_1) and an accommodating (C_2) type of Commission

---

the status quo and is at least of a compromising type. If C_1 is an accommodating type of Commission, then C_2 is an accommodating type too, since $C_1 > C_2$. The national authority can simply propose P, and the Commission will not challenge.

[13] Both Commission types can be compromising, $C_1 > C_2$, so that they are willing to accept $c_1(q)$. The national authority is not able to distinguish both types. Consequently, it has to rely on its prior beliefs in making a decision, which, if it wrongly assumes that the Commission is type C_2, leads to a challenge. In other equilibria with compromising types the national authority makes the right guess about the Commission type.

the national authority proposes $y = c_1(q)$ as the new measure, which will not be challenged by the Commission. This measure will also pass the other domestic actors since by definition $c_1(q) > P$.

If

$$pu_a(P) + (1 - p)u_a(q) \geq u_a(c_1(q)),$$

the national authority proposes $y = P$. This proposal has a positive probability of being challenged. If the Commission's ideal point is C_1 instead of C_2, the Commission will challenge the measure leading to the status quo. If the Commission's ideal point is indeed C_2, the measure will not be challenged.

Accommodating Types

If both Commission types are accommodating (combination VI in Table 10.1), the national authority may not be able to determine the Commission's true preferences. Information about the Commission types and thus their preferences is not important, because the national authority knows that both types prefer the domestic policy. In equilibrium, the national authority proposes its most preferred domestic policy, which will not be reversed.

Policy Implications

This game-theoretical analysis provides interesting insights into how the Commission and the domestic actors affect implementing policies. The national authority is mostly able to identify the Commission's true preferences by using its initial interpretation as a signal. The moment the national authority knows what the Commission wants it is able to develop an implementing policy that is acceptable to all other domestic players, which is not challenged by the Commission. However, knowing these preferences does not necessarily lead to an implementing policy that deviates from the legislative status quo.

The formal argument made in this chapter reveals a number of conditions that are important for the outcome of the national implementation process. These conditions are as follows:

- **Condition 2 (Commission preference):** *the Commission prefers an interpretation that deviates from the legislative status quo.*
- **Condition 3 (domestic agreement to change):** *all domestic players prefer the same implementing policies that differ from the legislative status quo.*
- **Condition 4 (congruence):** *the Commission and the domestic players prefer a change of the European policy such that they jointly prefer alternative implementing policies.*

They indicate whether the Commission and the domestic players prefer a change from the legislative status quo as specified in a European directive. In addition, condition 4 implies some similarity of preferences so that a non-empty win set exists. If the Commission prefers more regulation while all domestic players prefer less this win set will be empty, blocking any deviation from the status quo. On the basis of these conditions, we know that, in principle, the players need to prefer similar implementing policies differing from the legislative status quo to allow for some domestic deviation. In this configuration, the Commission cannot be a guardian type because it is inconsistent with conditions 2 and 4. Still, the question remains as to whether the domestic players are able to determine what the Commission wants and therefore avoid challenges to their policy.

Mistakes in interpreting the Commission's true preferences are restricted to situations in which the Commission prefers a limited change to the existing policy, either as compromising types or as a combination of compromising and accommodating types. Moreover, these types are found between the legislative status quo and the preference of the national authority, and clustered around the right-most domestic player, if such a player exists. Keeping all other things equal, the outcome depends on the national authority's prior beliefs. For this purpose, I distinguish between two possible types of national authority: a *reformist* authority putting a sufficiently high likelihood that the Commission prefers a "lower" level of regulation (i.e. type C_2), and a *conservative* authority which believes with sufficiently high likelihood that the Commission prefers a "higher" value (i.e. type C_1), in our case closer to the status quo. As indicated by the model, a conservative authority will implement a limited deviation from the European policy, which will not be challenged. A reformist authority, however, will propose an implementing policy that differs more from the legislative status quo. This policy choice will have a likelihood of being challenged.

- **Condition 5 (beliefs of the national authority):** *the prior beliefs of the national authority are conservative.*

Using these conditions, we can state the main implication of the model developed in this chapter as follows:

- **Result (deviating implementing policies):** *if conditions 2–4 apply, and if condition 1 or condition 5 for compromising and accommodating types or condition 5 for only compromising types is satisfied, the domestic players adopt an implementing policy that differs from the legislative status quo.*

If the Commission prefers a deviating policy similar to the domestic actors, the national authority is able to determine that the Commission is not a guardian type and therefore prefers some changes away from the legislative status quo. In that case, the domestic actors will implement, to the best of their knowledge, a deviating policy. Furthermore, the main result of our analysis is based on the condition for separation or the condition that the national authority makes a conservative assessment that will not lead to a challenge. It translates into two mirror results based on the absence of some of the necessary conditions:

- **Corollary 1 (maintaining the legislative status quo):** *if one of the conditions 2–4 does not apply, the implementing policy reflects the legislative status quo.*

In this case, the national authority will not be able to successfully propose a deviating policy. The Commission and/or the domestic players do not prefer such a policy.

We must also focus on conditions 1 and 5, which concern whether the Commission may challenge the implementing policy. Still, domestic players might be "lucky" by guessing the right Commission type.

- **Corollary 2 (Commission challenge):** *if conditions 2–4 apply, while conditions 1 and 5 for compromising and accommodating types or condition 5 for compromising types do not apply, the implementing policy could be challenged.*

Discussion

The model developed in this chapter suggests that national implementing policy is shaped by domestic preference combined with uncertainty as to how the Commission will react. Does the Commission prefer the domestic policy to the legislative status quo, or not?

An example of such a national discussion that affected the content of the implementing policy was the application of the Transport Operator Directive (98/76/EC) in the Netherlands. A new element in this directive regulating the profession was that the permit of a transport operator must be withdrawn if a "serious offence" is committed, rather than "serious, repeated offences," as in the preceding directive (96/26/EC). Mastenbroek (2007: 137–144) describes this process. It was unclear to the domestic players what the new wording meant. Would an administrative fine also count as an offence, and would one offence be sufficient to revoke a permit?

The existing practice in the Netherlands consisted of a points system in which repeated offences over a period of 3 years could lead to the withdrawal of a permit.[14] With the introduction of the new directive, the participating actors were divided into two groups, which can be regarded as veto players. The policy units of the ministry, which were also involved in the negotiations on the new directive, had the impression that this practice would also fit the new directive. This *conservative* view was supported by established transport businesses because they were not keen on introducing a new system, which would increase the risk of losing their permit. Others, and particularly the officials of the legal department of the transport ministry, argued

[14] Interestingly, as Mastenbroek (2007: 142) shows, the implementation of the points system was set up in such a way that the responsible agency did not receive information from the courts on offences. As a consequence, the agency was not able to apply the system.

that this system had to be modified to bring it more in line with the actual wording of the new directive. This *reformist* view was supported by the largest trade union, which wanted to have an effective system that would also protect drivers against insincere employers. They suggested abolishing the points system and proposed a system in which judges deciding on offences could immediately revoke a permit. During the process one of the policy units, the Directorate-General on Road Haulage, changed its position and joined the reformist side.

How the directive's requirements should be enforced was a national matter, which was not further specified. The "competent authority" in a member state should withdraw the license of a transport operator if the requirements are no longer satisfied. A different issue is the interpretation of the good repute requirement, which is an important element of the directive. The European Commission did not provide much guidance, leaving the domestic players in the dark about whether it would allow for a conservative view or only accept a more reformist domestic policy closer to the legislative status quo. In terms of the model developed in this chapter, the Commission's types were "compromising" by supporting the reformist group that wanted to adopt a strict interpretation of the new requirement, or "accommodating" in the sense of willing to support the existing system of repeated offences. In the end, "the relevant policy expert decided that the existing positions would suffice for 'Brussels'" (Mastenbroek 2007: 143). The prior belief was that the Commission was quite satisfied with the way the Dutch implemented the common transport policy, making it rather unlikely that the Commission would challenge the domestic players. The current practice of repeated offences was maintained. This was a lucky guess because the Commission did not challenge the Netherlands.

Still, the question remains whether the Netherlands transposed the good repute requirement of the Transport Operator Directive in a correct manner. Mastenbroek interviewed several experts on this issue. "Of the nine interviewees addressing this issue, only two interviewees are convinced that transposition was complete and correct. The others indicated that there were problems with the provisions for good repute, as these still implied repeated offences" (Mastenbroek 2007: 144). Differently put, 78% of the experts felt that this was a case of incorrect transposition (and subsequent implementation).

The transposition of the Road Haulage Operator Directive in the Netherlands is only one case. However, more systematic evidence shows that the Commission often does not challenge a member state in cases of incorrect transposition. In their empirical study on social policy directives, Hartlapp and Falkner (2009) report that the Commission did not start infringement procedure in several cases of non-compliance. At this point, a distinction has to be made between cases of non-notification, in which a member state failed to report one or more measures to transpose a directive into their national legal order, and cases of incomplete or incorrect transposition. The latter cases are of interest here, because they point to a deviation between the legislative status quo and the domestic implementation policy. Focusing on social policy directives, Hartlapp and Falkner found that only in 51% of these cases of incomplete or incorrect transposition did the Commission open an infringement procedure. Furthermore, these cases are unevenly distributed over the various directives. Especially in the case of the parental leave directive, ten cases of non-compliance were identified of which only three were taken to Court. In the case of the directive on part-time work, they identified six cases of non-compliance, while none was taken to Court. This remarkable behaviour of the Commission can be explained using the model presented in this chapter. If the Commission generously supports the main cause of these policies, and thus becomes an accommodating type, it will generously permit all kinds of deviations from the legislative status quo. Domestic actors in the member states therefore do not need to fear the Commission allowing them to fine-tune their national implementing policies.

Conclusions

So far, the implementation of European policy has not received much attention in the political science literature, partly because of its complexity in terms of the involvement of several layers of government and rather diverse national and even subnational implementation practices (Versluis 2007). Veto player theory, as developed by Tsebelis (2002), may help in theorizing on this topic, but it requires several adaptations. First, one has to step away from a formally determined definition of a player, allowing other actors to play a role in a model of implementation. Secondly, the theory requires a multi-layered structure in which European as well as domestic actors play a role (Marks et al. 1996). In this chapter, I specify veto player theory by developing a model on the implementation of European directives.

The model developed in this chapter applies the notion of veto players to actors who have de facto decision-making power on the implementation of European policy. In this way, the model accounts for the rich and diverse practices in EU member states, in which various political and administrative actors, sometimes together with private ones, determine national policy. In addition, the model incorporates the Union's multi-level context by focusing on the interactions between domestic players and the European Commission. Being unaware of the Commission's true preferences, the domestic actors have to decide whether and to what extent they will adopt an implementing policy that deviates from the legislative status quo. Specified in this way, veto player theory may help in understanding how European policy is implemented nationally and what causes policy drift, that is, changes in policy between the moment of formal adoption and actual implementation.

The analysis in this chapter suggests that a national implementing policy deviates from the legislative status quo if four necessary conditions are satisfied. The conditions state that when the domestic actors and the Commission jointly prefer a change away from the legislative status quo, and the domestic actors are able to set an implementing policy that will not be challenged by the Commission (by either identifying its type or by setting a relatively conservative policy), there will be deviations in the implementation process.

Only when both Commission types prefer a moderate deviation from the legislative status quo, may the national authority be unable to determine what the

Commission prefers, and it will then have to rely on its initial thoughts. The authority may underestimate the Commission's true preferences by adopting a too conservative implementing policy. In that case, the Commission will enjoy the benefit of having an implementing policy that will be relatively close to its true preferences. The authority may also overestimate the Commission preferences by falsely inferring that the Commission is too moderate. This will lead to a challenge of the domestic implementing policy.

The trade-off between having a better implementing policy and the risk of a Commission challenge is a matter of national "taste." A conservative national authority will propose an implementing policy that only marginally deviates from the legislative status quo without the risk of a challenge. A reformist national authority will propose a more ambitious policy that better fits to the national context, but against the risk of a Commission challenge. In selecting the player that takes the lead in the national implementation process, domestic players have a choice about how this dilemma is resolved. Several factors may shape this choice. If domestic players are concerned about whether they obey European law, as Falkner et al. (2005) suggest for some European member states, they may want to appoint a conservative national authority. If they are more risk taking, the likelihood of a challenge will be less of a concern. Also the way the domestic policy sector is structured may play a role. If this sector consists of a relatively small number of domestic players, the selection of the leading authority is more likely to be the result of a power struggle over the implementing policy, downplaying the risks of a challenge. In a more pluralistic policy sector in which power is distributed over many domestic players, these players may be more concerned about whether their policy will be accepted by the Commission. In short, characteristics of the national policy sector may feed into assessment of risk and the way in which uncertain domestic players set their priors.

The model developed in this chapter is a first step and needs to be further elaborated. Here we have only analyzed the interactions between the Commission and one member state, which is a simplification. If the Commission is playing against several member states with different domestic preferences, the Commission's signal to one member state can be used by the others to determine the Commission's true preferences. This may reduce the Commission's abilities to use information strategically to shape domestic policy. Another element that is worth considering is the Commission's limited abilities to monitor domestic policy choices. If the Commission is not able to determine what the true domestic policy is and relies on a signal from one of the domestic players, domestic players may shift their implementing policy away from the policy as adopted by the European Union. This dynamic is, for example, analyzed by Dimitrova and Steunenberg (2009), who show that informal policies implemented on the ground may substantially differ from the formal policy adopted by national policy makers.

The analysis in this chapter illustrates the multi-level structure of European policy making. This is reflected in the interactions between domestic players and the Commission guiding and monitoring this process. While domestic players have veto power nationally, based on the structure of the game, they still depend on the Commission. In this way, their veto power is not absolute, but conditional on the power of the "supranational" player. At the same time, the power of the Commission is limited as well, because this player may only act when the domestic players deviate too much from the legislative status quo. This limitation is a result of the "constitutional" agreement among the member states on the authority of supranational players. The structure therefore reflects the "checks and balances" that are common to any power-sharing arrangement in politics. It also emphasizes that policy games, as the one analyzed in this chapter, are ultimately embedded in broader power games among constituting players. As a consequence, veto power in a policy game is conditional.

Acknowledgements I thank the participants of the conference "Reform processes and policy change: How do veto players determine decision making in modern democracies" (14–16 May 2009, Mannheim), and the 2009 Conference of the Dutch Political Science Association (28–29 May 2009, Berg en Dal), and particularly Daniel Finke, for helpful comments.

References

Asser Instituut (2004) Implementatie EG richtlijnen vergeleken: Een onderzoek naar de implementatiepraktijk in een aantal EU-lidstaten in het bijzonder op het terrein van het maritiem vervoer. T.M.C. Asser Instituut, Den Haag

Banks JS (1991) Signaling games in political science. Harwood Academic, Chur

Börzel TA (2003) Guarding the treaty: the compliance strategies of the European Commission. In: Börzel TA, Cichowski RA (eds) The state of the European Union: Law, politics and society, vol 6. Oxford University Press, Oxford, pp 197–220

Carter JR, Schap D (1987) Executive veto, legislative override, and structure-induced equilibrium. Public Choice 52:227–244

Crombez C (1996) Legislative procedures in the European community. Br J Polit Sci 26:199–228

Dearden JA, Husted TA (1990) Executive budget proposal, executive veto, legislative override and uncertainty: a comparative analysis of the budgetary process. Public Choice 65:1–19

Dimitrova A, Steunenberg B (2000) The search for convergence of national policies in the European Union: an impossible quest? EU Polit 1:201–226

Dimitrova A, Steunenberg B (2009) Living in parallel universes? The implementation of EU rules on cultural heritage in Bulgaria. Paper presented at the 2009 General Conference of ECPR in Potsdam

Dowding K (2002) Rational choice and institutional change: an overview of current theories. In: Steunenberg B (ed) Widening the European Union: the politics of institutional reform and change. Routledge, London, pp 21–38

Falkner G, Treib O, Hartlapp M, Leiber S (2005) Complying with Europe? The impact of minimum harmonization and soft law in the member states. Cambridge University Press, Cambridge

Franchino F (2004) Delegating powers in the European community. Br J Polit Sci 34:269–293

Franchino F (2007) The powers of the union: delegation in the EU. Cambridge University Press, Cambridge

Giuliani M (2003) Europeanization in comparative perspective: institutional fit and national adaptation. In: Featherstone K, Radaelli C (eds) The politics of Europeanization. Oxford University Press, Oxford, pp 134–155

Hartlapp M, Falkner G (2009). Problems of operationalisation and data in EU compliance research. EU Polit 10:281–304

Héritier A (2001) Differential Europe: The European Union impact on national policymaking. In: Héritier A et al (eds) Differential Europe: the European Union impact on national policymaking. Rowman and Littlefield, Lanham, MA, pp 1–21

Kaeding M (2006) Determinants of transposition delay in the European Union. J Public Policy 26:229–253

Kiewiet DR, McCubbins MD (1988) Presidential influence on congressional appropriations decisions. Am J Polit Sci 32:713–736

König T, Luetgert B (2009) Troubles with transposition: Explaining trends in member state notification failure and timelines. Br J Polit Sci 39:163–194

Linos K (2007) How can international organizations shape national welfare states? Evidence from compliance with European Union directives. Comp Polit Stud 40:547–570

Marks G, Hooghe L, Blank K (1996) European integration from the 1980s: state-centric v. multilevel governance. J Common Market Stud 34:341–378

Mastenbroek E (2003) Surviving the deadline: the transposition of EU directives in the Netherlands. EU Polit 4:371–395

Mastenbroek E (2007) The politics of compliance: explaining the transposition of EC directives in the Netherlands. PhD thesis, Leiden University, Leiden

Matthews SA (1989) Veto threats: rhetoric in a bargaining game. Q J Econ 104:347–369

Mbaye H (2001) Why national states comply with supranational law: Explaining implementation infringements in the European Union 1972–1993. EU Polit 2:259–281

Ostrom E (1986) An agenda for the study of institutions. Public Choice 48:3–25

Romeijn M (2008) Compliance with EU social policies: Work in progress. PhD thesis, Radboud University Nijmegen, Nijmegen

Schmidt SK (2000) Only an agenda setter? The European Commission's power over the Council of Ministers. EU Pol 1:37–61

Shepsle KA, Weingast BR (1981) Structure-induced equilibrium and legislative choice. Public Choice 37:503–519

Steunenberg B (1994) Decision making under different institutional arrangements: legislation by the European community. J Theor Inst Econ 150:642–669

Steunenberg B (1996) Agent discretion, regulatory policymaking, and different institutional arrangements. Public Choice 86:309–339

Steunenberg B (2007) A policy solution to the European Union's transposition puzzle, Interaction of interests in different domestic arenas. West Eur Polit 30:23–49

Steunenberg B (2010) Is big brother watching? Commission oversight on the national implementation of EC directives. Eu Polit, forthcoming

Steunenberg B, Kaeding M (2009) "As time goes by": explaining the transposition of maritime directives. Eur J Polit Res 48:432–454

Steunenberg B, Rhinard M (2005) Hare or turtle? Member states catching up with the transposition of EC directives. Working paper, Leiden University, Leiden

Steunenberg B, Voermans W (2006) The transposition of EU directives. A comparative study of instruments, techniques and processes in six member states. Leiden University/WODC, Leiden

Thomson R, Torenvlied R, Arregui J (2007) The paradox of compliance: Infringements and delays in transposing European Union directives. Br J Polit Sci 37:685–709

Tsebelis G (1994) The power of the European Parliament as a conditional agenda setter. Am Polit Sci Rev 88:128–142

Tsebelis G (1995) Decision making in political systems: veto players in presidentialism, parliamentarism, multicameralism and multipartism. Br J Polit Sci 25:289–325

Tsebelis G (2002) Veto players: how political institutions work. Princeton University Press/Russell Sage Foundation, Princeton, NJ

Tsebelis G, Garrett G (1997) Agenda setting, vetoes and the European Union's co-decision procedure. Legist Stud 3:74–92

Tsebelis G, Garrett G (2000) Legislative politics in the European Union. EU Polit 1:9–35

Versluis E (2007) Even rules, uneven practices, opening the 'Black Box' of EU Law in action. West Eur Polit 30:50–67

Chapter 11
Strategic Voting in a Bicameral Setting*

Simon Hug

Introduction

How bicameralism affects reform processes specifically and policy outcomes more generally is a debated issue. While a recent review of bicameralism (Cutrone and McCarty 2006) concluded that in the absence of malapportionement or other ways in which the representatives might differ the two (or more) chambers had no effect, the studies presented by Rogers (2001, 1998) suggest that bicameralism might have an effect due to enhanced information provision in parliaments with two chambers. On the other hand Tsebelis and Money's (1997) analysis of politics in a bicameral parliament suggests that policy changes should become harder, under the assumption, however, that policy preferences differ between the two chambers (see also Tsebelis 1995).

These studies offering a general view of bicameralism and its effects do not, however, look more closely at the interactions between the members of the two chambers. Especially, in bicameral parliaments with a well-developed navette system and a conciliation committee, these interactions are likely to be of a strategic nature. Interest in strategic voting by MPs in general has, however, ebbed and flowed, mostly the former. Many scholars have found comfort in Krehbiel and Rivers's (1990) critique of work on strategic voting in parliaments (in particular in Congress), arguing that in the absence of a fixed agenda and partial information on the preferences of MPs strategic voting is unlikely. In many other parliaments, however, fixed agendas and information provided by political parties are more likely to prevail (see for instance Bütikofer and Hug 2008). However a large neglected aspect

*Some early thoughts of this study were presented at a seminar at the University of Mannheim, at the Annual Meeting of the Midwest Political Science Association in Chicago (April 2–5, 2009) and at the conference "Reform processes and policy change: How do veto players determine decision-making in modern democracies" University of Mannheim (May 14–16, 2009).

S. Hug (✉)
Département de science politique, Faculté des sciences économiques et sociales,
Université de Genève, Geneva, Switzerland
e-mail: simon.hug@unige.ch

T. König et al. (eds.), *Reform Processes and Policy Change: Veto Players and Decision-Making in Modern Democracies*, Studies in Public Choice 16,
DOI 10.1007/978-1-4419-5809-9_11,

regarding strategic voting relates to the chamber structure (though see Gross 1982; Miller 1984). Strictly speaking the analysis of strategic voting as championed by McKelvey and Niemi (1978) (based on Farquharson 1969) and more or less applied by, for instance, Bjurulf and Niemi (1978), Enelow and Koehler (1980), Enelow (1981), Denzau, Riker and Shepsle (1985), Calvert and Fenno (1994) relies on a final vote occurring in a given chamber. If this is the case as in much of Bjurulf and Niemi's (1978) analysis, this approach causes no problems. In bicameral settings, like the US Congress (Enelow and Koehler 1980; Enelow 1981; Denzau, Riker and Shepsle 1985; Krehbiel and Rivers 1990; Calvert and Fenno 1994) or the Swiss parliament (Bütikofer and Hug 2008) an analysis of strategic voting only makes sense when considering the bicameral sequence and voting procedure.[1]

Considering voting by MPs in a bicameral context goes in the same direction as recent work by Londregan (2000), Clinton and Meirowitz (2004), Cox and McCubbins (2005) and Carey (2008) (see also, e.g., Rosenthal and Voeten 2004; Spirling and McLean 2006; Carrubba, Gabel and Hug 2008) suggesting that votes in parliament have to be considered as embedded in the larger process of law-making. Important in this context are also, as Clinton and Meirowitz (2004) suggest, aspects of strategic voting. However, techniques used to analyze roll call votes do not consider this embedded nature of votes in parliaments (for exceptions, see Londregan 2000; Clinton and Meirowitz 2004). Given this, it is unclear what the roll call analyses actually tell us about MPs in a bicameral setting.

To gain a better understanding of bicameralism and its effect on reform processes one needs to assess whether MPs in two chambers engage in strategic interactions. Drawing on Martin's (2001) model of the bicameral US Congress and offering some initial results from a game with incomplete information, I wish to discuss the conditions under which strategic behavior across chambers may occur and, as a consequence, may affect our analyses of roll call data. Under certain conditions concerning the agenda power of the two chambers sophisticated voting by MPs is expected under rather mild conditions. But if agenda powers are vested in both chambers, the analysis suggests that sophisticated behavior, while still possible at the MP-level, is more likely off the floor of parliament, for instance in committees and in party caucuses, as suggested by Krehbiel and Rivers (1990)

In the next section, I review the literature on roll call votes as it relates to bicameral parliamentary settings. In section "Bicameral Setting", I then briefly discuss different bicameral settings in which sophisticated behavior may occur. The section "Sophisticated Voting in a Bicameral Setting: Theory" is devoted to a theoretical analysis of the conditions for sophisticated voting in a bicameral structure. Finally, I discuss the results on offer conclusions.

[1] Interestingly, none of the classical works on Congress seem to mention this complication, with the sole exceptions, to my knowledge, of the early work by Gross (1982) and Miller (1984) as well as the contribution of Martin (2001).

Roll Call Votes, Sophisticated Behavior and Bicameral Parliaments

The analysis of roll call votes in parliaments has progressed considerably over recent decades. On the one hand the methodological sophistication has increased dramatically, as demonstrated by, among others, Heckman and Snyder (1997), Poole (2000), Bailey and Chang (2001), Martin and Quinn (2002), and Clinton, Jackman and Rivers (2004) (for a review see Poole 2005). On the other hand, while initially very focused on analyses of the US Congress, roll call votes are increasingly also used as empirical material in comparative research (see for example Carey 2008).[2]

Much of this research, however, does not reflect on the context in which roll call votes occur. First, and foremost, roll call votes may only form a very selective subset of all votes taken in a parliament, and this subset, as more and more empirical evidence suggests, may bias our inferences (e.g., Carrubba, Gabel, Murrah, Clough, Montegomery and Schambach 2006; Roberts 2007; Carrubba, Gabel and Hug 2008; Chiou and Yang 2008; Thiem 2009; Hug 2010 (forthcoming)). The strongest empirical evidence for such bias appears in Roberts (2007) and Hug (2010 (forthcoming)) who show for the US Congress or the Swiss parliament respectively, that behavior in roll call votes differs systematically compared to behavior in other votes.

Second, as work for instance by Londregan (2000), Martin (2001), Clinton and Meirowitz (2004), Bütikofer and Hug (2008), and Hoyland and Hagemann (2010 (forthcoming)) shows, roll call votes take place in a specific decision-making process, and as many analyses of roll call votes consider them as independent observations, this context may again bias our inferences.[3] This decision-making context determines on the one hand what votes will be taken on the floor (and thus potentially be observed as roll call votes) (e.g., Londregan 2000; Clinton 2006; Penn 2008) through various gate-keeping powers,[4] and on the other hand may lead to sophisticated behavior by MPs (e.g., Volden 1998; Martin 2001; Clinton and Meirowitz 2004; Bütikofer and Hug 2008; Penn 2009).

While work on sophisticated behavior in parliaments has seen a series of Theoretical contributions (e.g., McKelvey and Niemi 1978; Enelow and Koehler 1980; Enelow 1981; Denzau, Riker and Shepsle 1985; Calvert and Fenno 1994) and empirical contributions (e.g., Bjurulf and Niemi 1978) in the aftermath of Farquharson (1969) seminal work, a critical article by Krehbiel and Rivers (1990) has largely (and for a considerable time) put a lid on studying sophisticated voting

[2] Comparative, in this context, may mean both work on parliaments other than the US Congress, and work comparing different legislatures.

[3] Related to this problem is obviously the effect of party discipline, which may lead to odd estimates of ideal-points based on roll call votes (see Rosenthal and Voeten 2004; Spirling and McLean 2006, 2007).

[4] See, however, Martin and Quinn (2005) argument that at least Bayesian ideal-point estimates of Supreme Court justices are not unduly affected by the latter's gate-keeping powers.

in parliaments.[5] Their critique of work on sophisticated behavior by MPs focuses on the following points. For MPs to be able to engage in sophisticated behavior, the agenda has to be fixed, and the MPs need to be reasonably well informed on the preferences of their colleagues. Discussing this issue in the context of the US Congress they argue that the important malleability of the agenda on the floor simply makes sophisticated behavior unlikely. Much more likely, according to them, is sophisticated behavior before voting occur on the floor, either through gatekeeping (see for instance Clinton 2006) or agenda-control (see for instance Cox and McCubbins 2005). If sophisticated voting is occurring all the same on the floor, it will often be observationally equivalent to sincere behavior, or sophisticated sincerity in Austen-Smiths terms (for the theoretical basis, see Austen-Smith 1987).

While this criticism may well apply to the US Congress (though see Calvert and Fenno 1994; Martin 2001; Clinton and Meirowitz 2004), it is far from certain that it implies the absence of all sophisticated floor behavior in parliaments around the world. On the contrary, agenda control by political parties (Bräuninger and Debus 2009; Cox and McCubbins 2010 (forthcoming)) and the role of information provider suggest that sophisticated behavior may well be quite frequent, especially in parliamentary systems (see for instance Bütikofer and Hug 2008).

Most work on sophisticated behavior relies implicitly (or explicitly) on McKelvey and Niemi's (1978), who based on Farquharson's (1969) contribution, propose analyzing voting in terms of sophisticated equivalents. Hence, working back through the agenda tree, each alternative is replaced by the outcome of the tree starting at the branches of the respective decisions. This implies, however, that the ultimate decision node is well identified (a critical point in addition to the points raised by Krehbiel and Rivers (1990)). As almost all empirical and theoretical analyses focus on a single chamber, but this ultimate decision node may not be as easily identified, or even be uncertain, for instance because of the possible use of conciliation committees in the case of bicameral disagreement.[6] Hence, ignoring the bicameral context may bias our analyses of sophisticated behavior on the chamber floors, especially if they rely in one way or the other on the idea of "sincere preferences" finding their expression in chamber final passage votes (except, obviously, on reports from the conciliation committee or on bills already adopted in the other chamber).

This bicameral context is, however, almost completely ignored. Perhaps, many scholars agree with Cutrone and McCarty (2006, 193) who conclude

> "Regardless of the theoretical framework or the collective action problem to be solved, we find that both positive and normative arguments in favor of bicameralism tend to

---

[5] Only recently a series of scholars have attempted to identify instances of strategic behavior (e.g., Jenkins and Munger 2003; Finocchiaro and Jenkins 2008; Leemann 2009). See also the related literature on log-rolling nicely reviewed by Stratmann (1997), who also devises a test for cyclical behavior in parliaments (Stratmann 1996).

[6] The only model dealing with this aspect that I am aware of, namely Martin's (2001), "solves" this problem by having an exogenous bill adopted if a conciliation committee needs to be called (see below for more details).

be weak and underdeveloped. Most of the effects of bicameralism are due primarily to quite distinct institutional choices, such as malapproportionment and super-majoritarianism, which correlate empirically with bicameralism."

Their conclusion is based on a discussion of a selected set of theoretical contributions[7] and an argument that the results of many empirical studies cannot really attribute a "causal effect" to the chamber structure.[8] Probably relying on this conclusion, most scholars seem not to have considered the bicameral structure when analyzing roll call votes. At most, some authors have attempted to sharpen our understanding of roll call votes by comparing them across chambers for various empirical analyses (see for instance Levitt 1996; Bailey and Chang 2001; Bailey 2007; Bütikofer and Hug 2010).

An early study by Gross (1982) and a rejoinder by Miller (1984) demonstrated that analyses of sophisticated voting focusing on one chamber in a bicameral setting is often inappropriate.[9] Martin's (2001) work is the only recent study that considers sophisticated voting in a separation of powers system, and thus by implication in a bicameral parliament.[10] His model presumes that a congressman has to vote on an exogenous bill A, knowing that another chamber still has a say, and both a president and the supreme court may invalidate the adopted bill. In case of a rejection, the status quo Q is the outcome, while in case of acceptance a compromise adopted (implicitly) by the conciliation committee will result. Analyzing this simple game in a one-dimensional policy space, Martin (2001) can derive implications concerning the likelihood of sophisticated behavior (distinguishing it also from "sophisticated sincerity") and finds considerable empirical support from empirical data on the US Congress.[11] The main limitation of Martin (2001) model stems from the quite constraining assumptions on which it is built. First of all, the agenda in this game is fixed with exogenously given alternatives, and the role of the conciliation committee in the event of disagreement between the chambers is rather arbitrary. Second, the information available to the main player in this game is complete and perfect. Hence, by assumption, Martin (2001) deals with a situation, which in the eyes of Krehbiel and Rivers (1990) may allow for sophisticated behavior, but should not

[7] For instance, they fail to consider Gross's (1982), Miller's (1984) and Martin's (2001) work on sophisticated behavior in a bicameral setting.

[8] See Heller (2007) for a review focusing on the empirical results (e.g., Levmore 1992; Heller 2001; Congleton 2003).

[9] Interestingly, these studies are hardly referred to in the current literature.

[10] Interesting to note is that Martin's (2001) article is almost exclusively cited (at least according to *Google Scholar*) by scholars dealing with the Supreme Court. For some reason, this important contribution has not found an audience among congressional (or legislative) scholars.

[11] In some sense related is Hoyland and Hagemann's (2010 (forthcoming)) study on bicameralism in the European Union. They can demonstrate that Council votes (i.e., votes in the upper house) affect the way in which the European parliament (the lower house) votes. While their focus is on the particularities of the so-called co-decision procedure, their work still suggests that separate analyses of one chamber may be misleading.

apply to the US Congress.[12] Despite these limitations, his model provides a fruitful starting point to assess different institutional setups discussed in the next section.

Bicameral Settings

Bicameralism differs in practice considerably in terms of the distribution of powers.[13] Implicit in Martin's (2001) model is a bicameral system in which one chamber has the proposal right, and diverging bills automatically lead to the adoption of a compromise bill, in which the difference between the two chambers are split.[14] Work on bicameral parliaments (e.g., Trivelli 1974; Tsebelis and Money 1997; Patterson and Mughan 1999) suggests, however, that there is a wide variety of arrangements, which may even differ according to the policy field.

Given Martin's (2001) model, three elements seem most important for what follows. First of all, is one chamber limited in its proposal rights (which is implicit in Martin's (2001) model)? Second, in case of bicameral disagreement, is there a conciliation committee which may propose a compromise proposal? Third, are the proposals endogenous or not?

In terms of the first criteria we may distinguish the following sets:

- Bicameral parliaments where one of the chambers only has the right to veto (but in some cases may be overridden). Examples: British House of Lords, European Parliament in the case of the ascent procedure (see Hix 2005), the Dutch upper house (see Timmermans, Scholten and Oostlander 2008), the German Bundesrat in the case of *Einspruchsgesetze* (see Ismayr 2008), etc.
- Bicameral parliaments where both chambers have the right to amend proposals and their agreement is required. Examples: German parliament in the case of laws requiring the consent of the Bundesrat (see Ismayr 2008), US Congress, Swiss parliament (see Jegher 1999), European parliament in the case of co-decision (see Hix 2005).[15]

---

[12] In his empirical analysis, however, Martin (2001) attempts to deal with the first point by limiting his analysis to a subset of votes where the assumption largely holds, and the results carry over.

[13] Cutrone and McCarty (2006, 180), in their review chapter on bicameralism, adopt an unnecessarily stringent definition of bicameralism by limiting it to parliaments where the two chambers have equal powers. Obviously, such a stringent definition, if applied indiscriminately, would eliminate almost all bicameral systems from consideration (for a description of the wide diversity of bicameral competencies, see Trivelli 1974; Tsebelis and Money 1997; Patterson and Mughan 1999).

[14] This is very similar to Tsebelis and Money's (1997) setup, where the bargain of the conciliation committee is characterized with the Nash bargaining solution (for the relationship between the mean and the Nash bargaining solution see Achen 2006).

[15] Though see Hoyland and Hagemann (2010 (forthcoming)) analysis suggesting that the Council has in this case conditional agenda-setting control (for a related argument concerning the cooperation procedure but regarding the EP, see Tsebelis 1994).

These two sets may be further subdivided according to the other two criteria. For each combination, however, clearly empirical examples may be found (see Tsebelis and Money 1997; Patterson and Mughan 1999).

Sophisticated Voting in a Bicameral Setting: Theory

In this section I explore two simple setups, one relying on Martin's (2001) model, to assess under what conditions sophisticated voting in a bicameral system may occur, both under complete information (as in Martin's (2001) model) and incomplete information.

Complete Information

The starting point of the complete information setup is Martin's (2001) model of strategic voting in a separation of powers system. His model is based on a one-dimensional policy space, over whose elements actors have single-peaked preferences (linear tent-preferences). In his setup apart a legislator and an "other chamber" two additional actors are present, namely a president and a judiciary. For simplicity, and because my focus is on bicameralism, I omit these.

Based on this simplification, the sequence of play is as follows:

1. An exogenous bill A is presented ($A < Q$ where Q is the status quo).
2. Member C with ideal-point x_C votes for A or Q. If she votes for Q the game ends, and the status quo Q is maintained.
3. If C votes for A the compromise bill of the conciliation committee between A and the other chamber's preferred policy x_O, i.e., $\frac{A+x_O}{2}$ results.

In this setup the decision of C, specifically whether to vote sincerely or sophisticatedly, depends on the preference configurations. Her utility from the two options are the following:

$$EU_C(A) = -|x_C - \frac{x_O + A}{2}| \tag{11.1}$$

$$EU_C(\neg A) = -|x_C - Q| \tag{11.2}$$

Hence, C will vote "sophisticatedly" for A if the following condition holds:

$$p(A) = 1 \text{ if } EU_C(A) \geq EU_C(\neg A) \tag{11.3}$$

$$p(A) = 1 \text{ if } -|x_C - \frac{x_O + A}{2}| \geq -|x_C - Q|. \tag{11.4}$$

The following four situations exhaust all preference configurations under the assumptions of the game:[16]

(a) $x_C \leq \frac{x_Q+A}{2}$ and $x_C \leq Q$
In that case C votes sincerely for A as long as $x_C \leq \frac{A+Q}{2}$ and sophisticatedly for A if $Q \geq \frac{x_Q+A}{2}$.
Hence, differences between sincere and sophisticated behavior appear if

(1) $x_C \leq \frac{A+Q}{2}$ and $Q < \frac{x_Q+A}{2}$ (sincere vote A, sophisticated vote Q).
(2) $x_C > \frac{A+Q}{2}$ and $Q \geq \frac{x_Q+A}{2}$ (sincere vote Q, sophisticated vote A).

(b) $x_C > \frac{x_Q+A}{2}$ and $x_C > Q$
Under these conditions C votes sincerely always for Q and sophisticatedly for A if $Q < \frac{x_Q+A}{2}$
Hence, differences between sincere and sophisticated behavior appear if

(1) $Q < \frac{x_Q+A}{2}$ (sincere vote Q, sophisticated vote A)

(c) $x_C \leq \frac{x_Q+A}{2}$ and $x_C > Q$
Under these conditions C votes sincerely always for Q and sophisticatedly for A if $Q \leq 2x_C - \frac{x_Q+A}{2}$
Hence, differences between sincere and sophisticated behavior appear if

(1) $Q \leq 2x_C - \frac{x_Q+A}{2}$ (sincere vote Q, sophisticated vote A)

(d) $x_C > \frac{x_Q+A}{2}$ and $x_C \leq Q$
In that case C votes sincerely for A as long as $x_C \leq \frac{A+Q}{2}$ and sophisticatedly for A if $Q > 2x_C - \frac{x_Q+A}{2}$.
Hence differences between sincere and sophisticated behavior appear if

(1) $x_C \leq \frac{A+Q}{2}$ and $Q \leq 2x_C - \frac{x_Q+A}{2}$ (sincere vote A, sophisticated vote Q).
(2) $x_C > \frac{A+Q}{2}$ and $Q > 2x_C - \frac{x_Q+A}{2}$ (sincere vote Q, sophisticated vote A).

Figure 11.1 illustrates the preference configurations under the four scenarios that lead to sophisticated behavior. In situation (a) there are two sets of preference configurations for C and O that lead to sophisticated behavior. The first one, depicted above the line, leads to a sincere vote by C for A but a sophisticated vote for Q. In the preference configuration depicted below the line, the sincere and sophisticated votes are inversed. Under conditions (b) the preference configurations leading to differences between sincere and sophisticated behavior are of one type, as depicted in panel (b) of Fig. 11.1. For conditions (c) again only one set of preference configurations leads to a sincere vote for A and a sophisticated vote for Q as depicted in panel (c) of Fig. 11.1. Finally, in the last configuration (d)) again two preference configurations would generate differences between sincere and sophisticated voting.

[16] The detailed derivations for the results appear in the appendix.

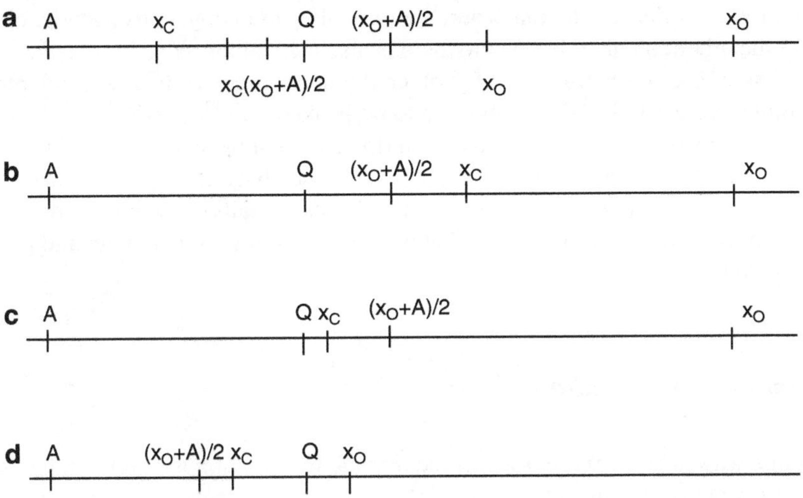

Fig. 11.1 Conditions under which C's sophisticated voting differs from sincere voting

The set depicted in panel (d) generates a sincere vote Q and a sophisticated vote for A, while an extreme value for x_O to the left of A would generate the inverse pattern.

The added value in terms of implications of these results compared to Martin's (2001) is limited if nonexistent. They underline again that preference divergences between C and the other chamber drive sophisticated behavior of C that is observably different from sincere behavior. Considering now a set of institutional variations based on the discussion earlier we can consider the following additional situations.

First, the agenda is exogenously fixed, both chambers vote according to a closed rule, and there is no conciliation committee. The sequence of play looks as follows:

1. An exogenous bill A is presented with $A < Q$, where Q is the status quo.
2. Member C with ideal-point x_C votes for A or Q.
3. The median voter of the other chamber with ideal-point x_O votes for A or Q.
4. If both chambers accept A, the latter option becomes law, if one of them rejects Q results.

In this scenario, quite clearly, C will never engage in sophisticated voting. A weakly dominant strategy, whatever the preference configuration, is to vote for her preferred alternative.

Next consider a situation where there is an endogenous agenda, closed rule in the other chamber and no conciliation committee.

In that case the situation looks like a simple veto player argument (Tsebelis 1995), where the agenda-setter (i.e., the first chamber) adopts the most preferred bill that is still acceptable to the other chamber.

Finally, consider a situation where there is also an endogenous agenda, closed rule in the other chamber, but where there is also a conciliation committee.

In that case C votes for A or Q if other chamber agrees with A, A is adopted if not compromise bill $\frac{x_Q+A}{2}$ is submitted to both chambers.[17]

While considering these various scenarios shows how sensitive the likelihood of sophisticated voting is to institutional details, the analyses are also considerably constrained by the simplifications of the institutional details of the bicameral setting and the informational assumption. That is, the assumption of complete and perfect information.

Incomplete Information

A simple way to address the issue of incomplete information is to rely on the work of McKelvey and Niemi's (1978) on sophisticated equivalents and employ some of the basic insights presented by Enelow (1981).

For simplicity, assume that two proposals A_1 and A_2 are voted on to replace the status quo Q. As an illustration, consider the situation where chamber 1 has the preference order $A_1 > A_2 > Q$ while chamber 2 has either $A_2 > Q > A_1$ or $A_2 > A_1 > Q$. The prior belief of chamber 1 ($p(Q)$) corresponds to the probability that chamber 2 has the first preference ordering and $1 - p(Q)$ that it will be the second ordering.

Consider the following sequence of play:

- Chamber 1 votes A_1 against A_2 and then the winner against Q.
- Provided one of the proposals beats Q the second chamber votes in the same sequence. If both adopt the same bill, the latter is the end result, otherwise the status quo Q will prevail.

In this case chamber 1 expected utility for the two votes is the following:

$$EU_1(\text{voting } A_1) = (p(Q) * U(Q)) + (1 - p(Q)) * U(A_1)$$
$$EU_1(\text{voting} A_2) = U(A_2).$$

This is obviously exactly the same setup as the suggestion of Enelow and Koehler's (1980) that sophisticated voting will occur depending on the prior belief of chamber 1.[18] What this setup allows, however, is to consider strategic voting both under the assumption of signalling (Banks 1991) and screening (Calvert 1986).

---

[17] It may seem odd that C does not vote on the proposal of the conciliation committee. Such a vote, however, is anticipated by C in the decision to vote for A, hence adding such a vote would be redundant.

[18] In Enelow and Koehler's (1980) the prior beliefs concern the behavior of other members of the same chamber.

Discussion

The limited theoretical considerations of sophisticated voting in a bicameral setting suggest that the bicameral sequence of decision making cannot simply be ignored. The model of Martin's (2001) and the extensions presented here, as well as the early work by Gross (1982) and Miller (1984) show that sophisticated voting is quite likely across chambers. This even more so, when incomplete information is assumed, as in the model of Enelow's (1981) dealing with an unicameral setting.

Martin's (2001) model, without the extension presented earlier, and the set-up in Enelow Enelow's (1981), are, however, limited in several regards. While their strength is the demonstration that sophisticated behavior may occur in bicameral settings, these results are obtained with fixed agendas (in both cases) and perfect knowledge of the preferences of all actors involved (in Martin's (2001) model). In a bicameral setting, however, as the one extension briefly discussed earlier, sophisticated voting is also possible if one chamber has agenda control and the other chamber has only veto power.[19] From a theoretical point of view, the situation seems more difficult where both chambers have agenda control and possible intercameral disagreements are settled by a conciliation committee. In that case, it is only very late in the game that the agenda tree is fixed sufficiently to allow observable sophisticated behavior. The conditions under which such behavior should be expected still need to be theoretically analyzed.

Comfort can be found, however, in the empirical evidence presented by Martin (2001). His analyses, though they only constitute an indirect test, suggest that even in the "inhospitable" environment of the US Congress sophisticated voting across chambers seems to occur. Similarly, Bütikofer and Hug (2008) provide evidence that on two specific bills for which they have precise preference information, MPs in the Swiss lower house behaved in part strategically. The analysis focuses, because of data availability, on only one of the two chambers with the puzzling result that not all MPs finally voted according to their sincere preferences. Given that in some instances the upper chamber still had to give its approval, this might be (very) indirect empirical evidence for strategic voting in a bicameral setting. Consequently, future extensions of the theoretical model should be tested empirically along similar lines as the tests proposed by Bütikofer and Hug (2008), i.e., by using exogenous preference measures for the alternatives considered in a parliament.

Conclusion

The main contention of this chapter is that roll call votes do not take place in a vacuum. While various scholars have already raised this point, few have considered an important aspect of parliament, namely its cameral structure. Bi- or multi-cameral

---

[19] As shown above, empirical examples for such a distribution of powers exist among the bicameral parliaments around the world.

structures create conditions for additional sophisticated behavior, which has not been dealt with sufficiently so far.

Simple theoretical models suggest, however, that conditions allowing for such behavior may very well exist. However, these conditions depend on the distribution of powers across chambers. Hence, if these conditions are likely to be fulfilled, also the bicameral structure of parliaments may raise doubts about the conclusions generated by simple-minded analyses of roll call votes.

Consequently, roll call vote analyses, whether in terms of ideal-point estimations or party cohesion, have to consider the context of the floor voting in much more detail to be sure that the inferences we draw are not systematically biased.

Acknowledgements I wish to thank the participants at these events, especially Marcelo Jenny, as well as Bjørn Hoyland for the helpful comments and the Swiss National Science Foundation (Grant No 100012-111909) for its generous funding.

Appendix

Below I present the more detailed calculations to determine the conditions under which C votes for A in the four different preference configurations (see earlier).

(a) $x_C \leq \frac{x_O+A}{2}$ and $x_C \leq Q$
In that case C votes for A

$$x_C - \frac{x_O + A}{2} \geq x_C - Q$$
$$\rightarrow Q \geq \frac{x_O + A}{2} \tag{11.5}$$

(b) $x_C > \frac{x_O+A}{2}$ and $x_C > Q$
In that case C votes for A

$$\frac{x_O + A}{2} - x_C \geq Q - x_C$$
$$\rightarrow Q \leq \frac{x_O + A}{2} \tag{11.6}$$

c) $x_C \leq \frac{x_O+A}{2}$ and $x_C > Q$
In that case C votes for A

$$x_C - \frac{x_O + A}{2} \geq Q - x_C$$
$$\rightarrow Q \leq 2x_C - \frac{x_O + A}{2} \tag{11.7}$$

d) $x_C > \frac{x_O+A}{2}$ and $x_C \leq Q$
In that case C votes for A

$$\frac{x_O + A}{2} - x_C \geq x_C - Q$$
$$\rightarrow Q > 2x_C - \frac{x_O + A}{2} \tag{11.8}$$

References

Achen CH (2006) Institutional realism and bargaining models. In: Thomson R, Stokman FN, Achen C, König T (eds) The European union decides. Cambridge University Press, Cambridge

Austen-Smith D (1987) Sophisticated sincerity: voting over endogenous agendas. Am Polit Sci Rev 81(4):1323–1329

Bailey M (2007) Comparable preference estimates across time and institutions for the court, congress and presidency. Am J Polit Sci 51(3):433–448

Bailey M, Chang K (2001) Comparing presidents, senators, and justices: inter-institutional preference estimation. J Law Econ Organ 17(2):477–506

Banks JS (1991) Signaling games in political science. Harwood Academic, Chur

Bjurulf BoH, Niemi RG (1978) Strategic voting in Scandinavian Parliaments. Scan Polit Stud 1(1):5–22

Bruninger T, Debus M (2009) Legislative agenda-setting in parliamentary democracies. Eur J Polit Res 48(6):804–839

Bütikofer S, Hug S (2008) Strategic behavior in the Swiss Parliament. Paper prepared for presentation at the Anual Meeting of the American Political Science Association, Boston, 27–31 August 2008

Bütikofer S, Hug S (2010) The Swiss upper house. "Chambre de Réflexion" or Conservative Renegades. J Legis Stud 16(2):176–194

Calvert RL (1986) Models of imperfect information in politics. Harwood Academic, Chur

Calvert RL, Fenno RF Jr (1994) Strategy and sophisticated voting in the senate. J Polit 56(2): 349–376

Carey JM (2008) Legislative voting and accountability. Cambridge University Press, New York

Carrubba CJ, Gabel M, Murrah L, Clough R, Montegomery E, Schambach R (2006) Off the record: unrecorded legislative votes, selection bias, and roll-call vote analysis. Br J Polit Sci 36:691–704

Carrubba CJ, Gabel M, Hug S (2008) Legislative voting behavior, seen and unseen: adjusting for selection effects in roll call vote analysis. Legis Stud Q 33:543–572

Chiou F-Y, Yang W (2008) Strategic choices of roll call requests. Paper presented at the annual meeting of the MPSA Annual National Conference, Palmer House Hotel, Hilton, Chicago, IL.

Clinton JD (2006) Testing lawmaking theories with (endogenous) roll calls, 90th–106th U.S. house. Department of Politics, Princeton University

Clinton JD, Meirowitz A (2004) Testing explanations of strategic voting in legislatures: a reexamination of the compromise of 1790. Am J Polit Sci 48(4):675–689

Clinton JD, Jackman S, Rivers D (2004) The statistical analysis of roll call voting: a unified approach. Am Polit Sci Rev 98(2):355–370

Congleton RD (2003) On the merits of bicameral legislatures: policy predictability within partisan polities. In: Holler MJ, Kliemt H, Schmidtchen D, Streit ME (eds) Year book of new political economy, vol 22. Mohr Siebeck, Tübingen, pp 29–49

Cox GW, McCubbins MD (2005) Setting the agenda: responsible party government in the U.S. house of representatives. Cambridge University Press, Cambridge

Cox, GW, McCubbins MD (2010) (forthcoming). Setting the agenda: parliaments, procedural cartels and policy making. Cambridge University Press, New York
Cutrone M, McCarty N (2006) Does bicameralism matter? In: Weingast BR, Wittman DA (eds) The Oxford handbook of political economy. Oxford University Press, Oxford, pp 357–372
Denzau A, Riker WH, Shepsle KA (1985) Farquharson and fenno: sophisticated voting and home style. Am Polit Sci Rev 79(4):1117–1134
Enelow JM (1981) Saving amendments, killer amendments, and an expected utility theory of sophisticated voting. J Polit 43:1062–1089
Enelow JM, Koehler DH (1980) The amendment in legislative strategy: sophisticated voting in the U.S. congress. J Polit 5:396–413
Farquharson R (1969) Theory of voting. Yale University Press, New Haven
Finocchiaro CJ, Jenkins JA (2008) In search of killer amendments in the modern U.S. house. Legis Stud Q 33:263–294
Gross DR (1982) Bicameralism and the theory of voting. West Polit Q 35:511–526
Heckman JJ, Snyder JM Jr (1997) Linear probability models of the demand for attributes with an empirical application to estimating the preferences of legislators. Rand J Econ 28(0 special issue):S142–S189
Heller WB (2001) Political denials: the policy effect of intercameral partisan differences in bicameral parliamentary systems. J Law Econ Organ 17(1):34–61
Heller WB (2007) Divided politics: bicameralism, parties, and policy in democratic legislatures. Annu Rev Polit Sci 10:245–269
Hix S (2005) The political system of the European Union, 2nd Edn. St. Martin's Press, New York
Hoyland B, Hagemann S (2010) (forthcoming). Bicameral politics in the Euopean Union. J Common Mark Stud
Hug S (2010) Selection effects in roll call votes. Br J Polit Sci 40(1):225–235
Ismayr W (2008) Gesetzgebung im politischen system Deutschlands. In: Ismayr W (ed) Gesetzgebung in Westeuropa : EU-Staaten und Europäische Union VS Verlag für Sozialwissenschaften, Wiesbaden, pp 383–429
Jegher A (1999) Bundesversammlung und Gesetzgebung. Der Einfluss von institutionellen, politischen und inhaltlichen Faktoren auf die Gesetzgebungstätigkeit der Eidgenössischen Räte. Haupt, Bern
Jenkins JA, Munger MC (2003) Investigating the incidence of killer amendments in congress. J Polit 65:498–517
Krehbiel K, Rivers D (1990) Sophisticated voting in congress: a reconsideration. J of Polit 52:548–578
Leemann L (2009) Catch me if you can. Recovering sophisticated voting in the lower house of Switzerland. Paper prepared for the Annual Swiss Political Science Meeting, St. Gallen, Jan 2009
Levitt SD (1996) How do senators vote? Disentangling the role of voter preferences, party affiliation, and senator ideology. Am Econ Rev 86(3):425–441
Levmore S (1992) Bicameralism: when are two decisions better than one? Int Rev Law Econ 12:145–162
Londregan J (2000) Legislative institutions and ideology in Chile. Cambridge University Press, New York
Martin AD (2001) Congressional decision making and the separation of powers. Am Polit Sci Rev 95(2):361–378
Martin AD, Quinn KM (2002) Dynamic ideal point estimation via Markov Chain Monte Carlo for the U.S. Supreme Court, 1953–1999. Polit Anal 10:134–153
Martin AD, Quinn KM (2005) Can ideal point estimates be used as explanatory variables? Washington University and Harvard University, St. Louis and Cambridge
McKelvey RD, Niemi RG (1978) A multistage game representation of sophisticated voting for binary procedures. J Econ Theory 18:1–22
Miller NR (1984) Bicameralism and the theory of voting a comment. West Polit Q 37(4):641–647

Patterson SC, Mughan A (eds) (1999) Senates: bicameralism in the contemporary world. Ohio State University Press, Columbus
Penn EM (2008) A distributive N-amendment game with endogenous agenda formation. Public Choice 136(1):201–213
Penn EM (2009) A model of farsighted voting. Am J Polit Sci 53(1):36–54
Poole K (2000) Nonparametric unfolding of binary choice data. Polit Anal 8(3):211–237
Poole K (2005) Spatial models of parliamentary voting. Cambridge University Press, New York
Roberts JM (2007) The statistical analysis of roll-call data: a cautionary tale. Legis Stud Q 32:341–360
Rogers JR (1998) Bicameral sequence: theory and state legislative evidence. Am J Polit Sci 42(Oct 4):1025–1060
Rogers JR (2001) An informational rationale for congruent bicameralism. J Theor Polit 12(2): 129–157
Rosenthal H, Erik V (2004) Analyzing roll calls with perfect spatial voting. Am J Polit Sci 48:620–632
Spirling A, Iain M (2006) The rights and wrongs of roll calls. Gov Opposition 41(4):581–588
Spirling A, Iain M (2007) UK OC OK? Interpreting optimal classification scores for the U.K. house of commons. Polit Anal 15(1):85–96
Stratmann T (1996) Instability in collective decisions? A test for cyclical majorities. Public Choice 88:15–28
Stratmann T (1997) Logrolling. In: Mueller DC (ed) Perspectives on public choice. A handbook. Cambridge University Press, Cambridge
Thiem J (2009) Nationale Parteien im Europischen Parlament. Delegation, Kontrolle und politischer Einfluss. VS Verlag, Wiesbaden
Timmermans A, Scholten P, Oostlander S (2008) Gesetzgebung im Politischen System der Niederlande. In: Ismayr W (ed) Gesetzgebung in Westeuropa: EU-Staaten und Europische Union. VS Verlag fr Sozialwissenschaften, Wiesbaden
Trivelli L (1974) Le bicamérisme: institutions comparées. Etude historique, statistique et critique des rapports entre le Conseil National et le Conseil des Etats. Université de Lausanne, Lausanne
Tsebelis G (1994) The power of the European Parliament as a conditional agenda setter. Am Polit Sci Rev 88(1):128–142
Tsebelis G (1995) Decision making in political systems: veto players in presidentialism, parliamentarism, multicamerialism and multipartyism. Br J Polit Sci 25:289–325
Tsebelis G, Money J (1997) Bicameralism. Cambridge University Press, New York
Volden C (1998) Sophisticated voting in supermajoritarian settings. J Polit 60(1):149–173

Chapter 12
Game Theoretic Models and the Empirical Analysis of EU Policy Making: Strategic Interaction, Collective Decisions, and Statistical Inference

Dirk Junge

Introduction

Veto players theories and related approaches have become increasingly influential in policy research. Since the pioneering work by Tsebelis (Tsebelis 1995; 2002), a considerable number of studies has applied the veto players approach to analyze how political decision making and legislative institutions work and how policy outcomes are produced in a variety of political systems (Bawn 1999; Bräuninger and König 1999; Crombez 1997; Hallerberg 2002; Hug and Tsebelis 2002; König 2001; Steunenberg 1994; Tsebelis 1994; 1995; 1999; Tsebelis and Money 1997 and the contributions in this book). The strong micro foundations, the parsimony and the ability to derive comparatively unambiguous predictions have contributed to the popularity of this approach.

In recent years there have been increasing efforts in European Union research to assess the performance of veto player theories empirically based on a larger number of cases in order to find out more about their explanatory power and the extent their theoretical arguments can be generalized to different decision-making situations (de Mesquita and Stokman 1994; König and Pöter 2001; Selck 2004; Thomson et al. 2006). In particular, researchers have started to apply formal models of EU policy making to data directly in order to test their predictions in a most rigid and comprehensive way and minimize the gap between the theoretical model to be tested and the empirical model that is used for that test. In this way, it is hoped to gain new insights into whether the theories fit the data and describe real world policy making processes appropriately.

However, making inferences on the explanatory power of game–theoretic models is difficult and can present problems that may invalidate the findings (Achen 2006a: 271; Morton 1998:117; Signorino 1999; Smith 1999). Yet, these problems have so far not received much attention in EU policy research. This chapter discusses how approaches to model testing in EU policy research can be improved

D. Junge (✉)
University of Mannheim, Germany
e-mail: djunge@mail.uni-mannheim.de

T. König et al. (eds.), *Reform Processes and Policy Change: Veto Players and Decision-Making in Modern Democracies*, Studies in Public Choice 16,
DOI 10.1007/978-1-4419-5809-9_12,

and proposes a potential alternative based on explicit stochastic modeling of EU legislative negotiations. I use the quantal-response approach introduced to political science by McKelvey and Palfrey (1996, 1998) to derive a stochastic version of a veto players model of EU policy making and employ this model to reassess the explanatory power of the veto players account based on detailed data on EU legislative initiatives (Thomson et al. 2006). This quantal response model can be used for direct tests of a broad range of veto players models. It makes it possible to determine the explanatory power and the contribution of the key arguments such as agenda-setting, the core and the win-set in empirical tests based on standard tools of statistics.

The results show that the veto players approach makes a significant contribution to our understanding of EU policy outcomes and clearly outperforms atheoretic models that assume random data generating processes – which is traditionally regarded as an important evaluation criterion for statistical models. Moreover, the key arguments of the veto players account seem to influence policy outcomes in the way theoretically expected: the win-set, the amendment-proof set and the agenda-setter draw outcomes towards their location in the policy space. The approach may thus not only help to test the explanatory power of veto players theories but also to identify which parts of the models are particularly weak, or do not fit the data studied very well. It therefore provides comparatively precise and comprehensive information on how veto players theories perform and in what respect they could be improved.

Game Theoretic Models and Empirical Inference

There is an ongoing debate in the methodological literature on how the empirical performance of game–theoretical models can best be assessed and what inferences can and should be drawn from different kinds of tests (Carrubba et al. 2007a,b; Signorino and Yilmaz 2003; Signorino 1999; Smith 1999). The fundamental problem is that the often complex patterns of strategic interaction these models describe are usually difficult to capture by conventional statistical methods such as regression analyses (Signorino and Yilmaz 2003). But ignoring this important aspect of the theories can easily lead to flawed conclusions (Signorino 1999; Smith 1999).

Several approaches have been discussed in the literature to remedy this problem. Some authors analyze point predictions of nonstatistical game–theoretical models to draw conclusions on their explanatory power (de Mesquita and Stokman 1994; Erikson and Romero 1990; Thomson et al. 2006), others suggest to use comparative static analysis or extend conventional regression models with appropriate interaction terms to correct potential misspecifications (Carrubba et al. 2007a,b; Segal et al. 1992). A more recent proposal is to employ stochastic game theory and estimate the theoretical models directly (Aragones and Palfrey 2004; McKelvey 1991; McKelvey and Palfrey 1996; 1998). While studies of EU policy making have started to assess game–theoretical models in empirical analyses, the methodological debates on the pitfalls of these approaches have so far received surprisingly little attention.

In EU policy research empirical applications of game–theoretical models almost exclusively focus on the evaluation of point predictions of nonstatistical models. König and Pöter (2001), Selck (2004) and Steunenberg and Selck (2006) assess and compare the explanatory power of different procedural veto player models on this basis that differ in their assumptions how the formal rights of the cooperation and codecision procedure shape policy outcomes, Arregui et al. (2006) and König and Proksch (2006) test exchange models in which actors exchange positions, resources, and rights to best accommodate their interests, Bailer and Schneider (2006) and Schneider et al. (2007) assess the predictions of bargaining models that focus on the negotiation process between the actors involved, and Arregui et al. (2006) and Achen (2006b) test models that consider policy outcomes as a form of compromise that simply averages actors ideal positions. Further examples of such applications in EU policy research include the challenge model by Bueno de Mesquita (de Mesquita and Stokman 1994, Arregui et al. 2006) and models that take coalition formation as the starting point of the analysis (Boekhoorn et al. 2006).These studies cover the most influential game–theoretical explanations of EU policy making and many of our insights about the empirical performance of these explanations come from this research.

But deriving inferences on the explanatory power of the theories and their arguments from nonstatistical models faces considerable limitations. One of the most fundamental problems is the so-called zero-likelihood problem (see, for example, Morton 1999: 117). The root of this problem is the deterministic nature of the theoretical models these studies employ. They derive point predictions on the outcome of policy making that are then used for model evaluation. However, by definition, those models regard these point predictions as the only possible outcome of the policy making process. All alternatives are treated as theoretically impossible results that should never occur according to the theory. To see the implications for model evaluation consider the following example.

Figure 12.1 shows a very simple procedural spatial model of policy making. In the model seven actors (M1–M7) face a decision on a policy proposal and it is assumed that they have to agree on that proposal in order to adopt it. The ellipses in the figure show the indifference curves of the actors with respect to the status quo: all policy options inside these ellipses are preferred by the actors to the status quo and would be adopted by the respective actor if otherwise the decision making process would lead to a maintenance of the status quo. As is typical for many procedural models of policy making, the agenda is set by a strong agenda setter who makes a proposal under closed rule that the other actors cannot change. According to the spatial logic of the model the agenda setter makes a proposal the other actors would prefer to the status quo but is as close as possible to the ideal position of the agenda setter. In the model described in the figure, this is the proposal P, which is the outcome prediction of the model. Now assume that the observed outcome of the policy process is O1. What does this mean for the quality of the model predictions? In order to answer this question one would require information about the extent to which these observations are consistent with the model and can be expected as the result of the theoretically assumed data generating process, but deterministic model

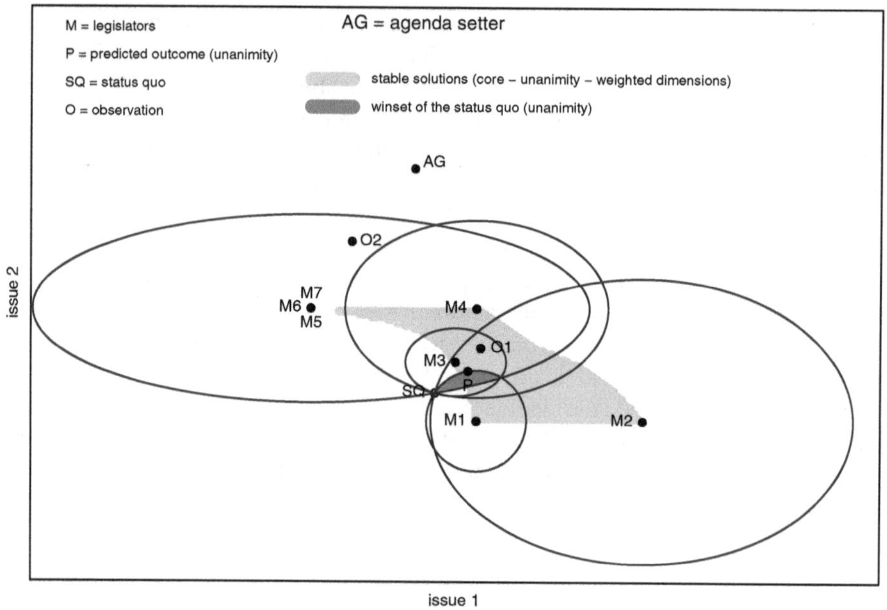

Fig. 12.1 The zero likelihood problem: Limits of statistical inference from non-statistical models

do not provide such information. They predict a particular outcome but do not make a statement on any alternative observation or allow any conclusions on such alternatives. Assume now that the observed outcome is not O1 but O2. Does this imply that the model now actually predicts the outcome better? The problem is that the deterministic model does not allow such a conclusion. All observations that deviate from the model predictions are not defined as possible outcomes of the decision making process given the model assumptions, no matter what these observations are- and immediately falsify it (Quinn and Westveld 2004).

In empirical analysis, deviations from the model predictions typically do occur and the zero-likelihood problem refers to the inability of deterministic models to cope with such models in an appropriate way. If the model is at least to some extent incorrect (as is practically always the case) an important question is how far the model predictions deviate from the empirical observation, respectively, how big the error of the model is and to what extent it is consistent with the data. Deterministic models do not answer this question. But such an answer would provide the basis of standard statistical procedure to assess the error of the model, its explanatory power and perform competitive tests (Achen 2006a: 271–272). This raises the general question of what inferences can and should be drawn from the results of deterministic model assessments on the explanatory power of the models.

Most empirical evaluations of game–theoretical EU policy making models use distance measures between observed and predicted outcome as an indicator for the model's error and its explanatory power. But such a measure is inconsistent with the theoretical assumptions of deterministic models for the reasons described earlier and does not make it possible to distinguish appropriately between different deviations from the theoretical arguments and to make inferences on error sizes. Moreover, it is not clear what such an error should substantially mean for the quality of the model. One would expect that such an indicator shows larger errors the more the theoretical arguments deviate from the observations and smaller errors in the opposite case. But this is not true for the distance measure employed as indicator in most game–theoretical models of EU policy making. The reason for this is that outcome predictions often result from a complex interaction of decisions at different stages of the legislative process in these theories, and deviations from the theoretically assumed behavior do not alter the predictions of the models in a easily predictable way and accordingly the distance between observed and predicted outcomes cannot be expected to increase with these deviations (nor even in a linear way). On the contrary, large distances between observed and predicted behavior can be caused by small deviations from the behavioral arguments, while small once can also be caused by big deviations. Figures 12.2 and 12.3 provide an example this complicated relationship between theoretical arguments and predicted outcomes in spatial models for two simple decision making situations.

For simplicity I assume that two actors (M1, M2) have to decide about the proposal of an agenda-setter, and agreement of both is required for adoption and the proposal cannot be renegotiated. The ellipses in the figure describe the indifference curves of the actors with respect to the status quo. If the dotted indifference curve truly describes the actors' behavior, the agenda-setter would choose exactly

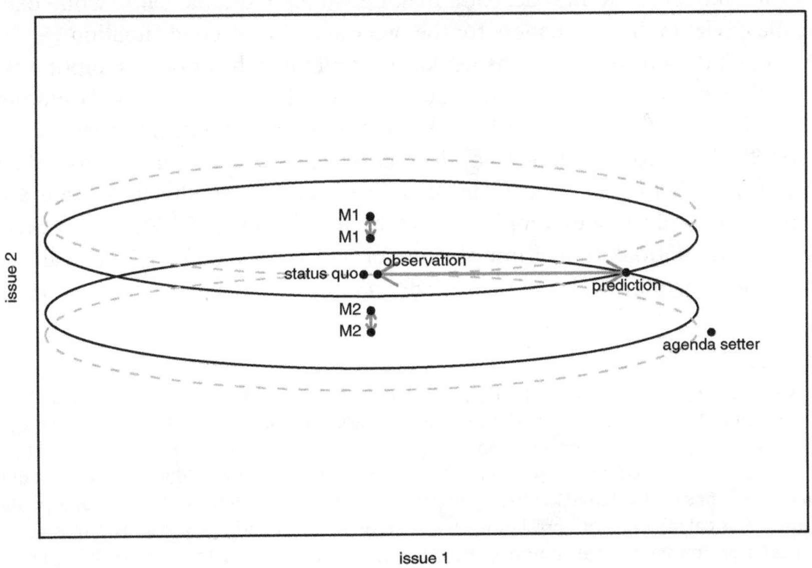

Fig. 12.2 Distance measures and the error of theoretical arguments: Robustness and implications of the indicator I

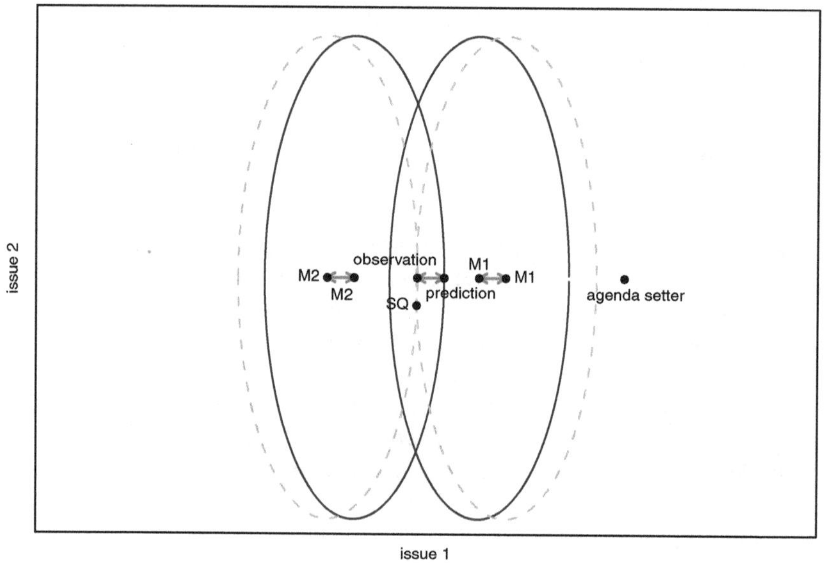

Fig. 12.3 Distance measures and the error of theoretical arguments robustness and implications of the indicator II

the observed outcome and the model is perfectly consistent with the observations. However, a slight deviation from this assumption (black curve) changes the prediction of the model in the first decision making situation dramatically, while exactly the same deviation hardly matters for the outcome in the second situation.

Although in both situations the deviation from the behavioral assumption is the same and all errors in the model are caused by this deviation, the widely employed distance measure shows a very different error. To what extent the observations deviate from the behavioral arguments of the theory is, therefore, by no means indicated by the distance between predicted and observed outcome and this measure is a very poor indicator of the models empirical performance. [1] Achen (2006a, 271) acknowledges these limitations of deterministic models in EU policy research and calls them scientifically incomplete because of their inability to make statistical statements

[1] A workaround proposed in some studies is to transform the distance measure and calculate more sophisticated criteria to evaluate model predictions based on the distance between observed and predicted outcomes (for an overview, see Achen 2006a). These include quasi hit rates that report how often a prediction come "close" to the observation measured by its distance, the calculation of pseudo R^2 that is also based on the aggregation of distances between observed and predicted outcomes, and calculations of correlations between predictions and outcomes. But it is not clear how these transformations can improve the empirical assessment of the models substantially if the transformed measure is already flawed. Other known limitations of the distance indicator of empirical model performance include a bias in favor of models that predict outcomes close to the mean of the particular scale employed to measure actor positions de Mesquita (2004); Junge and König (2007, 134)

on the size of the error and the explanatory power of the models due to the zero-likelihood problem. Because of these problems, direct tests of (point) predictions of theoretic analyses can hardly be recommended for the purpose of the empirical evaluation of policy making theories in quantitative studies (Morton 1999; Quinn and Westveld 2004, 117).

A simpler statistical approach to testing models that include claims on strategic interaction as a central element is to use conventional statistical regression techniques. One option would be to simply include the factors that are expected to influence the outcome of the game–theoretic model as independent variables in a regression analysis. For example, empirical applications of veto players analyses sometimes evaluate the effects of different arguments such as the number of veto players or the heterogeneity of interests in this way. However, treating these arguments as separate aspects of the model predictions that can be tested independently clearly misstates what the theory actually claims. In fact, veto players theory is very specific on how the distribution of interests, rights, and legislative procedures depend on each other and ignoring or misspecifying this conditionality may lead to flawed results of the analysis. More generally, regression analyses of this type have been criticized because they ignore or misspecify the often complex patterns of interaction that are an integral part of the game–theoretic models and particularly dense in applications to policy making (Signorino 1999; Smith 1999). Therefore, such analyses risk distorting the results of theory tests.

In order to address this problem of conventional regression techniques, comparative statics analyses have more recently been (re-) advanced (Carrubba et al. 2007a, b; Segal et al. 1992). The basic idea is to derive predictions on the impact of strategic behavior from the game–theoretic model and include it as interaction terms in conventional regression models. If the decision making process can be described as a sequence of decisions by single individuals and a regression model exists for each of these decisions (e.g., logistic regression in the case of a binary decision made by a single individual), the effects of strategic interaction can also be modeled by combining these models, i.e., applying the respective regressions sequentially starting from the last decision (Bas et al. 2008).

However, if employed for the analysis of policy making these approaches may face limitations for at least two reasons. First, if the theoretic model is complex (as is typically the case for policy making models) the interaction terms necessary to take strategic interactions into account increase disproportionally (Signorino and Yilmaz 2003). Second, theories of policy making typically involve nontrivial decision rules whose effect on policy outcomes is difficult to specify in conventional regression analyses. In particular, the policy making process is often difficult to capture by a sequence of single decisions as required by the approach proposed by Bas et al. (2008). For example, in European Union research, the data on legislative initiatives that will be employed in the empirical analysis suggests that the decision making situations which a regression model would also have to take into account include highly case specific policy spaces that differ by the number of dimensions and actors involved, the salience they attach to issues, the distributions of policy positions and coalitions, the set and distribution of options they can choose from, and the relevant decision making procedure – and their nontrivial implications for policy stability, policy change, the power of the agenda-setter, and policy outcomes. Capturing these characteristics without explicit game–theoretic modelling is not trivial.

Though comparative statics analysis is a classical and valuable approach for the assessment of formal models, it may not be easy to apply for the kind of analysis and data that policy studies are typically interested in. In this chapter I therefore use direct estimation of game–theoretical models is particularly well-suited for the analysis of collective decisions as it allows statistically valid inferences while taking all characteristics of the theoretical models into account and remaining comparatively parsimonious. I focus on the most frequently used approach in game–theory that allows for direct estimation: quantal response theory (McKelvey and Palfrey 1996; 1998).

Quantal Response Theory and the Statistical Analysis of EU Policy Making

Quantal response models can be interpreted as a generalization of deterministic game–theoretic models, that can describe different forms of bounded rationality apart from completely rational behavior (Goeree et al. 2004). The basic assumption is that actors do not always play optimal strategies but play better strategies with a higher probability than worse ones and anticipate that other actors do likewise (McKelvey and Palfrey 1996; 1998). This results in probabilistic decision making where every option has a probability greater than zero to be the outcome of the decision making process. As a consequence these models avoid the zero likelihood problem because they are able to assign a likelihood to every observed outcome from the model that can be used for conventional statistical inference (Quinn and Westveld 2004). While quantal response models have their roots in the experimental and statistical literature (see, for example, McFadden (1981); Ochs (1995)) political scientists have begun to apply them to observational data to explain the outcomes of strategic interaction. Signorino (1999) for example uses such a model to explain the outbreak of war between two countries based on data on 707 European dyads between 1815 and 1970. He concludes that the popular model by de Mesquita and Lalman (1992) cannot explain the outbreak of war if the strategic interaction in this model is taken into account. This result stands in contrast to previous nonstrategic analyses of the same model. Signorino and Tarar (2006) test an extended version of the rational deterrence hypothesis by employing a quantal response model and they show that alliances, balance of power, nuclear weapons, armaments, and the level of trade ties reduce the likelihood of conflict between two states if strategic interaction is taken into account. Guarnaschelli et al. (2000) analyze strategic interactions in decisions of juries that seek to find out whether a defendant is guilty or not.

Policy making in the European Union can be considered as a very suitable example of strategic interaction in political decisions that involve a larger number of actors. Many theories of EU policy making (and in particular the game–theoretical approaches on which the chapter focuses) assume that actors behave strategically in the EU legislative decision making process. For example, procedural models (described later in greater detail) assume that the legislative process starts with the initiative of the Commission that attempts to anticipate whether its proposal will be adopted or amended in the subsequent stages. Amendments in turn take into account whether these amendments are likely to be adopted in the final vote by all veto players. The final outcome of the legislative process is the result of this complex pattern of strategic interactions. Quantal response models allow taking such complex interaction structures into account. In the remainder of the chapter, I apply this approach to test a conventional veto players model based on detailed data on EU legislative initiatives (Thomson et al. 2006). I show how a quantal response version of this model can be developed and how it can statistically be estimated and tested.

Comprehensive analyses of EU policy making that employ the idea of veto players have first been introduced by Tsebelis (1994) and Steunenberg (1994) and now usually focus on the two most important procedures in EU legislative decision making under which more than 90% of laws have been negotiated since 1984 (König et al. 2006): the codecision procedure and the consultation procedure. In the theoretical literature, there is a debate on how the codecision procedure is best interpreted. This debate focuses on the question which actor can decisively shape the agenda in the legislative process. Some models suggest that this is the Commission (Crombez 2003; Steunenberg 2001), others that it is the Council president (Steunenberg 1994) and still others argue that the European Parliament is the decisive agenda setter in the codecision procedure (Steunenberg 1997). In contrast, the game–theoretic interpretation of the consultation procedure , the second of the two most important decision making procedures in the EU, is identical in all of the models: The legislative process starts with an initiative of the Commission who makes a proposal to the Council and the EP. The Council then decides whether it adopts the proposal with the required majority or proposes an amendment that requires unanimity for adoption. While the EP has a veto right in the codecision procedure and can even act as the decisive agenda setter (depending on the respective interpretation of the codecision procedure) it has no such powers in the consultation procedure and effectively plays no role in the theoretical model.

The empirical analysis employs quantal response models for the purpose of evaluation. These models belong to the class of game–theoretical models and assume that actors seek to take the consequences of their decisions into account and find best responses to the decisions of other actors. Equilibrium behavior can be determined by backward induction starting at the last stage of the legislative process. I will focus on a detailed analysis of a veto player model that adopts the view that the parliament is the decisive agenda-setter in the codecision procedure, show in detail, how the stochastic model can be derived from the game–theoretic arguments, implemented and statistically estimated and how it can be used to make comprehensive inferences about the empirical performance of the veto players model and its arguments based on standard tools of statistics. The implementation follows the ideas by Rubinstein (1982), Baron and Ferejohn (1989) and Banks and Duggan (2000) on how legislative games with different sequential decision making and proposal stages can be modelled, which links the approach to a much larger number of potential applications.

Modeling the Win-Set

In the last stage of decision making the members of the Council and, in the Codecision procedure, the European Parliament decide whether they adopt the final proposal or not. In the case of adoption the final proposal is the outcome of the legislative process, in the case of rejection, there is no policy change and the outcome of the legislative process is the status quo. Decision makers, thus, face a binary decision at the last stage of the legislative process between the proposal (px) and the status quo (sq). Assuming spatial preferences the utility UW the actors derive from the adoption of px and sq, respectively, depends on the distance between their ideal position and the status quo and their ideal position and the new policy proposal.

$$\mathrm{UW}_i(px) = \sqrt{\sum_{d=1}^{D}(sq_d - ip_{i,d})^2} - \sqrt{\sum_{d=1}^{D}(px_d - ip_{i,d})^2} \tag{12.1}$$

$$\mathrm{UW}_i(sq) = 0 \tag{12.2}$$

where d indexes the dimensions of the policy space and i the actor. The probability that actor i adopts proposal px in the final vote equals according to the logistic quantal response model:

$$\mathrm{PW}_i(px) = \frac{e^{\lambda_w \cdot \mathrm{UW}_i(px)}}{e^{\lambda_w \cdot \mathrm{UW}_i(px)} + e^{\lambda_w \cdot \mathrm{UW}_i(sq)}}. \tag{12.3}$$

The parameter λ_w indicates to what extent the decisions of actors deviate from the theoretically assumed behavior at the level of the win-set, i.e., to what extent the decision of actors follows the assumptions of the spatial decision making model, respectively, to what extent the spatial preferences assumed in the model determine the decision. More generally, if parameter $\lambda = \infty$ the actor decides completely consistently with the predictions of the model and chooses the better alternative with a probability of 1. If $\lambda = -\infty$ his behavior completely contradicts the theory and he makes exactly the opposite decision and chooses the worst option with a probability of 1. If $\lambda = 0$ he chooses each alternative with equal probability independent of the assumed preferences. The estimation of the parameter λ, therefore, provides information to what extent the observed behavior is consistent with the theory and allows the model to adjust to different patterns of decision making. A policy proposal is adopted if the formally required majorities in the Council and the European Parliament agree to it. The probability of a unanimous adoption (u) equals the product of the individual probabilities for agreement of the political actors:

$$\mathrm{PW}(px|u) = \prod_{i=1}^{I} \mathrm{PW}_i(px) \tag{12.4}$$

Calculating the probability of adoption in the case of qualified majority voting is more complicated. Because every actor has an at least a slightly greater than zero probability to agree to any policy proposal in the quantal response model, every theoretically possible (not necessarily winning) coalition C (e.g., France and UK agree to a proposal, all others reject it) has a probability greater than zero to occur. The probability of adopting a specific proposal under qualified majority rule is the sum of the probabilities of all voting coalitions CW in which the required majority agrees to that proposal.

$$\mathrm{PW}(px|qmv) = \sum_{cw=1}^{CW} P(C_{cw}) \tag{12.5}$$

The winning coalitions may also reflect voting weights of member states and these weights can be taken into account in this way.

Modeling the Amendment-Proof Set

In the penultimate stage of the legislative process, policy makers have to decide whether to amend the proposal of the agenda setter. They take the consequences of their decisions for the final stage of the policy making process into account and also that amendments delay the decision making process by one round, resulting in payoffs discounted by the factor d. Thus, their utilities UA from the initial proposal px and the amended proposal py at the stage of amendments is given by

$$\mathrm{UA}_i(px) = PW(px|VR) \cdot \mathrm{UW}_i(px) + (1 - PW(px|VR)) \cdot \mathrm{UW}_i(sq) \tag{12.6}$$

$$\mathrm{UA}_i(py) = (1-d) \cdot (PW(py|VR) \cdot \mathrm{UW}_i(py) + (1 - \mathrm{PW}(py|VR)) \cdot \mathrm{UW}_i(sq)) \tag{12.7}$$

where VR describes the voting rule applied in the final stage of decision making. The probability that a specific amendment py is proposed by the actor who is recognized as proposer also depends on the total set of options T he can choose from:

$$\mathrm{PA}_i(py) = \frac{e^{\lambda_a \cdot \mathrm{UA}_i(py)}}{\sum_{p=1}^{T} e^{\lambda_a \cdot \mathrm{UA}_i(p)}} \tag{12.8}$$

The total probability that this amendment is proposed is then the sum of the individual probabilities of making that proposal weighted by the probability wa_i of being recognized as the proposer in the amendment stage:

$$\mathrm{PA}(py) = \sum_{i=1}^{I} (\mathrm{PA}_i \cdot wa_i) \tag{12.9}$$

If the recognized proposer decides not to amend the initial proposal and opts for px the initial proposal is said to be stable or amendment-proof which is the case for all options in the policy space with a probability greater than zero in the quantal response model.

Modeling Agenda-Setting

The legislative process is assumed to start with a proposal of the agenda setter that effectively determines the agenda. In the model tested, this is the Commission in the consultation procedure and the European Parliament in the codecision procedure. Though it is acknowledged that the Commission formally initiates the legislative process in both procedures it is argued that in the codecision procedure the European Parliament can make counter proposals in later stages of the decision making process that are not constrained by the initial Commission proposal. Thus, according to this view, the European Parliament can be treated as the decisive agenda setter (Steunenberg 1997, Steunenberg and Selck 2006). The agenda setter makes a proposal that takes all possible amendments and decisions in later stages of the legislative process into account and the agenda setters preferences over the expected outcomes. This argument corresponds to the agenda-setter argument in conventional spatial models. The expected utility of the proposal px for the agendasetter at the stage of agenda-setting AS equals:

$$\mathrm{UAS}_i(px) = PA(px|px)\cdot \mathrm{UA}_i(px|px) + \sum_{p=1}^{T-px} PA(p|px)\cdot \mathrm{UA}_i(p|px), \quad (12.10)$$

where the first term describes the (undiscounted) expected utility of the initial proposal weighted by the probability that it passes and the second part the sum of the utilities of all alternative outcomes weighted by the probability that they occur. Expected utilities and probabilities of alternative proposals (respectively, passing) depend on which proposal is made first, because this determines which alternatives suffer from discounting in the expected utility calculations of the other actors – which in turn affects the expected utility calculations of the agenda setter. The agenda-setter seeks to exploit this characteristic according to the model and makes proposal px with the following probability:

$$\mathrm{PAS}_i(px) = \frac{e^{\lambda_{as}\cdot \mathrm{UAS}_i(px)}}{\sum_{p=1}^{T} e^{\lambda_{as}\cdot \mathrm{UAS}_i(p)}} \quad (12.11)$$

Depending on who is considered as the decisive agenda setter in the policy making process, the total expected probability that policy px is initially proposed is therefore:

$$PAS(px) = \sum_{i=1}^{I} (\mathrm{PAS}_i \cdot was_i) \quad (12.12)$$

where was_i defines the probability of actor i to draft the decisive proposal in the agenda-setting stage. In the application considered, the Commission is assumed to be the decisive agenda-setter in the consultation procedure and the European Parliament in the codecision procedure so a probability weight of 1 is accordingly assigned to these actors in the respective procedure (implying a weight of 0 for all other actors). The probability of observing a particular outcome according to the model is then the sum of the probability that the respective option has been proposed by the agenda setter, has not been amended and finally been adopted and the probability that this outcome is the result of a successful amendment that has received the required majorities of votes in the final stage of decision making. This probability is later referred to as the likelihood of the observation under the model.

An Empirical Application: Policy Making in the European Union

Data

For the estimation and empirical test of the theoretical models I reanalyze data from the DEU project (Thomson et al. 2006). This facilitates comparisons with previous findings on the subject. The DEU study provides quantitative estimates for actors' interests on contested Commission proposals, which were initiated between 1999 and 2001 (Thomson and Stokman 2006).

In this study, experts first identified the controversial issues raised by each Commission proposal. Secondly, they indicated the policy position initially favored by each of the 15 member states, the Commission and the EP, and the levels of salience they each attached to those 174 issues from 66 Commission proposals. Each proposal defines a case when it attracted some public attention in the period under study. A second selection criterion was the existence of some controversy in the decision making of the proposal. None of the proposals is still pending, and only one has been rejected. On closer inspection of the DEU data, each proposal contains one or more contested issues with estimates for the actors' interests (policy positions and saliencies), including the location of the status quo and outcome. More specifically, one finds that 21% of all proposals are one-dimensional, 38% are two-dimensional, and 41% of the proposals have higher dimensional policy spaces with between three and six issues. For all cases, the actors have different saliencies, and because 79% of these cases are multidimensional, this should be reflected in the shape of the actors' utility functions. For each issue, the interviewees were asked to assign the extreme values on a scale from 0 to 100 to the actors with the extreme policy positions. They then located the actors with intermediate positions.

Like all empirical studies, the DEU data also contains missing values for more than half of the contested 162 issues, i.e., for the status quo and the policy position of at least one actor. Research on missing values emphasizes the superiority of multiple imputation techniques against listwise deletion, but the question is which imputation method should be applied. In the following, the currently most prominent imputation

Table 12.1 Characteristics and distribution of legislative proposals

		Number of initiatives	Percentage	Number of issues	Percentage
Legislative procedure codecision	QMV	14	29.17	35	33.02
	Unanimity	5	10.42	12	11.32
Consultation	QMV	18	37.5	42	39.62
	Unanimity	11	22.92	17	16.04
Instrument	Directives	20	41.67	47	44.34
	Regulations	23	47.92	50	47.17
	Decisions	5	10.42	9	8.49
Policy area	Agriculture	11	22.92	29	27.36
	Internal market	11	22.92	28	26.42
	Fisheries	6	12.50	11	10.38
	ECOFIN	5	10.42	8	7.55
	Justice & home affairs	2	4.17	3	2.83
	General	2	4.17	4	3.77
	Others	11	22.92	23	21.70
Total		48	100	106	100

algorithm AMELIA is employed for the imputation of missing actor positions (King et al. 2001). However, if proposals contain missing values for the status quo, I follow Steunenberg and Selck (2006) and drop them from the analysis. The sample is, therefore, reduced to 48 legislative initiatives. Table 12.1 shows the distribution of the data with respect to voting rule, legislative procedure, instrument and the number of issues.

In spite of the sample reduction to 48 cases, the relative proportion of cases in each subcategory remains approximately the same as in the original DEU data set. Furthermore, there are enough cases in most subcategories to estimate the effects for each group and to control for possible bias on the overall estimates.

Statistical Estimation and Results

I estimate the theoretic model by maximum likelihood estimation. The likelihood in this application describes the probability that the observed outcomes are actually produced by respective theoretic model and is maximized with respect to λ, i.e., the impact of the theoretically assumed preferences on the actually observed behavior and outcomes. An advantage of the statistical estimation is that, similar to regression analyses, it is possible to distinguish between different arguments of the theories in the estimation, their error and their contribution to the explanatory power of the model. In other words, one can identify the relevance the arguments of the theories on the adoption of policy proposals, the amendment of proposals and agenda setting for the explanation of policy outcomes in the model. To gain more information on the contribution of these arguments I split the λ coefficient into three parts, one for each decision making stage (i.e., agenda-setting, amendments and final passage votes), and estimate them separately. The coefficients indicate to what extent the behavior assumed by the theory with respect to agenda-setting, amendment-proof set and the win-set is consistent with the true data generating process. Positive coefficients indicate behavior that is on average consistent with the theoretical model, negative coefficients behavior that is on average the opposite of what is theoretically assumed and zero coefficients signal that the observed data is best described by completely random decisions. However, the absolute size of the coefficients is difficult to compare because the decision making options should differ more with respect to their utility for the actors in the final stages of the decision making process than in the first stages because of the decreasing level of uncertainty on and relevance of other actors actions (which is due to the stochastic nature of decisions) and the estimation of λ conditions on that utility. As a consequence, one would expect coefficients to be smaller in the final stages (e.g., voting) than in the first. The split of the λ coefficient therefore also helps to control for scaling effects in the model. Table 12.2 shows the results of the empirical estimation.[2]

The first row of the table shows that the coefficients for all arguments are significantly positive, meaning that the observations are consistent with these arguments of the theoretical model. The positive coefficients indicate that policy outcomes can rather be observed inside the win-set than outside, rather inside the amendment-proof set than outside and that the agenda-setter rather proposes policies that are close to his ideal position than far away, given they are inside the win-set and the amendment-proof set. These results are perfectly consistent with the predictions of veto players theory.

The statistical approach also makes it possible to assess the contribution of the different arguments in the model to its explanatory power. One way to identify this contribution is to assume random behavior for each of the decision making stages in turn and fix the respective coefficient to 0 in order to determine the marginal impact of each theoretical argument on the likelihood of the model that describes how likely the actual observations are given the model assumptions. The decrease

Table 12.2 Veto players theory: explanatory power and scaling of arguments

	Agenda-setting	Amendments	Final voting	Initiatives	Log-likelihood
Veto players model	79.67***	236.64***	1.59***	48	−352.9
Δloglik	−8.46	−11.23	−24.79	–	–
Random model	0	0	0	48	−382.3

*** significant at the 0.05 level based on testing against a model that assumes random decision making at the level of the respective argument

[2] Because there are comparatively few formal restrictions on amendments the set of stable outcomes is comparatively small in this model. I employ a discount factor of 0.2 for all players for the purpose of demonstration to compensate for this effect and increase stability in the predictions.

of the likelihood that results from assuming random behavior is given in the second row of Table 12.2. The results show that manipulating the final stage of legislation in the decision making model has by far the largest impact on the explanatory power of the model. This suggests that the location of veto players in the policy space have the largest impact on the location of the outcomes of the policy process. The influence of the amendment-proof set comes second while the influence of the agenda-setter appears weakest in this comparison. However, one reason for the results of this comparison is methodological: the arguments at the first stages of decision making (e.g., agenda-setting) can only explain the variance not already explained by the arguments at the subsequent stages of decision making in this set up and, therefore, their overall contribution appears lower. But an important conclusion can nevertheless be drawn from this comparison (and can be drawn because of this set-up): every single argument in the veto players model contributes to its explanatory power above the contribution of the other arguments already in the model to a significant extent.

Finally, the statistical estimation of the theoretical models also makes it possible to evaluate their overall performance by applying similar criteria for model evaluation. One of the most basic ideas for this purpose in statistics is to compare the explanatory power of the theoretical model to what would be explained by a completely atheoretic random data generating process. At the very least, one would require the theoretical model to outperform the random data generating process in this comparison in order to be acceptable. There are different ways to implement this idea for evaluating strategic decision making models but one way would be to employ a model that assumes completely random decision making behavior at all stages of the decision making process for that purpose. In the application considered, this assumption is met if all coefficients of the theoretic model are set to 0. Table 12.2 shows that the veto players model meets this basic criterion and clearly outperforms the random data generating process described in the third row of the table. The difference of the log-likelihoods between the models amounts to 29.4, implying that observing the data at hand is $e^{29.4}$ more likely if we assume that the veto players account is the true data generating process – which is a very strong result even if one takes the additional degrees of freedom of the veto players model into account and is clearly significant. Thus, while nonstatistical assessments of veto players models of EU policy making based on the same data set have often come to rather sceptical conclusions about its empirical performance (Achen 2006a; Schneider et al. 2006), the statistical assessment shows that the veto players account provides a valuable explanation of how policy making in the European Union works and how policy outcomes are produced.

Conclusion

Empirical inference on game–theoretic models of EU policy making models is a difficult task. In this chapter I have drawn attention to some methodological pitfalls that can seriously flaw the results of empirical analyses but have so far received little attention in EU policy research. I argue that quantal response analysis offers a powerful approach that can help to overcome these problems for several reasons. With respect to analyses of nonstatistical models of EU policy making it allows valid statistical inference on the explanatory power of the models, the impact of single theoretical arguments and model comparisons based on standard tools of statistics. With respect to quantal response analyses in other fields of political science it appears to be particular useful in policy research because it makes it possible to model complicated patterns of strategic interaction among larger number of actors within complex institutions while remaining comparatively parsimonious.

Another potential advantage of the approach is theoretical: Compared to deterministic modelling stochastic game theory can allow more robust theoretical analyses of collective decisions due to their probabilistic nature. For this reason they can deal with some common problems of collective choice analyses in a more comprehensive or even alternative way. This includes the hypothesized instability of collective choices that has challenged and strongly influenced theory building in rational choice institutionalism while the empirical evidence has remained controversial (McLean 2002). Stochastic approaches like the quantal response approach employed in this analysis provide a natural explanation for this phenomenon and may help to extend the range of theories that can (meaningfully) be developed and applied in policy research.

References

Achen CH (2006a) Evaluating political decision-making models. In: Thomson R, Stokman FN, Achen CH, König T (eds) The European Union decides. Cambridge University Press, Cambridge, pp. 264–298

Achen CH (2006b) Institutional realism and bargaining models. In: Thomson R, Stokman FN, Achen CH, König T (eds) The European Union decides. Cambridge University Press, Cambridge, pp. 86–123

Aragones E, Palfrey TR (2004) The effect of candidate quality on electoral equilibrium: an experimental study. Am Political Sci Rev 98(1):77–90

Arregui J, Stokman FN, Thomson R (2006) Compromise, exchange and challenge in the european union. In: Thomson R, Stokman FN, Achen CH, König T (eds) The European Union decides. Cambridge University Press, Cambridge, pp. 124–152

Bailer S (2004) Bargaining success in the european union: the impact of exogenous and endogenous power resources. Eur Union Politics 5(1):99–123

Bailer S, Schneider G (2006) Nash versus schelling? the importance of constraints in legislative bargaining. In: Thomson R, Stokman FN, Achen CH, König T (eds) The European Union decides. Cambridge University Press, Cambridge, pp. 153–177

Banks JS, Duggan J (2000) A bargaining model of collective choice. Am Political Sci Rev 94(1):73–88

Baron DP, Ferejohn JA (1989) Bargaining in legislatures. Am Political Sci Rev 83(4):1181–1206

Bas MA, Signorino CS, Walker RW (2008) Statistical backwards induction: a simple method for estimating recursive strategic models. Political Anal 16(1):21–40

Bawn K (1999) Money and majorities in the federel republic of germany: Evidence for a veto players model of government spending. Am J Political Sci 43(3):707–736

Boekhoorn V, Deemen AMAV, Hosli MO (2006) A cooperative approach to decision-making in the european union. In: Thomson R, Stokman FN, Achen CH, König T (eds) The European Union decides. Cambridge University Press, Cambridge, pp. 178–210
Bräuninger T, König T (1999) The checks and balances of party federalism. german federal government in a divided legislature. Eur J Political Res 36(2):207–234
Carrubba CJ, Yuen A, Zorn C (2007a) In defense of comparative statics: specifying empirical tests of models of strategic interaction. Political Anal 15(4):465–482
Carrubba CJ, Yuen A, Zorn C (2007b) Reply to signorino. Political Anal 15(4):502–504
Crombez C (1997) The co-decision procedure in the european union. Legis Stud Quart 22(1): 97–119
Crombez C (2003) The democratic deficit in the european union: Much ado about nothing? Eur Union Politics 4(1):101–120
de Mesquita BB (2004) Decision-making models, rigor and new puzzles. Eur Union Politics 5(1):125–138
de Mesquita BB, Lalman D (1992) War and reason : domestic and international imperatives. Yale University Press, New Haven, [Conn.] ; London
de Mesquita BB, Stokman FN (1994) European Community decision making: models, applications, and comparisons. Yale University Press, New Haven; London
Erikson RS, Romero DW (1990) Candidate equilibrium and the Behavioral-Model of the vote. Am Political Sci Rev 84(4):1103–1126
Goeree JK, Holt CA, Palfrey TR (2004) Regular quantal response equilibrium. Exp Econ 8(4): 347–367
Guarnaschelli S, McKelvey RD, Palfrey TR (2000) An experimental study of jury decision rules. Am Political Sci Rev 94(2):407–423
Hallerberg M (2002) Veto players and the choice of monetary institutions. Int Org 56(4):775–802
Hug S, Tsebelis G (2002) Veto players and referendums around the world. J Theor Politics 14(4):465–515
Junge D, König T (2007) What's wrong with EU spatial analysis? the accuracy and robustness of empirical applications to the interpretation of the legislative process and the specification of preferences. J Theor Politics 19(4):465–487
King G, Honaker J, Joseph A, Scheve K (2001) Analyzing incomplete political science data: An alternative algorithm for multiple imputation. Am Political Sci Rev 95(1):49–69
König T (2001) Bicameralism and party politics in germany. Political Stud 49(3):411–437
König T, Luetgert B, Dannwolf T (2006) Quantifying european legislative research. using CELEX and PRELEX in EU legislative studies. Eur Union Politics 7(4):553–574
König T, Pöter M (2001) Examining the EU legislative process. The relative importance of agenda and veto power. Eur Union Politics 2(3):329–351
König T, Proksch S (2006) Exchanging and voting in the council: endogenizing the spatial model of legislative politics. J Eur Public Policy 13(5):647–669
McFadden D (1981) Econometric models of probabilistic choice. In: Manski C, McFadden D (eds) Structural analysis of discrete data with econometric applications. The MIT Press, Cambridge MA
McKelvey RD (1991) An experimental test of a stochastic game model of committee bargaining. In: Palfrey TR (ed) Laboratory research in political economy, pages vi,323p. University of Michigan Press ; Manchester : Manchester University Press [distributor], Ann Arbor.
McKelvey RD, Palfrey TR (1996) A statistical theory of equilibrium in games. Jpn Econ Rev 47(2):186–209
McKelvey RD, Palfrey TR (1998) Quantal response equilibria for extensive form games. Exp Econ 1:9–41
McLean I (2002) Review article: William h. riker and the invention of heresthetic(s). Br J Political Sci 32:535–558
Morton RB (1999) Methods and models: a guide to the empirical analysis of formal models in political science. Cambridge University Press, Cambridge

Ochs J (1995) Games with unique, mixed strategy equilibria – an Experimental-Study. Games Econ Behav 10(1):202–217

Quinn K, Westveld A (2004) Bayesian inference for semiparametric quantal response equilibrium models. Working paper

Rubinstein A (1982) Perfect equilibrium in a bargaining model. Econometrica 50(1):97–109

Schneider G, Finke D, Baltz K (2007) With a little help from the state: interest intermediation in the domestic pre-negotiations of EU legislation. J Eur Public Policy 14(3):444–459

Schneider G, Steunenberg B, Widgren M (2006) Evidence with insight: what models contribute to EU research. In: Thomson R, Stokman FN, Achen CH, König T (eds) The European Union decides. Cambridge University Press, Cambridge, pp. 299–316

Segal JA, Cameron CM, Cover AD (1992) A spatial model of roll call voting – senators, constituents, presidents, and interest-groups in Supreme-Court confirmations. Am J Political Sci 36(1):96–121

Selck TJ (2004) The impact of procedure: analyzing European Union legislative decision-making. Cuvillier Verlag, Göttingen

Signorino CS (1999) Strategic interaction and the statistical analysis of international conflict. Am Political Sci Rev 93(2):279–297

Signorino CS, Tarar A (2006) A unified theory and test of extended immediate deterrence. Am J Political Sci 50(3):586–605

Signorino CS, Yilmaz K (2003) Strategic misspecification in regression models. Am J Political Sci 47(3):551–566

Smith A (1999) Testing theories of strategic choice: the example of crisis escalation. Am J Political Sci 43(4):1254–1283

Steunenberg B (1994) Decision making under different institutional arrangements: legislation by the european community. J Inst Theor Econ 150(4):642–669

Steunenberg B (1997) Codecision and its reform: a comparative analysis of decision-making rules in the european union. In: Steunenberg B, van Vught F (eds) Political institutions and public policy: Perspectives on European decision making. Kluwer Academic Publisher, Dortrecht, pp. 205–229

Steunenberg B (2001) Enlargement and institutional reform in the european union: separate or connected issues? Const Political Econ 12:349–368

Thomson R, Stokman F, Achen C, König T. (2006) The European Union decides, 1st edn. Political economy of institutions and decisions. Cambridge University Press, Cambridge [u.a.]

Thomson R, Stokman FN (2006) Research design: measuring actors' positions, saliences and capabilities. In: Thomson R, Stokman FN, Achen CH, König T (eds) The European Union decides. Cambridge University Press, Cambridge, pp. 25–53

Tsebelis G (1994) The power of the european parliament as a conditional agenda setter. Am Political Sci Rev 88(1):128–142

Tsebelis G (1995) Decision making in political systems: Veto players in presidentialism, parliamentarism, multicameralism und multipartyism. Br J Political Sci 25(3):289–325

Tsebelis G (1999) Veto players and law production in parliamentary democracies: an empirical analysis. Am Political Sci Rev 93(3):591–608

Tsebelis G (2002) Veto players : how political institutions work. Princeton University Press, Princeton, N.J.

Tsebelis G, Money J (1997) Bicameralism. Political economy of institutions and decisions. Cambridge University Press, Cambridge

Part V
Conclusion

Chapter 13
Veto Players, Reform Processes and Policy Change: Concluding Remarks

Thomas König and Marc Debus

The idea of editing a volume of studies focusing on policy change, reform processes, and veto players originates from two events in 2009 at the University of Mannheim: In spring, we were submitting a proposal for a collaborative research centre entitled "The Political Economy of Reforms" to the German National Science Foundation (DFG), which will be funded over a period of at least 4 years (SFB 884). This interdisciplinary project starts with the common observation that our societies will face enormous challenges in the twenty-first century due to climate change, aging societies, economic and financial globalisation, etc. At the level of political decision making, these challenges require sophisticated political reforms, as they have the potential to seriously disturb the economic, political, and social order of modern democracies. Yet, we observe that reform making is frequently delayed, compromised, or even aborted because of the lack of consensus in these democracies. With DFG support we will be able to investigate failure and success of reform making in the coming years, and veto player theory is one of the central perspectives we will apply to improve our understanding of reform making, including a particular focus on the aggregation of competing interests of the actors involved, the impact of contexts, and political processes in modern democracies.

The second event leading to this volume took place in summer 2009, when George Tsebelis came to the Mannheim Centre for European Social Research (MZES) as a visiting professor to finish our book on *Realizing the Impossible: Reforming the European Union*. In 2002, George Tsebelis published his seminal book "*Veto Players. How Political Institutions Work.* Princeton University Press/Russell Sage Foundation", in which he predicts that the likelihood for policy change does not increase in modern democracies when a higher number of veto players must

T. König (✉)
Department of Social Sciences University of Mannheim, Germany
and
MZES, University of Mannheim, Germany
e-mail: t.koenig@uni-mannheim.de

M. Debus
MZES, University of Mannheim, Germany
e-mail: marc.debus@mzes.uni-mannheim.de

T. König et al. (eds.), *Reform Processes and Policy Change: Veto Players and Decision-Making in Modern Democracies*, Studies in Public Choice 16,
DOI 10.1007/978-1-4419-5809-9_13,

agree on changing the status quo. During his visit we organised a conference on the effects of veto players for reform making in modern democracies and invited scholars to discuss their insights into the analytical power of veto player theory. The conference was held from May 14 to 16, 2009 at the MZES with the financial support of the Fritz Thyssen Foundation. It brought together more than 25 political scientists studying institutional designs of modern democracies, preferences of political actors, and the impact of both on patterns of reform making.

This book is therefore both an evaluation of the current state of veto player theory for the analysis of reform making in modern democracies and an excellent starting point for our long-term project on "The Political Economy of Reforms" at the University of Mannheim. Briefly summarised, the contributions of this book have provided further insights into three central aspects of veto player analysis for explaining reform making in modern democracies. Given Tsebelis' framework on the interaction between political actors' institutional power, their preferences, and the location of the status quo, they stress (1) the identification of veto players' preference for measuring their reform-making behaviour, (2) the interpretation of other phenomena in complex veto player systems, which can provide additional insight into reform making, and (3) the modelling of strategic reform-making behaviour in veto player systems. All contributions make use of the central argument of veto player theory stating that policy change, as the likelihood for changing the status quo, is determined by the interaction between the institutional characteristics of political decision making and the preferences of the political actors that control the prevalence of the status quo.

The contributions of the first section deal with methodological challenges concerning the identification of the preferences of political actors in these reform-making processes. Compared to the first generation of veto player analyses, which have devoted much attention to the interpretation of the institutional provisions of political systems, the identification of actors' preferences is becoming more important for testing the explanatory power of the theory. Many preference indicators still oversimplify the policy context in which veto players take their vote on political reforms, or are simply lacking variation in their measures. While the central variable of veto player analysis concerns policy change, the contributions of the second section of this book focus on other phenomena in complex veto player systems: cabinet governance and intra-governmental control mechanisms, cabinet survival, and legislative activity under coalition governments across the government-opposition divide. These phenomena are considered to provide further insights into the reform-making behaviour of political actors. The third section of this volume consists of contributions that take a closer look at the strategic behaviour of veto players. They ask what will happen when the relevant political actors in the reform-making process know the effects of the number and preferences of the other actors involved.

All contributions in this book share the view that veto players have a decisive impact on policy change and the way political actors agree on political reforms, whether and in which way they change the status quo, and how new initiatives are finally enacted. Besides the interpretation of the institutional settings and the role of veto players, the behavioural identification is becoming more important for explaining the problem-solving capacity of modern democracies, which currently face major economic and societal challenges. The central aim of this concluding chapter is to review the central arguments of veto player theory by comparing it with "classical' studies in comparative governance research. In a second step, we compare the contributions in this book by looking at their theoretical and empirical innovations and their main message with regard to reform making on the basis of reform pressure. Additionally, we discuss incentives for further research on the basis of the results presented throughout this book.

Veto Player Theory, Modern Democracies, and Reform Making

Modern democracies even with a high level of economic development are currently facing great challenges due to climate change, aging societies, economic globalisation, etc. These challenges not only comprise the economic sector but they also apply to the environmental and societal sectors, and since the worldwide economic and financial crisis in 2008 the monetary and financial sectors. Although there is widespread consensus that reforms are necessary to cope with the challenges in these policy sectors, the common view is that we repeatedly experience reform initiatives which are only partially thought through, often delayed for extended periods of time, and watered-down before being adopted. In important policy areas, e.g. labour market institutions, health care system, federal structure, or fiscal sustainability, the status quo often prevails in spite of high societal costs. This observation has stimulated debates on the feasibility of reforms in democracies, and the willingness and ability of political actors to alter the status quo in particular.

Traditional studies in comparative politics and governance can hardly contribute to this discussion by referring to typologies (Sartori 1976; Lijphart 1999). For example, Lijphart (1999) uses several indicators to produce his famous mapping of democratic political systems and argues that two dimensions structure the "patterns of democracy" in developed countries – strong vs. weak executives and federal vs. unitary organised political systems. In the end, Lijphart (1999) finds that consensual democracies provide a similar macro-economic performance to political systems that make most of their decisions on the basis of majority rule. Similarly, Powell (2006) concludes that electoral systems that are based on proportional representation work better in terms of representing the median voter's policy position inside the government. Briefly summarised, this traditional literature provides various classifications along different institutional characteristics, i.e. the type of regime (presidential vs. parliamentary) in general, or the type of electoral system (proportional representation vs. majority rule), party system (two-party vs. multi-party systems) and legislature (uni- vs. bicameralism) in particular.

A major weakness of these classifications is that they ignore the behavioural component of decision making, which may explain reform success or failure in the same category of institutional provision. On closer inspection of the behaviour of political actors, political parties or candidates are generally motivated and mainly interested in maximizing their chances to win (government) offices by presenting their reform positions in electoral campaigns (Downs 1957; Müller and Strøm 1999), which they have to implement by legislative decisions to remain credible in the eyes of the voters. In the simple idealistic world of the "responsible party government model" (Powell 2000, 2004), the actor/party who wins the parliamentary majority will implement their ideal reform position in legislative decision making later. This, however, is almost never the case, as Powell (2004: 96–99) illustrates for the "responsible party government" model. A simple reason is that the electoral system may translate the preferences of the voters in a way that the political party of the median voter is hardly represented in the (coalition) government formed after the election.

Apart from the electoral system, other institutional provisions such as a strong constitutional court, central bank, or second chamber with a majority holding a different policy preference can also alter the chances of a government to implement its ideal reform position without making further compromise. In modern democracies, additional institutions can push or hinder reforms because they distribute power across actors with different interests in the policy-making process, so that a situation of "legislative gridlock" may occur (Sundquist 1968, 1988; Mayhew 1974, 1991; Binder 1999). At this stage, George Tsebelis' theory of veto players steps in. Tsebelis (1995, 2002) argues that it may be misleading to examine various factors of decision making in isolation. Bicameralism and presidentialism, for instance, share common characteristics of decision making, so that it is not necessary to distinguish between them for explaining reform success or failure. Tsebelis' approach takes the factors of decision making into account by modelling explicitly the voting behaviour of actors who are decisive for changing the status quo. The basic argument is that the more actors are necessary for changing the status quo, the more difficult or even impossible are significant reforms. Conceptually, these actors can be divided into institutional veto players when their support for a change of the status quo is constitutionally required, and into partisan veto players with veto power because of their de facto role on the organisation of coalition government. According to Tsebelis (2002: 18), political parties, which are decisive for coalition government, are partisan veto players.

In comparative politics, veto player analysis has changed our views on the working of institutions. Prominent examples are the insight into conditional agenda-setting power of the European Parliament (Tsebelis 1994), the increasing capacity to act in political systems with non-cohesive actors (Tsebelis and Garrett 1996), and the stability inducing effect of bicameral political systems (Tsebelis and Money 1995). Methodologically, these insights are derived from studying the interplay between different institutions when it comes to the size of the win set and the power to set the political agenda. This does not mean that veto player analysis stands in contrast to insights from traditional studies. In a recent article, Scharpf (2006: 846) reconsidered his joint-decision trap of policy making (e.g. Scharpf 1988) by concluding that the consequences of the "joint decision trap" and "compulsory negotiation system" are very similar to the policy implications of veto player systems.

Apart from traditional comparative analysis, veto player analysis may also enrich our understanding of reform making. In the analysis of German federalism, for instance, it has become popular to refer to the second chamber, the Bundesrat, as a veto playing institution, which is made responsible for the so-called "Reform backlog" (e.g. Scharpf 2002; Benz 2004). This characterisation of the Bundesrat indeed played a decisive role in the discussion and, finally, the reform of German federalism in 2006. In this vein, several scholars argued that the large share of German consent law proposals, that is bills that need the support of a majority in both chambers, not only slows down the reform-making process but also results in ineffective compromises (see, e.g. Schmidt 2001; Zohlnhöfer 2009). For German bicameralism, however, König and Bräuninger (1997,1999) found that only the interaction between the institutional provisions of legislative decision making, partisan preferences, and the location of the status quo provides sufficient insights into domain-specific reform making. In line with veto player analysis, significant changes were made in societal affairs, which even required a qualified majority in both chambers, while legislative gridlock persisted in economic affairs in the 1980s and 1990s (König et al. 2003).

On closer inspection of the partisan preferences of German parties, governing in coalition governments and thus intra-governmental conflicts between the governing parties rather than the strength of the second chamber had a decisive impact on the reform backlog (König and Bräuninger 2005). In terms of budgetary politics, Bawn (1999) as well as König and Tröger (2005) also show that partisan veto players have an important role in shaping the budgetary distribution and have an effect on the level of state expenditure. From a comparative perspective, there is also evidence that not only the number of partisan veto players has an effect on legislative activity and policy outputs (e.g. Kreppel 1997; Hallerberg and Basinger 1998; O'Reilly 2005), but that the ideological and policy-area specific orientation and distance between partisan veto players is also decisive (Tsebelis 1999, 2002: 170–208; Basinger and Hallerberg 2004; Martin 2004; Martin and Vanberg 2004, 2005; König 2007; Bräuninger and Debus 2009).

Tsebelis' idea of using the number of veto players in a political system together with their preferences for formulating hypotheses on patterns of policy making and policy outcomes has therefore advanced our understanding of policy making in general and in comparative governance and political economy in particular. Studies on political decision making and policy change provide clear empirical evidence for one of the central expectations derived from veto player theory: the larger the policy distance between veto players, the smaller tends to be the win set of the status quo. In situations with a small win set, the ability to change the status quo decreases, so that first, law production decreases and/or becomes slower and, second, changes in the taxation level or government expenditures become less likely. This indicates that there is support for the well-known statement by Plott (1979; see also Ostrom 1986) that policy outcomes are mainly influenced by the interplay of physical possibilities with institutions and preferences, two further variables that play a key role in economics and political science. Thus, analysing political decision making beyond the traditionalist way of focussing on specific institutional characteristics sheds more light on the patterns of governmental decision making and their consequences for policy outcomes.

Having contrasted the basic aims and principles of veto player theory with "classical" approaches in research on comparative governance and policy making, we now turn to a comprehensive look at the findings presented and their incentives for future research on the role of veto players for political decision making and reform processes.

Summary of Findings

The contributions to this book provide several new insights into veto player analysis and reform making. First, they present new strategies for the identification of veto players' preference to measure their behavioural incentives for reform making; second, they interpret other phenomena in complex veto player systems, which can provide additional insight into reform making; and third, they introduce modelling of strategic reform-making behaviour in veto player systems. What have we learned from each of these contributions with regard to the impact of veto players on policy change and the implementation of reform policies?

Mark Hallerberg's study on empirical applications of veto player analysis and institutional effectiveness highlights the relevance of ideological distances and institutional settings, in particular, for legislatures in parliamentary democracies and political economy outputs in developed countries, while work on developing and transition countries is encouraging. Veto players affect the institutions that are chosen to structure decision making. Moreover, the effectiveness of those institutions depends on the ideological distance among veto players. Institutions put in place under a government with low ideological distance may not function well if the ideological distance increases under the next government. Hallerberg discusses this aspect with examples from the making of fiscal policy. In coalition governments formed between parties with very similar policy positions on economic and financial issues, for instance, the coalition parties prefer delegating decisions to one central player who considers the full tax burden. This would fit perfectly into the Laver and Shepsle (1996) world where each cabinet minister has full control over the policy domain their portfolio deals with. In coalitions with a high internal policy conflict in financial questions, in contrast, the participating parties prefer "fiscal contracts" which include clear rules on the budget that all parties in the government can monitor. What does this imply for the study of reform policies? The central aspect is that one has to consider internal mechanisms of governing in coalitions before drawing conclusions about the size of their win set on the basis of the degree of the intra-governmental veto player distance. More broadly speaking, the question is raised on the design of institutions because the configuration of veto players leads different types of coordination problems within government.

Before we come back to the questions of delegation and control mechanisms in coalition governments discussed in Chap. 4 by Wolfgang C. Müller and Thomas Meyer, the point raised by Mark Hallerberg has to be connected to the contributions by Detlef Jahn (Chap. 2) and by Thomas König, Bernd Luig, Sven-Oliver Proksch, and Jonathan Slapin (Chap. 3). The goal of Detlef Jahn's study is, first, to compare existing veto player indices and, in a second step, to provide new indices that include variation in policy preferences and in the institutional settings. Detlef Jahn's incentive to create a new measure for veto player strength over countries and over time arose from the observation that existing veto player indices hardly include sufficient information on the characteristics of the political and party system. The revised indices presented in the chapter contributed by Detlef Jahn will be helpful to conduct more refined empirical analyses of reform making because of the availability of new data that describe veto player systems in more detail.

The contribution by Thomas König, Bernd Luig, Sven-Oliver Proksch, and Jonathan Slapin discusses existing methods for estimating preferences of veto players and presents a novel approach that considers the context of reform making when identifying the preferences of veto players. Reliability concerns in traditional content analysis of party manifestos (CMP; see Budge et al. 2001; Klingemann et al. 2006; Volkens 2007) have led researchers to develop quantitative content analysis techniques to extract policy preferences of political actors (e.g. Laver and Garry 2000; Laver et al. 2003; Slapin and Proksch 2008). This contribution introduces an automated procedure for identifying policy-specific language in party manifestos using keywords from legislative initiatives. This facilitates significantly the quantitative estimation of veto player preferences on substantive policy dimensions.

The contributions in the second part of the book study "phenomena" that are either explained from a veto player perspective or have an influence on policy change in parliamentary systems with coalition governments. They specifically discuss, first, the origins of various intra-governmental control mechanisms by which partisan veto players in governments can ensure that their partners in government comply with the policy agreements and procedural rules they agreed on in the coalition negotiation process (Chap. 5 by Wolfgang C. Müller and Thomas Meyer). The authors argue that coalition governments typically face problems from (partially) conflicting preferences of the cabinet parties. For many reasons, including aspects of their political careers, individual ministers are likely to pursue party policies rather than coalition ones. Yet, the doctrine of collective cabinet responsibility ties the coalition as a whole to government policy. Wolfgang C. Müller and Thomas Meyer identify several mechanisms that help to establish coalition control over individual ministers, that is, aspects such as contract design, screening, monitoring, and institutional checks. The authors of this chapter show that the countries' experience with specific control mechanisms, the coalition's bargaining environment, the actors' policy preferences, and political institutions determine whether coalition parties are willing to bear the costs of negotiating compromises. Like the findings of Mark Hallerberg, this also points to the role of intra-governmental institutional control mechanisms that are mostly ignored in empirical analysis of reform making under coalition governments.

Thomas Saalfeld's study referred to coalition politics and the determinants of the survival of coalition cabinets from a veto player perspective (Chap. 6). On the basis of Tsebelis (2002) and an unpublished study by the same author (2006) on the impact of legislative agenda control of governments on the formation, policy-making ability and (ultimately) durability of coalition cabinets over a legislative period, Thomas Saalfeld finds evidence for the importance of the number of veto players as predictors of coalition stability. Although the ideological distance between veto players is not of statistical significance for explaining cabinet duration, there is substantial evidence for the importance of agenda powers for the survival of minority cabinets. This implies that veto player theory is distinctive not only by emphasizing properties of the partisan veto players (number, preference diversity, and cohesion) rather than the parliamentary bargaining environment they operate in. Thomas Saalfeld also shows that even minority cabinets can be relatively stable if the partisan veto players are able to employ positional and institutional advantages as well as the government's agenda powers vis-à-vis parliament to compensate for their lack of parliamentary strength.

Thomas Bräuninger and Marc Debus analyse the determinants of bipartisan policy output in terms of legislative activity in countries with coalition governments. The authors of Chap. 7 argue that there are incentives for MPs for working together across partisan and coalitional lines. On the basis of a two-stage legislative model that covers the proposal and voting stage of a bill, Bräuninger and Debus identify the policy-area-specific heterogeneity inside the government and between government and opposition as a decisive variable, which should effect the introduction and the chances for success of a bipartisan law proposal. Their results for Belgium and Germany show that distances between policy positions in an issue area play a decisive role for bipartisan bills. They are more likely to be introduced when policy conflict within the government coalitions is large, while the veto player distance between government parties has a negative effect on the success of bipartisan bills. As argued in the contribution by König et al. (Chap. 4), general ideological measures such as the overall left-right dimension cannot account for policy making because of ignoring the cabinet structure.

Chapter 8 focuses on a further anomaly in legislative decision making by referring to the European level. The aim of the study by Thomas König and Dirk Junge is to analyse why member states with veto power usually support policy change proposed by a Commission initiative when their own position is located closer to the status quo. To get an answer, the authors investigate the voting preferences and logrolling opportunities of the EU member states on 48 Commission proposals. The principal finding of the authors of Chap. 8 is that models that derive actors' voting preferences from the policy space of each Commission proposal can hardly explain the consensus in the Council. The main reason for this result is that the Commission attempts to avoid a divided Council by initiating proposals for which member states favour a change of the status quo in the same direction. In the event of Council controversies about the size of policy change, König and Junge have shown that member states can solve their conflicts by mutually benefiting from logrolling across proposals that either belong to the same policy domain or are negotiated during the same period. Hence, inter-temporal and domain-specific logrolling can provide a powerful explanation for consensus even in a contested Council. The latter highlights the finding from previous chapters that legislative activity and political decision-making has to be analysed separately for each policy area.

The contributions subsumed in the third part of the book basically look at policy making in a strategic way. That is, political actors may anticipate the effects veto players have in the reform-making process. The four contributions that belong to this kind of research focus on the empirical evaluation of law-making theories (Chap. 9 by Luigi Curini and Francesco Zucchini), on a model of implementation strategies of European policy on the national level (Chap. 10 by Bernhard Steunenberg), on sophisticated voting in bicameral systems (Chap. 11 Simon Hug) and, finally, on the employment of quantal response theory in legislation (Chap. 12 by Dirk Junge). In their analysis of roll call votes in the Italian parliament, Luigi Curini and Francesco Zucchini test the explanatory power of veto player theory as compared to other models of legislative decision making (e.g. Krehbiel et al. 2005, Cox and McCubbins 2005). Their main finding is that, in contrast to models that focus on the median legislator and therewith on the parties that control these MPs, the governmental veto player model works better, which indicates that the agreement of all government parties is necessary for policy change. Like the contributions by Hallerberg, König et al., and Bräuninger and Debus, this result also highlights the importance of partisan veto players. In line with Wolfgang C. Müller and Thomas Meyer (Chap. 5), Curini and Zucchini also point to the characteristic of governing in coalitions by looking at mechanisms that help establishing a coalition government.

Bernard Steunenberg's study on the interplay of domestic actors and monitoring by the European Commission and its effect on the implementation of European policy widens the scope of analysis by looking at strategic decision making in multilevel systems. In principal, Steunenberg conceives the implementation process as a strategic game, in which the domestic actors decide about an implementation policy in consideration of the Commission's reaction. Hereby, domestic actors have incomplete information about the discretion of the Commission. His theoretically derived result, which is supported by a case study from the Netherlands, implies that one has to step away from a formally determined definition of a veto player so that other actors can play a role in a model of implementation. This indicates that national policy is shaped by domestic preferences and that these have to be combined with information on the uncertainty about how the Commission will react. Therefore, the theory requires a multi-layered structure in which European as well as domestic actors can play a role.

The contribution by Simon Hug in Chap. 11 highlights the importance of bicameral systems for strategic voting. Hug argues that bicameralism is a variant of veto players and that voting behaviour of MPs cannot only be analysed chamber-by-chamber. Instead, the whole legislative process has to be included when analysing policy making in bicameral systems. Thus, when referring to roll call votes, which are widely used in empirical political science to estimate the policy preferences of MPs (see Chap. 9 by Curini and Zuchhini; see also Poole and Rosenthal 1997; Hix et al. 2006; Clinton et al. 2004), one has to take the context of each MP's decision making into account. This argument corresponds to König et al. in Chap. 4 when bicameral systems raise incentives that MPs behave strategically.

Finally, the contribution by Dirk Junge finds that probabilistic decision-making models can have considerable advantages in applied policy research because they make it possible to assess even complex strategic interactions and institutional arrangements directly in a very parsimonious way. Thus, they can provide precise information about how competing legislative theories perform and how interests, rights, and procedures affect legislative outcomes even if many actors are involved, non-trivial decision rules and complex interaction structures apply.

Priorities for Future Research

The studies in this book used the framework of veto player theory to analyse the behaviour of political actors in reform-making processes and the determinants of policy outcomes. The main message is that the institutional arrangement of a political system in terms of the number of veto players and their policy preferences provide a solid base for determining the likelihood for significant change. Additionally, some contributions provided new methods for measuring policy preferences and indices for the strength of veto players in a comparative and sophisticated way. Furthermore, the studies provided in this book give some answers to the list of critical aspects of veto player theory (e.g. Ganghof 2003). A central challenge still concerns the correct interpretation of the decision-making procedure, which constitutes institutional and partisan veto players. Besides bicameral structures, the question is whether one should define supreme courts, central banks, etc. a priori as veto players? Jahn presents two new veto player indices that abstain from including supreme courts, but rather identify changes in the political system of the countries over time.

The veto player index of Tsebelis, for instance, does not incorporate changes in a country's institutional setting. Detlef Jahn includes this time-variant aspect, so that in his veto player index the second chambers of Sweden and Denmark are included only until their abolishment. Another example is the status change of the Belgian Senate. After the constitutional reform in 1993, the Belgian Senate lost power and it is therefore only considered as a veto player until 1993 by Jahn's new index. In addition, Jahn used the time-variant data from the CMP to identify changes in the ideological distance between veto players. While König et al. demand the use of data on party positions that take programmatic shifts into account, the quality of the data by the CMP project has been questioned in recent years (e.g. Mikhaylov et al. 2008; Benoit et al. 2009). The various ways of estimating party policy positions in addition to the availability of a number of datasets that cover these positions brings us to a second point raised by Ganghof in his 2003 article. From his perspective, the assignment of policy positions to veto players on the basis of the results of expert surveys and election manifestos, in particular, is not yet fully developed. Ganghof (2003: 10) argued that parties formulate their preferences with regard to their primary goal – that is, maximising votes to increase the probability to win control over governmental offices – and not with regard to the final outcome of decision-making process.

While there is still no solution for measuring the "true" preferences of political actors with regard to the final policy outcomes, the approach by König et al.

incorporates information on the legislative process when estimating the policy positions of German parties from 1983 to 1994. This contextual information derived from a combination of election manifestos and key words from law proposals brings us at least closer to the ideal conception of the estimation of "real" policy preferences of political actors. For bringing new insight into the "black box" of governmental decision making and for evaluating models like one of the "responsible party government", one objective for future research will be to develop methods to generate datasets that take into account the preferences of voters and their reform expectations. Voters should have different positions on policy reforms because they serve the material interests of some citizens often at the cost of others (Erikson et al. 2002). The expectations are straightforward: voters who think of increasing their utility from a reform will promote and support them, whereas reform losers will try to avoid or reject them.

New datasets on reform policy making should include a common measurement of preferences on the individual level and thus of the electorate and political actors such as candidates, parties, and governments on specific reform proposals and on common policy dimensions, so that the positions of all relevant political actors are comparable. Until know, issue-specific information on voter positions is often not comparable to the type of information commonly used in the analysis of parties and party systems (e.g. Shikano 2006). Establishing a set of standardised questions on key dimensions of policy conflict or on specific policy reforms will allow researchers to locate and map voters, political parties, and governments on the same policy dimensions and make inferences on that basis.

There are of course further open questions besides a theoretically based data collection that set incentives for future research. First, there is the equivalence problem: Are veto players of equal strength? Ganghof and Bräuniger (2006) propose a differentiation between strong and weak veto players on the basis of their power as warranted by a country's constitution. Their argument is in line with the conclusion by Hallerberg in Chap. 2, which calls for the inclusion of all institutional arrangements and thus not only of "full" veto players. Thus, incorporating information on the degree of strength of veto players is one incentive for both theoretical and empirical modelling. Saalfeld highlighted in his contribution the problems for measuring the policy position of the status quo and the policy direction of exogenous shocks. While this aspect is clearly of relevance for analysing reforms and thus the degree of policy change, there are no standard solutions for this problem. One fruitful starting point could be the analysis of policy programmes that are normally formulated during or after the coalition negotiation talks, like government declarations or coalition agreements (for studies that focus on this aspect, see König et al. 1999; Warwick 2001; Timmermans 2006; Debus 2008; Müller and Strøm 2008) or the content analysis of legislative bills and laws (e.g. König and Luig 2009).

Taking a closer look at the reform environment and the differentiation between specific policy areas when looking at reform policy making seems a further fruitful starting point for further research. On that basis, bargaining approaches like logrolling models can be evaluated in a better way. If a coalition government between a conservative and a social democratic party agrees, for instance, on market-liberal reforms of the welfare state and on the implementation of progressive social policies like gay marriage, one may argue that such changes of the status quo are only possible when clear rules inside the negotiated coalition agreement exist and policy area saliencies between coalition parties are different. The latter, however, requires the analysis of contextual features of the party system and of the environment of reform proposals like the preferences and expectations of voters and party supporters on the one hand and a detailed knowledge on the country-specific patterns of legislative decision making on the other (e.g. Carrubba and Volden 2000).

Relaxing the unitary actor assumption could be of relevance for policy making in veto player systems. If we can identify intra-party groups and their preferences, it seems promising to include them in a "unified" model that seeks to analyse the origins of policy making until the actual output of policy making. Such a theoretical design would include questions on how calls for new policies are put on the political agenda. Here, exogenous events and how they shape the position of the status quo and the media should play a major role. A second step would study how intra-party factions make use of calls for reform policies to shift to positions of their party and/or the government into a position they prefer.

Finally, future research should pay attention to the time dimension by comparing the original reform proposal potential with the final policy outcome. In evaluating the time line from the initiation of a reform proposal until its adoption or failure, one can analyse which stages in the political process are crucial for the survival of an attempt to change the status quo (e.g. Martin and Vanberg 2005). What kind of role is played by institutional events like mid-term elections or the occurrence of international crisis or wars like in the aftermath of September 11 for reform policies on various issue dimensions? A second consideration could be the individual perspective and the utility for a political actor to implement reforms. Reforms involve costs, typically in their early stages, and generate benefits, typically only after some time (Przeworski 1991). Whether reforms make sense from the point of view of the individual decision maker or those affected by the reforms depends on the consistency of their time horizons. Decision makers who are unlikely to reap the benefits of reform but who would have to shoulder their (electoral or office) costs are unlikely to engage in reforms (e.g. Haggard and Kaufman 1995; Hellman 1998). At the same time decision takers who are unlikely to benefit from reforms but need to carry their (financial) burdens are unlikely to support reforms (e.g. Lewis-Beck 1986; Lewis-Beck and Stegmaier 2000; Van der Brug et al. 2007; Duch and Stevenson 2006, 2008).

The research outlined here focuses on combining the preferences of political actors (i.e. voters, parties, and governments) with institutional constraints, the time line of policy making, and the broader environment of a political system, and veto player theory marks an ideal starting point for developing the necessary theoretical underpinning.

References

Basinger S, Hallerberg M (2004) Remodeling the competition for capital: how domestic politics erases the race to the bottom. Am Polit Sci Rev 98(2):261–276

Bawn K (1999) Money and majorities in the Federal Republic of Germany: evidence for a veto players model of government spending. Am J Polit Sci 43(3):707–736

Benoit K, Laver M, Mikhaylov S (2009) Treating words as data with error: estimating uncertainty in the comparative manifesto project measures. Am J Polit Sci 53(2):495–513

Benz A (2004) Path-dependent institutions and strategic veto players – national parliaments in the European Union. West Eur Polit 27(5):875–900

Binder SA (1999) The dynamics of legislative gridlock, 1947–96. Am Polit Sci Rev 93(3):519–533

Bräuninger T, Debus M (2009) Legislative agenda-setting in parliamentary democracies. Eur J Polit Res 48(6):804–839

Budge I, Klingemann H-D, Volkens A, Bara J, Tanenbaum E (2001) Mapping policy preferences. Estimates for parties, electors and governments 1945–1998. Oxford University Press, Oxford

Carrubba C, Volden C (2000) Coalitional politics and logrolling in legislative institutions. Am J Polit Sci 44(2):261–277

Clinton J, Jackman S, Rivers D (2004) The statistical analysis of roll call data. Am Polit Sci Rev 98(2):355–370

Cox GW, McCubbins MD (2005) Setting the agenda: responsible party government in the US House of Representatives. Cambridge University Press, Cambridge

Debus M (2008) Office and policy payoffs in coalition governments. Party Polit 14(5):515–538

Downs A (1957) An economic theory of democracy. Harper, New York

Duch RM, Stevenson RT (2006) Assessing the magnitude of the economic vote over time and across nations. Elect Stud 25(3):528–547

Duch RM, Stevenson RT (2008) The economic vote: how political and economic institutions condition election results. Oxford University Press, Oxford

Erikson RS, MacKuen MB, Stimson JA (2002) The macro polity. Cambridge University Press, Cambridge

Ganghof S (2003) Promises and pitfalls of veto player analysis. Swiss Polit Sci Rev 9(1):1–25

Ganghof S, Bräuninger T (2006) Government Status and legislative behaviour: Partisan veto players in Australia, Denmark, Finland and Germany. Party Polit 12(4):521–539

Haggard S, Kaufman RR (1995) The political economy of democratic transitions. Princeton University Press, Princeton

Hallerberg M, Basinger S (1998) Internationalization and changes in tax policy in OECD countries: the importance of domestic veto players. Comp Polit Stud 31(3):321–353

Hellman JS (1998) Winners take all: the politics of partial reform in postcommunist transitions. World Polit 50 (2):203–234

Hix S, Noury A, Roland G (2006) Dimensions of politics in the European parliament. Am J Polit Sci 50(2):494–511

Klingemann H-D, Volkens A, Bara J, Budge I, McDonald M (2006) Mapping policy preferences II: estimates for parties, electors and governments in central and eastern Europe, European Union and OECD 1990–2003. Routledge, London

König T (2007) Divergence or convergence? From ever-growing to ever-slowing European legislative decision making. Eur J Polit Res 46(3):417–444

König T, Bräuninger T (1997) Wie wichtig sind die Länder für die Politik der Bundesregierung bei Einspruchs- und Zustimmungsgesetzen? Zeitschrift für Parlamentsfragen 28(4):605–628

König T, Bräuninger T (1999) Finnland auf dem Weg zum Mehrheitssystem? Eine vergleichende Analyse der politischen Willensbildung vor und nach den finnischen Verfassungsreformen der 90er Jahre. Polit Vierteljahresschr 40(1):40–64

König T, Bräuninger T (2005) Gesetzgebung im Föderalismus. Speyerer Forschungsberichte 237. Deutsches Forschungsinstitut für Öffentliche Verwaltung, Speyer

König T, Luig B (2009) German 'LexIconSpace': policy positions and their legislative context. Ger Polit 18(3):345–364
König T, Tröger V (2005) Budgetary politics and veto players. Swiss Polit Sci Rev 11(4):47–75
König T, Blume T, Luig B (2003) Policy change without government change? German gridlock after the 2002 election. Germ Polit 12(2):86–146
König T, Volkens A, Bräuninger T (1999) Regierungserklärungen von 1949 bis 1998. Eine vergleichende Untersuchung ihrer regierungsinternen und -externen Bestimmungsfaktoren. Zeitschrift für Parlamentsfragen 30(3):641–659
Krehbiel K, Meirowitz A, Woon J (2005) Testing theories of lawmaking. In: Smith DA, Duggan J (eds) Social choice and strategic decisions: essays in honor of Jeffrey S. Banks. Springer, New York, pp 249–269
Kreppel A (1997) The impact of parties in government on legislative output in Italy. Eur J Polit Res 31(3):327–350
Laver M, Garry J (2000) Estimating policy positions from political texts. Am J Polit Sci 44(3): 619–634
Laver M, Shepsle KA (1996) Making and breaking governments. Cambridge University Press, Cambridge
Laver M, Benoit K, Garry J (2003) Extracting policy positions from political texts using words as data. Am Polit Sci Rev 97(2):311–331
Lewis-Beck MS (1986) Comparative economic voting: Britain, France, Germany, Italy. Am J Polit Sci 30(2): 315–346
Lewis-Beck MS, Stegmaier M (2000) Economic determinants of electoral outcomes. Annu Rev Polit Sci 3:183–219
Lijphart A (1999) Patterns of democracy. Yale University Press, New Haven
Martin LW (2004) The government agenda in parliamentary democracies. Am J Polit Sci 48(3):445–461
Martin LW, Vanberg G (2004) Policing the bargain: coalition government and parliamentary scrutiny. Am J Polit Sci 48(1):13–27
Martin LW, Vanberg G (2005) Coalition policymaking and legislative review. Am Polit Sci Rev 99(1):93–106
Mayhew DR (1974) Congress: the electoral connection. Yale University Press, New Haven
Mayhew DR (1991) Divided we govern: party control, lawmaking, and investigations, 1946–1990. Yale University Press, New Haven
Mikhaylov S, Laver M, Benoit K (2008) Coder reliability and misclassification in comparative manifesto project codings. Paper presented at the 66th MPSA Annual National Conference, Palmer House Hilton Hotel and Towers, 3–6 April 2008
Müller WC, Strøm K (eds) (1999) Policy, office or votes? How political parties in western Europe make hard decisions. Cambridge University Press, Cambridge
Müller WC, Strøm K (2008) Coalition agreements and cabinet governance. In: Strøm K, Müller WC, Bergman T (eds) Cabinets and coalition bargaining: the democratic life cycle in western Europe. Oxford University Press, Oxford, pp 159–199
O'Reilly RF (2005) Veto points, veto players, and international trade policy. Comp Polit Stud 38(6):652–675
Ostrom E (1986) An agenda for the study of institutions. Public Choice 48(1):3–25
Plott CR (1979) The application of laboratory experimental methods to public choice. In: Russell CS (ed) Collective decision making: applications from public choice theory. Johns Hopkins University Press, Baltimore, pp 137–160
Poole KT, Rosenthal H (1997) Congress: a political-economic history of roll call voting. Oxford University Press, New York
Powell GB (2000) Elections as instruments of democracy: majoritarian and proportional visions. Yale University Press, New Haven
Powell GB (2004) The chain of responsiveness. J Democracy 15(4):91–105
Powell GB (2006): Election laws and representative governments: beyond votes and seats. Br J Polit Sci 36(2):291–315

Przeworski A (1991) Democracy and the market: political and economic reforms in eastern Europe and Latin America. Cambridge University Press, Cambridge

Sartori G (1976) Parties and party systems. Cambridge University Press, Cambridge

Scharpf FW (1988) Von Fug und Unfug institutioneller Erklärungen. Replik zu Josef Schmid. Wo schnappt die Politikverflechtungsfalle eigentlich zu? Polit Vierteljahresschr 29(2):271–275

Scharpf FW (2002) The European social model: coping with the challenges of diversity. J Common Mark Stud 40(4):645–670

Scharpf FW (2006) The joint-decision trap revisited. J Common Mark Stud 44(4):845–864

Schmidt MG (2001) Thesen zur Reform des Föderalismus der Bundesrepublik Deutschland. Polit Vierteljahresschr 42(3):474–491

Shikano S (2006) Modellgestützte Rekonstruktion und Simulation des Ergebnisses der Bundestagswahl 2005. In: Bräuninger T, Behnke J (eds) Jahrbuch für Handlungs- und Entscheidungstheorie. Band 4: Schwerpunkt Parteienwettbewerb und Wahlen. VS Verlag für Sozialwissenschaft, Wiesbaden, pp 47–78

Slapin J, Proksch S-O (2008) A scaling model for estimating time-series party positions from texts. Am J Polit Sci 52(3):705-722

Sundquist J (1968) Politics and policy. Brookings, Washington

Sundquist J (1988) Needed: a political theory for the new era of coalition government in the United States. Polit Sci Q 103(4):613–635

Timmermans A (2006) Standing apart and sitting together: enforcing coalition agreements in multiparty systems. Eur J Polit Res 45(2):263–283

Tsebelis G (1994) The power of the European parliament as conditional agenda-setter. Am Polit Sci Rev 88(1):128–142

Tsebelis G (1995) Decision Making in Political Systems: Veto Players in Presidentialism, Parliamentarism, Multicameralism and Multipartyism. Br J Polit Sci 25(3):289–325

Tsebelis G (1999) Veto players and law production in parliamentary democracies: an empirical analysis. Am Polit Sci Rev 93(3):591–608

Tsebelis G (2002) Veto players. How political institutions work. Princeton University Press, Princeton

Tsebelis G (2006) Coalition theory: a veto players approach. Unpublished Manuscript. University of Los Angeles

Tsebelis G, Money J (1995) Bicameral negotiations: the Navette system in France. Br J Polit Sci 25(1):101–129

Tsebelis G, Garrett G (1996) Agenda setting power, power indices, and decision making in the European Union. International Review of Law and Economics 16(3):345–361

Van der Brug W, van der Eijk C, Franklin M (2007) The economy and the vote: economic conditions and elections in fifteen countries. Cambridge University Press, Cambridge

Volkens A (2007) Strengths and weaknesses of approaches to measuring policy positions of parties. Elect Stud 26(1):108–120

Warwick PV (2001) Coalition policy in parliamentary democracies. Who gets how much and why. Comp Polit Stud 34(10):1212–1236

Zohlnhöfer R (2009) Der Politikverflechtungsfalle entwischt? Die Effekte der Föderalismusreform I auf die Gesetzgebung. Zeitschrift für Politikwissenschaft 19(1):39–76

Kolibri 360 GmbH
Ferdinand-Jühlke-Straße 7
99095 Erfurt, Deutschland
produktsicherheit@kolibri360.de